Advances on Income Inequality and Concentration Measures

This impressive collection from some of today's leading distributional analysts provides an overview on a wide range of economic, statistical and sociological relationships that have been opened up for scientific study by the work of two turn-of-the-20th-century social scientists: C. Gini and M. O. Lorenz.

In particular the main themes are related to: (i) innovation in the theory and methods on income inequality and concentration analysis; (ii) inequality decomposition; and (iii) to worldwide empirical applications in applied economic analysis. Such research themes constitute a consistent and relevant part of the recent economic, econometric and statistical methods and applications in the international scientific literature. They also play a seminal role in policymaking given the importance of inequality and poverty reduction, of the improvement of living conditions within a framework of sustainable economic development. The editors of this volume explore three key areas: scientific quality, capacity of representing the leading paths of the present scientific research and the existence of a sort of scientific '*fil rouge*' among the contributions in order to propose a homogenous, useful and updated book.

With contributions from figures such as Barry Arnold and Frank Cowell, the resulting book deserves its place on the bookshelf of serious mathematical economists everywhere. It will appeal to economists, statisticians and sociologists with interests in socio-economic behaviour; and is also useful for government statisticians, policymakers at international, national and sub-national levels.

Gianni Betti is Associate Professor of Economic Statistics at the University of Siena.

Achille Lemmi is Professor of Economic Statistics at the University of Siena.

Routledge Frontiers of Political Economy

Advances on Income Inequality and Concentration Measures

Edited by Gianni Betti and Achille Lemmi

Routledge
Taylor & Francis Group

LONDON AND NEW YORK

First published 2008
by Routledge
2 Park Square, Milton Park, Abingdon, Oxon, OX14 4RN

Simultaneously published in the USA and Canada
by Routledge
605 Third Avenue, New York, NY 10017

*Routledge is an imprint of the Taylor & Francis Group,
an informa business*

Typeset in Times New Roman by
RefineCatch Limited, Bungay, Suffolk

British Library Cataloguing in Publication Data
A catalogue record for this book is available from the British Library

Library of Congress Cataloging in Publication Data
Advances on income inequality and concentration measures / edited by
Gianni Betti and Achille Lemmi.
       p. cm.
Includes bibliographical references and index.
    1. Income distribution–Mathematical models.   2. Lorenz curve.
3. Gini coefficient.   4. Poverty–Mathematical models.   I. Betti, Gianni.
II. Lemmi, Achille.
    HB523.A314 2008
    339.201′51924–dc22

                                                          2007044226

ISBN 13: 978-0-415-56947-7 (pbk)
ISBN 13: 978-0-415-44337-1 (hbk)

Contents

Contributors

Gordon Anderson, Economics Department, University of Toronto, Canada.

Barry C. Arnold, Department of Statistics, University of California, Riverside, USA.

Gianni Betti, Department of Quantitative Methods and C.R.I.DI.RE. 'Camilo Dagum', University of Siena, Italy.

Hilde Bojer, Department of Economics, University of Oslo, Norway.

Quentin L. Burrell, Isle of Man International Business School, UK.

Frank A. Cowell, London School of Economics, UK.

Elisabetta Croci Angelini, Department of Studies on Economic Development, University of Macerata, Italy.

Camilo Dagum, Department of Statistics, University of Bologna, Italy, and Emeritus Professor, University of Ottawa, Canada.

Joseph Deutsch, Department of Economics, Bar-Ilan University, Ramat-Gan, Israel.

Yuri Dikhanov, World Bank, Washington, USA.

Francesco Farina, Department of Economic Policy, Finance and Development, University of Siena, Italy.

Héctor R. Gertel, Facultad de Ciencias Económicas, Universidad Nacional de Córdoba, Argentina.

Roberto F. Giuliodori, Facultad de Ciencias Económicas, Universidad Nacional de Córdoba, Argentina.

Almas Heshmati, University of Kurdistan Hawler, Hawler, Federal Region of Kurdistan, Iraq.

Christian Kleiber, WWZ, Universität Basel, Basel, Switzerland.

Samuel Kotz, Department of Engineering Management and Systems Engineering, The George Washington University, Washington, USA.

Peter J. Lambert, Department of Economics, University of Oregon, USA.

Achille Lemmi, Department of Quantitative Methods and C.R.I.DI.RE. 'Camilo Dagum', University of Siena, Italy.

Tim F. Liao, Department Sociology, University of Illinois, USA.

Esfandiar Maasoumi, Department of Economics, Southern Methodist University, Dallas, USA.

Daniel L. Millimet, Department of Economics, Southern Methodist University, USA.

Süleyman Özmucur, University of Pennsylvania, USA.

Alejandro Rodríguez, Facultad de Ciencias Económicas, Universidad Nacional de Córdoba, Argentina.

Ernesto Savaglio, DMQTE, University 'G. D' Annunzio' of Pescara, and Department of Economics, University of Siena, Italy.

Jacques Silber, Department of Economics, Bar-Ilan University, Ramat-Gan, Israel.

Daniel J. Slottje, Department of Economics, Southern Methodist University, and FTI Consulting, Inc., USA.

Stefano Vannucci, Department of Economics, University of Siena, Italy.

Michael Ward, World Bank, Washington, USA.

Figures

Tables

Acknowledgements

Barry C. Arnold is grateful to Ludolf Meester for having improved the quality of the present version of Chapter 2.

Esfandiar Maasoumi and Almas Heshmati thank the editors for valuable comments, as well as participants at numerous seminars. An extended version of Chapter 3 is available at: http://faculty.smu.edu/maasoumi and http://www.iza.org/.

An earlier version of Chapter 13 was presented at the American Sociological Association Methodology Conference, Ann Arbor, MI, 22–24 April 2004. Tim Liao expresses appreciation to Camilo Dagum for his comments at the Siena Conference, that showed the need for a second stratification index, and to Estela Bee Dagum for her comments at the same conference, that led to the updated current simulated samples. Comments by Stephen Jenkins on an earlier version of the Chapter are also appreciated.

Hilde Bojer is grateful to Tony Atkinson and Erik Biørn for friendly and useful comments. The tables and graphs of Chapter 14 for the years 1982–2002 are based on the author's computations using data from the Surveys of Income and Wealth of Statistics Norway. The data were obtained through the Norwegian Social Sciences Data service (NSD). Results for the years 1970 to 1979 were computed by Statistics Norway to the author's specifications. Neither Statistics Norway nor NSD is in any way responsible for the author's use of the data.

Elisabetta Croci Angelini and Francesco Farina wish to thank MIUR for financial support (PRIN 2004) and Simone Bertoli, Marisa Civardi, Chris Gilbert and Renata Targetti Lenti for helpful comments on previous versions of Chapter 15.

Süleyman Özmucur and Jacques Silber would like to thank the participants of the International Conference in Memory of Two Eminent Social Scientists, C. Gini and M. O. Lorenz, that took place at the Certosa di Pontignano on 23–26 May 2005 for their useful comments. A previous version of Chapter 18 was completed while Jacques Silber was a Sabbatical Fellow at the World Institute for Development Economics Research (WIDER), Helsinki.

The editors are particularly grateful to the authors of the various chapters for their commitment and for their desire to contribute to the creation of the book. Special thanks go to colleagues Laura Neri and Vijay Verma for their constant support and worthwhile suggestions. Many thanks also to Francesca Ballini, Janet Donovan and Valentino Mazza for dealing with the editorial and linguistic aspects of the book.

Abbreviations

CDF	Cumulative Distribution Function
DD	Directional Distance
DDR	Directional Distance Ratio
DF	Disutility Function
E	Expectation Operator
GDD	Gross Directional Distance
GEM	Generalized Entropy Measure
GMD	Gini Mean Difference
GR	Gini Ratio
ID	Income Distribution
IDM	Income Distribution Model
IIM	Income Inequality Measure
LC	Lorenz Curve
ME	Mathematical Expectation
NDD	Net Directional Distance
PDF	Probability Distribution Function
SW	Social Welfare
SWF	Social Welfare Function
UF	Utility Function

Part I

Introduction

1 Editors' introduction

Gianni Betti and Achille Lemmi

More than a hundred years ago, in 1905, two relevant scientific events took place: (i) Corrado Gini defended his outstanding doctoral thesis on the statistical analysis of birth by gender at the University of Bologna (Italy) and (ii) Max Otto Lorenz, a year after having been awarded a Ph. D. in Economics at the University of Wisconsin (USA), published a remarkable paper on methods of measuring the concentration of income and wealth, in the former series of the *Journal of the American Statistical Association*, two events, strictly independent but capable of influencing socio-economic sciences the world over in a permanent way. In fact, the Lorenz paper has greatly influenced further development in probability theory, stochastic dominance and economic analysis, while Gini's interest in income inequality started with criticism of the Pareto inequality parameter (in the sense of its re-interpretation and mathematical proof as an equality and not an inequality parameter) and continued with his proposition of the famous income inequality ratio published in 1914.

These two analytic elements, namely the Lorenz curve and the Gini inequality ratio, have represented and still represent the basic starting point for every scholar interested in welfare economics, labour economics, development economics, social and economic statistics, quantitative sociology and political science. Moreover, they are of frequent and relevant use in many other scientific disciplines (e.g. engineering, probability theory, environmental analyses, and ecology) that a definition of 'fundamental scientific' tools is proper and adequate.

This is the reason why an international scientific conference was organized, in the second half of May 2005, at the University of Siena, so as to celebrate these two eminent social scientists, one hundred years after the events mentioned above had taken place. The success of the conference was greater than expected due mainly to both the quality of the contributions presented and discussed, and to the widespread participation from all over the world (not simply Europe and the USA but also South America, the Middle and Far East and Oceania).

There are at least two reasons for the success of the conference: (i) the quality of the scientific committee of the conference and in particular the contributions of Professors Samuel Kotz and Camilo Dagum, the real brains and hearts of the scientific event, and (ii) the importance of the scientific contribution of Gini and Lorenz '. . . evergreen after 100 years . . .' as Barry C. Arnold points out in the second chapter of this book.

Unfortunately Professor Kotz did not attend the conference for health reasons; the presence of his authoritative figure was underlined in the introductory conference speech given by Professor Dagum, charged with such a task given his long-lasting experience of scientific cooperation with the University of Siena and in particular with the Research Centre on Income Distribution of this University. The centre was created with his fundamental support and it now bears his name; he passed away a few months after the conclusion of the conference.

The scientific commemoration of Camilo Dagum has registered various, important and suitable initiatives; this book contains his most complete and updated contribution to the Gini approach to inequality analysis and measurement. His last passionate contribution to Corrado Gini, as passion and humanity, strictly connected to a rigorous scientific method, constantly represented the leading characteristic of Professor Dagum, an authoritative academic scientist capable of creating profound relationships of friendship and of mutual cooperation.

This book is deeply influenced by such an approach to inequality analysis and measurement, in the sense that it represents a modern, multi-faced and truly advanced collection of original papers on inequality within the Gini-Lorenz logical approach. At first sight this choice could be considered a limitation of the book within the framework of inequality analysis, since the latter can be treated following different, important and authoritative, widely diffused alternative approaches.[1] But full comprehensiveness is far from being the main objective of the book; instead it aims at representing the main schools of thought in current scientific research in inequality analysis within the Gini-Lorenz original approach, following a precise *fil rouge* among original contributions related to (i) innovation in the theory and methods on income inequality and concentration analysis, (ii) inequality decomposition and (iii) worldwide empirical analysis in applied economics.

The book is composed of 18 chapters grouped into four parts. After this Introduction, Chapters 2 and 3, written respectively by Barry C. Arnold and Frank A. Cowell complete the introductory section.

Barry C. Arnold celebrates **The Lorenz curve: evergreen after 100 years**. The author begins by reminding us how Lorenz's (1905) suggestion of a graphical manner in which to compare inequality in finite populations in terms of nested curves turned out to be remarkably well accepted. In fact, scholars continue to learn about and to utilize concepts derived from and intimately related to this curve. There is still work to be done related to Lorenz . . . ordering especially in higher dimensions. Moreover, many, perhaps unexpected, areas in which Lorenz . . . ordering ideas can be profitably used do exist. A small sample of such scenarios is included in the chapter.

Frank A. Cowell, in his contribution on **Gini, deprivation and complaints**, underlines how recent insights from the philosopher Larry Temkin have suggested a new basis for the measurement of income inequality, founded on the notion of individual 'complaints' about income distribution. Under certain specifications of the relationship between complaints and personal incomes it can be shown that a concept similar to the concept of deprivation thus emerges. In turn, deprivation is related to the Gini index and to poverty. The chapter examines the relationships between the Gini index and Lorenz's orderings on the one hand, and deprivation, poverty and complaints on the other.

Starting Part II on Theory and Methods, Esfandiar Maasoumi and Almas Heshmati focus their attention on **Evaluating dominance ranking of PSID incomes by various household attributes**. In this chapter the authors examine the dynamic evolution of incomes, both disposable and gross, for several groups in the PSID panel data at several points from 1968 to 1997. They employ the extended Kolmogorov-Smirnov tests of First and Second Order Stochastic Dominance (SD) as firstly implemented by Maasoumi and Heshmati (2000). In that paper they did not impose the Least Favorable Case (LFC) of the composite null hypotheses of SD orders. This is in contrast to simulation and bootstrap-based techniques that do so, resulting in tests that are not asymptotically similar or unbiased. The new approach is also different from the subsampling technique of Linton *et al.* (2005) who obtain critical values for these tests under very general sampling schemes. They offer partial control for many individual/family specific attributes, such as age, gender, education, number of children, work and marital status, by comparing group cells. This avoids having to specify and estimate models of dependence of incomes on these attributes, but lacks the multiple controls that exists when adopting such techniques. The authors find a surprising number of strong rankings, both between groups and over time, in gross income and, to a lesser extent, in 'disposable' incomes.

In Chapter 5 Gordon Anderson takes a look at **Indices and tests for Alienation based upon Gini type and Distributional Overlap Measures**. In this chapter Alienation Indices developed from the Gini coefficient together with Alienation Indices based upon a measure of distributional overlap (or lack of it) are outlined, their properties are examined and the indices are extended to multivariate situations. The indices are exemplified in examining alienation between the rich and the poor, and between location (the North and the South) and racial (White and non-White) divides, in the UK, with respect to before and after housing-cost measures of income.

Quentin L. Burrell's Chapter 6 is devoted to **Measuring relative equality of concentration between different income/wealth distributions**. The chapter begins with a recent paper where the author introduced two new measures – both based on the Gini mean difference – for measuring the similarity of concentration of productivity between different distributions. The first was derived from Dagum's notion of relative economic affluence (REA); the second – in some ways analogous to the correlation coefficient – is a new approach giving the so-called co-concentration coefficient (C-CC). Models and methods adopted in the field of informetrics – very roughly, the 'metric' aspects of 'information systems' – are very often based upon, or have direct analogies with, or at the very least are inspired by, ones from econometrics and it is the purpose of this chapter to suggest ways in which these new measures of similarity could be useful in, for instance, studies of income distributions (i) between different countries and (ii) over different periods of time. The measures are illustrated using exponential, Pareto, Weibull and Singh-Maddala distributions. Samuel Kotz's chapter gives a clear presentation of **Information matrices for some bivariate Pareto distributions**. Pareto distributions are the very popular and the widely applied distributions in the field of income and wealth modelling. They are very versatile and a variety of uncertainties can be usefully modelled by them. Some of the other application areas include extreme values, failure times, and modelling of birth rates and infant mortality rates, as well as reliability. In this chapter the authors consider four of the most popular bivariate Pareto distributions and derive the corresponding Fisher information matrices.

Ernesto Savaglio and Stefano Vannucci are the authors of Chapter 8: **On Lorenz preorders and opportunity inequality in finite environments**. The assessment of inequality in resource allocation by means of Lorenz preorders is both well established for univariate distributions and highly problematic for multivariate ones. The main reason for this is that, if the relevant variables are real-valued, the univariate case allows a natural total ordering of individual endowments, while any multivariate distribution, real-valued or otherwise, typically admits only partial orderings (e.g. dominance orderings) of the latter. That problem also arises in a discrete setting, namely when the resources to be allocated amount to a finite set of items/opportunities. That is so because it is by no means obvious if and how the set-inclusion partial preorder might be extended to a total preorder of opportunity sets. However, such an extension is apparently required in order to make it possible to define a Lorenz-like preorder of opportunity distributions amenable to characterizations via simple progressive Pigou-Dalton transfers as established by the classic Hardy-Littlewood-Polya (1929, 1934), theorem for real-valued income distributions. The chapter is devoted to a critical review of the existent literature on the problem of importing such 'nice' Lorenz-like preorders in finite settings.

Part III on Inequality decomposition contains four chapters; the first, Chapter 9, written by Camilo Dagum, contains his most complete and updated contribution to the Gini approach to inequality analysis and measurement, i.e. **Inequality decomposition, directional economic distance, metric distance, and Gini dissimilarity between income distributions**. Pareto (1895) specified his Type I model and advanced an inequality interpretation of his shape parameter a, which was later corrected by Gini (1909). Lorenz (1905) introduced the distribution of the mass of income as a function of the cumulative distribution function of the economic units as an efficient tool for analysing income inequality. These seminal contributions opened up a new field of research: the size distribution of income and wealth; moreover, they stimulated further development in probability, statistics, econometrics and applied economics.

Dagum's chapter purports to discuss, analyse and critically evaluate: (i) the decomposition approach of the generalized entropy measure of inequality, showing the serious shortcomings of all its variants (Theil index included) in accounting for the contribution of the between-groups inequality; (ii) the Gini ratio decomposition, which offers the advantage of accounting for the overlapping between income distributions; (iii) the directional distance ratio between binary combinations of income distributions, showing its superiority in relation to the decomposition approach and the further advantage of providing sound policy implications; and (iv) the distance function between income distributions and its relationship to the Gini dissimilarity index.

Chapter 10, written by Joseph Deutsch and Jacques Silber, discusses **The Shapley value and the decomposition of inequality by population subgroups with special emphasis on the Gini index**. This chapter proposes a generalization of the breakdown of income inequality by population subgroups that is based on the idea that either the within- or the between-groups inequality should be considered as a residual. This generalization of the inequality decomposition uses the concept of Shapley value and it is applied to the Gini index, which assumes that the ranking of individuals also plays a role. The chapter includes an empirical illustration using Israeli income data for the years 1990 and 1998.

Héctor R. Gertel, Roberto F. Giuliodori and Alejandro Rodríguez's presentation of the **Analysis of the short term impact of the Argentine Social Assistance Program *'Plan Jefes y Jefas'* on income inequality applying the Dagum Decomposition Analysis of the Gini Ratio**[2] is reported in Chapter 11. Extreme poverty levels were seen in Argentina after the severe crisis unleashed at the end of 2001. This was worsened by a deep production standstill, which made the national, provincial, and municipal governments face the need to generate programmes for comprehensive support for families, especially in relation to all essential aspects. This would enable the eradication of the high levels of indigence, and favour social inclusion so as to mitigate, at least partly, the extreme household income inequality in an increasing polarized society. The *'Jefes y Jefas de Hogar'* Programme is a social assistance programme, focused on the unemployed heads of households with dependents under the age of 18 or with disabled individuals of any age, that the national government started as of May 2002. In the chapter it is argued that a rigorous short-run measure of its contribution to enhance income distribution, by reducing income inequality across regions and groups, can be derived from a Gini coefficient decomposition procedure, such as the one introduced by Dagum (1997).

The chapter written by Tim F. Liao deals with the topic of **The Gini unbound: analyzing class inequality with model-based clustering**. For students of social and economic inequality, the most widely used measure is none other than the Gini index (or Gini inequality ratio). Whereas some other measures of inequality have certain characteristics that may be useful, such as the straightforward decomposability of the generalized entropy measures, the Gini index has remained the most popular, at least in part due to its ease in interpretation. However, the Gini index has some limitation in measuring inequality. It is less sensitive to how the population is stratified than how individual values differ. The twin purposes of this chapter are to explain the limitation and to propose a model-based method-latent class/clustering analysis for understanding and measuring inequality. The latent cluster approach has the major advantages of being able to identify potential 'classes' of individuals who share similar levels of income (or another attribute) and to assess the fit to the empirical data of alternative models of different assumptions and varying number of latent classes. The author distinguishes class inequality from individual inequality, the type that is better measured by the Gini index. Once the classes are estimated, the number of estimated classes obtained from the best-fitting model facilitates the decomposition of the Gini index into individual and class inequality. Class inequality is then measured by a stratification index based on the decomposition of the overall Gini into between-class and within-class inequality components. Therefore, the Gini index is extended and assisted by model-based clustering for measuring class inequality, thereby fulfilling its potential applicability.

Part IV on the Lorenz curve and Gini measures in applied economics starts with the chapter by Christian Kleiber on **The Lorenz curve in economics and econometrics.** This chapter surveys selected applications of the Lorenz curve and related stochastic orders in economics and econometrics, with a bias towards problems in statistical distribution theory. These include characterizations of income distributions in terms of families of inequality measures, Lorenz ordering of multiparameter distributions in terms of their parameters, and probability inequalities for distributions of quadratic forms.

In Chapter 14 Hilde Bojer presents an application on **Income inequality and the economic position of women in Norway 1970–2002.** In the period from 1970 to 2002 Norwegian women moved out of the home and into the paid labour market. The chapter investigates the effect of this social change on women's economic position and on individual income inequality. It argues that the distribution of individual incomes is of equal interest to household incomes as targets of public policy. Inequality is measured by the generalized entropy measure. The data are taken from the triennial, later annual, income surveys carried out by Statistics Norway in that period, giving reliable data on income for samples varying from 6,000 to 30,000 women and men. Women's average income compared to that of men increased from 27 per cent to 60 per cent. Total individual income inequality decreased strongly from 1970 to 1990, and decreased very slightly from 1990 to 2002. But this total covers very different developments for women and men. Inequality of employees remained unchanged during the whole period, both for women and men, when capital income is disregarded.

Chapter 15 by Elisabetta Croci Angelini and Francesco Farina is devoted to **Technological choices under institutional constraints: measuring the impact on earnings dispersion.** Increasing attention has been recently devoted in the literature to wage dispersion in Europe. Nevertheless, a wholly comprehensive analysis of the many factors contributing to the evolution of wage disparities is lacking. The overwhelming majority of studies concern labour market institutions. Even when research work is conducted at the most aggregated level – the overall trend of wage inequality in European countries – the opinion on the findings is sharply divided. It is apparent that interactions are more complex and other factors are to be taken into account, first of all technical change. In fact, the role of technology has been recognized but mainly in association with trade. Harsher competition in the international markets triggered by trade openness is alleged to depress the wage and employment levels of low-skilled workers in the advanced countries. The aim of the chapter is to contribute to filling this gap, by measuring the role of technical change in determining wage differentials across sectors and skill groups. The computation of the decomposition of the Theil index and a Gini-based indicator for earnings dispersion (EDI) are expected to convey information on two major determinants of wage differentials: (i) technical change; (ii) labour market institutions. Yuri Dikhanov and Michael Ward's study on **Redistributing global income to benefit the poor** is presented in Chapter 16. Implicit in the seminal works of Gini and Lorenz lies the fundamental notion of social justice. Both drew attention to the economic and social significance of redistributing income in the interests of obtaining a better social balance. Their work underlined the need to strengthen the longer-term sustainability of civil society and justified the implementation of progressive taxation measures to bring about a desired greater equality. It is in the spirit of the work of Gini and Lorenz, therefore, that this chapter goes beyond the narrower prescriptive policy requirements of the state for matching continuous density functions relating the global population to aggregate annual world income by means of the amalgamation of regional income distributions based on aggregated national data.

These 'true' distributions based on micro household survey data depict, simultaneously, for both global and selected regional geographical levels, changes in individual income against changes in total income over successive decennial periods from 1970 to 2000. A projection using adjustments to the past observed trends and specific assumptions about the future performances of major economic areas is made so as to estimate the degree of global inequality in the year 2015.

Daniel L. Millimet, Daniel J. Slottje and Peter J. Lambert present a work on **Inequality aversion, Income inequality, and social policy in the US:**

1947–1998. The chapter analyses inequality aversion in the US from 1947 to 1998 and identifies factors explaining the variation over this period. This is accomplished by utilizing the 'natural rate' of subjective inequality hypothesis put forth by Lambert *et al.* (2003). Under this hypothesis, one may solve the explicit time-specific values of the inequality aversion parameter that are consistent with the hypothesized natural rate. Building on Lambert *et al.*, the authors present evidence consistent with the existence of a natural rate of subjective inequality over time in the US by verifying that years with low (high) tolerance for inequality have low (high) inequality as measured by the Gini coefficient. Next, they explore the socio-economic factors accounting for the observed differences in inequality aversion over time. Among other things they find important effects of the political affiliation of governmental officials, public expenditure, per capita income and economic growth. Moreover, they document several interesting correlations between inequality aversion and social policies such as the minimum wage, government expenditure on education, and government-established poverty thresholds. Finally, they use the natural rate hypothesis to shed new light on the connection between inequality and short-run economic growth.

Finally, Chapter 18, written by Süleyman Özmucur and Jacques Silber, presents an application on **Internal migration, household size and income inequality in Turkey**. This chapter analyses the impact of internal migration on income inequality in Turkey. It emphasizes the separate effects on inequality of changes in household size and in income when individuals move from rural to urban areas or between regions. The empirical analysis is based on the 1994 Income Survey. From the study it appears that there are two reasons why internal migration from rural to urban areas and between regions induces an increase in the inequality of per capita income, whether one looks at inequality between households or individuals. First, the inequality of total household income is higher in urban areas; second, that of the size of households is higher in rural areas.

References

Dagum, C. (1997). 'A new approach to the decomposition of the Gini income inequality ratio', *Empirical Economics*, 22: 515–531.

Gini, C. (1909). 'Il diverso accrescimento delle classi sociali e la concentrazione della ricchezza', *Giornale degli Economisti*, XXXVIII, 69–83.

Gini, C. (1914). 'Sulla la misura della concentrazione e della variabilità dei caratteri', *Atti del Reale Istituto Veneto di Scienze, Lettere e Arti*.

Hardy, G.H., J.E. Littlewood and G. Polya (1929). 'Some simple inequalities satisfied by convex functions', *Messenger of Mathematics*, 58: 145–152.

Hardy, G.H., J.E. Littlewood and G. Polya (1934). *Inequalities*, 1st ed., London: Cambridge University Press.

Lambert, P.J., D.L. Millimet and D.J. Slottje (2003) 'Inequality aversion and the natural rate of subjective inequality', *Journal of Public Economics* 87: 1061–90.

Lemmi A. (1999), 'Comment to F.A. Cowell, Estimation of Inequality Indices', in

Silber, J. (ed.), *Handbook on Income Inequality Measurement*, Kluwer Academic Publishers: Boston/Dordrecht/London, pp. 286–289.

Lorenz, M.O. (1905). 'Methods of measuring concentration of wealth', *Journal of the American Statistical Association*, 9: 209–219.

Maasoumi, E. and Heshmati, H. (2000). 'Stochastic dominance amongst Swedish income distributions', *Econometric Reviews*, 19,3: 287–320.

Pareto, V. (1895). 'La legge della domanda', *Giornale degli Economisti*, 59–68.

Notes

1 We refer to the contributions of those scholars who extended the seminal work of A. B. Atkinson on decomposable entropy-based inequality measures (Lemmi 1999: 287).

2 The original paper presented at the International Conference in Memory of Two Eminent Social Scientists, C. Gini and M. O. Lorenz, that took place at the Certosa di Pontignano on 23–26 May 2005 mentioned above, received the prize of the Italian Statistical Society (Società Italiana di Statistica, SIS) for the best contribution of authors from an emerging country.

2   The Lorenz curve

Evergreen after 100 years

Barry C. Arnold

2.1 Introduction

In 1905, Max Lorenz proposed a simple graphical means to summarize the inequality of wealth in a finite population of individuals. Known subsequently as the Lorenz curve, it has survived well and indeed still occupies a preeminent place in discussion of the quantification of inequality. It was a simple, but a very good, idea. Subsequent investigations have provided useful interpretations of why it does so well in capturing our conceptions of what really constitutes inequality. Some of these insights will be discussed below. The mathematical concept known as majorization arrived somewhat later on the scene. Its close relationship with the ordering proposed by Lorenz in his pioneering paper has been apparent for many years, although it is difficult to pinpoint precisely when this nexus was first noted. Nevertheless, the deep understanding of the majorization partial order developed initially by Hardy, Littlewood and Polya (1929, 1934), has been seamlessly transformed to give us a spectrum of useful results and viewpoints on the 'true nature' of Lorenz's curve and its associated ordering of inequality in distinct populations or in populations viewed at different points in time. An important contribution to our understanding of the Lorenz curve, and an important reason for its continued and growing acceptance among economists, was found in Dalton's (1920) careful discussion of criteria that might be arguably accepted as being clearly desirable features of any measure of inequality and of any method for comparison of inequality between populations. The Lorenz curve may well have flourished without the contributions of Dalton, Hardy, Littlewood and Polya but it could not fail to flourish in the presence of such inputs. Indeed it seems that very few people question the fact that nested Lorenz curves signal a clear differential in inequality. What has kept the field of income inequality full of lively controversy is the question of what to do when, or how to interpret situations in which Lorenz curves cross.

The first focus of the present chapter will be on the role of the Lorenz curve in an income inequality context. But it must, and will, be remarked that inequality (often with a different name such as diversity, variability, etc.) is of interest in many other contexts. Moreover, thanks to the development of the mathematical consequences of majorization, it has been apparent that the majorization partial ordering or, almost equivalently, the Lorenz order has an ever-expanding role to play in the study of a spectrum of optimization settings that involve unexpected appearances of Schur convex functions. The need for a multivariate version of Lorenz's curve and his partial order rapidly become apparent. But how to achieve this desirable goal has proved to be elusive. In the mathematics literature, the parallel problem of defining multivariate majorization was receiving attention. In the mathematical context several variant interpretations of plausible multivariate majorization concepts were introduced but no productive suggestions were made regarding how to provide a multivariate version of the graphical tool that Lorenz had provided in giving us his 'curve'. Graphical techniques are of course limited by the dimensions available to us when graphing, but it was clear that some graphical extension of Lorenz's curve should be available at least in the bivariate case. Lorenz's curve was to celebrate its 90th birthday, however, before such a suitable extension was made available. The resulting Lorenz zonoid and Lorenz zonoid ordering, provided initially by Koshevoy (1995) and investigated thoroughly by Koshevoy and Mosler (Mosler 2002), has infused new multidimensional vigor into the evergreen Lorenz curve concept. Lively future development can be confidently predicted as we argue about what to do when Lorenz zonoids are *not* nested, assuming that we generally agree that nested zonoids do reflect a basic inequality ordering in higher dimensions that successfully mirrors the univariate ordering originally proposed by Lorenz. 'As the bow is bent concentration increases'.

2.2 Lorenz's curve (1905)

It all goes back to a brief paper published by Max Lorenz in the *Publication of the American Statistical Association* (later to be known as the *Journal of the American Statistical Society*) in June 1905 (Lorenz 1905). The paper is only nine pages long. The major thrust of the paper is the presentation of discussion of the spectrum of summary inequality measures being used at that time. He recognizes the fact that logarithmic analysis of income distributions has been popularized (especially by Pareto) but he regards logarithmic curves as 'treacherous'. In the last three pages of the paper he describes what will become the Lorenz curve. Actually there are only 35 lines of text and two diagrams devoted to the topic. It has all grown from that! These Lorenz curves provided originally by Lorenz will look a little strange to the modern reader. He has the axes interchanged (or rather, subsequently authors have interchanged the axes on his curves).

Lorenz began with a data set which provided, for a small selection of values, the proportion of the total population earning less than the given value together with the proportion of the total wealth of the population accruing to those individuals. The percentage of the population was plotted against the y axis and the proportion of the total wealth was plotted against the x axis. He then joined the points by a smooth curve, though he gave no hint as to how this interpolating curve was selected. Today we would likely interchange the axes in the diagram and interpolate linearly to obtain what we call the Lorenz curve.

If we have data available on every member of a finite population of n individuals then we can identify the Lorenz curve as being one defined by first ordering the wealths of the individuals from smallest to largest (denoted by $x_{1:n}, x_{2:n}, \ldots, x_{n:n}$) and then plotting the points:

$$\left(\frac{j}{n}, \frac{\sum_{i=1}^{j} x_{i:n}}{\sum_{i=1}^{n} x_{i:n}} \right), j = 1, 2, \ldots, n.$$

In addition we plot the point $(0,0)$ and linearly interpolate the $n + 1$ points to obtain the familiar bow shaped curve. If two populations have nested Lorenz curves, i.e. if the bow it bent more for one of the populations, then a clear indication is provided that one population exhibits more inequality than the other. If we denote the two population vectors by $\underline{x}$ and $\underline{y}$ and their corresponding Lorenz curves by $L_x (u)$ and $L_y (u)$ then our assertion is that if $L_x (u) \leq L_y (u), \forall u \in (0,1)$ then $\underline{x}$ exhibits at least as much inequality as $\underline{y}$. It may be remarked that use of Lorenz curves allows comparison between populations of different sizes.

To Lorenz it was clear that the Lorenz ordering was a sensible way to quantify inequality orderings. But he really gave no insight as to why it should be self-evident or, if you wish, why it is even plausible. To justify the paramount role that the Lorenz order has played in inequality discussions, we need to move ahead to relate it to Dalton's (1920) inequality principles. But before doing so, we will sidestep to consider the parallel concept of majorization.

2.3 Majorization

At some date prior to 1929, the partial ordering on $\Re^n$ known as majorization was introduced. By 1929, Hardy, Littlewood and Polya were showing its relationship to Schur's averages but they did not use the name majorization. The sufficient conditions for majorization were known as the Muirhead conditions (though Muirhead 1903 introduced the condition in the context of vectors of integers only).

For any vector $\underline{x} \in \Re^n$ we will denote its coordinates written in nondecreasing order by $(x_{1:n}, x_{2:n}, \ldots, x_{n:n})$. We will write our results in terms of an ordering from smallest to largest (to mesh nicely with the Lorenz ordering associated with Lorenz's curve) but it must be remarked that, in the mathematics literature, most of the discussion of majorization involves vectors arranged from largest to smallest.

Definition 2.1 Let $\underline{x}, \underline{y} \in \mathfrak{R}^n$. We will say that $\underline{x}$ is majorized by $\underline{y}$ and write $\underline{x} \prec \underline{y}$ if:

$$\sum_{i=1}^{k} x_{i:n} \geq \sum_{i=1}^{k} y_{i:n}, k = 1, 2, \ldots, n-1$$

and:

$$\sum_{i=1}^{n} x_{i:n} = \sum_{i=1}^{n} y_{i:n}.$$

Schur (1923) introduced the concept of an 'averaging'.

Definition 2.2 Let $\underline{x}, \underline{y} \in \mathfrak{R}^n$. We will say that x is an averaging of y if there exists an $n \times n$ doubly stochastic matrix P such that $\underline{x} = P\underline{y}$ (the vectors involved here are interpreted as column vectors). Functions which are monotone with respect to majorization are called Schur convex functions.

Definition 2.3 Let. $A \subset \mathfrak{R}^n$. A function $g : A \to \mathfrak{R}$ is said to be Schur convex on A if $g(\underline{x}) \leq g(\underline{y})$ for every pair $\underline{x}, \underline{y} \in A$ for which $\underline{x} \prec \underline{y}$.

The following basic results on majorization may be found in Hardy, Littlewood and Polya (1934) or, for a more modern treatment, in Marshall and Olkin (1979).

Theorem 2.1 Let $\underline{x}, \underline{y} \in \mathfrak{R}^n$. The following are equivalent:

(i) $\underline{x} \prec \underline{y}$.
(ii) $\underline{x}$ is an averaging of y (i.e. $\underline{x} = P\underline{y}$ for some doubly stochastic matrix P).

(iii) $\sum_{i=1}^{n} h(x_i) \leq \sum_{i=1}^{n} h(y_i)$ for every continuous convex function $h : \mathfrak{R} \to \mathfrak{R}$.

(iv) $\sum_{i=1}^{n} (x_i - c)^{+} \leq \sum_{i=1}^{n} (y_i - c)^{+} \ \forall c \in \mathfrak{R}$ and $\sum_{i=1}^{n} x_i = \sum_{i=1}^{n} y_i$.

We will also use two results concerning the structure of $n \times n$ doubly stochastic matrices. The set of all $n \times n$ permutation matrices will be denoted by $\mathscr{P}^n$ and the class of all $n \times n$ permutation matrices that involve an interchange of just two coordinates will be denoted by $\mathscr{B}^n$. A matrix will be said to be a T-transition matrix if it is of the form:

$$\lambda I + (1 - \lambda)B \tag{2.1}$$

where $\lambda \in [0, 1]$ and $B \in \mathscr{B}^n$. The class of all T-transition matrices (or more evocatively, as we will see later, the class of Robin Hood matrices) will be denoted by $\mathcal{T}^n$. Finally the class of all $n \times n$ doubly stochastic matrices will be denoted by $\mathcal{S}^n$. We have:

Theorem 2.2

(a) (Birkhoff 1946). $\mathcal{P}^n$ is the set of extreme points of $\mathcal{S}^n$ and $\mathcal{S}^n$ is the convex hull of $\mathcal{P}^n$.

(b) (Hardy, Littlewood and Polya 1934). If $\underline{x} \prec \underline{y}$ then there exists a finite set of matrices in $\mathcal{T}^n$, say $T_1, T_2, \ldots, T_m$ such that $\underline{x} = T_1 T_2 \ldots T_m \underline{y}$ (in fact m will be $\leq n - 1$ here).

Finally we remark that in the light of Theorem 2.2(b) it is possible to verify Schur convexity of a function by considering only the effect of changes in the first two coordinates. Thus a differentiable function $g : I^n \to \mathfrak{R}$, where I is an interval, is Schur convex if:

(i)   g is a symmetric function of $x_1, x_2, \ldots, x_n$
(ii)   for every $\underline{x} \in I^n$

$$(x_1 - x_2)\left(\frac{\partial}{\partial x_1} g(\underline{x}) - \frac{\partial}{\partial x_2} g(\underline{x})\right) \geq 0. \tag{2.2}$$

2.4 Dalton's key principle

In his important paper on desirable properties of income inequality measures, Dalton (1920) proposed four principles. The important one for our purposes is the one that says that, if we take a small amount from an individual in a population and give it to a relatively poorer individual in the population, the result will be a decrease in inequality. In other words, Robin Hood, in taking from the rich and giving to the poor, is indeed reducing inequality. In honor of the celebrated hero of Sherwood Forest, we will call this the Robin Hood principle (it is also known as the Dalton or the Pigou-Dalton principle) and the operation as a Robin Hood transfer.

Referring back to the discussion in Section 2.3, it is clear that the effect of a Robin Hood transfer on a population vector $\underline{x}$ is to replace $\underline{x}$ by $T\underline{x}$ where T is a T-transition matrix (or Robin Hood matrix). Moreover, referring to Theorem 2.2(b), we will have $\underline{x} \prec \underline{y}$ iff $\underline{x}$ can be obtained from $\underline{y}$ by a finite series of Robin Hood transfers (from rich to poor).

2.5 The Lorenz order for finite populations

In the context of income and wealth inequality, it is natural to restrict attention to non-negative variables. We may then consider a vector $\underline{x} \in \mathfrak{R}^n_+$ and associate a Lorenz curve with this vector using Lorenz's definition (with linear interpolation between the points). We may note that for two vectors $\underline{x}, \underline{y} \in \mathfrak{R}^n_+$, the corresponding Lorenz curves satisfy, $L_{\underline{x}}(u) \leq L_{\underline{y}}(u), \forall u \in (0, 1)$ if and only if the standardized version of y is majorized by the standardized version of x. Standardization in this setting involves dividing each coordinate of x by the total $\sum_{i=1}^{n} x_i$, y being standardized in similar fashion so that the standardized vectors have coordinates which sum to one. Thus, many properties of the Lorenz order can be immediately deduced from corresponding results for majorization. There is an advantage to the use of the Lorenz order. It allows us to compare populations of different sizes. In fact, it is possible and natural to extend the Lorenz order to compare quite arbitrary distributions, as we shall observe in the next section. From the results described for majorization we can conclude that, if we wish to use a scale invariant measure of inequality and if we accept that a Robin Hood operation decreases inequality, we are forced to accept the Lorenz order (based on nested Lorenz curves) as an appropriate inequality partial ordering. The attractiveness of the Robin Hood principle and the fact that one can move from a lower Lorenz curve to a higher Lorenz curve via a finite sequence of Robin Hood operations, undoubtedly explains the almost universal appeal of the Lorenz order as a clear reflection of inequality ordering.

2.6 The general Lorenz order

Let $\mathcal{L}_+$ denote the class of all non-negative random variables with finite positive expectations. We define a partial order on $\mathcal{L}_+$ by first associating a Lorenz curve with each random variable in $\mathcal{L}_+$.

Definition 2.4 (Gastwirth 1971). Let $X \in \mathcal{L}_+$ with distribution function F_X and quantile function F_X^{-1}. The Lorenz curve L_X corresponding to X is defined by

$$L_X(u) = \frac{\int_0^u F_X^{-1}(v)dv}{\int_0^1 F_X^{-1}(v)dv}, \quad 0 \le u \le 1. \tag{2.3}$$

It is evident from (2.3) that a Lorenz curve will be continuous, non-decreasing convex function that is differentiable almost everywhere in $[0, 1]$. These are properties that we expect from a Lorenz curve following Lorenz's original description of such curves. If $x = (x_1, x_2, \ldots, x_n$ has non-negative coordinates (not all zero), then we can consider two Lorenz curves associated with this vector. First, we may use Lorenz's original definition. Secondly, we can consider a random variable X associated with selecting a coordinate of x at random with all coordinates equally likely. For such a random variable $\bar{X}$ we can use Definition 2.4 to determine its corresponding Lorenz curve. The same curve is arrived at in both manners. Thus, (2.3) can be viewed as a legitimate extension of Lorenz's original concept, including Lorenz's bow-shaped curve for finite populations as a special case, that can be interpreted as one corresponding to a random selection of a unit from a finite population. Our Lorenz order is then naturally defined in the space $\mathcal{L}_+$ as follows.

Definition 2.5 For X, $Y \in \mathcal{L}_+$, we write $X \leq_L Y$ if and only if $L_X(u) \geq L_Y(u)$, $\forall u \in [0, 1]$. Note that this ordering actually relates equivalence classes of random variables in $\mathcal{L}_+$, where two random variables are said to be equivalent if one is a constant multiple of the other.

By considering a non-negative random variable as a limit in distribution of random variables taking on a finite number of possible values we can develop an analog to Theorem 2.1 (which gave alternative necessary and sufficient conditions for majorization).

Theorem 2.3 Let X, $Y \in \mathcal{L}_+$ with $E(X) = E(Y)$. The following are equivalent.

(i) $X \leq_L Y$.
(ii) X is an averaging of Y in the sense that there exist jointly distributed random variables Y', Z' such that $Y =^d Y'$ and $X =^d E(Y' \mid Z')$.
(iii) $E(h(X)) \leq E(h(Y))$ for every continuous convex function $h : \mathfrak{R} \to \mathfrak{R}$.
(iv) $E((X - c)^+) \leq E((Y - c)^+)$, $\forall c \in \mathfrak{R}_+$.

2.7 Extremal patterns

Among the set of vectors $\underline{x} \in \mathfrak{R}_+^n$ with $\sum_{i=1}^n x_i = c > 0$, the extremal cases with respect to majorization are of the form $(c/n, c/n, \ldots, c/n)$ and $(0, 0, \ldots, 0)$ corresponding, in income terms, to distributions in which, respectively, the wealth is evenly distributed or is all in the hands of one individual.

Many summary measures of inequality are defined in terms of the Lorenz curve. Three examples are:

(i) The Gini index, G, defined to be two times the area between the Lorenz curve and the egalitarian line (joining $(0,0)$ to $(1,1)$).
(ii) The Pietra index, P, defined to be the maximum vertical distance between the Lorenz curve and the egalitarian line.
(iii) The Kakwani index, K, defined to be the length of the Lorenz curve.

It is evident that all three measures, G, P and K, respect the Lorenz order. Moreover, by considering the extremal cases we may immediately identify bounds on these summary measures of inequality, thus:

$$0 \leq G \leq 1,$$
$$0 \leq P \leq 1 \tag{2.4}$$

And

$$\sqrt{2} \leq K \leq 2$$

(in order to obtain a measure whose values range from 0 to 1, Kakwani (1980) actually proposed using $(K - \sqrt{2})/(2 - \sqrt{2})$ as an inequality measure). But in fact any Schur convex function can be used as a summary measure of inequality by applying it to the vector $(x_1/\sum_{i=1}^{n} x_i, x_2/\sum_{i=1}^{n} x_i,$ $\ldots, x_n/\sum_{i=1}^{n} x_i)$. In particular, separable convex functions of the form $\sum_{i=1}^{n} g(x_i)$ where g is convex are often utilized. One of the first of such measures to be used involved the choice $g(x) = x^2$ and orders the inequality of populations in terms of their coefficients of variation. An alternative choice is $g(x) = x \log x$, the negative of the entropy function.

However, our interest in this and the following section is not in the use of the Lorenz order or its surrogate majorization, on its home grounds (income inequality comparisons), but we wish to highlight its potential role in disparate situations seemingly far removed from the income context. The remarkable diversity of such situations and the growing number of them, assure an evergreen future for Lorenz's curve and its associated partial order.

As a rule of thumb, if a problem deals with vectors in $\mathfrak{R}_+^n$ and if the extremal solution to that problem is a vector of the form $(c, c, \ldots, c)$ then we should look for the potential role of some Schur convex function and be on the lookout for a Lorenz ordering (or majorization) interpretation of the phenomenon in question. A more extensive collection of such examples may be found in Arnold (2007) (described specifically in terms of majorization), but it is hoped that the small selection presented below will serve to indicate some of the possibilities and will encourage readers to be on the lookout for more places for Max Lorenz's ordering to play a fruitful role.

2.8 Some examples

2.8.1 Time to absorption in a continuous time Markov chain

Consider a continuous time Markov chain with $n + 1$ states, of which n states, $\{1, 2, \ldots, n\}$, are transient and one state, $n + 1$, is absorbing. Consider the time T until absorption in state $n + 1$. The family of distributions of such absorption times is indexed by $\underline{a} = (a_1, a_2, \ldots, a_n)$ the initial probability distribution vector, and the matrix Q of intensities of transitions among the n transient states. Following Neuts (1975) we will say that T has a phase-type distribution with parameters $\underline{a}$ and Q and we write $T \sim PH(\underline{a}, Q)$.

We will say that T has a phase-type distribution of order n if n is the smallest integer such that the distribution can be identified with the time to absorption in a chain with n transient and one absorbing state. Perhaps the simplest example of a phase-type distribution of order n is provided by a gamma distribution with shape parameter n and intensity parameters l, i.e. a sum of n i.i.d. exponential (l) random variables. It corresponds to a chain which begins in state 1 (i.e. we have $\underline{a} = (1, 0, \ldots, 0)$) and progresses sequentially through the states $2, 3, \ldots, n + 1$ spending an independent exponential (l) time in each transient state. Denote such a simple phase-type random variable by T^*.

It is evident that phase-type distributions of order n with the same mean can exhibit considerable differences in their variability. For example, if in our simple example, instead of spending an exp(l) time in each state, the process spends an exp(l_i) time in state i, $i = 1, 2, \ldots, n$, it is well known that the choice $l_i = l$, $i = 1, 2, \ldots, n$ results in minimal variability in the sense of Lorenz ordering. In fact, O'Cinneide (1991) has verified that among *all* phase type distributions of order n, the simple gamma random variable $T^* \sim G(n, l)$ exhibits least variability as measured by the Lorenz order.

2.8.2 *Connected components of a random graph*

Following Ross (1981) consider a random graph with nodes $1, 2, \ldots, n$. We construct a random graph by drawing n arcs, each one emanating from one of the nodes. The arc beginning at node i ends at node $X(i)$ where the $X(i)$'s are independent identically distributed random variables with:

$$P(X_i = j) = p_j, j = 1, 2, \ldots, n \tag{2.5}$$

where $p_j \leq 0$ and $\sum_{j=1}^{n} p_j = 1$. Note that an arc might link a node to itself and note that several arcs might end at the same node (though they begin from separate nodes). The number of connected components of such a graph will be denoted by M. The possible values of M are clearly $1, 2, \ldots, n$ and the distribution of M will be governed by $\underline{p}$, the vector of probabilities appearing in (2.5). An extreme case, would involve $\underline{p} = (1, 0, \ldots, 0)$. In such a case all arcs will terminate at node 1 and we will have all nodes connected and $M = 1$ with probability 1. Thus, M is stochastically smallest when all the probability in $\underline{p}$ is concentrated at one point (in income terms, when one individual has all the money). We might conjecture that for each $m \in \{1, 2, \ldots, n\}$ the expression for $P(M \geq m)$ will be a Schur concave function of $\underline{p}$. The exact distribution of M is not easy to evaluate. However, Ross (1981) is able to provide an attractively simple expression for the expected values of M:

$$E(M) = \sum_{S} (|S| - 1)! \prod_{j \in S} p_j \tag{2.6}$$

where the summation is taken over every non-empty subset S of $\{1, 2, \ldots, n\}$. Using (2.6) he is able to verify that $E(M)$ is a Schur concave function of $\underline{p}$. Thus, to maximize the expected number of connected components of the graph we should set $p_j = 1/n$, $j = 1, 2, \ldots, n$.

Note that in this example it was not a priori obvious that $(1/n, 1/n, \ldots, 1/n)$ was an extremal choice for $\underline{p}$ but it was obvious that $(1, 0, \ldots, 0)$ was extremal and this motivated a search for a Schur convex or concave function.

2.8.3 Catchability

A closed ecological community such as an isolated island will contain an unknown number v of species of butterflies (for example). Butterflies are hunted until n individuals have been trapped. Let R denote the random number of different species represented among the n trapped butterflies. It is common practice to use the observed value of R to estimate the unknown parameter v. We may write $R = \sum_{i=1}^{v} I(X_i > 0)$, where $\underline{X} = (X_1, X_2, \ldots, X_v)$ is random vector with a multinomial distribution, i.e. $\underline{X} \sim multinominal\ (n, \underline{p})$. Here $\underline{p} = (p_1, p_2, \ldots, p_v)$ in which p_i denotes the probability that a particular trapped butterfly will be from species $i, i = 1, 2, \ldots, v$. Intuition suggests strongly that the distribution of R will depend on the variability in $\underline{p}$ (or on the inequality between the components of $\underline{p}$). p_i is often described as the catchability of species i. Under an equal catchability assumption (i.e. $p_i = 1/v$, $i = 1, 2, \ldots, v$}, we may expect many species to be represented among the n trapped butterflies, i.e. R will be large. At another extreme, if one species is 'trap happy' then we find most, if not all, of our trapped butterflies to be of that species, i.e. R will be small. Nayak and Christman (1992) show that for any $r = 1, 2, \ldots, n$ the quantity $P_{\underline{p}}(R \leq r)$, is indeed a Schur convex function of $\underline{p}$. From this it follows that the expected number of species represented in the sample, $E_{\underline{p}}(R)$, is a Schur concave function of $\underline{p}$. Consequently most of the estimates of v that are quite sensible assuming equal catchability will be negatively biased with the bias increasing as the variability in catchability increases.

It is possible to reinterpret these computations in the context of a simple random sample taken with replacement from a population broken into subpopulations of various sizes. Then R will represent the number of subpopulations represented in the sample. The model can also be invoked in a numismatic context where ancient coins come from an unknown number of minting locations.

2.9 To higher dimensions

It is natural to seek versions of inequality measures and orderings that can be used for multivariate income or wealth distributions. Thus, we may wish to model incomes of related individuals, incomes of individuals at different time points or incomes of one individual in various currencies. Given the attractiveness of Lorenz's partial order in the univariate setting, we are led to seek an appropriate k dimensional extension of Lorenz's curve. Some rather unsuccessful attempts at such a generalization can be found in the literature (e.g. Taguchi 1972; Arnold 1983). The perceived difficulty was due perhaps to an over emphasis on the Gastwirth definition of the Lorenz curve, (2.3), in terms of the quantile function F_X^{-1}. Such a definition involves ordering the observations and it appeared that some multivariate version of either order statistics or the quantile function would be required in order to take Lorenz's curve successfully to higher dimensions. Instead, the key lay in redefining the Lorenz curve in a manner that did not involve ordering the data.

As Lorenz did in the one dimensional case, we begin by considering a finite population of n individuals. However, now we assume that associated with the j'th individual is an m-dimensional wealth vector $\underline{x}_{(j)} = (x_{j1}, x_{j2}, \ldots, x_{jm})$ where, for example, $x_{j\ell}$ represents the wealth of individual j in currency ℓ, $\ell = 1, 2, \ldots, m$. Now, rather than consider only subpopulations consisting of relatively poor individuals, we will associate a point in $\Re^{m+1}_+$ with each sub-population of the full set of n individuals in the population. Associated with a particular subpopulation G including say t individuals we associate the vector:

$$\left(\frac{t}{n}, \frac{\sum_{j \in G} x_{j1}}{\sum_{j=1}^{n} x_{j1}}, \frac{\sum_{j \in G} x_{j2}}{\sum_{j=1}^{n} x_{j2}}, \ldots, \frac{\sum_{j \in G} x_{jm}}{\sum_{j=1}^{n} x_{jm}} \right) \qquad (2.7)$$

The first coordinate of this vector represents the proportion of the total population included in the group G, while coordinates $2, 3, \ldots, m + 1$ represent the proportion of the total wealth of the population held by individuals in group G for each of the m currencies under consideration.

The convex hull of the points of the form (2.7) constitutes the Lorenz zonoid of the population, introduced by Koshevoy (1995). Comparison of inequality between populations is then based on whether their corresponding Lorenz zonoids are nested. In a subsequent series of papers, Koshevoy and Mosler provided a natural extension of this concept to deal with quite general m-dimensional random variables (not just those taking on a finite number of values). Inter alia they provided links to other variability orderings and, in some cases, natural extensions of various univariate characterizations of the Lorenz order, such as those listed in Theorem 2.3 above. An excellent survey which includes discussion of this body of research may be found in Mosler (2002). The Lorenz zonoid order appears to be the compelling choice as a suitable m-dimensional analog of Lorenz's order, though it has a few perhaps unforeseen surprises for us. Intuitively the volume of the zonoid does provide an attractive summary measure of inequality (it actually coincides with the classical Gini index when wealth is one-dimensional). Moreover, a zero value for a measure of inequality is expected to be associated with an egalitarian distribution. When we deal with m currencies, the zonoid can have zero volume for some non-degenerate distributions. Mosler (2002) provides a variant definition to rectify this anomaly.

A second surprise is waiting for us if we consider the possibility of changing all the wealth of the individuals into one selected currency. An m-dimensional wealth random variable $\underline{X}$ will then have associated with it a one-dimensional random variable $c' \underline{X}$ where the c_ℓ's are non-negative quantities representing exchange rates. One idea for defining inequality among non-negative integrable m-dimensional random variables is based on such a currency exchange scenario. We will say that $\underline{X}$ is exchange rate Lorenz ordered with respect to $\underline{Y}$ if $\underline{c}' \underline{X} \leq_L \underline{c}' \underline{Y}$ in the usual univariate Lorenz order sense for every $\underline{c} \in \Re_+^m$.

Some candidate definitions for a Lorenz order among m-dimensional non-negative random vectors (with positive finite marginal expectations) are listed next.

(i) $\underline{X} \leq_L \underline{Y}$ if $L(\underline{X}) \subseteq L(\underline{Y})$ (where $L(\underline{X})$ denotes the Lorenz zonoid of $\underline{X}$).

(ii) $\underline{X} \leq_{L_1} \underline{Y}$ if $E\left(g\left(\dfrac{X_1}{E(X_1)}, \ldots, \dfrac{X_m}{E(X_m)}\right)\right) \leq E\left(g\left(\dfrac{Y_1}{E(Y_1)}, \ldots, \dfrac{Y_m}{E(Y_m)}\right)\right)$ for every continuous convex function $g : \Re_+^m \to \Re$ whose expectations exist.

(iii) $\underline{X} \leq_{L_2} \underline{Y}$ if $\underline{a}' \underline{X} \leq_L \underline{a}' \underline{Y} \, \forall \underline{a} \in \Re^m$.

(iv) $\underline{X} \leq_{L_3} \underline{Y}$ if $\underline{c}' \underline{X} \leq_L \underline{c}' \underline{Y} \, \forall \underline{c} \in \Re_+^m$.

(v) $\underline{X} \leq_{L_4} \underline{Y}$ if $X_\ell \leq_L Y_\ell, \, \ell = 1, 2, \ldots, m$.

Evidently the last three of these orderings are related in the sense that (iii) $\Rightarrow$ (iv) $\Rightarrow$ (v). Definition (v) could be labeled marginal Lorenz ordering. Our Lorenz zonoid order, (i), is actually equivalent to ordering (iii). Thus zonoid ordering implies but is not implied by exchange rate Lorenz ordering (or positive combinations Lorenz ordering in the terminology of Joe and Verducci 1992). Adding to its list of aliases, Mosler (2002) calls it the price Lorenz order. It would appear that in order to give the zonoid ordering an interpretation in terms of exchange rates we must consider some negative(!) exchange rates.

2.10 An evergreen future

On its one hundredth birthday, Lorenz's curve continues to generate interest and to be usefully applied in an amazingly broad spectrum of research areas. Open questions still abound, especially in the m-dimensional setting. And, of course, since in many instances Lorenz curves are not nested but cross once, twice or many times, considerable scope exists for consideration of Lorenz ordering over subsets of populations (e.g. studies of the poor, or the rich). The insights in that brief paper in 1905, coupled with inputs from mathematical discussions of majorization and its more abstract versions, continue to enable us to usefully grasp inequality, dispersion and variability concepts here, there and everywhere.

References

Arnold, B.C. (1983). *Pareto Distributions*, Burtonsville, MD: International Co-operative Publishing House.

Arnold, B.C. (2007). 'Majorization: Here, there and everywhere', *Statistical Science*, To appear.

Birkhoff, G. (1946). 'Three observations on linear algebra' (Spanish), *Univ. Nac. Tucuman. Revista A,* 5: 147–151.

Dalton, H. (1920). 'The measurement of the inequality of incomes', *Economics Journal*, 30: 348–361.

Gastwirth, J.L. (1971). 'A general definition of the Lorenz curve', *Econometrica*, 39: 1037–1039.

Hardy, G.H., J.E. Littlewood and G. Polya (1929). 'Some simple inequalities satisfied by convex functions', *Messenger of Mathematics*, 58: 145–152.

Hardy, G.H., J.E. Littlewood and G. Polya (1934, 1952). *Inequalities,* 1st ed., 2nd ed., London: Cambridge University Press.

Joe, H. and J. Verducci (1992). 'Multivariate majorization by positive combinations'. *Stochastic Inequalities (Seattle, WA, 1991)*, 159–181, *IMS Lecture Notes Monogr. Ser.,* 22, *Inst. Math. Statist., Hayward, CA.*

Kakwani, N.C. (1980). *Income Inequality and Poverty, Methods of Estimation and Policy Applications*, New York: Oxford University Press.

Koshevoy, G. (1995). 'Multivariate Lorenz majorization', *Social Choice and Welfare* 12: 93–102.

Lorenz, M.O. (1905). 'Methods of measuring concentration of wealth', *Journal of the American Statistical Association*, 9: 209–219.

Marshall, A.W. and I. Olkin (1979). *Inequalities: Theory of Majorization and its Applications, Mathematics in Science and Engineering*, 143, New York: Academic Press.

Mosler, K. (2002). *Multivariate Dispersion, Central Regions and Depth. The Lift Zonoid Approach, Lecture Notes in Statistics*, 165, Berlin: Springer-Verlag.

Muirhead, R.F. (1903). 'Some methods applicable to identities and inequalities of symmetric algebraic functions of n letters', *Proceedings of the Edinburgh Mathematical Society*, 21: 144–157.

Nayak, T.K. and M.C. Christman (1992). 'Effect of unequal catchability on estimates of the number of classes in a population', *Scandinavian Journal of Statistics*, 19: 281–287.

Neuts, M.F. (1975). 'Computational uses of the method of phases in the theory of queues', *Computational Mathematics and Applications*, 1: 151–166.

O'Cinneide, C.A. (1991). 'Phase-type distributions and majorization', *Annals of Applied Probability*, 1: 219–227.

Ross, S.M. (1981). 'A random graph', *Journal of Applied Probability*, 18 : 309–315.

Schur, I. (1923). 'Uber eine Klasse von Mittel bildungen mit Arwendungen die Determinanten-Theorie Sitzungsber', *Berlin Math. Gesellschaft* 23: 9–20.

Taguchi, T. (1972). 'On the two-dimensional concentration surface and extensions of concentration coefficient and Pareto distribution to the two-dimensional case (on an application of differential geometric methods to statistical analysis). I.', *Annals of the Institute of Statistical Mathematics*, 24: 355–381.

3 Gini, deprivation and complaints

Frank A. Cowell

3.1 Introduction

The early contributions of Gini and Lorenz have shaped the way the whole subject of income-distribution analysis has developed (Gini 1912, Lorenz 1905). Yet, over the last three or four decades, the Gini-Lorenz insights have been largely reinterpreted using the welfare-based approaches pioneered by Atkinson (1970) and Kolm (1969) taking their cue from the early work by Dalton (1920). This explicitly welfarist approach to the analysis of income distribution has influenced the development of research methodology and practical policy tools.

However, it is clear that a welfarist approach may not be necessary or even desirable: some have difficulty with issues such as the type of social consensus that supposedly underpins a social-welfare function; others may feel that coherent statements can be made about inequality comparisons without any reference to welfare. So alternative approaches to the subject have used analogies with information theory or on an explicit axiomatization of inequality that does not use the device of the social-welfare function.[1]

More recent work has attempted to reconsider the fundamental nature of income inequality and to examine the meaning of particular concepts in distributional analysis that lie outside the familiar territory of social-welfare analysis and information theory. Typically these focus on income differences rather than on individual income levels. The purpose of this chapter is to draw together results from a number of these recent contributions, to show the relationships between them and related work on deprivation and poverty, and to discuss the relationship with the original insights by Gini and Lorenz.

3.2 The setting

Let us begin by setting out a simplified framework of analysis for discussing the interconnected topics that form the theme of this chapter. For present purposes it is convenient to work with a fixed, finite population of economic agents who are identical in every respect other than income. The analysis can be extended to other empirically relevant cases by, for example, adjusting income using an equivalence scale and reweighting family units accordingly. Also, for many of the measures, we could use a more general distribution-function approach to present the results.

3.2.1 Population and income

Consider a given population of individuals

$$N := \{1, \ldots, n\}.$$

For each individual i there is an exogenously determined quantity to be known as 'income,' x_i.

The income distribution in the population is given by an n-vector

$$\mathbf{x} := (x_1, x_2, \ldots, x_n).$$

Let $\mathbb{R}$ denote the set of real numbers and let Ω_n^* be the set of ordered n-vectors:

$$\Omega_n^* := \{\mathbf{x} : \mathbf{x} \in \mathbb{R}^n, x_1 \le x_2 \le \ldots \le x_n\} \tag{3.1}$$

We may consider $\mathbf{x}$ to be taken from a connected subset $\mathbb{D}$ of Ω_n^*: one possibility is that $\mathbb{D}$ is the set of non-negative (ordered) n-vectors. This would be appropriate if 'income' is to be defined in a way that automatically rules out negative numbers; for example, if 'income' were in reality expenditure then it would be natural to assume $x_i \ge 0$. Some approaches choose to focus on a concept of individual welfare or utility which may, perhaps, be taken as a simple transform of individual income, in which case all that is required is a reinterpretation of $\mathbb{D}$.[2] Given the precise specification of $\mathbb{D}$ one can then, for example, represent inequality, poverty and other indices as functions from $\mathbb{D}$ to $\mathbb{R}$.

The methodology broadly consists in setting out a fairly parsimonious set of axioms that characterize the essential tools of distributional analysis. These tools can be summarized as:

- *Evaluation functions*. Perhaps the best known example of such a function is the Gini coefficient itself. This is one representative of a wide class that includes social-welfare functions, poverty measures and inequality measures.
- *Ranking criteria*. The prime example here is obviously the set of second-order ranking criteria associated with the Lorenz curve.

More specifically the idea is to find, for any specific problem in distributional analysis, a set of axioms that appropriately capture the principles that have an intuitive or ethical appeal for the problem in question and then to show that this specific set of axioms is necessary and sufficient for a particular evaluation function or ranking criterion to satisfy the stated principles.

3.2.2 The axiomatic approach

It might seem that the axiomatic approach is somewhat arbitrary. However, one of the arguments of this chapter is that there is a commonality of axioms across a number of topics that yield important insights on the connections between various principles of distributional analysis.

To begin with there are a few basic axioms that are frequently invoked to define the structure of evaluation functions and rankings. They are used so frequently that it makes sense to state a version of them here, before we have examined any of the specific distributional issues.

Let Φ be some evaluation function used for comparing income distributions, let δ, λ be scalars and $\mathbf{1} \in \mathbb{R}^n$ denote the vector $(1, 1, \ldots, 1)$.

Axiom 3.1 (Continuity) Φ *is a continuous function* $\mathbb{D} \to \mathbb{R}$.

Axiom 3.2 (Scale invariance) *For all* $\mathbf{x}$, $\mathbf{y} \in \mathbb{D}$, *and all* $\lambda > 0$ *such that* $\lambda\mathbf{x}$, $\lambda\mathbf{y} \in \mathbb{D}$: *if* $\Phi(\mathbf{x}) = \Phi(\mathbf{y})$ *then* $\Phi(\lambda\mathbf{x}) = \Phi(\lambda\mathbf{y})$.

Axiom 3.3 (Translation invariance) *For all* $\mathbf{x}$, $\mathbf{y} \in \mathbb{D}$ *and all* δ *such that* $\mathbf{x} + \delta\mathbf{1}$, $\mathbf{y} + \delta\mathbf{1} \in \mathbb{D}$: *if* $\Phi(\mathbf{x}) = \Phi(\mathbf{y})$ *then* $\Phi(\mathbf{x} + \delta\mathbf{1}) = \Phi(\mathbf{y} + \delta\mathbf{1})$.

Axioms 3.1 to 3.3 can readily be used for the characterization of ranking criteria rather than evaluation functions. These axioms, or modifications of them, endow the evaluation function Φ with a structure that turns out to be very useful for building a variety of tools for distributional analysis. Consider the use of these in characterizing a familiar inequality index.

For example characterization of the absolute Gini coefficient uses two more restrictive modifications of Axioms 3.2 and 3.3, namely:

Axiom 3.4 (Linear homogeneity) *For all* $\mathbf{x} \in \mathbb{D}$, *and all* $\lambda > 0$ *such that* $\lambda\mathbf{x} \in \mathbb{D}$: $\Phi(\lambda\mathbf{x}) = \lambda\Phi(\mathbf{x})$.

Axiom 3.5 (Translation independence) *For all* $\mathbf{x} \in \mathbb{D}$ *and all* δ *such that* $\mathbf{x} + \delta\mathbf{1} \in \mathbb{D}$: $\Phi(\mathbf{x} + \delta\mathbf{1}) = \Phi(\mathbf{x})$.

The absolute Gini is given by

$$I_{AG}(\mathbf{x}) := \frac{1}{n^2} \sum_{i=1}^{n} \sum_{j=i+1}^{n} [x_j - x_i] \tag{3.2}$$

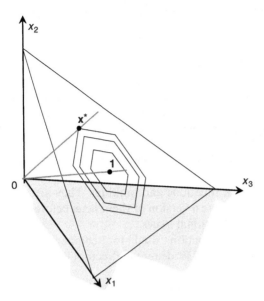

Figure 3.1 Contour map for the Gini, $n = 3$

and it has contours as illustrated in Figure 3.1. The triangular area is the simplex with the centroid $\mathbf{1} = (1, 1, 1)$ at which there is perfect equality. Let point $\mathbf{x}^*$ be some arbitrary income distribution; by Axiom 3.1, along any connected path from $\mathbf{x}^*$ to 1 inequality continuously approaches the value of perfect equality, conventionally normalized at 0; a point $\mathbf{x}^\lambda$ lying along the ray through $\mathbf{x}^*$ such that $\mathbf{x}^\lambda = \lambda\mathbf{x}^*$ will represent a distribution with inequality $\lambda I_{AG}(\mathbf{x}^*)$ (Axiom 3.4); a point lying along a line through $\mathbf{x}^*$ parallel to the ray through 1 represents a distribution with the same inequality as $\mathbf{x}^*$ (implied by Axiom 3.5).

What about ethical criteria such as the transfer principle? There are two approaches that have been adopted in the literature. The first is to build such a requirement in as an explicit principle for Φ. The second, and perhaps more satisfactory, is to allow it to emerge from the axiomatic structure: here the idea is to allow the structural axioms and other essential properties to characterize a general class of functions to which Φ belongs and then to consider the members of this class that may satisfy the particular ethical principle.

3.3 Deprivation

Income differences lie at the heart of the Gini approach to inequality. They are also central to the concept of 'relative deprivation' that has its origins in sociology (Runciman 1966). In the economics context the concept of deprivation can be seen as emerging naturally from the relationship between inequality measures and social-welfare functions. There are also intuitive and formal connections between deprivation and poverty analysis; in fact deprivation is structurally similar to the problem of poverty measurement which we will briefly consider first.

3.3.1 Poverty

Sen's approach to poverty (Sen 1976, 1979) makes the connection between poverty and deprivation explicit. His approach also assists the present discussion by making clear two key components of the problem: the identification of the poor and the aggregation of information about the poor. The aggregation of information can be into a single poverty index (an example of an evaluation function) or into a poverty ranking.

The question of income can be considered to lie outside the scope of the present discussion although in any application the distinction between, say, total family income and consumption expenditure may be crucial for the identification issue. Here income is just the quantity x used in section 3.2.

3.3.1.1 Identification and the reference point

The definition of a poverty line is a particularly convenient device because it automatically defines a reference point. Given a specific poverty line $z \in \mathbb{R}_+$ we can introduce the concept of the *poverty gap* for any person i

$$g_i(\mathbf{x}, z) = \begin{cases} z - x_i & \text{if } x_i \leq z \\ 0 & \text{otherwise} \end{cases}. \tag{3.3}$$

The poverty gap concept plays a central role in Sen's approach and is also at the heart of the Foster et al. (1984) analysis that developed the family of poverty indices (evaluation functions) given by

$$\frac{1}{n} \sum_{i=1}^{n} \left[\frac{g_i(\mathbf{x}, z)}{z} \right]^a \tag{3.4}$$

where a is a sensitivity index.

Let us define the cumulative poverty gap as

$$G_i(\mathbf{x}, z) := \frac{1}{n} \sum_{j=1}^{i} g_j(\mathbf{x}, z), \, i = 1, 2, \ldots, n \tag{3.5}$$

This then yields a key concept used for the purposes of ranking – the TIP curve (Jenkins and Lambert 1997) or poverty profile (Shorrocks 1998). This curve is formed by joining the points $(\frac{i}{n}, G_i(\mathbf{x}, z))$ and must be increasing and concave.

3.3.1.2 Axiomatic approach

The seminal paper by Sen (1976) was remarkable for its introduction of the Gini coefficient into the analysis of poverty. It is clear that this emerges from the specific assumptions that Sen introduced about the nature of poverty including an explicit introduction of an assumption that the weight to be placed on the gap $g_i(\mathbf{x}, z)$ in the aggregation process is to be proportional to i itself, i.e. proportional to i's position in the income distribution.

However, an alternative approach to the axiomatization of poverty has been provided by Ebert and Moyes (2002). The approach effectively examines the structure of rankings on $n + 1$ incomes – the n incomes of the agents $(x_1, x_2 \ldots, x_n)$ plus the poverty line z. They use Axioms 3.1 to 3.3 but apply them to this extended space of $n + 1$ incomes. To describe their contribution let us define p as the number of of people who are poor:

$$p(\mathbf{x}, z) := \# \{i : x_i \le z\}$$

and let P be the ordinal function representing the poverty ranking.[3] The following axioms are also required:

Axiom 3.6 (Focus) *For* $\mathbf{x} \in \mathbb{D}$ *and* $x_i > z$ *P is constant in* x_i.

Axiom 3.7 (Monotonicity) *For* $\mathbf{x} \in \mathbb{D}$ *and* $x_i \le z$ *P is strictly decreasing in* x_i.

Axiom 3.8 (Independence) *Let* $\mathbf{x}, \mathbf{y} \in \mathbb{D}$ *be such that* $P(\mathbf{x}, z) = P(\mathbf{y}, z)$, *and* $x_i = y_i$ *for some* $i \le p(\mathbf{x}, z)$; *then, for any* x° *such that* $x_{i-1} \le x^\circ \le x_{i+1}$
$$P(x_1, x_2, \ldots, x_{i-1}, x^\circ, x_{i+1} \ldots, x_n, z) = P(y_1, y_2, \ldots, y_{i-1}, x^\circ, y_{i+1} \ldots, y_n, z)$$

Then, Ebert and Moyes (2002) show the following:

Theorem 3.1 *Given Axioms 3.1–3.3 and 3.6–3.8 the function P representing the poverty ranking must satisfy*

$$\varphi \left(\frac{1}{n} \sum_{i=1}^{n} \left[\frac{g_i(\mathbf{x}, z)}{z} \right]^a, z \right) \tag{3.6}$$

or

$$\varphi \left(\frac{1}{n} \sum_{i=1}^{n} g_i(\mathbf{x}, z)^a, z \right) \tag{3.7}$$

where $a > 0$ *and* φ *is continuous and increasing in its first argument.*

Clearly (3.6) is just a transformation of the Foster et al. (1984) index (3.4), while (3.7) is an 'absolute' counterpart of the 'relative' index (3.4).

3.3.2 *Individual deprivation*

The elements of a theory of individual deprivation are essentially the definition of income, the reference group, and an evaluation method. Again the definition of income can be set aside, for the same reasons as in section 3.3.1. The specification of the reference group can be based on intuition, on theories from the social sciences, or on an explicit axiomatization.

3.3.2.1 *The Yitzhaki approach*

The key insight for our purposes was provided by Yitzhaki (1979). With hindsight this can be seen as a natural extension of one aspect of the Sen approach to the structure of poverty. Yitzhaki originally specified his individual deprivation measure using a fairly general formulation. If x is an individual's income and F is the distribution function for the economy in question then, assuming that individuals are alike in all respects other than income, the deprivation felt by someone with income x is

$$d(x) := \int_x^\infty [1 - F(y)] \, dy \qquad (3.8)$$

Expression (3.8) is equivalent to

$$d(x) = \int_x^\infty [y - x] \, dF(y) \qquad (3.9)$$

In terms of the present notation, for a finite population (3.9) can be expressed as follows. Given the income distribution represented by the vector $\mathbf{x}$, the deprivation experienced by individual i is

$$d_i(\mathbf{x}) = \frac{1}{n} \sum_{j=i+1}^n [x_j - x_i] \qquad (3.10)$$

Furthermore, define the conditional mean

$$\mu_i(\mathbf{x}) := \frac{1}{n-i} \sum_{j=i+1}^n x_j; \qquad (3.11)$$

where we note in passing that the conventional mean is given by $\mu_0(\mathbf{x})$. Then (3.10) can be written equivalently as

$$d_i(\mathbf{x}) = \frac{n-i}{n} [\mu_i(\mathbf{x}) - x_i] \qquad (3.12)$$

The individual deprivation index $d_i(\mathbf{x})$ is evidently the counterpart to the "gap" concept (3.3) used in poverty analysis.

3.3.2.2 An axiomatic approach

However, the deprivation problem differs from the poverty in one important respect. The poverty line can be taken as exogenous information defining the poverty problem, but there is no counterpart to that in the deprivation problem. The poverty gap $g_i(\mathbf{x}, z)$ follows from this definition and scarcely needs axiomatization, although in the Ebert and Moyes (2002) formulation it follows from Axiom 3.3. In the case of deprivation one either has to assume (3.12) arbitrarily or find an appropriate method of axiomatizing it.

Nevertheless a suitable axiomatization of $d_i(\cdot)$ can be found using some of the same structure as for the characterization of poverty. Clearly the crucial component of the problem is the definition of a reference group.

Ebert and Moyes (2000) provide an axiomatization of individual deprivation whereby the index is to be defined for all logically possible reference groups for a given N. As an alternative Bossert and D'Ambrosio (2006) axiomatize the Yitzhaki index using an approach that differs from Ebert and Moyes (2000) in the way the reference group of an individual is to be represented. Although it is otherwise similar to Ebert and Moyes (2000), some of the other axioms have to be modified or replaced as a result of this alternative way of characterizing the reference group.

In the Bossert and D'Ambrosio (2006) approach the reference group for individual i is the "better-than" set

$$B_i(\mathbf{x}) = \{j \in N : x_j > x_i\}$$

Axiom 3.9 (Focus) *For all* $\mathbf{x}, \mathbf{y} \in \mathbb{D}$ *such that* $B_i(\mathbf{x}) = B_i(\mathbf{y})$ *and* $x_j = y_j$ *for all* $j \in B_i(\mathbf{x})$ *and* $x_i = y_i$ *then*

$$d_i(\mathbf{x}) = d_i(\mathbf{y})$$

Axiom 3.10 (Normalization) *For all* $x \in \mathbb{D}$, *and* $j \neq i$ *such that* $x_j = 1$ *and* $x_i = 0$, $i \neq j$

$$d_i(\mathbf{x}) = \frac{1}{n}$$

Axiom 3.11 (Additive decomposition) *For all* $x \in \mathbb{D}$, *let* B^1, B^2 *be any two mutually exclusive and exhaustive subsets of* $B_i(\mathbf{x})$ *and define vectors* x^1 *and* x^2 *such that*

$$x_j^t = \begin{cases} x_i & \text{if } i \in B^t \\ x_j & \text{otherwise} \end{cases}, \ t = 1, 2.$$

Then

$$d_i(\mathbf{x}) = d_i(\mathbf{x}^1) + d_i(\mathbf{x}^2).$$

Then Bossert and D'Ambrosio (2006) show:

Theorem 3.2 *Axioms 3.4, 3.5 and 3.9 to 3.11, for the case* $\Phi = d_i$ *give*

$$d_i(\mathbf{x}) = \frac{1}{n} \sum_{j \in B_i(\mathbf{x})} [x_j - x_i]$$

The above expression is clearly the Yitzhaki index of individual deprivation (3.10) again.

3.3.3 *Aggregate deprivation*

Now consider the required elements for an approach to a concept of aggregate deprivation; clearly we need the definition of individual deprivation and an aggregation method.

3.3.3.1 *A standard approach*

Perhaps the most obvious way to derive a measure of aggregate deprivation from the individual deprivation measures is just to add them up. Using the Yitzhaki notation, suppose the deprivation experienced by a person with income x is measured by (3.8) or (3.9). Writing $\mu(F)$ for the mean of the distribution given by the distribution function F, expressions (3.8) or (3.9) can also be written as

$$\mu(F) - x + xq - C(F; q) \tag{3.13}$$

where

$$q = F(x)$$

and C is the income-cumulation function

$$C(F; q) := \int_0^q x(t)dt.$$

Integrating (3.13) over the distribution F we get

$$= -\int_0^1 C(F; q)dq + \int_0^\infty x \int_0^x dF(y)dF(x);$$

then the aggregated value of deprivation for the distribution F is

$$\mu(F) - 2 \int_0^1 C(F; q)dq \tag{3.14}$$

which is the absolute Gini. In terms of the notation of section 3.2 we would have the simplified form of aggregate deprivation given by

$$\frac{1}{n} \sum_{i=1}^n d_i(\mathbf{x}) \tag{3.15}$$

which, on rearrangement, gives (3.2).

The form (3.14) shows the close relationship between this interpretation of deprivation and generalized-Lorenz rankings (Hey and Lambert 1980). Finally, note that (3.15) is an absolute index (because of translation invariance); we can obviously convert it into a relative index by dividing by the mean, in which case one gets the conventional Gini coefficient, which exhibits scale invariance and will decrease under uniform additions to all incomes.

3.3.3.2 Extensions

However, it may be worth considering alternative forms of aggregation of individual deprivation. In a manner similar to the Foster et al. (1984) aggregation of poverty gaps, the deprivation index suggested by Chakravarty and Chakraborty (1984) and developed further in Chakravarty and Mukherjee (1999b) aggregates individual deprivation as follows:

$$\left[\frac{1}{n} \sum_{i=1}^n d_i(\mathbf{x})^{\varepsilon} \right]^{\frac{1}{\varepsilon}} \tag{3.16}$$

where $d_i(\mathbf{x})$ is given by (3.12) and $\varepsilon \geq 1$ is a sensitivity parameter. A similar relative concept for aggregate deprivation has been suggested by Chakravarty and Mukherjee (1999a):[4]

$$1 - \left[\frac{1}{n} \sum_{i=1}^n \left[1 - \frac{d_i(\mathbf{x})}{\mu_0(\mathbf{x})} \right]^{\varepsilon} \right]^{\frac{1}{\varepsilon}} \tag{3.17}$$

where $\mu_0(\mathbf{x})$ is the mean for the whole distribution.[5]

3.3.3.3 Relationship with Gini

The role of the Gini coefficient in characterizing deprivation has become familiar in the literature. The fact that individuals' rank is incorporated into its definition can be seen as a natural interpretation of social disadvantage.[6] However, a further lesson from the deprivation literature is the fundamental importance of differences – a concept that underlies all the approaches[7] and is also central to the Gini coefficient and the various types of generalized Gini coefficients. Furthermore, the comparison between the poverty and relative deprivation approaches clearly draws attention to the concept of reference group and reference income, a point that is essential in the argument of section 3.4.

3.4 Complaints and income distribution

The philosopher Larry Temkin introduced an alternative way of perceiving the income distribution in terms of inequality (Temkin 1986, 1993). Once again the role of income differences is central to the argument and it is interesting to see how this alternative approach relates to the Gini-Lorenz approach and to the analysis of deprivation considered in section 3.3.

3.4.1 The nature of complaints

3.4.1.1 Individual complaints

The fundamental concept required for the Temkin approach is that of an individual agent's complaint. Like the concept of deprivation examined in section 3.3.2 the Temkin concept of complaint can be naturally expressed in terms of income differences. But what differences?[8]

The answer to this again depends on the concept of the reference group. Temkin identifies three, each associated with a specific reference income level

- Best-off person
- All those better off
- The average

We will examine the way each of these relates to the standard approaches to inequality measurement and to the notions of deprivation discussed earlier.

3.4.1.2 Aggregate complaint

Temkin (1993) suggested two approaches, simple summation – as we did for the basic deprivation index – or a weighted aggregation. We leave this question open until we have considered the individual interpretations of 'complaint.'

3.4.2 Best-off Person (BOP)

3.4.2.1 Axiomatic structure

Here individual i's complaint given the income distribution $\mathbf{x}$ is specified by the difference between i's income and that of the richest person:

$$k_i(\mathbf{x}) := x_n - x_i. \tag{3.18}$$

Of course there may be more than one richest person; so it is useful to define $r(\mathbf{x})$ as the lowest value of $j \in N$ such that $x_j = x_n$.

We can make the Temkin idea of complaint-based inequality specific by characterizing the shape of a family of inequality measures, using the approach of Cowell and Ebert (2004). Suppose the BOP-complaint version of the Temkin inequality index is an evaluation function T. Then Cowell and Ebert (2004) use the basic structural axioms given in section 3.2.2 (with Φ replaced by T) plus these:

Axiom 3.12 (Monotonicity) *For* $\mathbf{x} \in \mathbb{D}$ *and* $i < r(\mathbf{x})$ *T is strictly decreasing in x_i.*

Axiom 3.13 (Independence) *Let* $\mathbf{x}$, $\mathbf{y} \in \mathbb{D}$ *be such that* $T(\mathbf{x}) = T(\mathbf{y})$, $r(\mathbf{x}) = r(\mathbf{y}) = r > 2$ *and* $x_r = y_r$. *Then, for any* $i < r$, $x_i = y_i \Rightarrow$ $\forall a \in [x_{i-1}, x_{i+1}] \cap [y_{i-1}, y_{i+1}]$ *and* $\mathbf{x}_{-i}(a)$, $\mathbf{y}_{-i}(a) \in \mathbb{D}$: $T(\mathbf{x}_{-i}(a)) = T(\mathbf{y}_{-i}(a))$.

Axiom 3.14 (Normalization) $T(0, \ldots, 0, 1) = 1$

Note the similarity of Axioms 3.12 and 3.13 to Axioms 3.7 and 3.8 in the analysis of poverty. So a result similar to Theorem 3.1 emerges. Let Ω_n be the subset of Ω_n^* such that $x_{n-1} < x_n$ – there is a single richest person. Then, using the topmost income x_n as a reference point Cowell and Ebert (2004) show the following for the two cases of the space of incomes:

Theorem 3.3 *T satisfies Axioms 3.1, 3.4, 3.5 and 3.12 to 3.14 if and only if there are* $w_j > 0, j = 1, \ldots, n-1$, $\sum_{j=1}^{n-1} w_j = 1$ *and* $\varepsilon \in \mathbb{R}$ *such that, for all* $\mathbf{x} \in \mathbb{D}$:

Case 1 ($\mathbb{D} = \Omega_n$)

$$T_\varepsilon(\mathbf{x}) = \left[\sum_{j=1}^{n-1} w_j k_j(\mathbf{x})^\varepsilon \right]^{\frac{1}{\varepsilon}} \quad for\ \varepsilon \neq 0 \tag{3.19}$$

$$= \prod_{j=1}^{n-1} k_j(\mathbf{x})^{w_j} for\ \varepsilon = 0 \tag{3.20}$$

Case 2 ($\mathbb{D} = \Omega_n^*$) *Condition (3.19) holds and* $\varepsilon > 0$.

3.4.2.2 Inequality measures

The parameters $w_1, \ldots, w_{n-1}$ and ε characterize the whole family of BOP-complaint inequality indices. All of them satisfy the transfer principle (Dalton 1920) if the richest person is included in the income transfer but not all will satisfy the transfer principle for an arbitrary pair of persons. However, Cowell and Ebert (2004) also show:

Theorem 3.4 *T_ε satisfies the transfer principle for any arbitrary pair of persons if and only if*

- $w_{j+1} \leq w_j$ *and* $\varepsilon > 1$ *or*
- $w_{j+1} < w_j$ *and* $\varepsilon = 1$

To illustrate the relationship of this class to the familiar Gini coefficient, examine Figure 3.2 that depicts iso-inequality contour maps for the case $n = 3$ with a fixed overall income level. Part (a) shows the contours for (absolute or relative) Gini, as shown in Figure 3.1; part (b) shows the contour map for one particular Temkin index that is clearly equivalent to those of the extended-Gini as discussed in section 3.3.3.

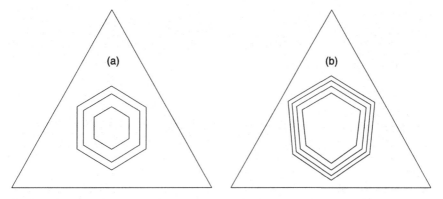

Figure 3.2 Contours for (a) Gini and (b) Temkin, $\varepsilon = 1$; $w_1 = 0.75$, $w_2 = 0.25$

3.4.2.3 Ranking

Apart from the behaviour of a typical complaint-inequality index it is natural to consider how the concept of complaint may be used in providing a ranking criterion. We need the counterpart to the Lorenz insight that is provided, in the poverty context, by the TIP curve or poverty profile given in (3.5). So, analogously, for any $\mathbf{x} \in \mathbb{D}$ we can define the cumulation of complaints recursively as

$$K_i(\mathbf{x}) := \sum_{j=1}^{i} k_j(\mathbf{x}), \, i = 1, 2, \ldots, n \tag{3.21}$$

This concept can be used to draw the 'cumulative complaint contour' (CCC) of a distribution $\mathbf{x}$, formed by joining the points $(\frac{i}{n}, K_i(\mathbf{x}))$ and has essentially the same properties as the TIP curve. If CCC($\mathbf{x}$) lies on or above CCC($\mathbf{y}$) then distribution $\mathbf{x}$ exhibits more BOP-complaint inequality than distribution $\mathbf{y}$.[9]

To see what this means consider the subclass of BOP-complaint inequality indices that satisfy the conventional transfer principle (see Theorem 3.4 above). Let $\mathcal{T} := \mathcal{T}_0 \cup \mathcal{T}_1$ where

$$\mathcal{T}_0 := \left\{ T_\varepsilon : \varepsilon > 1, \sum_{j=1}^{n-1} w_j = 1, \, w_j \geq w_{j+1} > 0 \right\}$$

$$\mathcal{T}_1 := \left\{ T_1 : \sum_{j=1}^{n-1} w_j = 1, \, w_j > w_{j+1} > 0 \right\}$$

There is a close relationship between this class $\mathcal{T}$ and an inequality-ranking principle $\succcurlyeq_T$ defined in terms of the complaint cumulations:

Definition 3.1 *For any* $\mathbf{x}, \mathbf{y} \in \mathbb{D}$ *distribution* $\mathbf{x}$ *exhibits more complaint-inequality than* $\mathbf{y}$ $(\mathbf{x} \succcurlyeq_T \mathbf{y})$ *if and only if*

$$K_i(\mathbf{x}) \geq K_i(\mathbf{y}) \text{ for } i = 1, 2, \ldots, n$$

where K_i *is given by (3.21).*

Theorem 3.5 *For any* $\mathbf{x}, \mathbf{y} \in \mathbb{D}$: $\mathbf{x} \succcurlyeq_T \mathbf{y} \Leftrightarrow T_\varepsilon(\mathbf{x}) \geq T_\varepsilon(\mathbf{y})$, *for all* $T_\varepsilon \in \mathcal{T}$.

The proof – reproduced in the appendix – relies on the fact that one can transform the CCC problem into one that is effectively an income-cumulation problem: the ranking $\succcurlyeq_T$ is closely related to the standard generalized-Lorenz ranking criterion $\succcurlyeq_{GL}$ (Shorrocks 1983).

3.4.3 All those better off (ATBO)

The analysis of section 3.4.2 can be adapted to the second type of complaint where each individual uses as his reference point the average income of all those who are better off. Unlike BOP the reference point is different for each person. Using the conditional mean (3.11) one obtains the ATBO-complaint as

$$k_i(\mathbf{x}) := \mu_i(\mathbf{x}) - x_i. \tag{3.22}$$

This will generate a set of ATBO-complaint indices of the form (3.19, 3.20) but with individual complaints k_i given by (3.22) rather than (3.18). This is clearly the ATBO counterpart of the family and is essentially the same as the Chakravarty version of deprivation given by (3.16).[10]

3.4.4 Average income (AVE)

For completeness let us also consider the possibility of AVE-complaint inequality indices. Here the reference point is, $\mu_0(\mathbf{x})$, the mean for the whole distribution. By analogy with (3.18) and (3.22) one now has

$$k_i(\mathbf{x}) : = \mu_0(\mathbf{x}) - x_i. \tag{3.23}$$

as the individual 'complaint' concept. But, as Devooght (2003) has pointed out, where incomes are greater than the mean, it is unclear what meaning is to be given to 'complaint.' Nevertheless, in this case the counterpart of (3.19, 3.20) is

$$\left. \begin{array}{c} \left[\displaystyle\sum_{j=1}^{n} w_j \left| k_j(\mathbf{x}) \right|^{\varepsilon} \right]^{\frac{1}{\varepsilon}} \quad \text{for } \varepsilon \neq 0, \\ \\ \displaystyle\prod_{j=1}^{n} \left| k_j(\mathbf{x}) \right|^{w_j} \quad \text{for } \varepsilon = 0. \end{array} \right\} \tag{3.24}$$

The family (3.24) is related to the Ebert (1988) class of inequality measures.

3.5 Conclusion

The focus of Gini's original contribution on income differences is fundamental. This focus is now widely recognized not only in the analysis of deprivation and of poverty but also in recent approaches to inequality that have incorporated the concept of complaint about income distribution. Likewise Lorenz's contribution, so closely associated in the literature with Gini's work, is also fundamental to recent contributions: a generalization of the Lorenz ranking works for both poverty orderings and complaint orderings.

Recent advances in the analysis of relative deprivation, poverty and complaint inequality show that these separate problems share a common structure. As we have seen many of the same axioms are conventionally used in the approach to characterizing measures for each of the three problems. However, they are not just an artefact of the methodology adopted by those who have recently worked on the formalization of these concepts. It is clear from the original contributions in each of these areas that individual deprivation, d_i, the individual poverty gap g_i, and individual complaint k_i are all examples of fundamental income differences that lie at the heart of the thinking about these issues: indeed in many respects the indices that incorporate the income-difference concepts can be obtained from another with little more than a change in notation. It is legitimate to see this modern body of work as part of the intellectual legacy of Gini and Lorenz.

Notes

1 See for example Theil (1967) on information theory, Bourguignon (1979), Cowell (1980), Shorrocks (1980) on axiomatic approaches.
2 However, this is not an innocuous assumption. Individual utility may well be a function of other people's incomes or utilities as well, in which case the relationship between simple properties of orderings and welfare properties may no longer hold; see Amiel and Cowell (1994).
3 We may use a continuous function P in view of Axiom 3.1; the statement $P(\mathbf{x}, z) \geq P(\mathbf{y}, z)$ should be read as 'for the poverty line z distribution $\mathbf{x}$ exhibits greater poverty than distribution $\mathbf{y}$.'
4 D'Ambrosio and Frick (2004) take the concept a stage further. They examine the relationship between (a) relative deprivation/satisfaction, i.e. the gaps between the individual's income and the incomes of all individuals richer/poorer than him and (b) self-reported level of satisfaction with income and life.
5 The approach is similar to the paper by Duclos and Grégoire (2002) who use the so-called S-Gini coefficient in the specification of a class of poverty indices that combine normative concerns for absolute and relative deprivation. Their indices are distinguished by a parameter that captures the ethical sensitivity of poverty measurement to 'exclusion' or 'relative-deprivation' aversion. The connection with the Chakravarty approaches can be seen if one writes the S-Gini as

$$\frac{1}{n} \sum_{i=1}^{n} \frac{d_i(\mathbf{x})}{\mu_0(\mathbf{x})} w_i(\upsilon)$$

where the weights are given by

$$w_i(\upsilon) := \upsilon [\upsilon - 1] \left[1 - \frac{i}{n} \right]^{\upsilon - 2}$$

6 For other developments of the basic deprivation concept and its welfare interpretation see Berrebi and Silber (1985, 1989), Chakravarty and Mukherjee (1998), Stark and Yitzhaki (1988), Yitzhaki (1979, 1980, 1982).
7 Podder (1996) provides an alternative approach to aggregate deprivation that does not appear to use the basic structural axioms in that he examines utility comparisons not income differences. However, we can see this as the basic idea applied to a utility transformation of income. The main idea is preserved if one just redefines $\mathbb{D}$ in terms of the space of utilities. Likewise in Chakravarty and Moyes (2003) deprivation is formulated in terms of utility rather than just in terms of income and they use this to examine the incidence of taxation on the amount of deprivation felt in the society.
8 Note that the complaint is not the same as the (dis)utility of deprivation, as in Podder (1996) or Chakravarty and Moyes (2003). Rather, the complaint exists as an independent entity:

To say that the best-off have nothing to complain about is in no way to impugn their moral sensibilities. They may be just as concerned about the inequality in their world as anyone else. Nor is it to deny that, insofar as one is concerned about inequality, one might have a complaint about them being as well off as they are. It is only to recognize that, since they are at least as well off as every other member of their world, they have nothing to complain about. Similarly, to say that the worst-off have a complaint is not to claim that they will in fact complain (they may not). It is only to recognize that it is a bad thing (unjust or unfair) for them to be worse off than the other members of their world through no fault of their own (Temkin 1986, p.102).

9 Chakravarty et al. (2003) introduce the idea of target shortfall orderings. Here one associates with each income x° a subgroup containing all persons whose incomes are not higher than x° and a person's target shortfall in a subgroup is the gap between the subgroup highest income and his own income. They establish an absolute target shortfall ordering, which, under constancy of population size and total income, implies the Lorenz and CCC orderings.

10 There is a superficial difference in that the summation in (3.19) runs from 1 to $n-1$ whereas in (3.16) it is from 1 to n. However, given that complaint or deprivation is zero at the top and that (3.16) restricts the value of ε, this distinction is irrelevant.

References

Amiel, Y. and F. A. Cowell (1994). Monotonicity, dominance and the Pareto principle. *Economics Letters 45*, 447–450.

Atkinson, A. B. (1970). On the measurement of inequality. *Journal of Economic Theory 2*, 244–263.

Berrebi, Z. M. and J. Silber (1985). Income inequality indices and deprivation: a generalization. *Quarterly Journal of Economics 100*, 807–810.

Berrebi, Z. M. and J. Silber (1989). Deprivation, the Gini index of inequality and the flatness of an income distribution. *Mathematical Social Sciences 18*(12), 229–237.

Bossert, W. and C. D'Ambrosio (2006). Reference groups and individual deprivation. *Economics Letters 90*, 421–426.

Bourguignon, F. (1979). Decomposable income inequality measures. *Econometrica 47*, 901–920.

Chakravarty, S. R. (1998). Relative deprivation and satisfaction orderings. *Keio Economic Studies 34*, 17–31.

Chakravarty, S. R. and A. B. Chakraborty (1984). On indices of relative deprivation. *Economics Letters 14*, 283–287.

Chakravarty, S. R. and P. Moyes (2003). Individual welfare, social deprivation and income taxation. *Economic Theory 21*, 843–869.

Chakravarty, S. R. and D. Mukherjee (1998). Lorenz transformation, utilitarian deprivation rule and equal sacrifice principle. *The Manchester School 66*, 521–531.

Chakravarty, S. R. and D. Mukherjee (1999a). Measures of deprivation and their meaning in terms of social satisfaction. *Theory and Decision 47*, 89–100.

Chakravarty, S. R. and D. Mukherjee (1999b). Ranking income distributions by deprivation orderings. *Social Indicators Research 46*, 125–135.

Chakravarty, S. R., C. D'Ambrosio, and P. Muliere (2003, March). Target shortfall orderings and indices. DIW Discussion Paper 340, German Institute for Economic Research, Königin-Luise-Str. 5, 14195 Berlin, Germany.

Cowell, F. A. (1980). On the structure of additive inequality measures. *Review of Economic Studies 47*, 521–531.

Cowell, F. A. and U. Ebert (2004). Complaints and inequality. *Social Choice and Welfare 23*, 71–89.

Dalton, H. (1920). Measurement of the inequality of incomes. *The Economic Journal 30*, 348–361.

D'Ambrosio, C. and J. R. Frick (2004, October). Subjective well-being and relative deprivation: An empirical link. IZA Discussion Paper 1351, Forschungsinstitut zur Zukunft der Arbeit.

Devooght, K. (2003). Measuring inequality by counting 'complaints': theory and empirics. *Economics and Philosophy 19*, 241–263.

Duclos, J.-Y. and P. Grégoire (2002). Absolute and relative deprivation and the measurement of poverty. *Review of Income and Wealth 48*, 471–492.

Ebert, U. (1988). A family of aggregative compromise inequality measure. *International Economic Review 29*(5), 363–376.

Ebert, U. and P. Moyes (2000). An axiomatic characterization of Yitzhaki's index of individual deprivation. *Economics Letters 68*(3), 263–270.

Ebert, U. and P. Moyes (2002). A simple axiomatization of the Foster-Greer-Thorbecke poverty orderings. *Journal of Public Economic Theory 4*, 455–473.

Foster, J. E., J. Greer, and E. Thorbecke (1984). A class of decomposable poverty measures. *Econometrica 52*, 761–776.

Gini, C. (1912). Variabilità e mutabilità. *Studi Economico-Giuridici dell'Università di Cagliari 3*, 1–158.

Hey, J. D. and P. J. Lambert (1980). Relative deprivation and the Gini coefficient: comment. *Quarterly Journal of Economics 95*, 567–573, and reply by Yitzhaki.

Jenkins, S. P. and P. J. Lambert (1997). Three 'I's of poverty curves, with an analysis of UK poverty trends. *Oxford Economic Papers 49*, 317–327.

Kolm, S.-C. (1969). The optimal production of social justice. In J. Margolis and H. Guitton (Eds.), *Public Economics*, pp. 145–200. London: Macmillan.

Lorenz, M. O. (1905). Methods for measuring concentration of wealth. *Journal of the American Statistical Association 9*, 209–219.

Podder, N. (1996). Relative deprivation, envy and economic inequality. *Kyklos 49*, 353–376.

Runciman, W. G. (1966). *Relative Deprivation and Social Justice*. London: Routledge.

Sen, A. K. (1976). Poverty: An ordinal approach to measurement. *Econometrica 44*, 219–231.

Sen, A. K. (1979). Issues in the measurement of poverty. *Scandinavian Journal of Economics 91*, 285–307.

Shorrocks, A. F. (1980). The class of additively decomposable inequality measures. *Econometrica 48*, 613–625.

Shorrocks, A. F. (1983). Ranking income distributions. *Economica 50*, 3–17.

Shorrocks, A. F. (1998). Deprivation profiles and deprivation indices. In S. P. Jenkins, A. Kapteyn, and B. M. S. Van Praag (Eds.), *The Distribution of Welfare and Household Production: International Perspectives*, Chapter 11, pp. 250–267. Cambridge: Cambridge University Press.

Stark, O. and S. Yitzhaki (1988). The migration response to relative deprivation. *Journal of Population Economics 1*.

Temkin, L. S. (1986). Inequality. *Philosophy and Public Affairs 15*, 99–121.

Temkin, L. S. (1993). *Inequality*. Oxford: Oxford University Press.

Theil, H. (1967). *Economics and Information Theory*. Amsterdam: North Holland.

Yitzhaki, S. (1979). Relative deprivation and the Gini coefficient. *Quarterly Journal of Economics 93*, 321–324.

Yitzhaki, S. (1980). Relative deprivation and the Gini coefficient: reply. *Quarterly Journal of Economics 95*, 575–576.

Yitzhaki, S. (1982). Relative deprivation and economic welfare. *European Economic Review 17*(1), 99–114.

Appendix

Proof of ranking result

First introduce the following lemma:

Lemma 3.1 *For any* $\mathbf{x}, \mathbf{y} \in \mathbb{D}$: $\mathbf{x} \geqslant_T \mathbf{y} \Leftrightarrow [\mathbf{y} - y_n \mathbf{1}] \geqslant_{GL} [\mathbf{x} - x_n \mathbf{1}]$.
Proof. By Definition 3.1 we have

$$\mathbf{x} \geqslant_T \mathbf{y} \Leftrightarrow \sum_{j=1}^{i} [x_n - x_j] \geq \sum_{j=1}^{i} [y_n - y_j], \, i = 1, 2, \ldots, n-1.$$

This is equivalent to

$$\frac{1}{n} \sum_{j=1}^{i} [y_j - y_n] \geq \frac{1}{n} \sum_{j=1}^{i} [x_j - x_n], \, i = 1, 2, \ldots, n \tag{3.25}$$

which means that $[\mathbf{y} - y_n \mathbf{1}] \geqslant_{GL} [\mathbf{x} - x_n \mathbf{1}]$. ∎

This then enables us to establish Theorem 3.5.

Proof. Consider $- T_\varepsilon(\cdot)$ as a function of $\mathbf{x} - x_n \mathbf{1}$: it is clearly symmetric, non-decreasing and concave in $\mathbf{x} - x_n \mathbf{1}$. So, using Lemma 3.1 and Theorem 3.2 of Shorrocks (1983), we find that $\mathbf{x} \geqslant_T \mathbf{y}$ implies

$$- T_\varepsilon(\mathbf{y}) \geq - T_\varepsilon(\mathbf{x}).$$

Now consider a subfamily of indices with typical member $T^{a,i} \in \mathcal{T}$ where

$$T^{a,i}(\mathbf{x}) := \sum_{j=1}^{n-1} w_j [x_n - x_j] \tag{3.26}$$

$$w_j = \begin{cases} \dfrac{1}{i}\left[1 - \dfrac{2aj}{[n-1][i+1]}\right] & \text{for } j = 1, \ldots, i \\[4mm] \dfrac{2a[n-j]}{[n-1][n-i][n-i-1]} & \text{for } j = i+1, \ldots, n-1. \end{cases} \tag{3.27}$$

Each $T^{a,i}$ is an instance of the case $\varepsilon = 1$ in (3.19). By assumption

$$T^{a,i}(\mathbf{x}) \geq T^{a,i}(\mathbf{y}), \ i = 1, \ldots, n-1. \tag{3.28}$$

However from (3.26) and (3.27) we have

$$\lim_{a \to 0} T^{a,i}(\mathbf{x}) = K_i(\mathbf{x})$$

and so, letting $a \to 0$, (3.28) implies

$$K_i(\mathbf{x}) \geq K_i(\mathbf{y}), \ i = 1, \ldots, n-1. \tag{3.29}$$

Hence $\mathbf{x} \succcurlyeq_T \mathbf{y}$. ∎

Part II
Theory and methods

4 Evaluating dominance ranking of PSID incomes by various household attributes

Esfandiar Maasoumi and Almas Heshmati

4.1 Introduction

In this chapter we examine the existence of uniform weak orders between welfare outcomes measured by total real incomes. Partial *strong* orders are commonly used on the basis of specific utility functions and their corresponding indices. The latter is the predominant form of evaluation and is done when one employs indices of inequality or poverty in welfare, mean-variance analysis in finance, or performance indices such as average scores or wages in program evaluation. Such strong orderings do not command consensus. Based on the expected utility paradigm, Stochastic Dominance (SD), Lorenz and General Lorenz are examples of 'orderings' that attempt to resolve this problem.

These relations are defined over relatively large classes of utility functions and represent 'majority' preferences. In evaluating distributed outcomes, as in all program and event evaluation exercises, average outcomes mask the differential impact on different participants and render index-based assessments as blunt instruments for policy analysis. SD analysis reveals all of the distributional changes, especially amongst the target groups.

We follow an alternative bootstrap procedure for estimating the probability of rejection of the SD hypotheses with a suitably extended Kolmogorov-Smirnov (KS) test for first and second order stochastic dominance. Alternative simulation and bootstrap implementations of this test have been examined by several authors including McFadden (1989), Klecan, McFadden and McFadden (1991), and Barrett and Donald (2003). The most general approach to date is given by Linton *et al.* (2005) who allow for very general sampling schemes based on subsampling. Accommodating generic dependence between the variables which are to be ranked is especially necessary in substantive empirical settings where incomes are compared before and after taxes (or some other policy decision), or returns on different funds are compared in the same or interconnected markets. We employ matched pairs over time to preserve dependence, but looking at the observed waves of the PSID (Michegan Panel Study of Income Dynamics), separated by several years, likely removes the dependence problem in the cases we consider here.

Our approach is similar to Linton *et al.* (2005) in one aspect. We too do not impose the boundary of the null of dominance. We obtain unconstrained estimates of the probabilities of non-rejection in the actual samples. This allows a classical 'hypothesis testing' by confidence intervals that avoids the 'null hypothesis bias' of the frequentist method. All the other alternative implementations of the KS test, such as McFadden (1989), Barret and Donald (2003), and Chernozukov (2002), impose a subset of composite boundary of the null, the so-called 'Least Favorable Case' (LFC) of identical distributions, and estimate the asymptotic critical values of the classical KS test. Such tests would be biased and not 'similar' on the boundary.

Let X_1 and X_2 be two variables (incomes, returns/prospects) at either two different points in time, or for different regions or countries, or with or without a program (treatment). Let X_{ki}, $i = 1, \ldots$, N; k = 1, 2 denote the not necessarily i.i.d. observations. Let U_1 denote the class of all von Neumann-Morgenstern-type utility functions, u, such that $u' \geq 0$, (increasing). Also, let U_2 denote the class of all utility functions in U_1 for which $u'' \leq 0$ (strict concavity), and U_3 denote a subset of U_2 for which $u''' \geq 0$. Let $X_{(1p)}$ and $X_{(2p)}$ denote the p-th quantiles, and $F_1(x)$ and $F_2(x)$ denote the cumulative distribution functions, respectively.

Definition 4.1 X_1 First Order Stochastic Dominates X_2, denoted X_1 FSD X_2, if any of the following equivalent conditions holds:

$$E[u(X_1)] \geq E[u(X_2)] \text{ for all } u \ \varepsilon \ U_1, \text{ with strict inequality for some } u; \text{ or} \quad (4.1)$$

$$F_1(x) \leq F_2(x) \text{ for all } x \text{ with strict inequality for some } x; \text{ or} \quad (4.2)$$

$$X_{(1p)} \geq X_{(2p)} \text{ for all } 0 \leq p \leq 1, \text{ with strict inequality for some } p. \quad (4.3)$$

Definition 4.2 X_1 Second Order Stochastic Dominates X_2, denoted X_1 SSD X_2, if any of the following equivalent conditions holds:

$$E[u(X_1)] \geq E[u(X_2)] \text{ for all } u \in U_2, \text{ with strict inequality for some } u; \text{ or} \quad (4.4)$$

$$\int_{-\infty}^{x} F_1(t)dt \leq \int_{-\infty}^{x} F_2(t)dt \text{ for all } x \text{ with strict inequality for some } x; \text{ or} \quad (4.5)$$

$$\Phi_1(p) = \int_{0}^{p} X_{(1t)} \, dt \geq \Phi_2(p) = \int_{0}^{p} X_{(2t)}dt \text{ for all } 0 \leq p \leq 1, \text{ with strict}$$

inequality for some value(s) p. $\quad (4.6)$

Weak orders of SD obtain by eliminating the requirement of strict inequality at some point. When these conditions are not met, as when Generalized Lorenz Curves of two distributions cross, unambiguous first and second order SD is not possible. Any strong ordering by specific *indices* that correspond to the utility functions U_1 and U_2 classes will generally not enjoy consensus. Whitmore introduced the concept of third order stochastic dominance (TSD) in finance; see, for example, Whitmore and Findley (1978). Shorrocks and Foster (1987) showed that the addition of a 'transfer sensitivity' requirement leads to TSD ranking of income distributions. This requirement is stronger than the Pigou-Dalton principle of transfers since it makes regressive transfers less desirable at lower income levels. Higher order SD relations correspond to increasingly smaller subsets of U_2.

The statistical problems of conducting stochastic and Lorenz-type dominance are quite formidable; see for example, Anderson (1996), Davidson and Duclos (2000), Kaur *et al.* (1994), Dardanoni and Forcina (2000), Bishop *et al.* (1992), and Crawford (1999). Maasoumi (2001) contains a discussion of some of these alternative approaches. Davidson and Duclous (2000) is the most general example of formulating the SD nulls as multiple comparisons of partial moments and offers tests for higher order SD. The joint test of SD hypothesis based on quantiles follows the Chi-bar squared distribution techniques; see Fisher, Wilson and Xu (1995). Tse and Zhang (2000) provide some Monte Carlo evidence on the power of some of these *alternative* tests. There are just a handful of papers that have pursued the more general objective of consistency against all alternatives, as in Linton *et al.* (2005).

Since the asymptotic null distribution of these tests depends on the unknown distributions, McFadden (1989) and Klecan, McFadden and McFadden (1991) proposed a Monte Carlo permutation procedure for the computation of critical values that is only useful for i.i.d. observations and exchangeable variables. Barrett and Donald (2003) propose an alternative simulation method based on an idea of Hansen (1996) for deriving critical values in the case where the prospects are mutually independent, and the data are i.i.d. The methods relying on standard bootstrap or simulation typically try to mimic the asymptotic null distributions in the Least Favorable Case (LFC) of the equal distribution functions. However, even the boundary of the null hypothesis of SD is a set that is larger than the LFC region; thus such LFC-based tests are not asymptotically similar on the boundary of the null hypothesis. On the other hand, the LMW-test in Linton *et al.* (2005) is based on a subsampling procedure which approximates the true sampling distribution under the composite null hypothesis and is asymptotically similar on the boundary. Consequently, the LMW-test might be asymptotically more powerful than the bootstrap-based or simulation-based tests for some local alternatives.

Our approach fixes the critical value (zero) at the boundary of our null, and estimates the associated 'significance level' by bootstrapping the sample or its blocks. This renders our tests 'asymptotically similar' and unbiased on the boundary. This is similar in spirit to inference based on p-values. This method could also be used to compare the two distributions up to any desired quantile, for instance, for poverty rankings.

4.2 The test statistics

Suppose that there are two prospects X_1, X_2 and let $A = \{X_k : k = 1,2\}$. Let $\{X_{ki} : i = 1,2, \ldots, N\}$ be realizations of X_k for k = 1, 2. These values could be 'residuals' of income, say, 'purged' of the influence of certain desired attributes, such as age, education, and gender. When data are limited one may want to use a model to control for such attributes. Here we follow an alternative of grouping the data into subsets, say of families with different sizes, or by educational attainment, and then make comparisons across homogenous populations.[1] For k = 1, 2 define:

$$F_k(x, \theta) = P(X_{ki}(\theta) \le x) \tag{4.7}$$

And:

$$\bar{F}_{kN}(x, \theta) = \frac{1}{N} \sum_{i=1}^{N} 1(X_{ki}(\theta) \le x). \tag{4.8}$$

We denote $F_k(x) = F_k(x, \theta_{k0})$ and $\bar{F}_{kN}(x, \theta_{k0})$, and let $F(x_1, x_2)$ be the joint c.d.f. of $(X_1, X_2)'$. Now define the following functionals of the joint distribution:

$$d = \min_{k \ne l} \sup_{x \in \chi} [F_k(x) - F_l(x)] \tag{4.9}$$

$$s = \min_{k \ne l} \sup_{x \in \chi} \int_{-\infty}^{x} [F_k(t) - F_l(t)]dt \tag{4.10}$$

where χ denotes a given set contained in the union of the supports of X_{ki} for k = 1,2. Without loss of generality we assume that the supports are bounded. The hypotheses of interest are:

$$H_0^d : d \le 0 \text{ vs. } H_1^d : d > 0$$
$$H_0^s : s \le 0 \text{ vs. } H_1^s : s > 0$$

The null hypothesis H_0^d implies that the prospects in A are not first-degree stochastically maximal, i.e., there exists at least one prospect in A which first-degree dominates the others. Likewise for the second order case. The test statistics are the empirical analogues of (4.9)–(4.10), given below:

$$D_N = \min_{k \ne l} \sup_{x \in \chi} \sqrt{N} [\bar{F}_{kN}(x, \dot{\theta}_k) - \bar{F}_{lN}(x, \dot{\theta}_l)] \tag{4.11}$$

$$S_N = \min_{k \ne l} \sup_{x \in \chi} \sqrt{N} \int_{-\infty}^{x} [\bar{F}_{kN}(t, \dot{\theta}_k) - \bar{F}_{lN}(t, \dot{\theta}_l)]dt \tag{4.12}$$

We next discuss the issue of how to compute the supremum in D_N and S_N, and the integrals in S_N. There have been a number of suggestions in the literature that exploit the step-function nature of $\bar{F}_{kN}(t, \theta)$. The supremum in D_N can be (exactly) replaced by a maximum taken over all the distinct points in the combined sample. Regarding the computation of S_N, Klecan *et al.* (1991) propose a recursive algorithm for exact computation of S_N; see also Barrett and Donald (2003) for an extension to third order dominance.

To reduce the computation time, it may be preferable to compute approximations to the suprema in D_N, S_N based on taking maxima over some smaller grid of points $X_J = \{x_1, \ldots, x_J\}$ where $J < n$. Provided the set of evaluation points becomes dense in the joint support, the distribution theory is unaffected by using this approximation. In our applications we report Probability $\{D_N \leq 0\}$ and Probability $S_N \leq 0\}$ and are able to identify which distribution dominates, if any. These are the maximum test sizes associated with our critical value of 'zero' which is clearly the boundary of our null that *includes* the LFC. Thus we are reporting the critical level associated with this non-rejection region. These critical levels can be shown as in Linton *et al.* (2005) to be 'conservative' since, in the limit, they are at least as large as the corresponding levels for the asymptotic test on the boundary. Importantly, we do not impose the LFC on our bootstrap resampling.

4.3 Testing for SD in PSID

4.3.1 Data

We compare five waves of the Michegon Panel Study of Income Dynamics (PSID)[2] in the years 1968, 1978, 1988, 1993, and 1997. Two definitions of income are used: gross and disposable incomes. For each year the 'gross income' represents 'husband and wife' or total family income including wages, interest, welfare payments, and unemployment receipts. 'Disposable income' is measured as gross income including transfer payments less family taxes. Incomes of spouses are added together and adjusted for family size to obtain per capita equivalent household incomes. Following a tradition in the literature we have chosen a weight of 1.0 for adult family members and 0.50 for children below the age of 18. Incomes and taxes are transformed to fixed 1993 prices using the urban consumer price index.

We do not have access to disposable income for 1993 and 1997 as these are not publicly available to download. The first four years are final releases, while the last, 1997, is early-release data. The years were chosen to be representative as well as sufficiently far apart so that policy/events would have the time to produce measurable effects. Nevertheless, some of our 'unconditional' comparisons reflect snapshots of points in time. In addition to unconditional comparison of household income distribution over time, incomes are compared conditional on a number of household characteristics. A household is identified by the household's head.[3] Head is defined as the husband in families with couples. When income distributions of groups are compared, the income variable is an average per capita income of individual/ household head income over the period 1968–1993. Thus these comparisons are better than snapshots at points in time as they take out some transitory movements. This kind of aggregation is meant to avoid misleading results and follows the reasoning in mobility analysis with Maasoumi-Shorrocks-Zandvakili indices; see, for example, Maasoumi and Zandvakili (1990).

The household characteristics that we control for are: age, marital status, working status, racial status, gender, occupation, number of children, level of education, length of unemployment, and geographical mobility. Household characteristics are the head characteristics. Since these characteristics of head may differ over time, we have chosen to use those of 1993 as a reference, but mean gross and mean disposable incomes are defined as average of per capita income for the years 1968–1993 and 1968–1988, respectively. The 1997 gross income data were excluded as they are early-release.

In defining age groups we have taken productivity into account. The sample is divided into four groups: 18–35; 36–50; 51–65; and 66 and more. The heads by marital status are classified into three groups: married; single (or widowed); and divorced (including separated, or spouse-absent). The working status includes three groups: working, temporarily laid off; unemployed; and retired, housewife, student and others. The racial groups are three: white; black; and 'Indian, Spanish, Asian, others'. Sex is the head of household gender: male and female. There are four occupational groups: professional and managers; self-employed unincorporated 'businessmen'; other occupations; and not in the labor force. The number of children is divided into four groups: families with no children; one child; two children; and three and more children. Education is the head's total years of schooling grouped into: 0–11 years; 12-plus grades; and college degree and higher. Unemployment is defined by the length of unemployment period in number of hours. The variable was transformed into months of unemployment (180 hours per month) divided into three groups: 0–1 month; 2–3 months; and more than three months. Finally, geographical mobility is classified into three groups: head living in the same state where he/she grew up; same region where grew up; and different state and region where grew up.

Our analysis is carried out in two parts. Part one is 'unconditional' tests for SD over the years for the entire distribution of incomes, with no controls for attributes, for both gross and disposable incomes. Part two is 'conditional' by having controls for the above attributes. The analysis and comparison of results are carried out both with and without PSID population weights. The weight variable is the sampling weight provided by PSID meant to make these samples more 'representative' of the US population. They reflect the frequency of household types in the population and are used to produce unbiased estimation of the descriptive statistics. It is generally agreed that for inference about the 'US population', one must focus on the weighted results.

Summary of the number of observations by income definition and various subgroups of household is given in Table 12 of Maasoumi and Heshmati (2005), hereafter MH. Since not all the families are in all years, we take only a balanced panel. This results in reduction in the number of observations. The summary statistics (number of observations, mean and standard deviation) of the two income definitions in weighted and unweighted forms including the number of balanced observations are given in the first part of each table. We include only two of the tables here because of space limitations. All are available in the longer version of the paper on the authors' webpages.

4.3.2 Unconditional analysis

Consider Table 4.1. The first part summarizes our data by years of observation. The balanced number of households observed all five years is 3897.[4] The mean real gross income is continuously increasing over time from $12,483 in 1968 to $19,632 in 1997, as is the dispersion in income, increasing from $10,818 to $20,904. Increases in the dispersion of income are more pronounced in 1988 and 1997. The coefficient of variation increased from 86.6 to 106.5 indicating growing income 'dispersion'. The level of real disposable income, ranging between $11,252 and $12,409, is 88–90 per cent of gross income. It is increasing over time reflecting reduced share of income taxes and transfers. The dispersion in disposable income is somewhat smaller than in gross income indicating income equalization effects of taxes and transfers.

Accounting for population weights increases both the gross and disposable mean incomes over time, in the range $14,786–$22,231 to $13,208–$18,027, respectively. The temporal patterns are the same but level differences are large compared to the unweighted summaries. The difference is a reflection of higher weights being associated with higher income households.

Concerning temporal patterns of the household attributes we note that the percentage share of households with zero income has increased from 0.1 per cent in 1968 to 1.4 per cent in 1993. Households without children or with fewer than two children have increased in number, while those with three or more children have decreased. The share of female-headed households is large and varies from 28 per cent to 31 per cent. Significant variations in the age groups in the form of a shift from the lower-age groups to the upper-age groups is evident over time. The relative share of blacks has been reduced over time, while those of 'other' race groups has increased. The share of working population is decreasing, while the share of unemployed and those not in the labor force is increasing. In the latter years, fewer persons are in marriage, while the unmarried, divorced, and separated are increasing in number. The number of household heads with a medium level of education is increasing significantly relative to those holding a college degree. Major changes in population occurs in the share of retired and those not in the labor force. The share of heads with no unemployment record is decreasing, while those with more than three months of unemployment increasing. The

Table 4.1 Comparisons of gross and disposable incomes by YEAR of observation

	unweighted observations								weighted observations							
	gross income				disposable income				gross income				disposable income			
variable	n	mean	std	prob	n	mean	std	prob	n	mean	std	prob	n	mean	std	prob
1968	3897	12483	10818		3897	11252	8802		71348	14786	11674		71348	13208	9406	
1978	3897	14819	12344		3897	12997	9292		63751	17883	13989		63751	15441	10244	
1988	3897	17377	16700		3897	15408	12409		69608	20518	19820		69608	18027	14077	
1993	3897	18704	17069		.	.	.		67454	21960	19207		.	.	.	
1997	3897	19632	20904		.	.	.		59328	22231	22823		.	.	.	
variable	mean	std	prob		n	mean	std	prob	n	mean	std	prob	mean	std	prob	
1968(x) vs. 1978 (y):																
FSDxoy	0.1019	0.0111	0.000		3897	0.1153	0.0115	0.000	71348	0.1151	0.0027	0.000	0.1190	0.0027	0.000	
FSDyox	0.0002	0.0008	0.381		3897	0.0023	0.0020	0.103	63751	−0.0002	0.0002	0.930	0.0001	0.0005	0.558	
FOmax	0.0002	0.0008	0.381		3897	0.0023	0.0020	0.103	69608	−0.0002	0.0002	0.930	0.0001	0.0005	0.558	
SSDxoy	0.3394	0.0399	0.000		.	0.3503	0.0368	0.000	67454	0.4589	0.0106	0.000	0.4379	0.0102	0.000	
SSDyox	−0.0653	0.0102	1.000		.	−0.0693	0.0090	1.000	59328	−0.0539	0.0022	1.000	−0.0508	0.0018	1.000	
SOmax	−0.0653	0.0102	1.000		.	−0.0693	0.0090	1.000		−0.0539	0.0022	1.000	−0.0508	0.0018	1.000	
1968(x) vs. 1988 (y):																
FSDxoy	0.1828	0.0109	0.000		3897	0.1702	0.0101	0.000	71348	0.1753	0.0026	0.000	0.1873	0.0025	0.000	
FSDyox	−0.0007	0.0008	0.821		3897	−0.0009	0.0009	0.842	63751	−0.0020	0.0002	1.000	−0.0023	0.0002	1.000	
FOmax	−0.0007	0.0008	0.821		3897	−0.0009	0.0009	0.842	69608	−0.0020	0.0002	1.000	−0.0023	0.0002	1.000	
SSDxoy	0.3353	0.0224	0.000		.	0.5374	0.0321	0.000	67454	0.4049	0.0062	0.000	0.6082	0.0084	0.000	
SSDyox	−0.1828	0.0109	1.000		.	−0.1484	0.0107	1.000	59328	−0.1753	0.0026	1.000	−0.0943	0.0023	1.000	
SOmax	−0.1828	0.0109	1.000		.	−0.1484	0.0107	1.000		−0.1753	0.0026	1.000	−0.0943	0.0023	1.000	

variable	mean	std	prob	mean	std	prob	mean	std	prob	mean	std	prob
1968(x) vs. 1993 (y):												
FSDxoy	0.1989	0.0107	0.000	.	.	.	0.2001	0.0024	0.000	.	.	.
FSDyox	−0.0010	0.0005	0.987	.	.	.	−0.0019	0.0002	1.000	.	.	.
FOmax	−0.0010	0.0005	0.987	.	.	.	−0.0019	0.0002	1.000	.	.	.
SSDxoy	0.6717	0.0345	0.000	.	.	.	0.7536	0.0089	0.000	.	.	.
SSDyox	−0.1987	0.0109	1.000	.	.	.	−0.1415	0.0025	1.000	.	.	.
SOmax	−0.1987	0.0109	1.000	.	.	.	−0.1415	0.0025	1.000	.	.	.
1968(x) vs. 1997 (y):												
FSDxoy	0.2165	0.0110	0.000	.	.	.	0.1895	0.0027	0.000	.	.	.
FSDyox	−0.0005	0.0004	0.961	.	.	.	−0.0006	0.0001	1.000	.	.	.
FOmax	−0.0005	0.0004	0.961	.	.	.	−0.0006	0.0001	1.000	.	.	.
SSDxoy	0.4945	0.0270	0.000	.	.	.	0.5295	0.0072	0.000	.	.	.
SSDyox	−0.2165	0.0110	1.000	.	.	.	−0.1895	0.0027	1.000	.	.	.
SOmax	−0.2165	0.0110	1.000	.	.	.	−0.1895	0.0027	1.000	.	.	.
1978(x) vs. 1988 (y):												
FSDxoy	0.0782	0.0111	0.000	0.0862	0.0101	0.000	0.0675	0.0020	0.000	0.0855	0.0021	0.000
FSDyox	0.0001	0.0012	0.491	−0.0008	0.0009	0.814	0.0005	0.0004	0.097	−0.0017	0.0003	1.000
FOmax	0.0001	0.0012	0.491	−0.0008	0.0009	0.814	0.0005	0.0004	0.097	−0.0017	0.0003	1.000
SSDxoy	0.1835	0.0232	0.000	0.3135	0.0325	0.000	0.1926	0.0067	0.000	0.3283	0.0088	0.000
SSDyox	−0.0781	0.0113	1.000	−0.0471	0.0104	1.000	−0.0541	0.0028	1.000	−0.0102	0.0022	1.000
SOmax	−0.0781	0.0113	1.000	−0.0471	0.0104	1.000	−0.0541	0.0028	1.000	−0.0102	0.0022	1.000
1978(x) vs. 1993 (y):												
FSDxoy	0.1070	0.0096	0.000	.	.	.	0.0971	0.0022	0.000	.	.	.
FSDyox	−0.0009	0.0006	0.934	.	.	.	−0.0019	0.0002	1.000	.	.	.
FOmax	−0.0009	0.0006	0.934	.	.	.	−0.0019	0.0002	1.000	.	.	.
SSDxoy	0.4276	0.0354	0.000	.	.	.	0.4328	0.0100	0.000	.	.	.
SSDyox	−0.0965	0.0108	1.000	.	.	.	−0.0537	0.0024	1.000	.	.	.
SOmax	−0.0965	0.0108	1.000	.	.	.	−0.0537	0.0024	1.000	.	.	.

variable	mean	std	prob	mean	std	prob	mean	std	prob	mean	std	prob
1978(x) vs. 1997 (y):												
FSDxoy	0.1095	0.0113	0.000	.	.	.	0.0859	0.0023	0.000	.	.	.
FSDyox	-0.0005	0.0004	0.961	.	.	.	-0.0006	0.0001	1.000	.	.	.
FOmax	-0.0005	0.0004	0.961	.	.	.	-0.0006	0.0001	1.000	.	.	.
SSDxoy	0.3363	0.0278	0.000	.	.	.	0.3112	0.0077	0.000	.	.	.
SSDyox	-0.1094	0.0114	1.000	.	.	.	-0.0667	0.0028	1.000	.	.	.
SOmax	-0.1094	0.0114	1.000	.	.	.	-0.0667	0.0028	1.000	.	.	.
1988(x) vs. 1993 (y):												
FSDxoy	0.0336	0.0096	0.000	.	.	.	0.0335	0.0024	0.000	.	.	.
FSDyox	0.0013	0.0007	0.002	.	.	.	0.0024	0.0002	0.000	.	.	.
FOmax	0.0013	0.0007	0.002	.	.	.	0.0024	0.0002	0.000	.	.	.
SSDxoy	0.1043	0.0254	0.000	.	.	.	0.1219	0.0069	0.000	.	.	.
SSDyox	-0.0304	0.0117	0.994	.	.	.	-0.0329	0.0027	1.000	.	.	.
SOmax	-0.0304	0.0117	0.994	.	.	.	-0.0329	0.0027	1.000	.	.	.
1988(x) vs. 1997 (y):												
FSDxoy	0.0346	0.0090	0.000	.	.	.	0.0228	0.0015	0.000	.	.	.
FSDyox	0.0005	0.0007	0.222	.	.	.	0.0015	0.0002	0.000	.	.	.
FOmax	0.0005	0.0007	0.222	.	.	.	0.0015	0.0002	0.000	.	.	.
SSDxoy	0.1485	0.0299	0.000	.	.	.	0.1148	0.0083	0.000	.	.	.
SSDyox	-0.0312	0.0117	0.996	.	.	.	-0.0138	0.0028	1.000	.	.	.
SOmax	-0.0312	0.0117	0.996	.	.	.	-0.0138	0.0028	1.000	.	.	.
1993(x) vs. 1997 (y):												
FSDxoy	0.0125	0.0060	0.000	.	.	.	0.0064	0.0007	0.000	.	.	.
FSDyox	0.0045	0.0062	0.336	.	.	.	0.0180	0.0028	0.000	.	.	.
FOmax	0.0030	0.0038	0.336	.	.	.	0.0064	0.0007	0.000	.	.	.
SSDxoy	0.0593	0.0307	0.030	.	.	.	0.0137	0.0082	0.048	.	.	.
SSDyox	0.0000	0.0143	0.523	.	.	.	0.0302	0.0049	0.000	.	.	.
SOmax	-0.0019	0.0121	0.553	.	.	.	0.0132	0.0075	0.048	.	.	.

Notes

a FSDxoy denotes first order stochastic dominance of X over Y, and SSDxoy is similarly defined for second order dominance of X over Y.

b The FOmax and SOmax denote the joint tests of X vs. Y and Y vs. X., referred to as maximality.

within- and between-state mobility is constant while between-state mobility is increasing at the expense of within-region mobility. For frequency distribution by household characteristics see the extended version.

Results in Table 4.1 are based on data where household attributes are ignored. The test results are based on a selection of years (1968, 1978, 1988, 1993, and 1997). Consecutive time patterns of dominance using annual waves may differ from the current non-consecutive ones.

All results are based on 1,000 bootstrap samples, 5 per cent income partitions, first taking into account population weights and then without accounting for population weights. In comparing two distributions, the first group is denoted the 'X' distribution, and the second by 'Y' distribution. Thus 'FSDxoy' denotes 'first order stochastic dominance of X over Y', and 'SSDxoy' is similarly defined for second order dominance of X over Y. The 'FOmax' and 'SOmax' denote the joint tests of X vs. Y and Y vs. X., referred to as 'maximality' by McFadden (1989).

4.3.2.1 Test results for the whole distribution over time

In the second part of Table 4.1, our test statistics are summarized by their mean and standard errors, as well as the probability of the test statistic being negative or zero (the null).

For (unweighted) **gross income**, several cases (5 out of 10) of first order and second order (9 out of 10) dominance are observed for recent years over earlier years. The exceptions are 1968 vs. 1978, 1978 vs. 1988, 1988 vs. 1993 and 1993 vs. 1997 where there is no FSD, while in the case of 1993 vs. 1997 no SSD either. The latter two years are found to be second order maximal (unrankable). The same patterns hold for **disposable income** distributions, where latter years SSD earlier years. One difference is that 1988 first order dominates 1978 at the 81 per cent level. Type I error would be too large perhaps, but power is enhanced. Taxes and transfers appear to cause a general right separation in the CDFs, but we do not have formal tests of the significance associated with this aspect of what is depicted in Figures 4.1a and 4.1b. The level of significance is higher in the disposable income cases compared to gross incomes. Figure 4.1A depicts the corresponding sample CDFs and cumulated CDFs which indicate *apparent* SD rankings or lack thereof.

The test results based on the population weighted data are basically the same as those from the unweighted cases. A few distinctions to be mentioned are. First, we observe FSD of gross income in 1978 over 1968. Second, the degree of significance for weighted data is systematically higher compared to those for unweighted data. It appears that, in the presence of dominance, 'significance' is an increasing function of the number of observation (weights) in the annual samples.

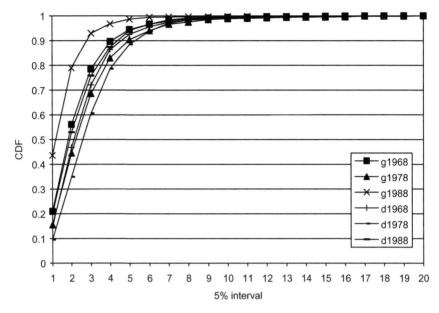

Figure 4.1a Weighted CDF of gross (g) and disposable (d) incomes by years of
observation

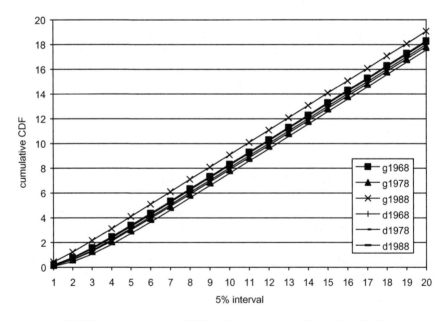

Figure 4.1b Weighted cumulative CDF of gross (g) and disposable (d) incomes by
years of observation

4.3.3 Conditional analysis

4.3.3.1 Introduction

As mentioned previously, the households are distinguished by the household head characteristics in 1993, but mean gross and mean disposable incomes are defined as period average of per capita incomes. The characteristics that we condition on include those of head: age, marital status, working status, race, gender, occupation, number of children, level of education, length of unemployment, and geographical mobility. But we only report a few of these cases in this shortened chapter.

4.3.3.2 Test results for age groups

Table 4.2 summarizes the results for age groups (18–35, 36–50, 51–65, 65–), for weighted and unweighted observations, and for gross and disposable incomes. The mean gross income is somewhat increasing with working age, but so is its dispersion. After taxes and transfers no notable change in this pattern is found. The mean disposable income constantly lies below gross income in all age groups. There are no cases of FSD between age groups. As expected the two middle age groups' gross incomes SSD those of the very young, but this ranking vanishes with disposable incomes suggesting significant income equalization impact of transfers and taxes. The weighting of observations is inconsequential. For disposable incomes, however, we note an SSD of the weighted 18–35 over the 66+ age group. Without controlling for other factors, such as marital status, education or employment, it appears that the younger households are better off than the 'retired'. A further disaggregation of age groups might be necessary to reveal the existence and magnitude of further between-group transfers. The disposable incomes of age groups are generally second order maximal, implying that they may be ranked only at higher levels than SSD. A neat result of Davidson and Duclos (2000) suggests that, if two distributions have an FSD ranking for some part of the (lower) support, they are rankable at some higher order. The results reveal a sometimes stark distinction between an apparent dominance and its lack of statistical significance. They also suggest, but we have not tested, the possibility that almost all the disposable incomes FSD or SSD the gross income distributions. With the exception of the peak income group, 36–55, this appears to cut across all age groups. It is worth recalling that SD rankings are transitive. See Figure 4.2a and 4.2b for CDFs.

4.3.3.3 Test results by marital status

In Table 3 of MH (2005), they report the test results for the head's marital status. The mean gross and disposable incomes of the first two groups are somewhat higher than the third group who likely include many single mother

Table 4.2 Comparisons of mean period (gross 1968–1993 and disposable 1968–1988) incomes by AGE of household's head in 1993

| | unweighted observations | | | | | | weighted observations | | | | | |
| | gross income | | | disposable income | | | gross income | | | disposable income | | |
variable	n	mean	std	n	mean	std	n	mean	std	n	mean	std
18–35	1199	15471	6669	1199	13203	5937	17463	16430	6972	17463	13406	5957
36–50	1393	16394	6759	1393	13195	5501	22282	17338	7064	22282	13333	5550
51–65	647	16850	8475	647	13271	6061	13889	17933	8657	13889	13191	5990
65–	658	14380	6758	658	13248	6238	13820	14738	6261	13820	13132	5929

| | gross income | | | disposable income | | | gross income | | | disposable income | | |
variable	mean	std	prob	mean	std	prob	mean	std	prob	mean	std	prob
18–35(x) vs. 36–50 (y):												
FSDxoy	0.0740	0.0163	0.000	0.0282	0.0145	0.000	0.0693	0.0049	0.000	0.0254	0.0046	0.000
FSDyox	0.0046	0.0040	0.013	0.0214	0.0105	0.005	0.0015	0.0012	0.001	0.0327	0.0032	0.000
FOmax	0.0046	0.0040	0.013	0.0156	0.0072	0.005	0.0015	0.0012	0.001	0.0249	0.0040	0.000
SSDxoy	0.2413	0.0663	0.000	0.0647	0.0468	0.000	0.2291	0.0195	0.000	0.0495	0.0126	0.000
SSDyox	-0.0042	0.0019	0.996	0.0299	0.0449	0.453	-0.0040	0.0005	1.000	0.0375	0.0189	0.031
SOmax	-0.0042	0.0019	0.996	0.0088	0.0144	0.453	-0.0040	0.0005	1.000	0.0303	0.0122	0.031
18–35(x) vs. 51–65 (y):												
FSDxoy	0.0764	0.0207	0.000	0.0238	0.0120	0.002	0.0880	0.0055	0.000	0.0175	0.0025	0.000
FSDyox	0.0045	0.0070	0.078	0.0259	0.0154	0.001	0.0000	0.0001	0.300	0.0425	0.0034	0.000
FOmax	0.0045	0.0069	0.078	0.0152	0.0078	0.003	0.0000	0.0001	0.300	0.0175	0.0025	0.000
SSDxoy	0.2865	0.0822	0.000	0.0464	0.0449	0.021	0.3047	0.0200	0.000	0.0172	0.0027	0.000
SSDyox	-0.0021	0.0081	0.786	0.0522	0.0603	0.229	-0.0059	0.0006	1.000	0.1467	0.0222	0.000
SOmax	-0.0022	0.0080	0.786	0.0110	0.0122	0.250	-0.0059	0.0006	1.000	0.0172	0.0027	0.000

variable	mean	std	prob	mean	std	prob	mean	std	prob	mean	std	prob
18–35(x) vs. 66– (y):												
FSDxoy	0.0064	0.0045	0.000	0.0209	0.0121	0.001	0.0041	0.0005	0.000	0.0098	0.0025	0.000
FSDyox	0.0923	0.0215	0.000	0.0339	0.0179	0.002	0.1279	0.0056	0.000	0.0481	0.0047	0.000
FOmax	0.0064	0.0045	0.000	0.0158	0.0085	0.003	0.0041	0.0005	0.000	0.0098	0.0025	0.000
SSDxoy	0.0047	0.0033	0.000	0.0390	0.0561	0.263	0.0040	0.0005	0.000	-0.0024	0.0020	0.852
SSDyox	0.2820	0.0786	0.000	0.0704	0.0610	0.041	0.4155	0.0191	0.000	0.1395	0.0194	0.000
SOmax	0.0047	0.0033	0.000	0.0100	0.0154	0.304	0.0040	0.0005	0.000	-0.0024	0.0020	0.852
36–50(x) vs. 51–65 (y):												
FSDxoy	0.0417	0.0177	0.000	0.0202	0.0137	0.015	0.0430	0.0044	0.000	0.0083	0.0038	0.000
FSDyox	0.0293	0.0140	0.002	0.0311	0.0177	0.000	0.0174	0.0026	0.000	0.0476	0.0051	0.000
FOmax	0.0243	0.0115	0.002	0.0137	0.0084	0.015	0.0174	0.0026	0.000	0.0083	0.0038	0.000
SSDxoy	0.0917	0.0714	0.000	0.0266	0.0435	0.272	0.0981	0.0183	0.000	0.0071	0.0053	0.091
SSDyox	0.0444	0.0307	0.027	0.0736	0.0627	0.000	0.0173	0.0026	0.000	0.1037	0.0201	0.000
SOmax	0.0259	0.0201	0.027	0.0063	0.0108	0.272	0.0173	0.0026	0.000	0.0071	0.0053	0.091
36–50(x) vs. 66– (y):												
FSDxoy	0.0032	0.0034	0.000	0.0309	0.0126	0.000	0.0003	0.0004	0.000	0.0178	0.0031	0.000
FSDyox	0.1568	0.0219	0.000	0.0420	0.0189	0.000	0.1928	0.0055	0.000	0.0520	0.0054	0.000
FOmax	0.0032	0.0034	0.000	0.0251	0.0101	0.000	0.0003	0.0004	0.000	0.0178	0.0031	0.000
SSDxoy	0.0000	0.0000	0.000	0.0471	0.0662	0.359	0.0000	0.0000	0.000	-0.0041	0.0008	0.993
SSDyox	0.5306	0.0782	0.000	0.0992	0.0583	0.000	0.6629	0.0192	0.000	0.1235	0.0159	0.000
SOmax	0.0000	0.0000	0.000	0.0196	0.0266	0.359	0.0000	0.0000	0.000	-0.0041	0.0008	0.993
51–65(x) vs. 66– (y):												
FSDxoy	0.0015	0.0021	0.094	0.0256	0.0140	0.000	0.0000	0.0000	0.293	0.0204	0.0031	0.000
FSDyox	0.1633	0.0256	0.000	0.0325	0.0184	0.002	0.1836	0.0051	0.000	0.0402	0.0048	0.000
FOmax	0.0015	0.0021	0.094	0.0175	0.0094	0.002	0.0000	0.0000	0.293	0.0204	0.0031	0.000
SSDxoy	-0.0015	0.0015	0.641	0.0547	0.0697	0.269	-0.0029	0.0004	1.000	0.0398	0.0222	0.042
SSDyox	0.5496	0.0925	0.000	0.0769	0.0641	0.023	0.6937	0.0190	0.000	0.0574	0.0081	0.000
SOmax	-0.0015	0.0015	0.641	0.0151	0.0207	0.292	-0.0029	0.0004	1.000	0.0353	0.0165	0.042

Notes

a FSDxoy denotes first order stochastic dominance of X over Y, and SSDxoy is similarly defined for second order dominance of X over Y.

b The FOmax and SOmax denote the joint tests of X vs. Y and Y vs. X., referred to as maximality.

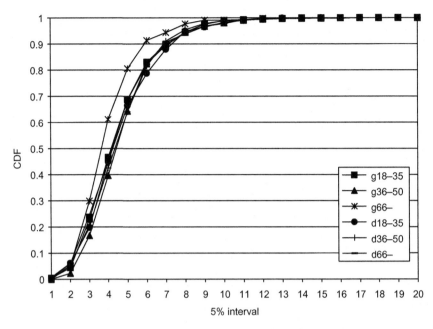

Figure 4.2a Weighted CDF of gross (g) and disposable (d) incomes by age groups

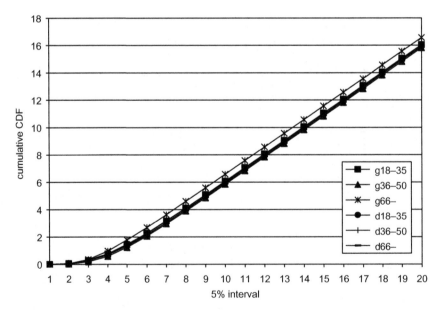

Figure 4.2b Weighted cumulative CDF of gross (G) and disposable (d) incomes by age groups

families. In general the between-group variations in mean and standard deviations are quite small. The pattern is very similar in comparing the samples with and without weighting. The married group second order dominates the unmarried at the 91 per cent level. The unmarried/married and other groups are maximal. In the weighted case, again the married second order dominate the unmarried, while others also second order dominate the unmarried. There is no evidence of any statistically significant FSD or SSD in terms of disposable income unconditional on the number of children. Later we will be discussing disposable income conditional on the number of children.

4.3.3.4 *Test results by working status*

In Table 4 of MH (2005), we have the test results by the working status of household heads. The mean gross income of the working category is higher than that of remaining non-working groups. Given the tax structure in the US one might expect much larger income differences. The small difference might be due to the relatively short unemployment spells in the US and the averaging of incomes over this period. For these reasons, the working group has on average a slightly lower disposable income than the unemployed. When we do not account for weight differences, the gross income of the working group second order dominates the 'others' not in the labor force, while the working vs. unemployed and the unemployed vs. others are unrankable. This means that there are some welfare functions in our functional classes that are so 'equality-preferring' that they make SD ranking of gross working incomes impossible. Clearly, there will be many indices in these situations that will provide complete ranking of these unrankable distributions.

The tests based on the unweighted observations on disposable incomes show no first and second order dominance relationship. Similar patterns hold in the weighted case, with the exception that the 'working' second order dominate 'others' in terms of both incomes. In the definition of unemployment, one does not account for the length of unemployment. This might partially explain the absence of dominance relations by working status. Later we will investigate the role of unemployment distinguished by the length of the spell. Again for distribution of incomes by working status see Figures 4A to 4D in MH (2005).

4.3.3.5 *Test results by racial status*

The heads are classified into three groups: white; black; others including Indian, Hispanic and Asians. In looking at the statistical summaries given in the first part of Table 5 in MH (2005), the gross income of the whites is above that of the 'other' groups when observations are not weighted. For the unweighted observations the mean disposable income of blacks is the highest. This surely demonstrates one of the better-known problems with the unweighted PSID observations. In the weighted form the position of groups is changed, 'others' showing higher gross income than white and blacks, respectively. The sample size is, however, small, and made smaller by our 'balancing' over these many years, and might be affected by outlier and missing observations. The test results show that unweighted white gross income distribution second order dominates the black incomes at the 92 per cent level, but is unrankable in comparison with others. As mentioned above, accounting for taxes and transfers changes the dominance rankings. Blacks' disposable incomes second order dominate the whites' at the 94 per cent level.

When *weighted* data are used, the same relationship between gross incomes of whites and blacks holds, but others second order dominate the white distribution. Here, the white disposable income distribution second order dominates the corresponding black distribution. Neglected within-group heterogeneity might be another quite significant problem here.

4.3.3.6 Test results by gender

Table 6 in MH (2005) indicates that mean gross incomes of males are greater than females' gross incomes, as is the within-group income dispersions. In terms of disposable income the positions are reversed with almost equal income dispersion. The share of males is 70 per cent of the total sample. The test results, based on unweighted data, show that male incomes second order dominate the female incomes at 99 per cent level, while no such dominance relation is found when disposable incomes are considered. With weighted data the males gross income still second order dominates females, but the position is reversed in favor of females when disposable incomes are considered. Welfare policies through taxes and transfers appear to have been successful in bringing about welfare parity between male and females. Graphs of CDFs are given in Figure 4.3a and 4.3b.

4.3.3.7 Test results by occupation

There are three occupation groups in Table 7 of MH (2005): professional and managers; other occupations; and not in labor force. Again the mean incomes differ in terms of gross incomes by occupation in favor of professionals, but the differences between groups vanish in terms of disposable incomes regardless of whether any observation weights are used or not. The test results indicate that professionals and managers second order dominate the remaining two groups when gross income is considered. The last two groups are not first and second order rankable, but clearly rankable at some higher level. The same dominance relationship holds but stronger when weighted data are used. No first or second order dominance is found between disposable incomes. Again, higher order ranks cannot be ruled out. Graphs of CDFs are given in MH (2005).

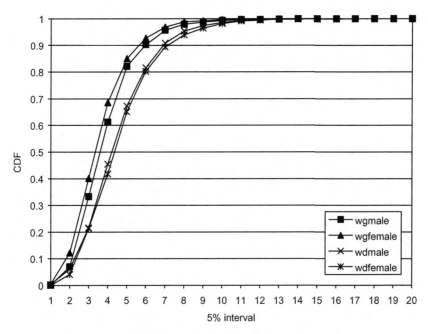

Figure 4.3a Weighted CDF of gross (g) and disposable (d) incomes by gender

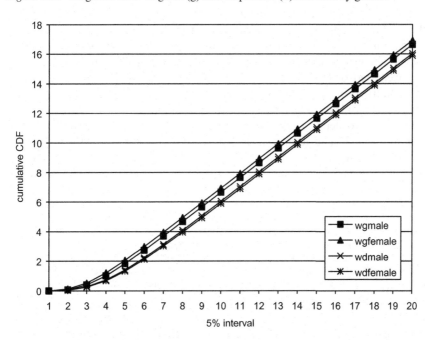

Figure 4.3b Weighted cumulative CDF of gross (g) and disposable (d) incomes by gender

4.3.3.8   Test results by number of children

Summary of the results for households grouped by the number of children into households with no children, one child, two children; and three and more is found in Table 8 of MH (2005). The mean gross income per capita and its dispersion are negative functions of the number of children. The relation is not obvious in disposable income terms. Despite the mean differences no group's gross or disposable incomes dominates another in the unweighted form. In the weighted case there are two exceptions, where heads with no children second order dominate the groups with one and two children, but not those with three and more. Note that the results are in line with the objectives of welfare policies designed to improve living conditions of families with children, but the absence of first and second order dominance is rather surprising. But these results are influenced by grouping the households by characteristics valid for 1993, while incomes refer to the original periods. Higher order ranking is possible.

4.3.3.9   Test results by years of schooling

Mean gross and disposable incomes are increasing function of years of schooling. Here education is defined as the head's total years of schooling grouped into: 0–11 years; 12+; and college degrees (Table 9 of MH 2005). The test results indicate that medium education level second order dominates the low level, and is in turn second order dominated by the high level of education. This is valid for gross income in both unweighted and weighted forms. The groups compared by unweighted disposable income are maximal. For weighted observations on disposable incomes, the holders of a college degree turned out to dominate by second order the 0–11 schooling group at the 91 per cent level. The remaining two groups are not first and second order rankable. In order to discern the effects of human capital on earnings one should use a finer grouping of the households, as well as test for higher SD orders. This finding is consistent with regression-based results attributing certain returns to schooling since indices can be found to obtain complete rankings when FSD and SSD are not present. See also Figures 9A to 9D in MH (2005).

4.3.3.10   Test results by length of unemployment

Households are grouped by the length of unemployment period into: 0–1 month; 2–3 months; and more than three months. Mean and dispersion of gross incomes decreases by the length of unemployment spells. Test results provided on Table 10 of MH (2005) indicate that the first group second order dominate the last group at 86 per cent level. No dominance relation is found for the unweighted disposable income data. The weight differences results in same relation in the case of gross income, while the second group second order dominates the first group in the case of disposable income. Other comparisons are first and second order maximal. Graphs of CDFs are given in MH (2005).

4.3.3.11 Test results by geographical mobility

The households by the last attribute, geographical mobility, are classified by location of the places they grow up into: living in the same state; same region; and different state and region (Table 11 in MH 2005). Mobility affects positively the per capita gross incomes. The effect is, however, small. Heads living in a different state and region than they grow up in second order dominates those growing up in the same state. Accounting for weight differences produces similar result, but in addition we find also second order dominance of heads growing up in the same region over those growing up in the same state. Non dominance relation is found in comparison of groups by per capita disposable incomes. CDFs are given in MH (2005).

In sum, for the conditional analysis we find that first order dominance is very rare, but second order dominance holds in several cases when we consider per capita household gross income. In most comparisons there is no evidence of any dominance relationship in disposable income terms. Accounting for differences in weights improves the significance level and even frequency of second order dominance relationship. In several cases the pattern of results is similar for households characterized by a number of attributes. For instance, it is surprising to find weak effects for gender, education, the number of children, or seniority on the distribution of 'gross income'. The 'post-tax' incomes show very similar mean and dispersion levels. This could be due to several reasons. The effect of price index, the 'per capita' equivalent transformation of incomes, and a possible impact of 'block' bootstrap resampling on how new entry and exit in the yearly samples is treated.

4.4 Concluding remarks

Based on our implementation of the KS-type FSD and SSD tests, we were able to show a perhaps surprising number of cases of dominance between unconditional income distributions, improving steadily until the 1990s. These rankings are due to many other factors that may explain income differentials between population subgroups. Ceteris paribus examination is offered here by conducting SD tests for incomes of different groups identified by numerous characteristics, including race, age, gender, and education. Future work will examine regression-based simultaneous controls which avoid the problem of small cell sizes that would arise in the grouping approach.

Notes

1 We have studied these residuals elsewhere.
2 The PSID data is available on http://www.isr.umich.edu/src/psid/ for free downloads. For a full description of the data please see the guide to various interviewing years' procedures and codebooks.
3 Some advocate the recent approach where the head is defined as the person with the highest income.
4 Elimination of the unbalanced households was necessary to conduct matched-bootstrapping, where we obtain re-samples of the same households over time.

References

Anderson, G.J. (1996), 'Nonparametric Tests of Stochastic Dominance in Income Distributions', *Econometrica*, 64: 1183–1193.

Barrett, G. and Donald, S. (2003), 'Consistent Tests for Stochastic Dominance', *Econometrica*, 71,1: 71–104.

Bishop, J.A., Formby, J.P. and Thisle, P.D. (1992), 'Convergence of the South and Non-South Income Distributions, 1969–1979', *American Economic Review*, 82: 262–272.

Chernozhukov, V. (2002), 'Inference on Quantile Regression Process, an Alternative', Working Paper, MIT.

Crawford, I. (1999), 'Nonparametric Tests of Stochastic Dominance in Bivariate Distributions with an Application to UK Data', Institute for Fiscal Studies, WP 28/99.

Dardanoni, V. and Forcina, A. (2000), 'Inference for Lorenz Curve Orderings', *Econometrics Journal*, 2: 49–75.

Davidson, R. and Duclos, J.Y. (2000), 'Statistical Inference for Stochastic Dominance and for the Measurement of Poverty and Inequality', *Econometrica*, 68: 1435–1464.

Fisher, G., Wilson, D. and Xu, K. (1998), 'An Empirical Analysis of Term Premiums Using Significance Tests for Stochastic Dominance', *Economics Letters*, 60: 195–203.

Hansen, B.E. (1996), 'Inference when a Nuisance Parameter is not Identified under the Null Hypothesis', *Econometrica*, 64: 413–430.

Kaur, A., Prakasa Rao, B.L.S. and Singh H. (1994), 'Testing for Second-Order Stochastic Dominance of Two Distributions', *Econometric Theory*, 10: 849–866.

Klecan, L., McFadden, R. and McFadden, D. (1991), 'A Robust Test for Stochastic Dominance', Working Paper, Department of Economics, MIT.

Linton, O., Maasoumi, E. and Whang, Y.J. (2005), 'Consistent Testing for Stochastic Dominance under General Sampling Schemes', *Review Of Economic Studies*, 72: 735–765.

Linton, O., Maasoumi, E. and Whang, Y.J. (2007), 'Corrigendum', Review of Economic Studies, 75: 1–5.

Maasoumi, E. (2001), 'Parametric and Nonparametric Tests of Limited Domain and Ordered Hypotheses in Economics', Chapter 25, in B. Baltagi (ed.) *A Companion to Econometric Theory*, London: Basil Blackwell.

Maasoumi, E. and Heshmati, A. (2005), 'Evaluating Dominance Ranking of PSID Incomes by Various Household Attributes', http://faculty.smu.edu/maasoumi and http://www.iza.org.

Maasoumi, E. and Zandvakili, S. (1990), 'Generalized Entropy Measures of Mobility for Different Sexes and Income Levels', *Journal of Econometrics*, 43: 121–133.

McFadden, D. (1989), 'Testing for Stochastic Dominance', in Part II of T. Formby and T.K. Seo (eds.) *Studies in the Economics of Uncertainty* (in honor of J. Hadar), Berlin: Springer-Verlag.

Shorrocks A. and Foster, J. (1987), 'Transfer Sensitive Inequality Measures', *Review of Economic Studies*, 54: 485–497.

Tse, Y.K. and Zhang, X.B. (2000), 'A Monte Carlo Investigation of Some Tests for Stochastic Dominance', Unpublished Manuscript, National University of Singapore.

Whitmore, G.A. and Findley, M.C. (1978), 'Stochastic Dominance: An Approach to Decision-Making under Risk', Heath, Lexington: Mars.

5 Indices and tests for alienation based upon Gini type and distributional overlap measures

Gordon Anderson

5.1 Introduction

The recent change from using both before and after housing cost measures of income to using just the former in calculating UK poverty and inequality measures has been the subject of some controversy (Brewer *et al.* 2004). For many of the poor, housing expenditures are not discretionary in nature as are other consumption goods. Their 'lumpy' nature implies that some agents are 'rationed' to a larger housing stock than they would otherwise choose. Furthermore, a large portion of housing stock is rent-controlled or owner-occupied so that measured housing cost differences may not reflect quality differences or opportunity costs. Thus each measure carries distinct information that in particular is pertinent to the situation of the poor relative to the rich and the abandonment of one of the measures implies a sacrifice of information on the status of the poor relative to the rich which may skew relative comparisons.

Within economics there is a growing interest in the examination of relative concepts such as deprivation, social exclusion, alienation, polarization and convergence (see Bossert, D'Ambrosio and Peragine 2007; Duclos, Esteban and Ray 2004, and papers cited therein). These concepts have much to do with the measurement of a sense of social distance between agents (Akerlov 1997), but more importantly they are concerned with the distances between (rather than within) identifiable groups of agents. (In the following discussion these will be generically referred to as the rich and poor clubs). Most conventional poverty measures adhere to the focus axiom in abstracting from the status of the 'non-poor' in the poverty calculus. In this context so-called relative poverty measures are considered relative in the sense that the income status of poor agents is compared to some notion of a poverty line. However, if the well-being of the poor is negatively affected by a sense of deprivation – that they are so much worse off than the rich – then a sense of the distance between the poor and the non-poor is required. 10 per cent–90 per cent gaps familiar in quantile regression and inequality measurement possess a flavor of what is required but they do not capture the specific status of the poor relative to the rich.

The issue here has much to do with notions of inequality between groups, something of which in a one-dimensional world Gini was particularly aware (Gini 1916) and which has found expression in subsequent work (Butler and Donald 1987; Deutsch and Silber 1997, 1999; Dagum 1980, 1987; Gastwirth 1975; Yitzhaki 1994). Note that in this environment the incomes of the poor are not necessarily always less than those of the rich. Gastwirth and Dagum (in looking at gender and racial clubs) consider respectively the probability that a poor person earns at least as much as a rich person and the probability that a rich person earns at least as much as a poor person. These are, of course, complementary; in fact they can be shown to sum to one and are related to the probability of transvariation introduced by Gini (1916), but these measures are hard to extend to a multidimensional framework.

In this chapter alienation indices developed from the Gini coefficient together with alienation indices based upon a measure of distributional overlap (or lack of it) are outlined, their properties examined and the indices are extended to multivariate situations. The indices are exemplified in examining alienation between the rich and the poor, and between location (the North and the South and racial White and non-White) divides in the UK with respect to before and after housing cost measures of income that have been the source of such controversy.

5.2 Univariate, Gini-based, alienation measures

Starting with the classic Gini inequality coefficient which, with x_i being the income of the i'th agent for agents $i = 1, \ldots, n$ and where for convenience and without loss of generality, incomes are arranged in ascending rank order, may be written as:

$$Gini = \frac{1}{2n^2 \mu} \sum_{i=1}^{n} \sum_{j=1}^{n} |x_i - x_j| \tag{5.1}$$

where μ is the mean of the x's. Suppose the poverty cut-off, which defines the rich and poor clubs, is somewhere between x_p and x_{p+1} where $p < n$, then Gini may be thought of as the average mean normalized differences between agents within the poor club, between agents within the rich club and between poor and rich club agents. Yitzhaki (1994) cites Lasswell (1965) in referring to this as perfect stratification, i.e. no overlapping between the clubs. In measuring alienation it is only the last group of comparisons that are relevant, i.e. the average normalized difference between the rich group and poor group agents. In this case the new statistic 'AGini' could be written as:

$$AGini = \frac{1}{p(n-p)\mu} \sum_{j=p+1}^{n} \sum_{i=1}^{p} (x_j - x_i) = \frac{1}{\mu} \left(\frac{\sum_{j=p+1}^{n} x_j}{n-p} - \frac{\sum_{i=1}^{p} x_i}{p} \right) \tag{5.2}$$

Clearly this is still a number greater than 0 (but it is no longer guaranteed to be less than 1) which reflects the mean normalized average distance between the poor group and the rich group. Indeed the formulae in (5.2) can be generalized to general group differences where stratification is imperfect. The income distribution is now presumed to be a mixture of two subgroup population distributions (poor and non-poor), where relationship to the poverty line is no longer the defining feature of the clubs. Using $I_{poor}(i)$ as an indicator function equaling 1 when the i'th person is from the poor club and 0 otherwise AGini becomes:

$$AGini = \frac{1}{\mu}(\Sigma\, x_i \left(\frac{I_{poor}\,(i)}{\sum_{j=1}^{n} I_{poor}\,(j)} - \frac{1 - I_{poor}\,(i)}{\sum_{j=1}^{n} (1 - I_{poor}\,(j))} \right) \tag{5.3}$$

which is the mean normalized difference between the subgroup means.

Observe that in (5.2) the same index would be arrived at if one were to work with $x_i - z$ and $x_j - z$, the corresponding distances from the poverty line z which facilitates a link to the well-known family of poverty and welfare indices introduced by Foster, Greer and Thorbecke (1984) as follows.[1] The theoretical representation of this family is given by:

$$P_a\,(x, z) = \int_0^z \left(\frac{z - x}{z} \right)^a dF\,(x) \tag{5.4}$$

where $F(x)$ is the cumulative density function (with p.d.f. $f(x)$) describing the population of incomes, z is the maximum of the poor and a is an index defining the nature of the poverty index and corresponds to a measure of poverty aversion. As a consequence P_0 corresponds to the poverty count, P_1 is a normalized measure of the intensity of relative deprivation and so on. P_i/P_0 may be construed as the expected value of a weighted function of the normalized income deficiency where the weights are the $(i-1)$'th power of the normalized income deficiency itself. Thus increasing i increases the weights attached to those furthest from the poverty line and interestingly as $a\,(= i)$ becomes very large the index becomes a Rawlsian measure in focusing almost entirely on the poorest agent. Along similar lines $W(x,z)$, an index of weighted relative distances of incomes above the poverty line, may be contemplated whose theoretical representation is of the form:

$$W_a\,(x, z) = \int_z^\infty \left(\frac{x - z}{z} \right)^a dF\,(x) \tag{5.5}$$

In this case W_0 corresponds to the proportion of the population above the poverty line W_1 is a normalized measure of relative well being of the non-poor, W_2 is a measure of the intensity of the relative well being of those above the poverty line, and so on. In this case as a becomes very large the index becomes almost entirely focused on the richest person, W_1/W_0 corresponds to the expected normalized income surplus over the maximum poverty income etc. For all $a > 0$ all of these indices are essentially measuring relative weighted distances from the poverty line and it is in this sense that they are considered relative measures. However, both W and P are completely uninformed with respect to the distribution of incomes in the other group which accords with the focus axiom alluded to earlier. For the purposes of reflecting the notion of alienation between the poor and non-poor groups this axiom needs to be violated. Indeed the population analogue of AGini can be shown to be a special case ($a = 1$) of a general class of alienation measures which, for pre-specified $a \geq 1$, is given by:

$$\left(\frac{z}{\mu}\right)^a \left(\frac{W_a}{W_0} - \frac{P_a}{P_0}\right) \tag{5.6}$$

These measures are related to, but not the same as, generalizations of the between-income distribution measures proposed by Dagum (1980) and Gastwirth (1975) which do not exist when clubs do not overlap. Inference for these concepts may be based upon extensions to the formulae developed in Davidson and Duclos (1997, 2000) and Zheng *et al.* (2000). However, they are very difficult to generalize to situations where club membership is defined in a multidimensional framework (see Anderson 2007 and references therein). Also there is a sense in which the indices are very moment-specific, for example AGini would be very effective at picking up alienation engendered by movements in subgroup or club; however, it would not be so effective in picking up alienation (or polarization) engendered by changes in within-subgroup variability. A perennial problem with the Gini coefficient is that it is not good at picking up marginal inter-temporal changes in income distributions, it tends to be inter-temporally very stable and rarely indicates significant changes. To examine this a small Monte Carlo study was performed,[2] an income distribution was simulated 1,000 times from exp(N(5.6, 0.77)) (calibrated on the data encountered in the following application) and subjected to growth rates of 3, 5, 7, 9 and 11 per cent. AGini's for a perfectly segmented society based upon a half median poverty line were calculated (their average value ranged from 0.9092 to 0.9129, the average value of standard normal test statistics for changes in the value of the AGini between years was 0.09). A similar exercise with overlapping poor and non-poor clubs yielded much lower AGini coefficients with average values of 0.12 and average values of the test statistic for differences of about 0.6. Basically, significant changes in the AGini coefficients over time rarely occurred without considerable changes in the income distribution structure. Intuitively the difficulty is that in both the perfectly segmented and imperfectly segmented situations the statistic is based upon the differences between two concepts that are themselves evolving slowly over time.

5.3 Distributional overlap: an alternative alienation measure

An attractive feature of these Gini-based alienation measures is that, like the Gini, they are unit-free (a consequence of the mean normalization). An alternative technique for assessing alienation between two groups is to evaluate how much the two populations have in common, that is to say how much they overlap. Such an index is also unit-free, readily extended to multivariate environments and is sensitive to subgroup distribution changes that are not location-based (see Anderson 2004). Furthermore since it focuses on tail-area effects it is likely to be more sensitive to changes over time (especially when policies are designed to influence the structure of the income distribution in its tail areas). Weitzman (1970) was the first to propose such an instrument. Such a measure corresponds to non-alienation and its negative or some negative function of it corresponds to a degree of alienation. Anderson, Ge and Leo (2004) propose an overlap measure as a measure of convergence and its complement as a measure of alienation. The extent to which two distributions $f(x)$ and $g(x)$ overlap is given by:

$$OV = \int_{-\infty}^{\infty} \min(f(x), g(x))dx$$

Clearly it is a number between 0 and 1 with 0 corresponding to no overlap and 1 to the perfect matching of the two distributions. It follows that AOVER $= 1 - $OV is a measure of the extent to which the distributions do not match or are alienated. When $f(x)$ and $f(y)$ are specified to the extent that all of their parameters can be estimated and the intersection points of $f(x)$ and $g(x)$ calculated OV can be estimated parametrically (see Anderson *et al.* 2005). When $f(\ )$ and $g(\ )$ are unknown, given independent samples from $f(\ )$ (represented by x) and $g(\ )$ (represented by y) of sizes n_x and n_y respectively, its empirical counterpart may be implemented by choosing $K + 1$ partitions of the range of x defined by $x_k, k = 1, \ldots, K$ and calculating:

$$OVEST = \max \left(\frac{I(x - x_K)}{n_x}, \frac{I(y - x_K)}{n_y} \right)$$
$$- \sum_{k=1}^{K} \min \left(\left(\frac{I(x - x_k)}{n_x} - \frac{I(x - x_{k-1})}{n_x} \right), \left(\frac{I(y - x_k)}{n_y} - \frac{I(y - x_{k-1})}{n_y} \right) \right)$$

Where $I(z)$ is an indicator function equal to 1 when $z \leq 0$ and 0 otherwise. The estimator and associated tests are most effective when the intersection points of the unknown distributions correspond with the chosen partition points.

Since $f(x)$ and $g(x)$ are unknown so will their intersection points be; however, they could be estimated by adapting kernel estimation techniques.

The parametric version depends upon the properties of the estimators for the distribution parameters; typically if the parameter estimates are consistent then so will OV be. The problem with the non-parametric version is that the estimator OVEST is inconsistent. There are two sources of inconsistency, the first arise when the chosen partition points do not coincide with the intersection points of the two distributions of interest. It is best understood by considering a closed interval [a, b] over which the $f(x)$ and $g(x)$ overlap and $f(x^*) = g(x^*)$ for an x^* inside the open interval (a, b) with $g(x) < f(x)$ for $x < x^*$ and $g(x) > f(x)$ for $x > x^*$. The component appropriate for the overlap measure is given by:

$$A = \int_a^{x^*} g(x)dx + \int_{x^*}^b f(x)dx$$

Whereas the component included in the calculation will be the smaller of either:

$$\int_a^b f(x)dx = A + \int_a^{x^*} (f(x) - g(x))dx$$

or:

$$\int_a^b g(x)dx = A + \int_{x8}^b (g(x) - (f(x))dx$$

In both cases the second right-hand side term is positive, overstating the degree of overlap. The other source of bias is related to the $Min(p,q)$ function where p and q are the respective independent estimators of the probability of being in an interval under $f(\ )$ and $g(\ )$. This bias derives from the fact that, in general for independent variables p and q, $E(p) \geq E(p|p < q)$. Since p is an unbiased estimator for $f(\ )$, the conditional estimator implicit in the min function will be downward-biased. Generally for independent p and q, with respective pdf's $j(p)$ and $k(q)$ (with cdf's $J(\ )$ and $K(\ )$), $E(p|p < q)$ is given by:

$$\int_0^1 \int_p^1 pj(p)k(q)dqdp = \int_0^1 pj(p)[1 - K(p)]dp = E(p) - \int_0^1 pj(p)(K(p)dp$$

Since the last term is never negative, the overlap measure is always biased downward. Anderson, Ge and Leo (2005) examine the properties of these estimators in a Monte Carlo study. The asymptotic normality of the test statistic was considered and could not be rejected for reasonably small samples ($n = 200$). Using kernel estimates for intersection points did not appear to yield a great advantage in terms of bias reduction (bias due to partition points and intersection points being non-coincident was of a small order as Table 5.1 indicates[3]). To examine the effect of the biases alienation measures based upon the overlap of two normal distributions were considered; Table 5.1 summarizes the results. In one scenario the distributions intersected once (essentially location-shifted distributions) in the other they intersected twice (scale-shifted distributions). Inconsistencies due to the approximation of the intersection points are of a much smaller order than those due to the use of the Min() function, the latter being proportionately more significant when there is either a great deal of overlap or when there is very little overlap. Proportionately the total bias is much more important when the alienation index (or overlap measure) is close to one or zero being close to 20 per cent in some cases.

5.4 Multivariate considerations

Extension to a multivariate measures can be somewhat problematic with regard to Gini-based alienation measures. Multivariate Gini coefficients have been developed (see Anderson 2004 and Koshevoy and Mosler 1997) but adapting them to the current context is complex; it requires defining club membership criteria for each characteristic but even then extending the analogy to multivariate measures of FGT indices is difficult. One approach is to take some weighted mean of the various AGini coefficients in each dimension (suppose there are K dimensions) but then the weights have to be determined (Anderson 2004). Two possibilities are an arithmetic or geometric mean AGini's, e.g.:

Table 5.1 Approximate absolute bias in the alienation measure

IA	Location shift			Scale shift		
	Total bias	$g(x) = f(x)$ bias	Proportionate bias	Total bias	Intersection bias	Proportionate bias
0.1	0.0183	0.0006	0.1830	0.0199	0.0030	0.1990
0.2	0.0117	0.0006	0.0585	0.0144	0.0036	0.0720
0.3	0.0087	0.0001	0.0290	0.0110	0.0020	0.0367
0.4	0.0109	−0.0007	0.0272	0.0117	−0.0014	0.0292
0.5	0.0185	−0.0018	0.0370	0.0167	−0.0062	0.0334
0.6	0.0312	−0.0032	0.0520	0.0260	−0.0121	0.0433
0.7	0.0489	−0.0047	0.0699	0.0394	−0.0192	0.0563
0.8	0.0711	−0.0065	0.0711	0.0568	−0.0272	0.0710
0.9	0.0977	−0.0084	0.0977	0.0778	−0.0360	0.0864

$$MAGINI = \prod_{k=1}^{K} \left(\frac{1}{p(n-p)} \sum_{i=1}^{p} \sum_{j=p+1}^{n} \frac{(x_{ik} - x_{jk})^2}{\bar{x}_k} \right)^{b_k} \ or$$

$$\frac{1}{p(n-p)} (2K)^{-0.5} \sum_{i=1}^{p} \sum_{j=p+1}^{n} \sqrt{\sum_{k=1}^{K} \frac{(x_{ik} - x_{jk})}{\bar{x}_k}} a_k$$

where in each case the weights a_k and β_k, which each sum to K have to be chosen by the investigator.[4] The former statistic with equal weights will be employed here. Extension to a multivariate alienation index is very straightforward:

$$MAOVER = 1 - \int_{-\infty}^{\infty} \int_{-\infty}^{\infty} \ldots \int_{-\infty}^{\infty} \min(f(x_1, x_2, \ldots x_K),$$

$$g(x_1, x_2, \ldots x_K)) dx \ dx \ldots dx_K$$

Unlike the multivariate Gini no weighting metric is required for this measure; however, the disadvantage of this type of measure arises when there is no overlap in one of the dimensions since the measure will be degenerate and record 'complete' alienation regardless of other overlapping covariates.

5.5 The application

Reducing relative poverty has been a policy target of the British government since 1998. Evaluation of the success (or otherwise) of policies has been clouded by controversy over the recent abandonment of some of the comparison instruments, more specifically the 'after housing cost' income measure (Brewer *et al.* 2004). Poverty measures had been based upon income measures both before and after housing costs, an acknowledgement of the concern that for many, housing expenditures are not discretionary in nature in the sense that other consumption goods are. The 'lumpy' nature of housing raises the possibility that the poor are 'rationed' to a larger housing stock than they would otherwise choose. Furthermore, between-agent housing cost differences may not reflect quality differences since they are not calculated on an opportunity cost/economic rent basis. This issue is of particular interest in the case of specific alienated poor groups, a large portion of which inhabit properties in the social rented sector where rents have been set with little regard to housing quality or market prices. The presumption has been that the distinction materially effects various welfare and poverty calculations and it would be interesting to compare the individual measures with the consequences of considering the joint impact of after housing cost incomes and housing costs. That is to say, does the distinction alter the extent to which the groups are alienated from the rest of society? That poverty level targets were expressed in relative (median income-based income cut-offs) rather than

Table 5.2 Means, medians, standard deviations, and sample sizes for non-poor and poor clubs for sample years

	1996		1998		2000		2002	
	Non-poor	Poor	Non-poor	Poor	Non-poor	Poor	Non-poor	Poor
Income before	309.7	88.0	342.7	94.5	382.4	98.9	391.0	103.0
housing costs	255.8	100.2	280.0	108.0	308.3	116.1	326.6	121.7
	234.7	32.7	290.7	36.9	366.9	44.8	303.9	47.8
	27626	2733	24710	2500	25408	2635	14948	1435
Income after	288.4	64.3	316.7	72.5	354.0	74.0	366.5	80.4
housing costs	238.9	81.2	258.5	89.7	284.6	95.5	306.1	101.7
	237.0	50.0	293.8	51.5	376.2	63.1	303.8	63.8
	25729	4630	23165	4045	24053	3990	14152	2231
Housing costs*	51.5	−0.8	58.5	−1.3	62.8	−2.6	58.8	−2.8
	42.4	5.3	48.1	5.2	51.5	5.6	48.7	5.1
	35.3	19.9	40.5	24.1	44.0	34.4	39.9	22.8
	21061	9298	18564	8646	18973	9070	10907	5476

Note Negative average housing costs for the poor arise because different equivalence scales are used for before and after housing costs concepts due to different household economies of scale effects in the income measurement concepts. This effect is particularly strong at the lower end of the income scale. Household size and composition was adjusted for on the basis of equivalence scales proposed in McClements (1977).

absolute (needs-based income cut-offs) terms is significant, probably reflecting the recent popular notion that poverty is a relative concept[5] (see Hills 2001, 2002). Indeed measures of the relative poverty of subgroups are an expression of how aspects of the subgroup income distribution differ from that of the rest of the population, summarized by the population median. This falls short of measuring differences between the income distributions of a subgroup and its complement in a complete sense; however, it is very much in the spirit of assessing subgroup alienation. Indeed, if the policy target is to make the subgroup and its complement more 'alike', measures of alienation or coherence are the appropriate comparison tool.

The data used in this study relate to United Kingdom household income from all sources net of direct taxes and is drawn from the annual Family Resources Survey. Two measures of income are used in the analysis, one before housing costs are deducted and one after housing costs are deducted. Until recently the UK government treated the measures as complementary indicators of living standards, presenting both in its 'Households Below Average Income' poverty audits. Table 5.2 provides summary statistics of the data. The issue first considered is how do standard poverty measures compare with relative poverty measures when the alienation of the poor is a matter of concern? Table 5.3 presents results for the years 1996–2002 comparing the poverty rate with the alienation measure for income before housing costs, income after housing costs, and housing cost measures. For the purposes of

Table 5.3 Comparing poverty rate with the alienation measure for sample years

	Before housing costs		After housing costs		Housing costs	
Year	Pov Rate	AGini	Pov Rate	AGini	Pov Rate	AGini
1996	0.0900	0.7651	0.1525	0.8817	0.3063	1.4722
1998	0.0919	0.7759	0.1487	0.8710	0.3178	1.5127
2000	0.0940	0.7968	0.1423	0.8905	0.3234	1.5699
2002	0.0876	0.7873	0.1362	0.9735	0.3342	1.6108

this exercise the poverty line was considered to be half the median income in the sample and membership of the poor and non-poor clubs defined by which side of the line a household is on. Since there is perfect segmentation, no overlap measure is available. Clearly the three measures have substantially different-shaped distributions and not surprisingly they present quite different pictures of the progress of poverty and alienation. In all cases alienation has increased over the period whereas the poverty rate has increased with respect to the income before housing costs deductions and housing costs measures but it has decreased with respect to the income after housing cost measure. The culprit in the increase in poverty is the increase in the portion of people whose housing expenditures are below half the median expenditure, lending credence to the view that before housing costs measures and after housing costs measures capture quite different aspects of the poor–non poor relationship.

An interesting feature of these results is that with the income before housing cost measure and the housing cost measure poverty and alienation move in step; increased alienation appears to be a concomitant of increased poverty. However, after housing costs have been deducted from income, the poverty and alienation measures move in opposite directions. Essentially, although the plight of the poor is improving with respect to this measure, the status of the non-poor is improving even more rapidly so that the gap between them, measured in terms of their average after housing costs expenditures, is widening.

A primary question is whether or not the between-period changes of the indices correspond to significant changes or trends in the respective measures. Table 5.4 reports the asymptotic standard normal tests and upper tail probabilities for poverty reduction and alienation reduction between comparison years. Negative values of the test statistics indicate increases over time, positive values denote reductions. Generally after housing costs measures exhibited reductions in poverty and alienation indices whereas housing costs measures indicated increases in alienation measures. Tests for significant changes in the AGini statistic are very much like a difference in means test and the changes in the poverty rate corresponds to a difference in population proportions test. Consistent with our limited Monte Carlo experiment, generally, changes in AGini indices are small relative to their variability so

Table 5.4 Standard normal, between-year, poverty reduction and AGini alienation reduction tests (upper-tail probabilities in brackets)

	Before housing costs		
	1996	*1998*	*2000*
1998	−0.7731 (0.7803)		
	−0.0351 (0.5140)		
2000	−1.6466 (0.9502)	−0.8438 (0.8006)	
	−0.0922 (0.5367)	−0.0570 (0.5227)	
2002	0.8803 (0.1894)	1.5129 (0.0652)	2.2462 (0.0123)
	−0.0506 (0.5202)	−0.0250 (0.5100)	0.0197 (0.4921)
	After housing costs		
	1996	*1998*	*2000*
1998	1.7887 (0.0368)		
	0.0234 (0.4907)		
2000	3.4811 (0.0002)	2.1258 (0.0168)	
	−0.0170 (0.5068)	−0.0368 (0.5147)	
2002	4.7601 (0.0000)	3.5952 (0.0002)	1.7887 (0.0368)
	0.0133 (0.4947)	−0.0040 (0.5016)	0.0252 (0.4899)
	Housing costs		
	1996	*1998*	*2000*
1998	−2.9696 (0.9985)		
	−0.1222 (0.5486)		
2000	−4.4630 (1.0000)	−1.4304 (0.9237)	
	−0.2348 (0.5928)	−0.1286 (0.5512)	
2002	−6.2079 (1.0000)	−3.5650 (0.9998)	−2.3441 (0.9905)
	−0.3733 (0.6455)	−0.2434 (0.5961)	−0.0861 (0.5343)

that changes are rarely statistically significant. This is not the case with the poverty rate measures which indicate substantial changes especially when housing costs are separated out from incomes. Perhaps the most striking feature of Table 5.5 is the significant, persistent and opposite signed trends in poverty rates in the After housing costs and Housing costs measurement concepts that to some degree net out in the Before housing costs variable. This again reinforces the view that the separation of income after housing costs and housing costs provides policymakers with quite distinct pieces of information.

Other group comparisons

Underlying these results there may be subgroup differences which merit consideration here; regional and racial differences will be considered presenting an opportunity to compare the overlap (AOVER) measure with AGini and their multivariate counterparts. Before and after housing costs income measures are reported together with the joint distribution of income after housing costs and housing costs. The regional analysis was based upon a partition of households in Northern locations (South Midlands and above excluding East Anglia) and southern locations (the complementary set). Interestingly, there is little accord between AGini and AOVER indices in the before and after housing cost analyses; there is, however, considerable accord in the multidimensional indices which both reflect an increasing alienation over time between the north and south.

Table 5.6 reports the significance of the changes over time. Again the AGini measures never altered significantly so the test statistics (available on

Table 5.5 Regional alienation

Year	Before housing costs		After housing costs		After housing costs and housing costs joint distribution	
	AGINI	AOVER	AGINI	AOVER	AGINI	AOVER
1996	0.1383	0.0800	0.1202	0.0759	0.1795	0.1958
1998	0.1705	0.0968	0.1526	0.0802	0.2130	0.2041
2000	0.1747	0.0889	0.1590	0.0739	0.2159	0.2041
2002	0.1455	0.1031	0.1144	0.0984	0.2171	0.2622

Table 5.6 Standard normal, between-year, AOVER alienation reduction tests (lower-tail probabilities in brackets)

	Before housing costs		
	1996	*1998*	*2000*
1998	3.4869 (0.9998)		
2000	1.9100 (0.9719)	−1.5707 (0.0581)	
2002	3.6509 (0.9999)	0.9578 (0.8309)	2.1884 (0.9857)

	After housing costs		
	1996	*1998*	*2000*
1998	0.9489 (0.8287)		
2000	−0.4505 (0.3262)	−1.3701 (0.0853)	
2002	3.6499 (0.9999)	2.8921 (0.9981)	3.9452 (1.0000)

	Joint distribution		
	1996	*1998*	*2000*
1998	1.2382 (0.8922)		
2000	1.2355 (0.8917)	−0.0128 (0.4949)	
2002	7.2537 (1.0000)	6.2219 (1.0000)	6.2591 (1.0000)

request) are not reported here. With respect to the AOVER measure, 2002 appears to have been a year of substantial alienation relative to all other years, especially when the income after housing costs and the joint income after housing costs and housing costs distributions are considered. Otherwise the previous years show little in the way of substantial differences between the years in any of the measurement categories.

An examination of racial alienation effects was based upon a partition of households into white and non-white (mixed households were included in the non-white group). With one or two exceptions trends in the AGINI and AOVER indices corresponded. While levels of the AOVER indices were much higher than those for the regional comparison, they were relatively more stable over time.

As for statistically significant changes, again the AGini inter-temporal differences were never significant but in this case neither were the AOVER statistics generally speaking. The joint distribution indices are never significant and the only significant univariate measure difference appears to be with respect to 1996/1998 comparison with − 3.2942 (0.0005) for the before housing cost measure and − 3.0127 (0.0013) for the after housing cost measure which corresponds to a substantial reduction in alienation over the period.

5.6 Conclusions

The use of concepts of alienation and exclusion have become commonplace in economics and instruments for measuring their extent are needed. Measures based upon the formulation of the Gini coefficient and upon the degree to which distributions overlap have been introduced, discussed and extended to multivariate situations. The Gini-based measure, calculated in the same spirit as Gini as the average distance between the elements in one population and those in another, can be shown to be the aggregate mean normalized difference in subgroup means. As such it has great intuitive appeal. However, it appears to exhibit great variability relative to its inter-temporal trend and hence does not appear to identify inter-temporal changes in the level of alienation very well in a statistical sense. In addition, extension to the multivariate environment is somewhat arbitrary depending as it does upon the

Table 5.7 Racial alienation

Year	Before housing costs		After housing costs		After housing costs and housing costs joint distribution	
	AGini	AIndex	AGini	AIndex	AGini	AIndex
1996	0.2405	0.2077	0.3082	0.2396	0.2750	0.9034
1998	0.1161	0.1557	0.1756	0.1891	0.2317	0.8976
2000	0.1240	0.1816	0.1780	0.2210	0.2248	0.8931
2002	0.1902	0.1776	0.2525	0.2225	0.2943	0.8948

choice of some weighting scheme between the characteristics. However, it does provide a tool of analysis when the distributions of interest do not overlap.

The overlap-based measure exhibits much less stochastic variability relative to its inter-temporal trend and hence appears more able to identify statistically significant trends. It also has great intuitive appeal and is more readily extended to multivariate environments in that it does not require the formulation of a between factor weighting scheme. However, two bias sources inherent in its calculation have been demonstrated, one due to not knowing intersection points of subgroup functions, the other to the conditional nature of the estimation process, but they do not impede its use as an index for between-period comparisons since the bias is systematically in one direction. Another drawback of this particular method is that it is non-informative when distributions being compared do not overlap.

The measures have been exemplified in considering alienation issues between various groups in the UK, based upon before and after housing cost income measurement concepts. Analysis of the alienation of the poor and non-poor groups (segmented by half the median income) indicated that traditional poverty measures (poverty counts based upon a half median income cut off) yielded different temporal profiles from alienation measures across the different measurement concepts. In terms of the poverty and alienation of the poverty group this highlights the notion that they are fundamentally different ideas. In terms of before and after housing cost income measures the results lend support to the view that ignoring one of the measures (the U.K. government's statistical agencies have recently moved to just using the before housing cost measure) implies that important information is being overlooked. There appears to be significant poverty reduction indicated by the after housing cost measure which is counterbalanced by significant poverty increases in the housing cost measure so that little evidence of a trend emerges from the before housing cost income measure.

More detailed analysis of alienation between the north and the south and between whites and non-whites over the 1996–2002 period has indicated significant alienation in the former but none in the latter. With respect to the north and south dichotomy there was a lack of accord between the univariate before and after housing cost income Gini-based and overlap measures but much accord in the joint measures.

Notes

1 See also Butler and Donald (1987).
2 Full details are available from the author upon request.
3 Indeed kernel estimation of an unknown number of intersection points proved troublesome of itself in smallish samples largely because the wrong number (generally too many) of intersection points was identified.
4 Alternative inequality measures have been proposed in Maasoumi (1986) and Tsui (1995) which could equally well be converted into alienation measures.

5 In fact, both groups experienced steady declines in absolute poverty throughout the 1990's, while trends in relative poverty rates have not been so obvious.

References

Akerlov, G.A. (1997), 'Social Distance and Social Decision', *Econometrica*, 65, 1005–1027.

Anderson, G.J. (2004), 'Toward an Empirical Analysis of Polarization' *Journal of Econometrics*, 122, 1–26.

Anderson, G.L. (2007), 'The Empirical Assessment of Multidimensional Welfare, Inequality and Poverty: Sample Weighted Multivariate Generalizations of the Kolmogorov-Smirnov Two-Sample Tests for Stochastic Dominance.', *Journal of Economic Inequality*, forthcoming.

Anderson, G.J., Y. Ge and T.W. Leo, (2005), 'Distributional Overlap: Simple, Multivariate, Parametric and Non-Parametric Tests for Alienation, Convergence and General Distributional Difference Issues', Mimeo Economics Department University of Toronto.

Bossert, W., C. D'Ambrosio and V. Peragine (2007), 'Deprivation and Social Exclusion', *Economica*, forthcoming.

Brewer, M., A. Goodman, M. Myck, J. Shaw and A. Shephard (2004), 'Poverty and Inequality in Britain: 2004' The Institute For Fiscal Studies Commentary, 96.

Butler, R.J. and J.B. McDonald (1987), 'Interdistributional Income Inequality', *Journal of Business and Economic Statistics*, 5, 13–18.

Dagum, C. (1980), 'Inequality Measures Between Income Distributions with Applications', *Econometrica*, 48, 1791–1803.

Dagum, C. (1987), 'Measuring the Economic Affluence Between Populations of Income Receivers', *Journal of Business and Economic Statistics*, 5, 5–12.

Davidson, R. and J.Y. Duclos (1997), 'Statistical Inference for the Measurement of the Incidence of Taxes and Transfers', *Econometrica* 65, 1453–1466.

Davidson, R. and J.Y. Duclos (2000), 'Statistical Inference for Stochastic Dominance and for the Measurement of Poverty and Inequality, *Econometrica*, 68, 1435–1464.

Deutsch, J. and J. Silber (1997), 'Gini's "Transvariazioni" and the Measurement of Inequality Within and Between Distributions', *Empirical Economics*, 22, 547–554.

Deutsch, J. and J. Silber (1999) 'Inequality Decomposition by Population Subgroup and the Analysis of Interdistributional Inequality', in J. Silber (Ed.), *Handbook of Income Inequality Measurement*, Kluwer, 363–397.

Duclos, J.Y., J. Esteban and D. Ray (2004), 'Polarization: Concepts, Measurement and Estimation', *Econometrica*, 72, 1737–1772.

Foster, J., J. Greer and E. Thorbecke (1984), 'A Class of Decomposable Poverty Measures', *Econometrica*, 52, 761–766.

Gastwirth, J.L. (1975), 'Statistical Measures of Earnings Differentials' *The American Statistician*, 29, 32–35.

Gini, C. (1916), 'Concetto di "Transvariazione" e le sue prime applicazioni', *Studi di Economia, Finanza e Statistica, editi del Giornale degli Economisti e Rivista di Statistica*.

Hills, J. (2001), 'Poverty and Social Security: What Rights? Whose Responsibilities?', in A. Park, J. Curtice, K. Thompson, L. Jarvis and C. Bromley (eds), *British Social Attitudes: The 18th Report – Public Policy, Social Ties*, London, Sage.

Hills, J. (2002), 'Following or Leading Public Opinion?', Social Security Policy and Public Attitudes Since 1997', *Fiscal Studies*, 23, 539–558.

Koshevoy, G. and K. Mosler, (1997). 'Multivariate Gini indices'. *Journal of Multivariate Analysis*, 60, 252–276.

Maasoumi, E. (1986), 'The Measurement and Decomposition of Multidimensional Inequality' *Econometrica*, 54, 771–779.

Tsui, K.Y. (1995), 'Multidimensional Generalizations of the Relative and Absolute Inequality Indices: The Atkinson-Kolm-Sen Approach'. *Journal of Economic Theory*, 67, 251–265.

Weitzman, M. (1970), 'Measures of Overlap of Income Distributions of White and Negro Families in the U.S.', Technical Paper 22, Bureau of the Census.

Yitzhaki, S., (1994), 'Economic Distance and Overlapping of Distributions,' *Journal of Econometrics*, 61, 147–159.

Zheng, B., J.P., Formby, W.J. Smith and V. Chow (2000), 'Inequality Orderings, Normalized Stochastic Dominance and Statistical Inference', *Journal of Business and Economic Statistics*, 18, 479–488.

6 Measuring relative equality of concentration between different income/wealth distributions

Quentin L. Burrell

6.1 Introduction

One of the most intuitively reasonable requirements of a measure of concentration of income/wealth within a population is that it should be invariant under scale transformations – the degree of inequality should be the same if incomes are measured in € or US$. The situation is rather different if we are comparing inequalities between populations. For instance, suppose we have two populations whose unit income distributions are identical, but with one measured in €, the other in US$. Then their 'within population' concentration measures will be the same and yet there is clearly a difference 'between populations' since if both were expressed in the same units, we would have two populations with different degrees of affluence.

Dagum (1987) sought to address this problem by introducing a measure of relative economic affluence (REA) based upon the Gini mean difference, defined as the average absolute difference between incomes of (randomly chosen) members of the two populations. It turns out that the REAs of two income distributions are the same if and only if the means of the two distributions are the same. The first of the new measures proposed by Burrell (2005a) is a simple adaptation of the REA; the second incorporates the Gini mean difference and the Gini coefficients of the two populations separately to give a normalized measure – somewhat analogous to the correlation coefficient – lying between 0 and 1, with the upper value being achieved if and only if the two population income distributions (measured in the same units) are identical. Although we will talk in terms of income distributions, the notions clearly extend to other fields.

6.2 Basic definitions

We imagine a population of individuals and let X denote the income of a randomly chosen individual. Suppose that the distribution of X in the population is given by the (absolutely) continuous probability density function (*pdf*) $f_X(x)$ defined on the non-negative real line. (Restricting attention to the absolutely continuous case is done purely for simplicity of presentation.)

Notation.

(i) $\mu_X = E[X] = $ mean of $X = \int\limits_0^\infty x f_X(x)dx;$

(ii) $\Phi_X(x) = P(X \geq x) = \int\limits_x^\infty f_X(y)dy = $ tail distribution function of X.

It is useful to recall that for a continuous non-negative random variable X we have:

$$E[X] = \int\limits_0^\infty \Phi_X(x)dx = \mu_X \qquad (6.1)$$

(see, for instance, Stirzaker 1994: 238). Without further comment we will always assume that the mean is finite. There are many different approaches to the measurement of concentration/inequality of (income) distributions and we refer the reader to Lambert (2001) and Kleiber and Kotz (2003) for further discussion.

Definition 6.1 The *Gini coefficient/index/ratio* for X is defined formally as:

$$\gamma_X = \frac{E[|X_1 - X_2|]}{2\mu_X}, \text{ where } X_1 \text{ and } X_2 \text{ are independent copies of } X.$$

(See the previous references, among many others, as well as the original presentation by Gini 1914).

The idea behind the definition is that we look at each pair of individuals within the population in turn, find the absolute difference between their incomes and then average out over all possible pairs. For purposes of calculation, the above definition is not very convenient. Of the many others available (see for instance Yitzhaki 1998), the one that best suits our purposes is given in the following:

Proposition 6.1

$$\gamma_X = 1 - \frac{\int\limits_0^\infty \Phi_X(x)^2 \, dx}{\mu_X} \qquad (6.2)$$

According to Kleiber and Kotz (2003), this is originally due to Arnold and Laguna (1977) 'at least in the non-Italian literature'. It was independently rediscovered by Dorfman (1979) in economics and by Burrell (1991, 1992a) in informetrics.

The Gini coefficient is usually held to be one of the, if not *the*, best inequality measures in that it obeys all seven of the 'desirable' properties proposed by Dalton (1920) for such a measure, see Dagum (1983). One of these properties is that it is invariant under scale, or is independent of the unit of measurement. This is clearly almost a necessary property in measuring inequality within a population. However, this property should not necessarily carry over to comparative studies of inequality between populations if different units of income are used. As an example, suppose that the income in two populations each follows an exponential distribution, measured in the same units but with different means. Then clearly the general level of income is greater in the population having the greater mean. On the other hand, since the exponential is a scale-parameter family, the Gini coefficient for each will be the same. Hence reliance on standard measurements of inequality such as the Gini coefficient is inappropriate for measuring relative inequality between populations. Instead, we follow Dagum (1987) to extend the Gini coefficient to become a measure of the overall inequality of income between two populations.

Let us denote the income of a randomly chosen individual from each population by X, Y, respectively. The mean and tail distribution function are defined as before and denoted μ_X, Φ_X respectively, and similarly for the Y population. The idea behind the construction of the Gini ratio between the two populations is exactly the same as that of the Gini coefficient for a single population, namely we look at pairs of individuals, but now one from each population, find the absolute difference between their incomes, measured in the same (monetary) units, and average this difference over all possible pairs. Thus we have the following:

Definition 6.2 The *Gini ratio* between the two populations, denoted by $G(X, Y)$, is given by $G(X, Y) = \dfrac{E[|X - Y|]}{\mu_X + \mu_Y}$, where X, Y are independent.

(The numerator of the above expression is what is referred to as the *Gini mean difference*, Dagum 1987).

The analogy with Definition 6.1 is clear. Indeed, the Gini coefficient becomes a special case since if X and Y have the same distribution then $G(X, Y) = G(X, X) = \gamma_X$ so that the (comparative) Gini ratio becomes the (single population) Gini coefficient. Note also that $0 \leq G(X, Y) < 1$, where we can get $G \to 1$ as a limiting case, see Dagum (1987).

Again, for purposes of calculation, the defining formula for the Gini ratio is not very convenient so that we make use of the following:

Theorem 6.1 With the above notation:

$$G(X, Y) = 1 - \frac{2 \int\limits_{0}^{\infty} \Phi_X(x)\, \Phi_Y(x)dx}{\mu_X + \mu_Y} \tag{6.3}$$

Proof. See Appendix 6.1.

Example. Suppose that X and Y are exponentially distributed with parameters λ and μ so that their means are $1/\lambda$ and $1/\mu$ and the tail distribution functions are given by $\Phi_X(x) = e^{-\lambda x}$ and $\Phi_Y(x) = e^{-\mu x}$ respectively.
Then elementary integration shows that

$$\int\limits_{0}^{\infty} \Phi_X(x)\, \Phi_Y(x)dx = \int\limits_{0}^{\infty} e^{-(\lambda + \mu)x}\, dx = \frac{1}{\lambda + \mu}.$$

From Theorem 6.1 it then follows that:

$$G(X, Y) = 1 - \frac{2/(\lambda + \mu)}{1/\lambda + 1/\mu} = 1 - \frac{2\lambda\mu}{(\lambda + \mu)^2} \tag{6.4}$$

Note that if we write $\beta = \mu/\lambda = E[X]/E[Y]$ then this can be written:

$$G(X, Y) = 1 - \frac{2\beta}{(1 + \beta)^2} = \frac{1 + \beta^2}{(1 + \beta)^2} = G(\beta), \text{ say.}$$

Thus the Gini ratio depends only upon the *relative* means of the two populations, as we would expect since the exponential is a simple scale family. The relationship is illustrated in Figure 6.1.

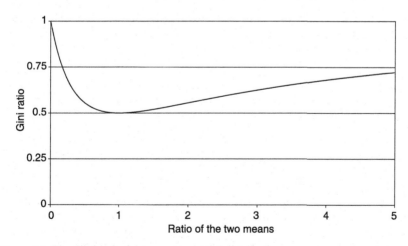

Figure 6.1 The Gini ratio for two exponential distributions

Note that the graph indicates a unique minimum at $\beta = 1$, corresponding to the two distributions being the same, in which case the Gini ratio assumes the Gini coefficient value of $\gamma_X = \frac{1}{2}$. Thus, if there is a difference in the means, then this is reflected in a Gini ratio value greater than $\frac{1}{2}$. Note also that $\lim_{a \to 0} G(a) = \lim_{a \to \infty} G(a) = 1$, and there is a point of inflection at $a = 2$.

6.3 Normalized measures

6.3.1 The relative concentration coefficient

In the paper in which he introduced the Gini ratio, Dagum (1987) proposed the notion of *relative economic affluence* (REA). We briefly recap Dagum's approach, but modifying some of his notation and terminology.

As described earlier, the Gini ratio is derived from the average absolute difference in income between the X-population and the Y-population. Dagum's relative measure results from splitting this difference into two components: the average *excess* income of members of the X-population over less affluent Y-sources, which we denote by $p(X, Y)$, or p_1 in Dagum's notation; and the average *excess* income of Y-sources over less affluent X-sources, denoted $p(Y, X)$, or Dagum's d_1. (These two components are in fact those considered in the proof of Theorem 6.1 in the Appendix.)

Definition 6.3 (Burrell 2005a) The relative concentration coefficient (RCC) between the X and Y populations is given by $D(X, Y) = p(X, Y)/p(Y, X)$ assuming, without loss of generality, that $E[X] \leq E[Y]$.

Note that this is just one minus the *relative economic affluence* (REA) defined by Dagum (1987: Definition 7). A useful alternative representation of $D(X, Y)$ is given in the following:

Proposition 6.2 Assuming, without loss of generality, that $E[Y] \geq E[X]$ the RCC is given by:

$$D(X, Y) = \frac{\mu_X - \int \Phi_X \Phi_Y}{\mu_Y - \int \Phi_X \Phi_Y} = \frac{\int \Phi_X (1 - \Phi_Y)}{\int (1 - \Phi_X) \Phi_Y}$$

Proof. See Burrell (2005a).

Corollary. $0 < D(X, Y) \leq \dfrac{\mu_X}{\mu_Y} \leq 1$ and $D(X, Y) = 1$ if and only if $E[X] = E[Y]$.

The proof is immediate, but see Burrell (2005a) for details.

Thus $D(X, Y)$ is normalized in that it lies between 0 and 1 and the upper bound is achieved if and only if the two means are the same. However, if the means are not the same then the upper bound is given by the ratio of the means and this leads us to make the following:

Definition 6.4 The (modified) RCC where wlog $E[Y] > E[X]$ is:

$$D^*(X, Y) = \frac{\mu_Y}{\mu_X} D(X, Y) = \frac{1 - (\int \Phi_X \Phi_Y)/\mu_X}{1 - (\int \Phi_X \Phi_Y)/\mu_Y} \qquad (6.5)$$

6.3.2 The co-concentration coefficient

Note that, although the Gini ratio already gives some sort of measure of the degree of similarity/dissimilarity between two income distributions so far as their concentration/inequality is concerned, it is not very informative on its own. One problem is that the ratio is minimized when the two distributions are the same whereas we would like a comparative measure to be *maximized* in this situation. This is easily resolved if we make the following:

Definition 6.5

(i) $\theta_X = 1 - \gamma_X = \dfrac{\displaystyle\int_0^\infty \Phi_X(x)^2\, dx}{\mu_X} \qquad (6.6)$

= *coefficient of equality* within the distribution of X

(ii) $H(X, Y) = 1 - G(X, Y) = \dfrac{2\displaystyle\int_0^\infty \Phi_X(x)\, \Phi_Y(x)\, dx}{\mu_X + \mu_Y} \qquad (6.7)$

= *equality ratio* between the distributions of X and Y.

Note that both θ_X and $H(X, Y)$ lie between 0 and 1 and that $\theta_X = 1$ corresponds to the case where all individuals have the same income. If all individuals across both populations have equal income, then $H(X, Y) = 1$. Also, zero values can only be achieved via a limiting process so that in practice both may be taken as being strictly greater than zero.

We can now construct a new measure that focuses on the degree of *equality* rather than *inequality* of concentration between the two populations.

Definition 6.6 The *co-concentration coefficient* (C-CC) is given by:

$$Q(X, Y) = \frac{H(X, Y)}{\sqrt{\theta_X \theta_Y}} = \frac{(1 - G(X, Y))}{\sqrt{(1 - \gamma_X)(1 - \gamma_Y)}} \qquad (6.8)$$

$$= \frac{2\int \Phi_X \Phi_Y}{\mu_X + \mu_Y} \sqrt{\frac{\mu_X \mu_Y}{(\int \Phi_X^2)(\int \Phi_Y^2)}} \qquad (6.9)$$

where the representation (6.9) follows from (6.8) together with (6.6) and (6.7). The following shows that this is a standardized measure and is (joint) scale invariant:

Theorem 6.2

(i) $0 < Q(X, Y) \le 1$
(ii) $Q(X, Y) = 1$ if and only if the two distributions are the same.
(iii) $Q(kX, kY) = Q(X, Y)$ for any constant k.

Proof. See Appendix 6.2.

Note. The equality of distributions required for the C-CC to achieve its upper bound is a much stronger condition than the equality of means required in the case of the RCC and, we would argue, a more natural requirement.

6.4 Some theoretical examples

6.4.1 Exponential distribution

Suppose that X and Y are exponentially distributed with parameters λ and μ so that their means are $1/\lambda$ and $1/\mu$. Then if $\lambda > \mu$, so that $E[Y] > E[X]$, we find from (6.5) and a little algebra, that the modified RCC is given by $D^*(X, Y) = \mu/\lambda = \beta < 1$. Similarly, if $\mu > \lambda$, we find $D^*(X, Y) = 1/\beta < 1$.

From the previous form of the Gini ratio and Gini coefficient, it follows immediately, by substitution into (6.7), that the C-CC is given by $Q(X, Y) = \dfrac{4\beta}{(1 + \beta)^2}$ where again the parameter β is the ratio between the two means. The behavior of the two measures as β varies is illustrated in Figure 6.2.

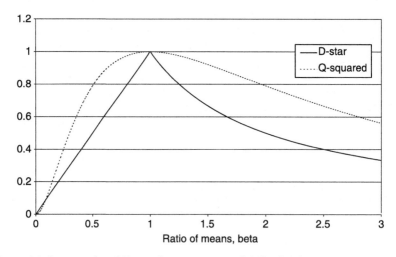

Figure 6.2 Q-squared and D-star for two exponential distributions

Remark. In practice we have found that the graph of $Q(X, Y)$ is fairly flat and so we recommend using its square for illustrative purposes. (This is analogous to using the R^2 measure, or coefficient of variation, rather than the basic correlation coefficient in correlation studies.)

Note that $D^* = Q^2 = 1$ when $\beta = 1$ and that both tend to zero as $\beta \to 0$ or $\beta \to \infty$. What is interesting is the different way that the two measures distinguish between different exponential distributions. Note how, as β moves away from 1, the sharply peaked D^* falls quickly below 1, while the smoothly varying Q^2 falls much more slowly. For instance, if we want the concentration measure to be at least 0.90, then for the modified RCC this requires $0.9 < \beta < 1.11$. To ensure a C-CC value of at least 0.9 we need just $0.519 < \beta < 1.925$.

6.4.2 Pareto distribution

The basic Pareto distribution with index $a > 0$ is defined by the pdf:

$$f(x) = \frac{a}{x^{1+a}} \text{ for } x > 1$$

or the tail distribution function, $\Phi(x) = 1$, if $x < 1$, $= 1 / x^a$, if $x > 1$.

The mean is $a/(a-1)$, provided $a > 1$. See, for example, Burrell (1992b), Kleiber and Kotz (2003: 71).

Hence if X is Pareto of index a and Y is Pareto of index β then:

$$\int_0^\infty \Phi_X(x)\,\Phi_Y(x)dx = 1 + \int_1^\infty \frac{1}{x^{a+\beta}}\,dx = 1 + \frac{1}{a+\beta-1} = \frac{a+\beta}{a+\beta-1}$$

Then from Theorem 6.1, we find:

$$G(X, Y) = 1 - \frac{\dfrac{2(a+\beta)}{(a+\beta-1)}}{\left(\dfrac{a}{a-1} + \dfrac{\beta}{\beta-1}\right)} \tag{6.10}$$

Note, therefore, that the Gini ratio depends on both a and β. This again should not be too surprising since the Pareto family is indexed by a shape rather than a scale parameter. If $a = \beta$ then the expression reduces to $G(X, Y) = \dfrac{1}{2a-1}$, which is the Gini coefficient for a Pareto distribution of index a, see Burrell (1992b), Kleiber and Kotz (2003: 78).

Although there does not seem to be a simpler algebraic expression for the ratio than that given above, fairly straightforward (if tedious!) calculus reveals the following general features:

Lemma (Burrell 2005a) Write $G(a)$ to denote the above $G(X, Y)$ for some chosen *fixed* value of $\beta > 1$. Then

(i) $G(a)$ has a unique minimum at $a = \beta + \sqrt{2\beta(\beta - 1)}$
(ii) $\lim\limits_{a \to 1} G(a) = 1$

(iii) $\lim\limits_{a \to \infty} G(a) = \dfrac{1}{2\beta - 1}.$

(Note that in (iii), the limiting value is the Gini coefficient for a population having a Pareto distribution of index β.)

Similar, though slightly longer, routine calculations with the previously given expressions for the Gini ratio of two Pareto distributions (6.10) and their means show that in this case the relative concentration coefficient is given by

$$D^*(X, Y) = \frac{a\,(a - 1)\,(2a - 1)}{\beta\,(\beta - 1)\,(2\beta - 1)}, \text{ where } 1 < a \le \beta.$$

One can similarly give explicit, but not particularly enlightening, algebraic expressions for the co-concentration coefficient $Q(X, Y)$. Instead, we give in Figures 6.3 and 6.4 graphs of $Q^2(X, Y)$ and $D^*(X, Y)$ as functions of a for

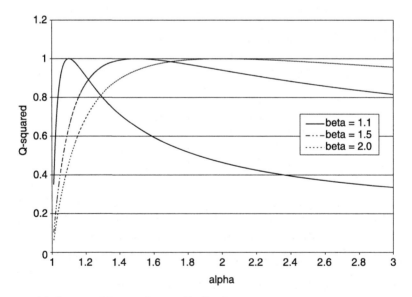

Figure 6.3 Q-squared for two Pareto distributions

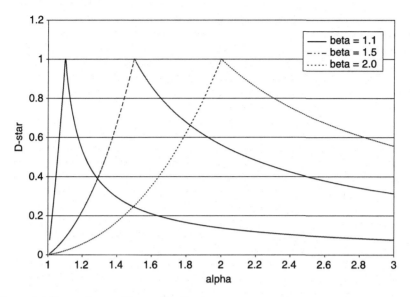

Figure 6.4 D-star for two Pareto distributions

β = 1.1, 1.5, 2. Again it is interesting to compare the different ways in which the two measures reflect the changes in a. For all cases the measures achieve their maximum values when $a = \beta$, i.e. when the two distributions, and hence their means, coincide. However, the RCC is sharply peaked around the maximum and falls away quickly while the C-CC declines slowly as a exceeds β.

6.4.3 *Weibull distribution*

Suppose that $X \sim$ Wei (a, β), i.e. X has a Weibull distribution with index a and scale parameter β, so that the tail distribution function of X is given by:

$$\Phi_X(x) = P(X > x) = \exp[-(x / \beta)^a)]$$

The mean of the distribution is well known to be $\mu_X = E[X] = \beta \Gamma\left(1 + \dfrac{1}{a}\right)$, which results from, or can be viewed as providing, the useful identity:

$$\int_0^\infty \exp[-(x/\beta)^a]\,dx = \beta\Gamma\left(1 + \frac{1}{a}\right) \tag{6.11}$$

Noting that $\Phi_X(x)^2 = \exp[-2(x/\beta)^a] = \exp[-(x/\lambda)^a]$, where $\lambda = \beta/2^{1/a}$, we can use the identity (6.11) to straight away write:

$$\int_0^\infty \Phi_X(x)^2\, dx = \left(\frac{\beta}{2^{1/a}}\right) \Gamma\left(1 + \frac{1}{a}\right).$$

It then follows that the Gini coefficient, using (6.2), is $\gamma_X = 1 - 2^{-1/a}$.

This is, of course, a well-known result; see, for example, Kleiber and Kotz (2003: 177) for an alternative derivation.

Similarly, if $X \sim$ Wei (a, β_1) and $Y \sim$ Wei (a, β_2) then:

$$\Phi_X(x)\Phi_Y(x) = \exp\left[-(x/\beta_1)^a - (x/\beta_2)^a\right] = \exp\left[-x^a\left(\frac{1}{\beta_1^{\ a}} + \frac{1}{\beta_2^{\ a}}\right)\right]$$

$$= \exp\left[-(x/\lambda)^a\right],$$

where now $\lambda = \dfrac{\beta_1\,\beta_2}{(\beta_1^{\ a} + \beta_2^{\ a})^{1/a}}$. It then follows from the identity (6.11) that:

$$\int_0^\infty \Phi_X(x)\,\Phi_Y(x)\, dx = \frac{\beta_1\,\beta_2}{(\beta_1^{\ a} + \beta_2^{\ a})^{1/a}}\, \Gamma\left(1 + \frac{1}{a}\right)$$

Of course, the above derivation can be much simplified if we recall that the Weibull parameter β is a scale parameter and that the measures we are considering are (joint) scale invariant, see Theorem 6.2(iii). Hence there is no loss in assuming that, say, $\beta_1 = \beta$ and $\beta_2 = 1$ throughout. With this assumption we find the equality ratio (Definition 6.5) as:

$$H(X,\ Y) = \frac{2\displaystyle\int_0^\infty \Phi_X(x)\,\Phi_Y(x)dx}{\mu_X + \mu_Y} = \frac{2\dfrac{\beta}{(1 + \beta^a)^{1/a}}\,\Gamma\left(1 + \dfrac{1}{a}\right)}{(1 + \beta)\,\Gamma\left(1 + \dfrac{1}{a}\right)} = \frac{2\beta}{(1 + \beta)\,(1 + \beta^a)^{1/a}}$$

Also, the product of the coefficients of equality is $\theta_X\,\theta_Y = 2^{-2/a}$ so that the co-concentration coefficient is:

$$Q(X,\ Y) = \frac{H(X,\ Y)}{\sqrt{\theta_X\theta_Y}} = \frac{2^{1 + 1/a}\,\beta}{(1 + \beta)\,(1 + \beta^a)^{1/a}} = \frac{2\beta}{(1 + \beta)}\left(\frac{2}{1 + \beta^a}\right)^{1/a}$$

(Note the particular case where $a = 1$ reduces to the exponential distribution described earlier.)

The graph of Q^2 as a function of the scaling ratio β is given in Figure 6.5 for various values of a. Note how in each case the peak, where $Q^2 = 1$, occurs when the scale ratio $\beta = 1$, which corresponds to the two distributions coinciding.

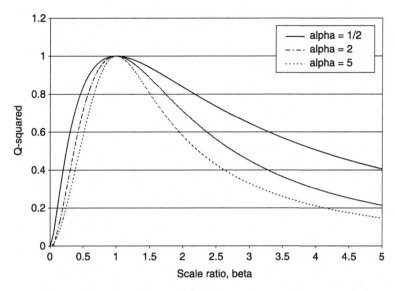

Figure 6.5 Q-squared for the Weibull distribution

For the modified relative concentration coefficient, using the formula (6.5) and the results above, routine algebra gives:

$$D^* (X, Y) = \frac{(1 + \beta^\alpha)^{1/\alpha} - 1}{(1 + \beta^\alpha)^{1/\alpha} - \beta} \text{ if } \beta \leq 1 = \frac{(1 + \beta^\alpha)^{1/\alpha} - \beta}{(1 + \beta^\alpha)^{1/\alpha} - 1} \text{ if } \beta > 1.$$

This is illustrated in Figure 6.6 over the same range and for the same values of α. Note the severely peaked nature of the graphs around $\beta = 1$ for $\alpha > 1$.

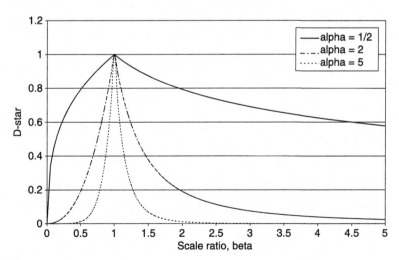

Figure 6.6 D-star for the Weibull distribution

The differences between the general forms of the graphs reflect the different emphases of the two measures in assessing differences/similarities in concentrations.

6.4.4 Singh-Maddala distribution

The Singh-Maddala (1975, 1976) distribution is a very flexible three-parameter income distribution model. (See Kleiber and Kotz 2003 for a concise treatment of its various attributes.) For our purposes, an attractive feature is the simple form of its tail distribution function. Indeed, adopting the Kleiber and Kotz notation, if $X \sim SM(a, b, q)$ then:

$$\Phi_X(x) = \left[1 + \left(\frac{x}{b}\right)^a\right]^{-q} \text{ and hence, as before,}$$

$$\mu_X = E[X] = \int_0^\infty \Phi_X(x)dx = \int_0^\infty \left[1 + \left(\frac{x}{b}\right)^a\right]^{-q} dx = \frac{b\Gamma(1 + 1/a)\,\Gamma(q - 1/a)}{\Gamma(q)} \quad (6.12)$$

The final equality of (6.12) provides our 'useful identity'. (Note that we have merely quoted the expression for the mean of the distribution; see Kleiber and Kotz 2003: 201 for details.) Clearly, then:

$$\int_0^\infty \Phi_X(x)^2\,dx = \int_0^\infty \left[1 + \left(\frac{x}{b}\right)^a\right]^{-2q} dx = \frac{b\Gamma(1 + 1/a)\,\Gamma(2q - 1/a)}{\Gamma(2q)}$$

using (6.12), so that the coefficient of equality is:

$$\theta_X = \frac{\Gamma(q)\,\Gamma(2q - 1/a)}{\Gamma(q - 1/a)\,\Gamma(2q)}$$

Also if $X \sim SM(a, b, q)$ and $Y \sim SM(a, b, p)$ then, using the same 'identity' in (6.12):

$$\int_0^\infty \Phi_X(x)\,\Phi_Y(x)dx = \int_0^\infty \left[1 + \left(\frac{x}{b}\right)^a\right]^{-(q+p)} dx = \frac{b\Gamma(1 + 1/a)\Gamma(q + p - 1/a)}{\Gamma(q + p)}$$

and the equality ratio is then:

$$H(X, Y) = \frac{2\int_0^\infty \Phi_X(x)\,\Phi_Y(x)dx}{\mu_X + \mu_Y} = \frac{2\Gamma(q + p - 1/a)}{\Gamma(q + p)}\left(\frac{\Gamma(q - 1/a)}{\Gamma(q)} + \frac{\Gamma(p - 1/a)}{\Gamma(p)}\right)^{-1}$$

Note that both the coefficient of equality and the equality ratio do not involve the parameter b, as should be expected since it is a scale parameter for the SM distribution. From the above, it is clearly straightforward to derive a general expression for the C-CC although it is rather cumbersome and not too enlightening. However, certain special cases simplify matters greatly. For instance, if we take $a = 1$ then we find after a little algebra that:

$$Q(X, Y) = \frac{\sqrt{(q - 1) (2q - 1) (p - 1) (2p - 1)}}{(q + p - 1) (q + p - 2)}$$

It is now straightforward to plot this as a function of $p > 1$ for any value of $q > 1$ (to ensure finite means). This is illustrated in Figure 6.7, again using the squared form of the function. Notice that here we get $Q^2 = 1$ when $p = q$, again corresponding to the two distributions coinciding.

For the modified RCC, rather than give the general form let us just stay with the special case where $a = 1$ as considered above. Routine calculation leads, for a given value of q, to $D^* = p/q$ if $p < q$, $D^* = q/p$ if $p > q$.

Thus the graph of D^* is linear in p for $p < q$ and is proportional to $1/p$ for $p > q$. See Figure 6.8 and again compare with the corresponding Figure 6.7 for the Q^2 measure. Our view is that, once again, D^* is rather harsh in distinguishing between the distributions, which is not surprising given that it hinges simply on the mean rather than the overall distribution.

Remark. The reason that the Singh-Maddala example works so neatly in the calculation of the C-CC above is that the tail distribution function is of the form $\Phi (x) = g(x)^a$ where a is the sole parameter of interest. This then gives

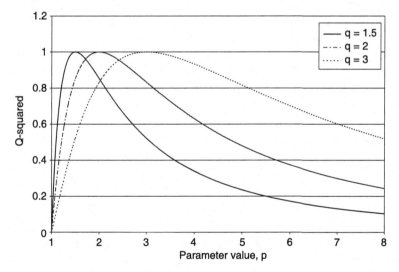

Figure 6.7 Q-squared for the Singh-Maddala distribution

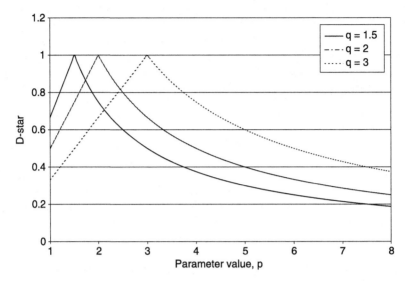

Figure 6.8 D-star for the Singh-Maddala distribution

the identity, $\int \Phi = \int g^a = \mu(a)$, say, and then $\int \Phi^2 = \int g^{2a} = \mu(2a)$. Also if X and Y belong to the same parametric family, with parameter values a, β respectively, then:

$$\int \Phi_X \Phi_Y = \int g^{a+\beta} = \mu(a + \beta)$$

Substituting into (6.8) then gives the C-CC as:

$$Q(X,\ Y) = \frac{2\mu\ (a + \beta)}{\mu(a) + \mu(\beta)} \sqrt{\frac{\mu(a)\mu(\beta)}{\mu(2a)\mu(2\beta)}}$$

Use of this formula allows us to straight away write down the C-CC for such as the exponential and Pareto distributions as well as the Singh-Maddala considered here.

6.5 Concluding remarks

In this chapter we have merely defined and given some simple theoretical examples of the Q^2 and D^* measures and have not made any investigation of their statistical properties, although we hope to have convinced the reader of the superiority of Q^2 as the more subtle measure. Nor have we considered empirical applications. The empirical analogues of the formulae for the two measures are given in Burrell (2005a,b, 2006, 2007). For possible applications within the current context, there would seem to be several possibilities including:

- Within informetrics, examples of comparative studies over several data sets have been given in Burrell (2005b, 2006), leading to a so-called co-concentration matrix. The analogous treatments of income/wealth distributions for different countries or for the same country during different years, maybe in 'real' terms, are obvious applications.
- It would seem that it could also be used in investigative studies to assess the effects of (proposed) taxation changes or degrees of inflation.
- Again from informetrics, much use is made of time-dependent stochastic models, in which case the entire distributional shape changes as the length of the time period increases. This means that concentration, as measured by the Gini index or illustrated via the Lorenz curve, also changes; see Burrell (1992a, b). An investigation of the behavior of the Q^2 measure in such circumstances has been reported in Burrell (2007). Are there similar models appropriate for income/wealth distributions? After all, if we double the period of observation, we (roughly) double the average income so how does the overall income distribution change so far as shape and concentration are concerned?

Any conclusions regarding the efficacy of the Q^2 measure must be tentative at this stage – anything definitive requires further experience of its application and interpretation – but we are hopeful that it might be a useful additional tool in comparative studies.

References

Arnold, B. C. and Laguna, L. (1977). 'On generalized Pareto distributions with applications to income data', *International Studies in Economics* 10, Department of Economics, Iowa State University, Ames, Iowa.

Burrell, Q. L. (1991). 'The Bradford distribution and the Gini index', *Scientometrics* 21, 181–194.

Burrell, Q. L. (1992a). 'The Gini index and the Leimkuhler curve for bibliometric processes', *Information Processing and Management* 28, 19–33.

Burrell, Q. L. (1992b). 'The dynamic nature of bibliometric processes: a case study', in I. K. Ravichandra Rao, ed. *Informetrics – 91: selected papers from the Third International Conference on Informetrics*, v 97–129, Bangalore, Ranganathan Endowment.

Burrell, Q. L. (2005a). 'Measuring similarity of concentration between different informetric distributions: Two new approaches', *Journal of the American Society for Information Science and Technology* 56, 704–714.

Burrell, Q. L. (2005b). 'An empirical study of the measurement of similarity of concentration between different informetric distributions', in P. Ingwersen and B. Larsen, eds. *Proceedings of ISSI 2005*, 129–139, Stockholm, Karolinska University Press.

Burrell, Q. L. (2006). 'Measuring concentration within and co-concentration between informetric distributions: An empirical study', *Scientometrics* 68(3), 441–456.

Burrell, Q. L. (2007). 'Time-dependent aspects of the co-concentration coefficient', *Scientometrics* 73(2), 161–174.

Dagum, C. (1983). 'Income inequality measures', in S. Kotz and N. S. Johnson, eds. *Encyclopedia of Statistical Sciences, Volume 4*, 34–40, New York, Wiley.

Dagum, C. (1987). 'Measuring the economic affluence between populations of income receivers', *Journal of Business and Economic Statistics* 5, 5–11.

Dalton, H. (1920). 'The measurement of inequality of incomes', *Economic Journal* 30, 348–361.

Dorfman, R. (1979). 'A formula for the Gini coefficient', *Review of Economics and Statistics* 61, 146–149.

Gini, C. (1914). 'Sulla misura della concentrazione e della variabilità dei caratteri', *Atti del Reale Istituto Veneto di Scienze, Lettere ed Arti* 73, 1203–1248.

Kleiber, C. and Kotz, S. (2003). *Statistical size distributions in economics and actuarial sciences*, New Jersey, Wiley.

Lambert, P. J. (2001). *The distribution and redistribution of income, 3 edition*, Manchester, Manchester University Press.

Singh, M. and Maddala, G. S. (1975). 'A stochastic process for income distributions and tests for income distribution functions', *ASA Proceedings of the Business and Economic Statistics Section*, 551–553.

Singh, M. and Maddala, G. S. (1976). 'A function for the size distribution of incomes', *Econometrica* 44, 963–970.

Stirzaker, D. (1994). *Elementary Probability*, Cambridge, Cambridge University Press.

Stuart, A., and Ord, J. K. (1987). *Kendall's Advanced Theory of Statistics. Volume 1: Distribution Theory, 5th edition*, London, Griffin.

Yitzhaki, S. (1998). 'More than a dozen alternative ways of spelling Gini', *Research on Income Inequality* 8, 13–30.

Appendix 6.1

Proof of Theorem 6.1

Although it is straightforward to give a general proof, either using Lebesgue-Stieltjes integration or via the expectation operator (see Dagum 1987), we prefer to use elementary methods and restrict attention to the (absolutely) continuous case. Suppose that X and Y are independent copies of the variables. Then:

$$E[|X - Y|] = \iint |x - y| f_X(x) f_Y(y) dx dy$$

Splitting the region of integration into $\{x > y\}$ and $\{y > x\}$, the former yields, let us say:

$$p(X, Y) = \iint_{x > y} (x - y) f_X(x) f_Y(y) dx dy = \int_0^\infty \left[\int_0^x (x - y) f_Y(y) dy \right] f_X(x) dx$$

$$= \int_0^\infty \left[x \int_0^x f_Y(y) dy - \int_0^x y f_Y(y) dy \right] f_X(x) dx$$

$$= \int_0^\infty \left[xF_Y(x) - \left(yF_Y(y) \mid_0^x - \int_0^x F_Y(y)dy \right) \right] f_X(x)dx$$

$$= \int_0^\infty \left[\int_0^x F_Y(y)dy \right] f_X(x)dx$$

$$= \int_0^\infty \left[\int_0^x f_X(x)F_Y(y)dy \right] dx$$

$$= \int_0^\infty \left[\int_y^\infty f_X(x)F_Y(y)dx \right] dy$$

$$= \int_0^\infty \Phi_X(y)F_Y(y)dy = \int_0^\infty \Phi_X(y)(1 - \Phi_Y(y))\, dy$$

Interchanging the roles of x and y in the above leads straight to:

$$p(Y, X) = \iint_{y > x} (y - x) f_X(x) f_Y(y) dx dy = \int_0^\infty \Phi_Y(y) F_X(y) dy$$

$$= \int_0^\infty \Phi_Y(y)(1 - \Phi_X(y))\, dy$$

Adding these two expressions gives:

$$E[|X - Y|] = p(X, Y) + p(Y, X) = \int \int |x - y| f_X(x) f_Y(y) dx dy$$

$$= \int_0^\infty \Phi_X(y)(1 - \Phi_Y(y))\, dy + \int_0^\infty \Phi_Y(y)(1 - \Phi_X(y))\, dy$$

$$= \int_0^\infty (\Phi_X(y) + \Phi_Y(y) - 2\Phi_X(y)\, \Phi_Y(y))\, dy$$

$$= \int \Phi_X + \int \Phi_Y - 2 \int \Phi_X \Phi_Y$$

$$= \mu_X + \mu_Y - 2 \int \Phi_X \Phi_Y \tag{6.A.1}$$

and the result follows.

Appendix 6.2

Proof of Theorem 6.2

(i) $H(X, Y) = 1 - G(X, Y) = \dfrac{2\displaystyle\int_0^\infty \Phi_X(x)\,\Phi_Y(x)dx}{\mu_X + \mu_Y}$, so that:

$$H(X, Y)^2 = \left(\frac{2\int \Phi_X \Phi_Y}{\mu_X + \mu_Y}\right)^2 = \frac{4\,(\int \Phi_X \Phi_Y)^2}{(\mu_X + \mu_Y)^2} \tag{6.A.2}$$

Now:

$$(\textstyle\int \Phi_X \Phi_Y)^2 \le (\int \Phi_X^2)\,(\int \Phi_Y^2) \tag{6.A.3}$$

by the Cauchy-Schwarz inequality, variants of which can be found in most introductory texts on analysis; see also Stuart and Ord (1987: 65). Also:

$$(\mu_X + \mu_Y)^2 = (\mu_X - \mu_Y)^2 + 4\mu_X\mu_Y \ge 4\mu_X\mu_Y \tag{6.A.4}$$

Combining (6.A.3) and (6.A.4) then gives, from (6.A.2):

$$H(X, Y)^2 = \frac{4(\int \Phi_X \Phi_Y)^2}{(\mu_X + \mu_Y)^2} \le \frac{(\int \Phi_X^2)\,(\int \Phi_Y^2)}{\mu_X\mu_Y} = \theta_X\theta_Y$$

and the result follows.

(ii) For $Q(X, Y) = 1$, both of the above inequalities (6.A.3) and (6.A.4) must be equalities. For the second, trivially the equality holds if and only if $\mu_X = \mu_Y$. The Cauchy-Schwarz inequality reduces to an equality if and only if there is a constant c such that, for all x, $\Phi_X(x) = c\Phi_Y(x)$. Then, using the note at the end of the end of the Proof of Theorem 1 above, this leads to $\mu_X = \int \Phi_X = c \int \Phi_Y = c\mu_Y$. Having established the requirement that the two means must be the same, this implies that $c = 1$ and hence the two distributions are the same.

7 Information matrices for some bivariate Pareto distributions

Samuel Kotz

7.1 Introduction[1]

Pareto distributions are the most popular and the most applied distributions in the field of income and wealth modeling. They are very versatile and a variety of uncertainties can be usefully modeled by them. Some of the other application areas include extreme values, failure times, modeling of birth rates and infant mortality rates, and reliability. In this chapter, we consider four of the most popular bivariate Pareto distributions:

- the bivariate Lomax distribution with the joint survivor function and joint pdf

$$\bar{F}(x, y) = \frac{1}{(1 + \theta x + \phi y)^a} \tag{7.1}$$

and

$$f(x, y) = \frac{a(a + 1)\theta\phi}{(1 + \theta x + \phi y)^{a+2}}, \tag{7.2}$$

respectively, for $x > 0$, $y > 0$, $\theta > 0$, $\phi > 0$ and $a > 0$.
- a variant of the above with the joint pdf

$$f(x, y) = \frac{b^{2a}\Gamma(2a + c)}{\Gamma(c)\Gamma^2(a)} \frac{x^{a-1} y^{a-1}}{(1 + bx + by)^{2a+c}} \tag{7.3}$$

for $x > 0$, $y > 0$, $a > 0$, $b > 0$ and $c > 0$.
- Muliere and Scarsini (1987)'s bivariate Pareto distribution with the joint pdf

$$f(x, y) = \begin{cases} \dfrac{\lambda_2(\lambda_0 + \lambda_1)}{\beta^2} \left(\dfrac{x}{\beta}\right)^{-(1 + \lambda_0 + \lambda_1)} \left(\dfrac{y}{\beta}\right)^{-(1 + \lambda_2)}, & \text{if } x > y, \\[3mm] \dfrac{\lambda_0}{\beta} \left(\dfrac{x}{\beta}\right)^{-(1 + \lambda_0 + \lambda_1 + \lambda_2)}, & \text{if } x = y, \\[3mm] \dfrac{\lambda_1(\lambda_0 + \lambda_2)}{\beta^2} \left(\dfrac{y}{\beta}\right)^{-(1 + \lambda_0 + \lambda_2)} \left(\dfrac{x}{\beta}\right)^{-(1 + \lambda_1)}, & \text{if } y > x \end{cases} \tag{7.4}$$

for $x \geq \beta$, $y \geq \beta$, $\lambda_0 > 0$, $\lambda_1 > 0$, $\lambda_2 > 0$ and $\beta > 0$.

- De Groot (1970)'s bivariate Pareto distribution with the joint pdf

$$f(x, y) = \gamma(\gamma + 1)(\xi - \eta)^{\gamma}(y - x)^{-(\gamma + 2)} \tag{7.5}$$

for $0 < x < \eta < \xi < y$ and $\gamma > 1$.

The aim is to calculate the Fisher information matrix corresponding to each of the distributions above. For a given observation (x, y), the Fisher information matrix is defined by

$$(I_{jk}) = \left\{ E \left(\frac{\partial \log L(\boldsymbol{\theta})}{\partial \theta_j} \frac{\partial \log L(\boldsymbol{\theta})}{\partial \theta_k} \right) \right\}$$

for $j = 1, 2, \ldots, p$ and $k = 1, 2, \ldots, p$, where $L(\boldsymbol{\theta}) = f(x, y)$ and $\boldsymbol{\theta} = (\theta_1, \theta_2, \ldots, \theta_p)$ are the parameters of the pdf f. It has the meaning "information about the parameters $\boldsymbol{\theta}$ contained in the observation (x, y)." The information matrix plays a significant role in statistical inference in connection with estimation, sufficiency and properties of variances of estimators. It is related to the covariance matrix of the estimate of $\boldsymbol{\theta}$ (being its inverse under certain conditions). See Cox and Hinkley (1974) for details.

The exact forms of the information matrix are derived in Sections 7.2, 7.3, 7.4 and 7.5: Some technical results required for the derivations are noted in Appendix. The calculations use the Euler psi function defined by

$$\Psi(a) = \frac{\log \Gamma(a)}{da}.$$

The properties of this special function can be found in Gradshteyn and Ryzhik (2000).

7.2 Information matrix for bivariate Lomax

If (x, y) is a single observation from (7.2) then the log-likelihood function can be written as

$$\log L(a, \theta, \phi) = \log \{a(a + 1)\theta\phi\} - (a + 2) \log (1 + \theta x + \phi y).$$

The first-order derivatives are:

$$\frac{\partial \log L}{\partial \theta} = \frac{1}{\theta} - (a + 2) \frac{x}{1 + \theta x + \phi y},$$

$$\frac{\partial \log L}{\partial \phi} = \frac{1}{\phi} - (a + 2) \frac{y}{1 + \theta x + \phi y},$$

and

$$\frac{\partial \log L}{\partial a} = \frac{1}{a} + \frac{1}{a + 1} - \log (1 + \theta x + \phi y).$$

The second-order derivatives are:

$$\frac{\partial^2 \log L}{\partial \theta^2} = -\frac{1}{\theta^2} + (a + 2) \frac{x^2}{(1 + \theta x + \phi y)^2},$$

$$\frac{\partial^2 \log L}{\partial \theta \partial \phi} = (a + 2) \frac{xy}{(1 + \theta x + \phi y)^2},$$

$$\frac{\partial^2 \log L}{\partial \theta \partial a} = -\frac{x}{1 + \theta x + \phi y},$$

$$\frac{\partial^2 \log L}{\partial \phi^2} = -\frac{1}{\phi^2} + (a + 2) \frac{y^2}{(1 + \theta x + \phi y)^2},$$

$$\frac{\partial^2 \log L}{\partial \phi \partial a} = -\frac{y}{1 + \theta x + \phi y},$$

and

$$\frac{\partial^2 \log L}{\partial a^2} = -\frac{1}{a^2} - \frac{1}{(a + 1)^2}.$$

Using the well-known formula

$$E (X^m Y^n \mid a) = mn \int_0^\infty \int_0^\infty x^{m-1} y^{n-1} (1 + \theta x + \phi y)^{-a} dy dx \qquad (7.6)$$

(where a denotes the shape parameter in (7.1)), we can express the elements of the Fisher information matrix as

$$E\left(-\frac{\partial^2 \log L}{\partial\theta^2}\right) = \frac{1}{\theta^2} - \frac{a+2}{3} E(X^3 Y \mid a+2),$$

$$E\left(-\frac{\partial^2 \log L}{\partial\theta\partial\phi}\right) = -\frac{a+2}{4} E(X^2 Y^2 \mid a+2),$$

$$E\left(-\frac{\partial^2 \log L}{\partial\theta\partial a}\right) = \frac{1}{2} E(X^2 Y \mid a+1),$$

$$E\left(-\frac{\partial^2 \log L}{\partial\phi^2}\right) = \frac{1}{\phi^2} - \frac{a+2}{3} E(X Y^3 \mid a+2),$$

$$E\left(-\frac{\partial^2 \log L}{\partial\phi\partial a}\right) = \frac{1}{2} E(X Y^2 \mid a+1),$$

and

$$E\left(-\frac{\partial^2 \log L}{\partial a^2}\right) = \frac{1}{a^2} + \frac{1}{(a+1)^2}.$$

By application of Lemma 7.1, the expectations above can be calculated as

$$E(X^3 Y \mid a+2) = \frac{3B(1, a+1) B(3, a-2)}{\theta^3 \phi},$$

$$E(XY^3 \mid a+2) = \frac{3B(3, a-1) B(1, a-2)}{\theta \phi^3},$$

$$E(X^2 Y^2 \mid a+2) = \frac{4B(2, a) B(2, a-2)}{\theta^2 \phi^2},$$

$$E(X^2 Y \mid a+1) = \frac{2B(1, a+1) B(2, a-1)}{\theta^2 \phi},$$

and

$$E(XY^2) = \frac{2B(2, a) B(1, a-1)}{\theta \phi^2}.$$

7.3 Information matrix for a variant of bivariate Lomax

If (x, y) is a single observation from (7.3) then the log-likelihood function can be written as

$$\log L(a, \theta, \phi) = \log [b^{2a} \Gamma(2a+c) / \{\Gamma^2(a)\Gamma(c)\}] - (a-1) \log x + (a-1)$$
$$\log y - (2a+c) \log (1 + bx + by).$$

The first-order derivatives are:

$$\frac{\partial \log L}{\partial a} = 2 \log b + 2\Psi (2a + c) - 2\Psi (a) + \log (xy) - 2 \log (1 + bx + by),$$

$$\frac{\partial \log L}{\partial b} = \frac{2a}{b} - \frac{(2a + c) (x + y)}{1 + bx + by},$$

and

$$\frac{\partial \log L}{\partial c} = \Psi(2a + c) - \Psi (c) - \log(1 + bx + by).$$

The second-order derivatives are:

$$\frac{\partial^2 \log L}{\partial a^2} = 4\Psi' (2a + c) - 2\Psi' (a),$$

$$\frac{\partial^2 \log L}{\partial a \partial b} = \frac{2}{b} - \frac{2(x + y)}{1 + bx + by},$$

$$\frac{\partial^2 \log L}{\partial a \partial c} = 2\Psi' (2a + c),$$

$$\frac{\partial^2 \log L}{\partial b^2} = -\frac{2a}{b^2} + \frac{(2a + c) (x + y)^2}{(1 + bx + by)^2},$$

$$\frac{\partial^2 \log L}{\partial b \partial c} = -\frac{x + y}{1 + bx + by},$$

and

$$\frac{\partial^2 \log L}{\partial c^2} = \Psi' (2a + c) - \Psi' (c).$$

The elements of the Fisher information matrix corresponding to the above second-order derivatives can be computed as follows: since certain second-order derivatives are constants, it is clear that

$$E\left(-\frac{\partial^2 \log L}{\partial a^2}\right) = 2\Psi' (a) - 4\Psi' (2a + c),$$

$$E\left(-\frac{\partial^2 \log L}{\partial a \partial c}\right) = -2\Psi' (2a + c),$$

and

$$E\left(-\frac{\partial^2 \log L}{\partial c^2}\right) = \Psi'(c) - \Psi'(2a + c).$$

Using the relation

$$E\left(X^m\, Y^n \mid c\right) = \frac{b^{2a}\Gamma(2a + c)}{\Gamma(c)\Gamma^2(a)} \int_0^\infty \int_0^\infty \frac{x^{m+a-1}y^{n+a-1}}{(1 + bx + by)^{2a+c}}\, dy\, dx \tag{7.7}$$

(where c denotes the shape parameter in (7.3)), the remaining elements of the Fisher information matrix can be expressed as

$$E\left(-\frac{\partial^2 \log L}{\partial a \partial b}\right) = -\frac{2}{b} + \frac{2c}{2a + c}\{E(X \mid c + 1) + E(Y \mid c + 1)\},$$

$$E\left(-\frac{\partial^2 \log L}{\partial b^2}\right) = \frac{2a}{b^2} - \frac{c(c + 1)}{2a + c + 1}\{E(X^2 \mid c + 2) + E(Y^2 \mid c + 2)$$
$$+ 2E(XY \mid c + 2)\},$$

and

$$\frac{\partial^2 \log L}{\partial b \partial c} = \frac{c}{2a + c}\{E(X \mid c + 1) + E(Y \mid c + 1)\}.$$

By application of Lemma 7.2, the expectations above can be calculated as

$$E(X^2 \mid c + 2) = \frac{a(a + 1)}{b^2 c(c + 1)},$$

$$E(Y^2 \mid c + 2) = \frac{a(a + 1)}{b^2 c(c + 1)},$$

$$E(XY \mid c + 2) = \frac{a^2}{b^2 c(c + 1)},$$

$$E(X \mid c + 1) = \frac{a}{bc},$$

and

$$E(Y \mid c + 1) = \frac{a}{bc}.$$

7.4 Information matrix for Muliere and Scarsini's bivariate Pareto

If (x, y) is single observation from (7.4) then the log-likelihood function can be written as

$$\log L\,(\lambda_0, \lambda_1, \lambda_2, \beta) = \begin{cases} \log\{\lambda_2\,(\lambda_0 + \lambda_1)\,\beta^{\lambda_0 + \lambda_1 + \lambda_2}\} - (\lambda_0 + \lambda_1 + 1)\log x - \\ \qquad\qquad (\lambda_2 + 1)\log y, \text{ if } x > y \geq \beta, \\ \log\{\lambda_0\beta^{\lambda_0 + \lambda_1 + \lambda_2}\} - (\lambda_0 + \lambda_1 + \lambda_2 + 1)\log x, \\ \qquad\qquad\qquad \text{if } x = y \geq \beta, \\ \log\{\lambda_1\,(\lambda_0 + \lambda_2)\beta^{\lambda_0 + \lambda_1 + \lambda_2}\} - (\lambda_0 + \lambda_2 + 1)\log x - \\ \qquad\qquad (\lambda_1 + 1)\log y, \text{ if } y > x \geq \beta. \end{cases}$$

The first-order derivatives are:

$$\frac{\partial \log L}{\partial \lambda_0} = \begin{cases} \dfrac{1}{\lambda_0 + \lambda_1} + \log \beta - \log x, & \text{if } x > y \geq \beta, \\ \dfrac{1}{\lambda_0} + \log \beta - \log x, & \text{if } x = y \geq \beta, \\ \dfrac{1}{\lambda_0 + \lambda_2} + \log \beta - \log y, & \text{if } y > x \geq \beta, \end{cases}$$

$$\frac{\partial \log L}{\partial \lambda_1} = \begin{cases} \dfrac{1}{\lambda_0 + \lambda_1} + \log \beta - \log x, & \text{if } x > y \geq \beta, \\ \log \beta - \log x, & \text{if } x = y \geq \beta, \\ \dfrac{1}{\lambda_1} + \log \beta - \log x, & \text{if } y > x \geq \beta, \end{cases}$$

$$\frac{\partial \log L}{\partial \lambda_2} = \begin{cases} \dfrac{1}{\lambda_2} + \log \beta - \log y, & \text{if } x > y \geq \beta, \\ \log \beta - \log x, & \text{if } x = y \geq \beta, \\ \dfrac{1}{\lambda_0 + \lambda_2} + \log \beta - \log y, & \text{if } y > x \geq \beta, \end{cases}$$

$$\frac{\partial \log L}{\partial \beta} = \frac{\lambda_0 + \lambda_1 + \lambda_2}{\beta},$$

$$\frac{\partial^2 \log L}{\partial \lambda_0^2} = \begin{cases} -\dfrac{1}{(\lambda_0 + \lambda_1)^2}, & \text{if } x > y \geq \beta, \\ -\dfrac{1}{\lambda_0^2}, & \text{if } x = y \geq \beta, \\ -\dfrac{1}{(\lambda_0 + \lambda_2)^2}, & \text{if } y > x \geq \beta, \end{cases}$$

$$\frac{\partial^2 \log L}{\partial \lambda_0 \partial \lambda_1} = \begin{cases} -\dfrac{1}{(\lambda_0 + \lambda_1)^2}, & \text{if } x > y \geq \beta, \\ 0, & \text{if } x = y \geq \beta, \\ 0, & \text{if } y > x \geq \beta, \end{cases}$$

$$\frac{\partial^2 \log L}{\partial \lambda_0 \partial \lambda_2} = \begin{cases} 0, & \text{if } x > y \geq \beta, \\ 0, & \text{if } x = y \geq \beta, \\ -\dfrac{1}{(\lambda_0 + \lambda_2)^2}, & \text{if } y > x \geq \beta, \end{cases}$$

$$\frac{\partial^2 \log L}{\partial \lambda_0 \partial \beta} = \frac{1}{\beta},$$

$$\frac{\partial^2 \log L}{\partial \lambda_1^2} = \begin{cases} -\dfrac{1}{(\lambda_0 + \lambda_1)^2}, & \text{if } x > y \geq \beta, \\ 0, & \text{if } x = y \geq \beta, \\ -\dfrac{1}{\lambda_1^2}, & \text{if } y > x \geq \beta, \end{cases}$$

$$\frac{\partial^2 \log L}{\partial \lambda_1 \partial \lambda_2} = 0,$$

$$\frac{\partial^2 \log L}{\partial \lambda_1 \partial \beta} = \frac{1}{\beta},$$

$$\frac{\partial^2 \log L}{\partial \lambda_2^2} = \begin{cases} -\dfrac{1}{\lambda_2^2}, & \text{if } x > y \geq \beta, \\ 0, & \text{if } x = y \geq \beta, \\ -\dfrac{1}{(\lambda_0 + \lambda_2)^2}, & \text{if } y > x \geq \beta, \end{cases}$$

$$\frac{\partial^2 \log L}{\partial \lambda_2 \partial \beta} = \frac{1}{\beta},$$

and

$$\frac{\partial^2 \log L}{\partial \beta^2} = -\frac{\lambda_0 + \lambda_1 + \lambda_2}{\beta^2}.$$

Since the second derivative with respect to λ_1 and λ_2 is zero it follows that the maximum likelihood estimates of the two parameters are independent. The elements of the Fisher information matrix corresponding to the non-zero second-order derivatives can be computed as follows: since certain second-order derivatives are constants, it is clear that

$$E\left(-\frac{\partial^2 \log L}{\partial \lambda_0 \partial \beta}\right) = -\frac{1}{\beta},$$

$$E\left(-\frac{\partial^2 \log L}{\partial \lambda_1 \partial \beta}\right) = -\frac{1}{\beta},$$

$$E\left(-\frac{\partial^2 \log L}{\partial \lambda_2 \partial \beta}\right) = -\frac{1}{\beta},$$

and

$$E\left(-\frac{\partial^2 \log L}{\partial \beta^2}\right) = \frac{\lambda_0 + \lambda_1 + \lambda_2}{\beta^2}.$$

Since

$$\Pr(X < Y) = \lambda_1 (\lambda_0 + \lambda_2) \beta^{\lambda_0 + \lambda_1 + \lambda_2} \int_\beta^\infty \int_x^\infty x^{-(\lambda_1 + 1)} y^{-(\lambda_0 + \lambda_2 + 1)} dy dx$$

$$= \lambda_1 \beta^{\lambda_0 + \lambda_1 + \lambda_2} \int_\beta^\infty x^{-(\lambda_0 + \lambda_1 + \lambda_2 + 1)} dx$$

$$= \frac{\lambda_1}{\lambda_0 + \lambda_1 + \lambda_2},$$

the elements of the information matrix can be computed as

$$E\left(-\frac{\partial^2 \log L}{\partial \lambda_0^2}\right) = \frac{\lambda_2}{(\lambda_0 + \lambda_1)^2 (\lambda_0 + \lambda_1 + \lambda_2)} + \frac{1}{\lambda_0 (\lambda_0 + \lambda_1 + \lambda_2)}$$

$$+ \frac{\lambda_1}{(\lambda_0 + \lambda_2)^2 (\lambda_0 + \lambda_1 + \lambda_2)},$$

$$E\left(-\frac{\partial^2 \log L}{\partial \lambda_0 \partial \lambda_1}\right) = \frac{\lambda_2}{(\lambda_0 + \lambda_1)^2 (\lambda_0 + \lambda_1 + \lambda_2)},$$

$$E\left(-\frac{\partial^2 \log L}{\partial \lambda_0 \partial \lambda_2}\right) = \frac{\lambda_1}{(\lambda_0 + \lambda_2)^2 (\lambda_0 + \lambda_1 + \lambda_2)},$$

$$E\left(-\frac{\partial^2 \log L}{\partial \lambda_1^2}\right) = \frac{\lambda_2}{(\lambda_0 + \lambda_1)^2 (\lambda_0 + \lambda_1 + \lambda_2)} + \frac{1}{\lambda_1 (\lambda_0 + \lambda_1 + \lambda_2)},$$

and

$$E\left(-\frac{\partial^2 \log L}{\partial \lambda_2^2}\right) = \frac{1}{\lambda_2 (\lambda_0 + \lambda_1 + \lambda_2)} + \frac{\lambda_1}{(\lambda_0 + \lambda_2)^2 (\lambda_0 + \lambda_1 + \lambda_2)}.$$

7.5 Information matrix for De Groots's bivariate Pareto

If (x, y) is a single observation from (7.5) then the log-likelihood function can be written as

$$\log L(\gamma, \xi, \eta) = \log \{\gamma(\gamma + 1) (\xi - \eta)^\gamma\} - (\gamma + 2) \log (y - x).$$

The first-order derivatives are:

$$\frac{\partial \log L}{\partial \gamma} = \frac{1}{\gamma} + \frac{1}{\gamma + 1} + \log (\xi - \eta) - \log (y - x),$$

$$\frac{\partial \log L}{\partial \xi} = \frac{\gamma}{\xi - \eta},$$

$$\frac{\partial \log L}{\partial \eta} = -\frac{\gamma}{\xi - \eta},$$

$$\frac{\partial^2 \log L}{\partial \gamma^2} = -\frac{1}{\gamma^2} - \frac{1}{(\gamma + 1)^2},$$

$$\frac{\partial^2 \log L}{\partial \gamma \partial \xi} = \frac{1}{\xi - \eta},$$

$$\frac{\partial^2 \log L}{\partial \gamma \partial \eta} = -\frac{1}{\xi - \eta},$$

$$\frac{\partial^2 \log L}{\partial \xi^2} = -\frac{\gamma}{(\xi - \eta)^2},$$

$$\frac{\partial^2 \log L}{\partial \xi \partial \eta} = \frac{\gamma}{(\xi - \eta)^2},$$

and

$$\frac{\partial^2 \log L}{\partial \eta^2} = -\frac{\gamma}{(\xi - \eta)^2}.$$

Since all of the second-order derivatives above are constants expressions for the elements of the Fisher information matrix are straightforward.

7.6 Appendix

We need the following technical lemmas to calculate the elements of the Fisher information matrix.

Lemma 7.1 *If X and Y are jointly distributed according to (7.2) then*

$$E(X^m Y^n) = \frac{mnB(n, a - n)B(m, a - m - n)}{\theta^m \phi^n}$$

for $m \geq 1$ and $n \geq 1$.

Proof. Using the formula (7.6), one can express

$$E(X^m Y^n) = mn \int_0^\infty \int_0^\infty x^{m-1} y^{n-1} (1 + \theta x + \phi y)^{-a} \, dy dx$$

$$= mn \int_0^\infty x^{m-1} \phi^{-a} \int_0^\infty y^{n-1} \left(y + \frac{1 + \theta x}{\phi} \right)^{-a} \, dy dx$$

$$= mn \int_0^\infty x^{m-1} \phi^{-a} \left(\frac{1 + \theta x}{\phi} \right)^{n-a} B(n, a - n) dx$$

$$= mnB(n, a - n)\theta^{n-a} \phi^{-n} \int_0^\infty x^{m-1} \left(x + \frac{1}{\theta} \right)^{n-a} \, dx$$

$$= mnB(n, a - n)\theta^{n-a} \phi^{-n} \left(\frac{1}{\theta} \right)^{m-a+n} B(m, a - m - n).$$

The result of the lemma follows. ▲

Lemma 7.2 *If X and Y are jointly distributed according to (7.3) then*

$$E(X^m Y^n) = \frac{\Gamma(m + a)\Gamma(n + a)\Gamma(c - m - n)}{b^{m+n}\gamma^2(a)\Gamma(c)}$$

for $m \geq 1$ and $n \geq 1$.

Proof. Using the formula (7.7), one can express

$$
E(X^m Y^n) = \frac{\Gamma(2a+c)}{b^{m+n}\Gamma(c)\,\Gamma^2(a)} \int_0^\infty \int_0^\infty \frac{(bx)^{m+a-1}(by)^{n+a-1}}{(1+bx+by)^{2a+c}}\, d(by)d(bx)
$$

$$
= \frac{\Gamma(2a+c)}{b^{m+n}\Gamma(c)\Gamma^2(a)} \int_0^\infty \int_0^\infty \frac{u^{m+a-1}v^{n+a-1}}{(1+u+v)^{2a+c}}\, dvdu
$$

$$
= \frac{\Gamma(2a+c)}{b^{m+n}\Gamma(c)\Gamma^2(a)} \int_0^\infty u^{m+a-1} \int_0^\infty \frac{v^{n+a-1}}{(1+u+v)^{2a+c}}\, dvdu
$$

$$
= \frac{\Gamma(2a+c)}{b^{m+n}\Gamma(c)\Gamma^2(a)} \int_0^\infty \frac{u^{m+a-1}}{(1+u)^{a+c-n}}\, B(a+c-n, n+a)du
$$

$$
= \frac{\Gamma(2a+c)}{b^{m+n}\Gamma(c)\Gamma^2(a)}\, B(a+m, c-m-n)\, B(a+c-n, n+a).
$$

The result of the lemma follows. ▲

Note

1 The Chapter is a joint work with Saralees Nadarajah.

References

Cox, D. R. and Hinkley, D. V. (1974). *Theoretical Statistics*. London: Chapman and Hall.

de Groot, M. H. (1970). *Optimal Statistical Decisions*. New York: McGraw-Hill.

Gradshteyn, I. S. and Ryzhik, I. M. (2000). *Table of Integrals, Series, and Products* (sixth edition). San Diego: Academic Press.

Muliere, P. and Scarsini, M. (1987). Characterization of a Marshall-Olkin type class of distributions. *Annals of the Institute of Statistical Mathematics*, **39**, 429–441.

8 On Lorenz preorders and opportunity inequality in finite environments

Ernesto Savaglio and Stefano Vannucci

8.1 Introduction

The assessment of inequality in resource allocation by means of Lorenz pre-orders is both well established for univariate distributions and highly problematic for multivariate ones. The main reason for such a state of affairs is the following: if the relevant variables are real-valued, the univariate case allows a natural *total* ordering of individual endowments, whereas any multivariate distribution, real-valued or otherwise, typically admits only *partial* rankings (e.g. dominance orderings) of the latter as natural and non-controversial. This problem also arises in a discrete setting, namely when the resources to be allocated amount to a finite set of items/opportunities. That is so because it is by no means obvious if and how the non-controversial *set-inclusion partial preorder* might be extended to a *total* preorder of opportunity sets in order to define a Lorenz-like preorder of opportunity distributions amenable to characterizations via simple progressive Pigou-Dalton transfers as established by the classic Hardy-Littlewood-Polya (henceforth HLP) theorem for real-valued (income) distributions. The present chapter is devoted to a critical review of the extant literature on the problem of importing such Lorenz-like preorders in finite settings.

8.2 Building Lorenz preorders in finite settings: a critical review

It is well known that early in the last century economists became interested in evaluating inequality of incomes or of wealth. Thus, in order to measure how desirable is a given distribution with respect to another one in terms of equality, it became important to determine on which basis one (income) distribution could be regarded as 'more even' than another one. The first statement of this kind was given clear embodiment by Max Otto Lorenz (1876–1959), an applied statistician, who was Director of the Bureau of Statistics in the United States and who developed in 1905 what is now well known as the *Lorenz curve*.

A second independent origin of Lorenz curve is in mathematical analysis and can be dated back to the work of Muirhead (1903) concerning a generalization of the arithmetic-geometric mean inequality. Consider a population of n individuals, whose income could be represented by a positive natural number. Order the individuals from the poorest to the richest to obtain a vector distribution $x_1, \ldots x_n$, where the generic x_i denotes the wealth of individual i, $i = 1, \ldots, n$. Then, plot the points, $\left(\dfrac{k}{n}, \dfrac{S_k}{S_n}\right)$, $k = 0, \ldots, n$, where S_0

$= 0$ and $S_k = \sum_{i=1}^{k} x_i$ is the total income of the poorest k individuals in the population. Hence, joining the points by line segments to obtain a curve connecting the origin with the point $(1, 1)$, we get a curve as M in Figure 8.1 below, that is convex and lies under the straight line E representing the distribution where all people get the same quantity of income. The closer a curve is to E, the more even is the distribution of income.

If $x_1, \ldots, x_n$ denote the incomes of individuals in the distribution of total income I that induce curve M and analogously $y_1, \ldots, y_n$ induce curve P, then according to the idea of Lorenz, $(x_1, \ldots, x_n)$ represents a 'more nearly equal' distribution of I than does $(y_1, \ldots, y_n)$ if and only if

$$\sum_{i=1}^{k} x_i \geq \sum_{i=1}^{k} y_i, \quad k = 1, \ldots, n-1 \tag{8.1}$$

and of course $\sum_{i=1}^{n} x_i = \sum_{i=1}^{n} y_i$

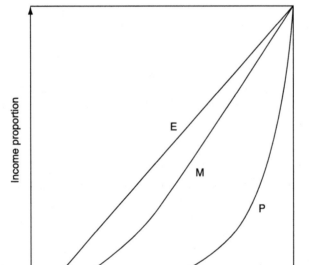

Figure 8.1 Lorenz curves

Muirhead (1903) was the first who identified the relation 8.1, which is now-adays denoted as $\mathbf{x} \prec \mathbf{y}$, read as '$\mathbf{x}$ Lorenz dominates $\mathbf{y}$' and the asymmetric component of a preorder on the space of all vector distributions in $\mathbb{R}^n$. More-over, Muirhead proved that if the components of $\mathbf{x}$ and $\mathbf{y}$ are nonnegative integers, then condition 8.1 is equivalent to the fact that distribution $\mathbf{x}$ can be derived from distribution y by a finite number of transfers of income which take place from the richer to the poorer individual and that must not be so large as to reverse the relative ranking of the two people involved in the transfer. This normative principle, now called Pigou-Dalton,[1] was actually first discussed by Muirhead (1903) and can be summarized as follows:

Definition 1. *Let* $\mathbf{y} = (y_1, \ldots, y_n) \in \mathbb{R}^N_+$, *then if* y_l *is the income of individual l,* $l = 1, \ldots, n$, $y_i < y_l$ *and an amount* δ *of income is transferred from individual l to i, than income inequality is diminished provided* $\delta \leq \dfrac{(y_l - y_i)}{2}$.

A sequence of Pigou-Dalton transfers produces an 'averaging' over a dis-tribution that is tantamount to pre-multiplying a column vector $\mathbf{y}$ by a doubly stochastic matrix[2] B in order to obtain a smoother distribution $\mathbf{x}$, namely $\mathbf{x} = B\mathbf{y}$. In his seminal work on Hadamard's determinant inequality, Schur (1923) proved that if $\mathbf{x} = B\mathbf{y}$ for some doubly stochastic matrix B, then $\sum_{i=1}^{n}$ $\varphi(x_i) \leq \sum_{i=1}^{n} \varphi(y_i)$ for any continuous concave function $\varphi : I \subseteq \mathbb{R} \to \mathbb{R}$.

Later, all the main elementary properties described above of the Lorenz preorder were summarized by the following classic result thanks to HLP (1934) (see also Marshall and Olkin (1979)), namely:

Theorem 1 (HLP (1934, 1952)). *Let* $\mathbf{x} = (x_1, \ldots, x_n)$, $\mathbf{y} = (y_1, \ldots, y_n) \in \mathbb{R}^N_+$. *Then, the following conditions are equivalent:*

i) $\mathbf{x} \prec \mathbf{y}$;

ii) $\mathbf{x}$ *can be derived from* $\mathbf{y}$ *through a finite sequence of transformations* $\mathbf{z}' = f(\mathbf{z})$ *of the following type:*

$z'_i = z_i + \delta$, $z'_j = z_j - \delta$ *with* $i \leq j$ *and* $z'_k = z_k$, *for* $k \neq i, j$ *and* $\delta > 0$ *provided* $\delta \leq \dfrac{(y_l - y_i)}{2}$;

iii) $f(\mathbf{y}) \geq f(\mathbf{x})$ *holds for any* $f : \mathbb{A} \subseteq \mathbb{R}^N_+ \to \mathbb{R}$ *of the following form: for each* $\mathbf{z} \in$

$\mathbb{A} f(\mathbf{z}) = \sum_{i=1}^{n} \varphi(z_i)$ *where* $\varphi : \mathbb{R} \to \mathbb{R}$ *is a continuous concave function.*[3]

As mentioned above, we review the main attempts to export Lorenz-like preorders into a finite setting. More precisely, we consider those Lorenz-style preorders of opportunity distributions which satisfy a counterpart of the foregoing HLP theorem. However, the Lorenz-based comparisons of univariate distributions are enabled by the *total* ordering induced by the perfect comparability of the individual incomes. On the contrary, individual endowments, namely multivariate distributions of personal goods/alternatives (hence opportunities), typically admit only *partial* non-controversial orderings. Therefore, a Lorenz preorder of opportunity distributions requires the preliminary definition of a *total* preorder on opportunity sets, an apparently controversial task. As a matter of fact, the problem of building up a Lorenz-like preorder, starting from a partial (pre)ordering in a finite setting, has not received yet in the literature the attention it deserves. The few exceptions include some works such as Hwang (1979), Lih (1982), Hwang and Rothblum (1993), which focus on Lorenz preorder when the set of population units is endowed with a fixed partial order.

Indeed, Hwang (1979) extends the classical concept of Lorenz (or dually majorization) preorder on a set of distributions to the case where the set of coordinates or equivalently of population units is partially ordered. His results rely, quite unexpectedly, on a classical theorem of Shapley on the existence of the core for every convex game and parallel the abovementioned result of Muirhead on the equivalence between the Lorenz preorder and a Pigou-Dalton finite sequence of transfers. Lih (1982) also extends the concept of majorization as introduced above (see 8.1) to the case of real-valued functions defined on a finite partially ordered set. More precisely, Lih defines the majorization preorder as follows: let $(P, \leq)$ denote a finite poset and Φ the set of all real-valued functions on $(P, \leq)$, if $a, \beta \in \Phi$ then a majorizes β if, for any order filter U of $(P, \leq)$, $a(U) \geqslant \beta(U)$ and $a(P) = \beta(P)$ where, for any $\gamma \in \Phi$, $\gamma(U) = \Sigma \{\gamma(x): x \in U\}$. In such a setting, he replicates the classical result of HLP reviewed above as Theorem 1.

Hwang and Rothblum (1993) provide a further extension of majorization and Schur convexity with respect to partial orders over the coordinates of an Euclidean space. They introduce the notion of 'pairwise connectedness' with respect to posets, which is actually a generalization of the Pigou-Dalton criterion of transfers, in order to achieve a characterization of Schur convexity (namely condition (*iii*) in Theorem 1), with respect to partial orders for the case when every Schur convex function is neither necessarily symmetric (as in Lih (1982) and in the original work of Schur (1923)) nor asymmetric (as in Hwang (1979)). They also provide necessary and sufficient conditions for Schur convexity which rely on two-coordinate local properties of functions. That result implies that conclusions about local behavior of functions can be drawn without being forced to check every pair of coordinates on the (symmetric) domain of the function. Hence, their characterization of majorization via Schur convexity applies to a wider class of functions than those which are continuously differentiable. In particular, Hwang and Rothblum extend the original Schur-(Ostrowski) theorem (see Marshall and Olkin (1979) chapter 3)). Such a generalized approach to majorization with a partial order of population units or dimensions might conceivably be extended to a finite environment.[4]

However, as mentioned above, the basic source of difficulty, and controversy, in the economic literature is uncertainty about the underlying 'basic' preorder on endowments or opportunity sets in a multidimensional setting. Indeed, let X denote the *finite* set of alternatives/opportunities, $N = \{1, \ldots, n\}$ the population of agents, and $\wp(X)$ the power set of X, i.e. the set of its *opportunity sets*, with $\#X \geq 3$, in order to avoid trivial qualifications. We are interested in those opportunity rankings $(\wp(X), \geqslant)$ that arise whenever all the alternatives are 'never bad'. Once this mild if not totally undisputed requirement is accepted, we may restrict our attention to those preorders of opportunity sets which satisfy:

Axiom 1 (*Set-Inclusion Monotonicity (MON)*). *For any $A, B \in \wp(X)$, $A \geqslant B$ whenever $A \supseteq B$.*

Clearly enough, *MON* is not to be confused with the much stronger and more controversial:

Axiom 2 (*Strict Set-Inclusion Monotonicity (SMON)*). *For any $A, B \in \wp(X)$, $A \geqslant B$ whenever $A \supset B$.*[5]

In the wake of Sen (1985), Pattanaik and Xu (1990) first addressed the ranking problem for finite opportunity sets following an axiomatic approach (see also Barberà, Bossert and Pattanaik (2004) for a critical review of the literature). That seminal work by Pattanaik and Xu focuses on those partial preorders $(\wp(X) \setminus \{\emptyset\}, \geqslant)$ on the set of *non-empty* opportunity sets which satisfy *SMON* as defined above as well as:

Axiom 3 (*Indifference between Singletons (IS)*). *For all $x, y \in X$, $\{x\} \sim \{y\}$,*

and

Axiom 4 (*Independence (IND)*). *For all $A, B \in \wp(X) \setminus \{\emptyset\}$ and $x \in X, x \notin A \cup B$ and $A \geqslant B$ if and only if $A \cup \{x\} \geqslant B \cup \{x\}$.*

Then, Pattanaik and Xu show that the cardinality-based total preorder $\geqslant_{\#}$ is the sole preorder satisfying those properties, namely $(\wp(X) \setminus \{\emptyset\}, \geqslant)$ is a preorder enjoying *SMON ,IS ,IND* if and only if for any, $A, B \in \wp(X) \setminus \{\emptyset\}$, $A \geqslant B$ precisely when $\#A \geqslant \#B$.

It turns out that the (total) cardinality-based preorder $\geqslant_{\#}$ does support a Lorenz-like preorder of opportunity distributions over a finite opportunity set, as shown by Ok and Kranich, namely:

Theorem 2 (Ok and Kranich (1998)). *If the underlying opportunity preorder is $(\wp(X), \geqslant_{\#})$, then for any pair of opportunity distributions $\mathbf{A}, \mathbf{B} \in (\wp(X))^{N}$,*

A $\prec$ **B** *iff* **A** *is reachable from* **B** *through a finite sequence of (suitably defined) Pigou-Dalton transfers or iff* $f(\mathbf{A}) \leq f(\mathbf{B})$ *for any (suitably defined) Schur-concave function f.*

Moreover, the cardinality-based preorder is the sole Strict Set-Inclusion Monotonic total preorder which supports such a Lorenz-like preorder of opportunity distributions, namely:

Theorem 3 (Ok (1997)). *Let* $(\wp(X), \succcurlyeq)$ *be a Strict Set-Inclusion Monotonic totally preordered set,[6] and for any pair of opportunity distributions* **A**, **B** $\in$ $(\wp(X))^N$, **A** $\prec$ **B** *iff* **A** *is reachable from* **B** *through a finite sequence of (suitably defined) Pigou-Dalton transfers and iff* $f(\mathbf{A}) \leq f(\mathbf{B})$ *for any (suitably defined) Schur-concave function f. Then* $\succcurlyeq = \succcurlyeq_{\#}$.

However, the cardinality-based preorder is typically regarded as a trivial and uninteresting ranking of opportunity sets. Indeed, rejection of the cardinality ranking is quite obvious if some relevant evaluations of (or preferences on) opportunities are available. But the cardinality-based preorder is also typically rejected as a ranking of opportunity sets in terms of *freedom of choice*, namely when reliable and detailed preferential information is not available or is deemed to be not relevant. We concur, but one should then ask: why is that so? The answer to the foregoing question is not entirely clear, but one of the main drawbacks of the cardinality-based preorder is arguably its failure to accommodate even a minimal diversity of judgments concerning the relevance of distinct opportunities.

Therefore, if a Lorenz-like preorder on opportunity distributions is to be defined starting from a freedom-of-choice-based ranking of opportunity sets, one should look for a class of preorders on opportunity sets that satisfy *MON* but not *SMON*, and accommodate a minimal diversity of judgments concerning the relevance of distinct opportunities.

In that vein, one may consider *set-inclusion filtral preorders (SIFPs)*. A SIFP on a finite set X of basic alternatives/opportunities amounts to the set-inclusion partial order as augmented with a *minimal opportunity threshold* which is induced by an order filter (to be defined below): under the threshold, opportunity sets are indifferent to each other and to the null opportunity set, while over the threshold the set-inclusion partial order is simply replicated.

As mentioned above, we shall rely on the definition of an *order filter of a poset* in order to capture the notion of a threshold in this setting. In fact, such an order filter amounts to a set that collects all the elements of the poset which are greater than some member of a specified list of *non-comparable* elements, the so-called *generators*. That list is also called the *basis* $\wp$ of the filter itself and corresponds to the set of minimally acceptable opportunity sets. The elements of the basis $\wp$ jointly constitute a threshold. In this way, we associate a threshold to each order filter as defined on the opportunity set. In particular, when $\wp$ is a singleton the order filter F is said to be *principal.* In particular, whenever X is finite, there is an one-to-one correspondence between order filters and antichains of $(\wp(X), \supseteq)$, hence between order filters and thresholds on the opportunity space. All this can be made precise by the following:

Definition 2 ((Principal) Order Filter of the Set-Inclusion Poset). *Let $\wp$ be an antichain of $(\wp(X), \supseteq)$, namely $\wp \subseteq \wp(X)$ and for any $b_i, b_j \in \wp$ if $b_i \neq b_j$ then not $b_i \supset b_j$. An order filter of $(\wp(X), \subseteq)$ with basis $\wp$ is a set $F = F(\wp) \subseteq \wp(X)$ such that:*

(1) *$\wp \subseteq F$ and*
(2) *for any $A, B \in Y$, if $A \in F$ and $B \supset A$ then $B \in F$.*

Whenever, $\#\wp = 1$, i.e. $\wp$ is a singleton, F is a principal *order filter.*

In other terms, the order filter collects all the elements of X which are not $\geqslant$-smaller than at least one element in the basis $\wp = \{b_1, \ldots, b_l\}$. Hence, an order filter of $(\wp(X), \supseteq)$ collects all the opportunity sets which are located above the threshold as specified by the basis $\wp \subseteq (\wp(X), \supseteq)$ and are therefore deemed acceptable according to the standard induced by $\wp$. Notice that each opportunity set in the filter's basis does correspond to minimally acceptable bundles of opportunities or equivalently to minimal amounts of freedom of choice. Hence, a (general) order filter accommodates the case where a few such 'minimal' bundles exist, while a principal order filter represents situations where the 'minimally' acceptable bundle of opportunities is unique. To put it in other terms, the case of (general) order filters embodies a degree of flexibility in opportunity appraisal which is conspicuously absent when the threshold is defined by a principal order filter. Nevertheless, we shall focus on the latter case since it turns out to be both more tractable and transparent. It should also be noticed that an opportunity set in the filter's basis that includes at least two elements/opportunities does represent a complementarity effect between the latter opportunities. Similarly, any opportunity set in the filter's basis and any element/opportunity which does not belong to the basis of the order filter behave as complementary goods.

Having defined (principal) order filters, we are now ready to introduce *set-inclusion filtral preorders (SIFPs)*, namely

Definition 3 (Set-Inclusion (Principal) Filtral Preorders (SIFPs)). *For any (principal) order filter F of $(\wp(X), \supseteq)$ the F-generated set-inclusion (principal) filtral preorder (SIFP) is the binary relation $\geqslant_F$ on $\wp(X)$ defined as follows: for any $A, B \in \wp(X)$, $A \geqslant_F B$ if and only if $A \supseteq B$ or $B \notin F$.[7]*

Thus, the order filter of a SIFP collects all the opportunity sets that meet a minimum standard, i.e. are located over or above the threshold: any opportunity set which does not meet the corresponding standard is simply not acceptable, namely is equivalent to the null set. Since the behavior of a SIFP over the threshold simply mimics set-inclusion, it is arguably *non-controversial*. But, the threshold itself can be chosen in many different ways: therefore SIFPs, unlike, for example, the cardinality preorder, also accommodate a non-negligible *diversity* of judgments concerning the most appropriate ranking of opportunity sets. Thus, SIFPs can be regarded as a format for opportunity rankings that, building upon a common and essentially 'objective' basis, gives some scope to a modicum of diversity in judgments.

It is easily checked that in general SIFPs satisfy *MON* but fail to satisfy *INS, IND* or *SMON*.[8]

On the other hand, a SIFP, principal or otherwise, is in general a *non-total* partial preorder. Then, in order to try and define a Lorenz-like preorder on the corresponding opportunity distributions in the standard manner outlined above, a total extension of a SIFP must be provided. In Savaglio and Vannucci (2007a), that is done through the *height function* of a SIFP, as defined below.

Definition 4. *Let F be a (principal) order filter of* $(\wp(X), \supseteq)$ *and* $\geqslant_F$ *the (principal) SIFP induced by F. Then, the* $\geqslant_F$*-induced height function*

$$h_{\geqslant_F} : \mathcal{P}(X) \to \mathbb{Z}_+$$

is defined as follows: for any $A \subseteq X$:

$$h_{\geqslant_F}(A) = \max \left\{ \begin{array}{l} \#\mathcal{C} : \mathcal{C} \text{ is a } \geqslant_F\text{-chain, such that} \\ A \in \mathcal{C} \text{ and } A >_F B \text{ for any } B \in \mathcal{C} \setminus \{A\} \end{array} \right\}.$$

In words, the height function assigns to each opportunity set A a nonnegative number, namely the size of the longest strictly ascending chain having A as its maximum.[9] Thus, the height of an opportunity set A in $(\wp(X), \geqslant_F)$ counts the number of opportunity sets which are below A according to preorder $\geqslant_F$, when considering the longest path ending in A. In terms of the Hasse diagram of $(\wp(X), \geqslant_F)$, we count *how many steps*, we go down following the vertical directions before getting to the threshold. Height functions are in general a very useful and standard tool in the theory of combinatorial posets. In our case the *height function* implicitly *provides a total extension of the relevant SIFP*, namely the resulting 'higher than' relation, denoted $(\wp(X), \geqslant_F^h)$. It has been proved (see Vannucci (2003)) that height-based extensions of *principal* SIFPs are amenable to a (filter-parametric) characterization in terms of the following properties:

Axiom 5 (*F-Restricted Indifference between Singletons (F-RIS)*). *A preordered set* $(\wp(X), \geqslant)$ *satisfies* F-RIS *if for all* $A \in F$ *and* $x, y \in X \setminus A$, $A \cup \{x\} \sim A \cup \{y\}$.

Axiom 6 (*F-Restricted Strict Monotonicity (F-RSM)*). $(\wp(X), \geqslant)$ *satisfies* F-RSM *if for all* $A \in F$ *and* $x, y \in X$ *such that* $x \neq y, y \notin A$ *entails* $A \cup \{x, y\} > A \cup \{x\}$.

Axiom 7 (*F-Restricted Independence (F-RIND)*). $(\wp(X), \geqslant)$ *satisfies* F-RIND *if for all* $A, B \in F$ *and* $x \in X$, $x \notin A \cup B$ *and* $A \geqslant B$ *if and only if* $A \cup \{x\} \geqslant B \cup \{x\}$.

Axiom 8 (*F-Threshold Effect (F-TE)*). $(\wp(X), \geqslant)$ *satisfies* F-TE *if and only if* $A > B \sim \emptyset$ *for all* $A, B \subseteq X$ *such that* $\emptyset \neq A \in F$ *and* $B \in \wp(X) \setminus F$.

It turns out that such a total height-based extension of the given SIFP allows us to replicate some of the basic results of the theory of income inequality measurement in the more general context of opportunity distributions. This is made precise by the following:

Theorem 4 (Savaglio and Vannucci (2007a)). *Let F be a principal order filter of* $(\wp(X), \supseteq)$, $\mathbf{A}, \mathbf{B} \in (\wp(X))^N$ *two opportunity distributions such that their height vectors* $h_{\geqslant F}(\mathbf{A})$, $h_{\geqslant F}(\mathbf{B})$ *are positive. Then,* $\mathbf{A} < \mathbf{B}$ *iff* $\mathbf{A}$ *is reachable from* $\mathbf{B}$ *through a finite sequence of (suitably defined) Pigou-Dalton transfers or iff* $f(\mathbf{A}) \leqslant f(\mathbf{B})$ *for any (suitably defined) Schur-concave function f.*

Reliance on the set-inclusion order as implied by SIFPs, however, is only satisfactory when at least some of the relevant resources are public, or at least non-rival goods. Savaglio and Vannucci (2007b) suggest one way to confirm the foregoing result while avoiding such a disturbing restriction. Indeed, if individual endowments are modeled via multisets[10] rather than sets, then the items in the basic set X could be rivalrous and excludable objects, namely as pure private goods. Thus, the very same problem considered above can be addressed starting from the strict dominance order for *multisets*, as augmented with a threshold, a sort of multidimensional (opportunity) poverty line below which each opportunity set is indifferent to the null set. Hence, in order to extend the basic results of the literature on inequality measurement in the multidimensional context of opportunity profiles, we provide a suitable reformulation of the Pigou-Dalton transfer principle and of the notion of Schur convexity in a multipartition context. A counterpart of the classic HLP characterization of the Lorenz preorder on finite multipartitions via simple Pigou-Dalton transfers is provided in the multiset framework. It is worth noticing that a partition of multisets, or *multipartition*, is a mathematical notion that mimics a multivariate distribution and that can be represented as a rectangular matrix with integer entries whose generic row i denotes the assignment of the annual vector of goods to the i-th agent (see 8.2 below). Such a matrix, induced by finite multiset-partitions, is exactly the framework used to study multidimensional inequality, i.e. the disparity of a population of N individuals distinguished for several attributes.

$$x \quad y \quad \ldots \quad w \ldots \quad z \qquad \leftarrow \text{goods}$$

people
$\downarrow$

$$\mathbf{m} = \begin{bmatrix} m_1(x) & m_1(y) & \ldots & m_1(z) \\ \cdot & \cdot & & \cdot \\ \cdot & \cdot & m_i(w) & \cdot \\ \cdot & \cdot & & \cdot \\ \cdot & \cdot & \cdot & \cdot \\ m_n(x) & \ldots & \cdot & m_n(z) \end{bmatrix} \tag{8.2}$$

Thus, the foregoing approach provides a majorization preorder of multi-profiles of goods that extends the classic unidimensional analysis of income inequality to a finite multivariate context. In particular, the componentwise strict dominance preorder of vectors, representing the assignment of the goods to the agents, supports a multipartition counterpart to the celebrated HLP Theorem. In a sense, Savaglio and Vannucci (2007b) provide a somewhat optimistic answer to the question: '*A lost paradise?*', raised by Trannoy (2006) and concerning the *possibility* of finding again '*the miracle of the HLP theorem*' in the multidimensional context.

8.3 Concluding remarks

Opportunity sets, as opposed to income levels, do not admit an obvious total (pre)order. When it comes to the assessment of inequality among opportunity distributions according to a Lorenz preorder, however, that is undoubtedly a rather fastidious inconvenience. Two basic strategies may be devised to escape the foregoing difficulty while sticking to the notion of a majorization preorder, namely (i) extending SIFPs to total preorders in a suitably 'natural' manner or (ii) reformulating (and generalizing) the Lorenz construct in order to adapt it to the general case of arbitrary non-total preorders.

Concerning strategy (i) we have shown by a class of examples, i.e. height-based total extensions of principal set-inclusion filtral preorders, that rankings of opportunity sets other than the cardinality-based ranking do support a Lorenz-like preorder of opportunity distributions.

By comparison, strategy (ii) is a quite radical move. Indeed, it can be shown that it demands a special tactic to cope with pairs of *non-isomorphic* lattices of order filters: thus, it goes to the very foundations of the Lorenz construct. An exploration of this attack route to the problem of opportunity inequality assessment is therefore best left as a topic for further research.

Notes

1 After Pigou, who hinted at it on p. 24 of his book *Wealth and Welfare* in 1912 and Dalton, who clearly described the notion of transfer in an income distribution context in a seminal work published on the *Economic Journal* in 1920.
2 Recall that a $n \times n$ doubly stochastic matrix B is a nonnegative square matrix where all row and column sums are equal to 1.

3 Functions $f(\cdot) = \Sigma \, \varphi\,(\cdot)$ as defined above are indeed called Schur concave in honor of Schur.
4 Hwang and Rothblum (1994) provide an example concerning *discrete* coherent systems composed of series modules.
5 As usual, $>$ and $\sim$ denote the asymmetric and symmetric components of $\geqslant$, respectively.
6 Or, alternatively, a totally preordered set satisfying another property called 'contraction consistency' (see Ok (1997) for a formal definition and a discussion of such a property).
7 Notice that, under the extremal or degenerate cases $F = \wp(X)$ and $F = \emptyset$, $(\wp(X), \geqslant_F)$ reduces to the set-inclusion order and the degenerate total preorder consisting of a single indifference class, respectively.
8 Or 'contraction consistency' as mentioned in note 6 above.
9 Recall that a chain of a preordered set $(Y, \geqslant)$ is a subset $Z \subseteq Y$ such that $(Z, \geqslant)$ is a totally preordered set.
10 A finite *multiset* on X is a function $m: X \to \mathbb{Z}_+$ such that $\Sigma_{x \in X} m(x) < \infty$. A partition of multiset m – or *multipartion* of m – on population N is a profile $\mathbf{m} = \{m_i\}_{i \in N}$ of multisets on X, such that for any $x \in X$: $\Sigma_{i \in N} m_i(x) = m(x)$.

References

Barberà, S., W. Bossert and P.K. Pattanaik (2004). Ranking Sets of Objects, in Barberà S., P. J. Hammond and C. Seidl (eds.): *Handbook of Utility Theory vol. II Extensions*, Kluwer Academic Publishers, 893–977.

Hardy, G., J. E. Littlewood and G. Pólya (1934, 1952). *Inequalities*, Cambridge: Cambridge University Press.

Hwang, F. K. (1979). Majorization on a Partially Ordered Set, *Proceedings of the American Mathematical Society* 76, 199–203.

Hwang, F. K. and U. Rothblum (1993). Majorization and Schur Convexity with respect to Partial Orders, *Mathematics of Operations Research* 18, 928–944.

Hwang, F. K. and U. Rothblum (1994). Optimality of Monotone Assemblies for Coherent Systems Composed of Series Modules, *Operations Research* 42, 709–720.

Lih, K. (1982). Majorization on Finite Partially Ordered Sets, *SIAM Journal of Algebraic and Discrete Methods* 4, vol. 3 495–503.

Marshall, A. W. and I. Olkin (1979). *Inequalities: Theory of Majorization and Its Applications*, New York: Academic Press.

Muirhead, R. F. (1903). Some Methods Applicable to Identities and Inequalities of Symmetric Algebraic Functions of *n* Letters, *Proceedings of Edinburgh Mathematical Society* 21, 144–157.

Ok, E. (1997). On Opportunity Inequality Measurement, *Journal of Economic Theory* 77, 300–329.

Ok, E. and L. Kranich (1998). The Measurement of Opportunity Inequality: A Cardinality-Based Approach, *Social Choice and Welfare* 15, 263–287.

Pattanaik, P. K. and Y. Xu (1990). On Ranking Opportunity Sets in Terms of Freedom of Choice, *Recherches Economiques de Louvain* 56, 383–390.

Savaglio, E. and S. Vannucci (2007a). Filtral Preorders and Opportunity Inequality, *Journal of Economic Theory* 132, 474–492.

Savaglio, E. and S. Vannucci (2007b). – On Multidimensional Inequality in Partitions of Multisets, Quaderno del Dipartimento di Economica Politica n.504 University of Siena.

Schur, I. (1923). Über eine Klasse von Mittelbildungen mit Anwendungen die Deter-minanten, *Theorie Sitzungsber. Berlin. Mathematische Gesellschaft* 22, 9–20.

Sen, A.K. (1985). *Commodities and Capabilities*, Amsterdam: North Holland.

Trannoy, A. (2006). Multidimensional Egalitarianism and the Dominance Approach: a Lost Paradise?, in Farina, F. and E. Savaglio (eds.), *Inequality and Economic Integration*, Routledge, London.

Vannucci, S. (2003). A Characterization of Height-Based Extensions of Principal Filtral Opportunity Rankings, Quaderno del Dipartimento di Economia Politica n.411 University of Siena.

Part III
Inequality decomposition

9 Inequality decomposition, directional economic distance, metric distance, and Gini dissimilarity between income distributions

Camilo Dagum

9.1 Introduction

In the history of economic thought, the highly relevant theme of income distribution recognizes two main strands of research, the functional and the personal distribution of income. Forerunner of the former are Cantillon (1755), A. R. J. Turgot and J. B. Say. In particular, Cantillon already considered four factors of production, that is, labor, capital, land and entrepreneur, being salary, interest, rent, and profit their respective rates of return. He rightly called *certain remuneration* salary, interest, and rent, while profit was referred to as an *uncertain remuneration.* It is worthwhile to observe that the addition of the certain remuneration plus the imputed profit, that is, the *ex-ante* uncertain or expected remuneration, determine the *ex-ante* value added. Adding to them the costs of raw materials and intermediate inputs determine the good or service price at factors cost. Instead, the selling price of a good or service determines its market price. Subtracting from it the certain remuneration plus the costs of raw materials and intermediate inputs determine the *ex-post* or realized profit, which can be positive, negative or null. Hence, *ex-post* profit is a residual.

Ricardo (1817) was the first to advance a formal theory of the functional distribution of income. On the other hand, Pareto (1895, 1896, 1897) was the first to specify, analyze and estimate a model of personal distribution of income and to advance a socio-demographic and economic foundation of it, and proposing as an income inequality measure his shape parameter a. Pareto made the wrong interpretation that income inequality is an increasing function of a (Dagum 1987). Gini (1909, 1910) proved that the Pareto inequality interpretation has to be reversed; that is, for the Pareto model, Gini proved that income inequality is a decreasing function of a. Afterward, Gini (1914, [1955], [2005]) proposed his well-known distribution-free inequality measure, the Gini ratio.

For almost a century, these two highly related strands of research, functional and personal income distributions, followed independent development, as two solitudes. By the 1970s there was concern to find a theoretical linkage between these two distributions. To the best of my knowledge, Dagum (1994, 1999a) is the first to offer a rigorous theoretico-empirical formalization of the linkage between functional and personal income distributions, beginning with the specification of his income-generating function as a function of human capital and wealth.

Pareto's and Gini's seminal contributions stimulated further research to develop more comprehensive personal income distribution models, with support given by the positive real numbers, and Dagum (1977) extended it to include the non negative real numbers. A parameter of Dagum model accounts for the relative frequency of economic units with null and negative incomes. The Gini ratio was also a great stimulus to pursue further research on income inequality. One line of research started with Theil (1967) who proposed an entropic measure of inequality and its decomposition into within-and between-group contributions to the total inequality of the population of economic units. In the same year, Bhattacharya and Mahalanobis (1967) proposed a decomposition of the Gini ratio. Dagum (1980) proposed a directional distance ratio between pair-wise groups of income distributions. Further development of this field of research includes topics such as wealth distribution models (Dagum 1993, 1994, 1999b, 2004, 2005a), personal human capital method of estimation and its distribution (Dagum and Vittadini 1996, Dagum and Slottje 2000, Dagum *et al.* 2003), and the measurement and evaluation of poverty (Sen 1976, Dagum *et al.* 1992 and Dagum and Costa 2004).

The scope of this study is manifold. In particular, (i) to discuss Dagum's directional distance and directional distance ratio between income distributions; (ii) to deal with the decomposition of Gini and the generalized entropy inequality ratios of a population partitioned into k groups, $k \geq 2$; and (iii) to discuss the limitations of metric distance functions to study asymmetric concepts such as the relative affluence of a group with respect to another that have a smaller average income than the first.

This chapter is organized as follows: Section 9.2 introduces and briefly discusses the Dagum fundamental equation of income. This is used in Section 9.4 to prove an outstanding feature of the Gini ratio, that is, that the product of the average income times the disutility function implied by the Gini ratio and formally derived in Section 9.4, is equal to the mathematical form of the second-order stochastic dominance; Section 9.3 presents the main decomposition approaches to analyze income inequalities between income distributions; Section 9.4 introduces a set of definitions and theorems needed for the development and interpretation of Dagum directional distance ratio and Gini inequality decomposition. The former is presented in Section 9.5, and the latter in Section 9.6. Section 9.7 deals with the decomposition of the generalized entropy measure of inequality; Section 9.8 discusses, within the scope of this research, a proposed metric distance function and shows that it is a member of the Gini set of dissimilarity measures. Working with the data of the Italian Sample Survey of Income and Wealth for Italy and its three regions, Section 9.9 estimates and analyzes the directional distance ratio, the Gini decomposition, and three particular cases of the generalized entropy ratio. Section 9.10 presents the conclusion.

9.2 The fundamental equation of income

Dagum (1990, 1993, 1995, 2005b) introduced the fundamental equation of income:

$$y = U[y, F(y)] + \mu V[y, F(y)], \tag{9.1}$$

and the following three factually supported propositions:

Proposition 9.1 Individual economic units and societies have a preference for more income and wealth.

Proposition 9.2 Societies have a preference for equity, that is, a preference to reward he economic units according to a socially accepted principle of distributive justice.

Proposition 9.3 Economic units make interpersonal comparisons of utilities and disutilities.

In equation (9.1), y denotes income; U stands for the utility function (UF), V for the disutility function (DF), $F(y)$ is the cumulative distribution function (CDF), and μ is the ME of income y. The UF $U(.)$ has the dimension of income whereas the DF $V(.)$ is dimensionless, and $\mu V(.)$, which stands for the loss function, has the income dimension. In the fundamental equation of income (9.1), the utility and disutility functions are stated as functions of income y and its CDF; hence, unlike the utilitarian UFs, it explicitly recognizes Proposition 9.3, that is, the existence of interpersonal comparisons of utilities and disutilities.

Given y and $F(y)$, $U(.)$ and $V(.)$ are also functions of μ and LC, because, if $E(Y) = \mu$ exists, then μ and the Lorenz curve $L(y)$ are univocally determined. Moreover, given μ, there is a one-to-one correspondence between $F(y)$ and $L(y)$. The only inequality measures that fulfill Proposition 9.3 are the Gini ratio and those based on Gini's approach, such as Bonferroni's, De Vergotini's, Amato's and Zenga's. Inequalities ratios such as the Pearson coefficient of variation, the variance of the log of income, all the members of the generalized entropy measure (GEM) and Atkinson ratio, have strictly utilitarian $U(\cdot)$ and $V(\cdot)$ functions. Based on this serious limitation, they have to be discarded. Furthermore, we will discuss later on other more damaging objections to these inequalities.

Applying Proposition 9.1 we deduce that U is a monotonic increasing function of y. Hence, the Proposition 9.1 can be used to state the first-order stochastic dominance, which is consistent with the Bernoulli Principle that requires only a non-decreasing utility function. As in our case, for a twice differentiable CDF and UF, it requires that UF be a monotonic increasing function of income.

Applying Proposition 9.1 and Proposition 9.2, and assuming the general observed case that income inequality is greater than the society preference for social equity (distributive justice), we derive that UF is a monotonic increasing and concave function of income. Hence, the first two total derivatives of U with respect to y satisfy the following inequalities:

$$dU/dy > 0, \ d^2U/dy^2 < 0 \quad \text{and } d^2U/dy^2 = -\mu dV^2/dy^2 \tag{9.2}$$

If the inequalities in (9.2) are satisfied, we can state the second-order stochastic dominance, which is equivalent to the Bernoulli Principle that requires a positive aversion to inequality.

Propositions 9.1 and 9.2 are consistent with well-accepted economic theory since Daniel Bernoulli (1738, [1954]) who specified the strictly utilitarian utility function $U(y) = \log y$ and called it *emolumentum*. He used this UF to solve the famous Saint Petersburg Paradox. Given Proposition 9.1 and Proposition 9.2, the CDF $F(y)$ is preferred to the CDF $G(y)$ if and only if:

$$E_F[U(Y, F(Y)] > E_G[U(Y, G(Y)], \quad \text{i.e.,} \tag{9.3}$$

$$\int_0^\infty U[y, F(y)]dF(y) > \int_0^\infty U[y, G(y)]dG(y). \tag{9.4}$$

Equations (9.3) and (9.4) correspond to the definition of the second-order stochastic dominance.

Taking ME in (9.1) we have:

$$E(Y) = E[U(Y, F(Y)] + \mu E[V(Y, F(Y)], \tag{9.5}$$

hence:

$$\mu = SW + \mu I, \tag{9.6}$$

where $E[U(.)]$ and $E[V(.)]$ define the social welfare function (SWF) and the income inequality measure (IIM) of the utility and disutility function specified in (9.5) (see Dagum 1990, 1993, 1998). SW has the dimension of income and I is dimensionless. Multiplying the latter by μ, it becomes of dimension one.

For societies that prefer more income and wealth (Proposition 9.1) and less inequality than the observed one (Proposition 9.2), assuming a twice differentiable CDF, it can be deduced from (9.1) and (9.2) that:

$dV/dy > 0$ and $d^2V/dy^2 > 0,$ (9.7)

therefore, $V[y, F(y)]$ is a monotonic increasing and convex function of y. Furthermore, given μ, there is a dual relationship between UF and DF, and SWF and IIM. In effect, given the UF and applying (9.1) we deduce its corresponding DF, and conversely. Similarly, given an IIM and applying (9.6) we deduce its corresponding SWF, and conversely.

It follows from (9.1) and (9.6) that the SWFs and IIMs are functionals that map the sets of UFs and DFs into the closed sets $[0,\mu]$ and $[0, 1]$, respectively. To apply the latter support to the members of the GEM we need to divide them by their corresponding maximum possible values (Dagum 1993). Therefore:

$SW: \{U[y, F(y)]\} \rightarrow [0, \mu]$ and (9.8)

$I: \{V[y, F(y)]\} \rightarrow [0, 1].$ (9.9)

The qualification of Proposition 9.2 constrains the observed income inequality to the general case of being greater than the income inequality that a society prefers according to a socially adopted principle of social justice. Hence, we are imposing a local, but not a wide-ranging validity to equation (9.6). If a society prefers more inequality than the observed, then we are in the first-order stochastic dominance case, which is consistent with the Bernoulli principle jointly with a relaxation of $U[y, F(y)]$ that requires it to be only a monotonic increasing function of income. Making an unjustifiable interpretation of J. Bentham (1789), Stuart Mill, Marshall, Pigou and a large number of today's economists ignore Proposition 9.2. To maximize SW they assume strictly additive and separable utilitarian UFs, which are increasing and concave functions of income. These unjustifiable assumptions lead to the counterfactual conclusion that SW is maximized when IIM tends to zero, which is a categorical mistake (Aristotle called it a $\mu\varepsilon\tau\alpha\beta\alpha\sigma\iota\varsigma$ $\varepsilon\iota\varsigma$ $\alpha\lambda\lambda o$ $\gamma\varepsilon\eta o\varsigma$). Then, without solution of continuity, they reached the conclusion that perfect income equality, meaning that all the economic units receive the mean income μ, is the ideal case (Kakwani 1980). Instead, it is nothing more and nothing less than the origin of the support of IIMs without any value judgment attached to it, unless we are dealing with a population of identical economic units in *nature and nurture*. Factual evidences, supported by biological science, tells us that the members of any society possess unequal endowment of attributes such as ability, intelligence, physical and mental health conditions, driving force, intellectual concentration, academic background, home cultural and educational background, social environment, wealth distribution and amount of human capital. In synthesis, they testimony the existence of unequal opportunities which determine unequal income distributions.

To assess the factual income inequalities has to be done with respect to a well-defined and socially accepted principle of social equity. An observed income distribution that fulfills the adopted principle of social justice, the maximum SW is attained for a value of the income inequality ratio greater than zero. Personally, I consider the most appealing and rigorous principle of social equity the one advanced over two centuries ago by the French economist and social philosopher Saint-Simon. He stated that a social justice principle consists in giving to each one according to his/her capacity and to each capacity according to his/her output.

9.3 The decomposition approach

To gain a broader insight into the inequality structure of a population we need to add to the scalar measure of inequality, some decomposition or disaggregation form of it. Among the most important decomposition approaches we have:

(i) The Lorenz curve, which allows the comparative analysis of income shares by quantiles and the frequently observed case of intersecting Lorenz curves. For instance, if in two different periods of time, the Lorenz curve L_1 intersects the Lorenz curve L_2 from above, it implies that, with respect to L_2, the lower and higher income groups of L_1 increased their income shares at the expense of a decrease in the income shares of the income groups in the neighborhood of the intersection point.

(ii) The decomposition of a population of economic units into specific groups derived from well-determined socioeconomic and geographic attributes, purporting to estimate a *directional distance ratio* (DDR) *between* the income distributions of all binary combinations of groups, and completing this information with the Gini ratio of the income distribution of each group. This approach was initiated by Dagum (1978, 1980, 1987, 1998).

(iii) The decomposition of the income inequality of a population into the contribution of the inequalities *within* and *between* groups (subpopulations). This approach was initiated by Theil (1967) for his entropic measure of inequality, and Bhattacharya and Mahalanobis (1967) for the Gini ratio.

(iv) The approach proposed by Ebert (1984) as an alternative to the Dagum directional distance ratio. It is based on a metric distance function, which is a particular case of Gini (1915, 1965) dissimilarity ratios. This approach lacks power to deal with the structure of inequalities between income distributions.

The sections that follow deal with points (ii), (iii) and (iv). First, we introduce some basic definitions and theorems needed to derive the decomposition of the Gini ratio and to provide the bases for the Dagum DDR between income distributions of all binary combinations of groups.

9.4 Directional distance ratio and Gini decomposition: basic definitions and theorems

We introduce a set of definitions and theorems to be used in the derivation of Dagum DDR between income distributions and in the decomposition of the Gini ratio. Some of these definitions and theorems were presented in Dagum (1980, 1987 and 1998).

Let n be the sample size of a population of income units. It is partitioned in k groups corresponding to k socioeconomic attributes such as gender, years of schooling, region and age. The r-th group is of size n_r, hence, $\sum_{r=1}^{k} n_r = n$.

To the n income units corresponds an n-order income vector representing the observed income distribution. Being the sample partitioned into k groups, to the r-group corresponds an n_r-order income vector, $r = 1, 2, \ldots, k$. Therefore:

$$y = (y_1, \ldots, y_i, \ldots, y_n) = (y_{11}, \ldots, y_{1n_1}, \ldots, y_{r1}, \ldots, y_{rn_r}, \ldots, y_{k1}, \ldots, y_{kn_k}) \tag{9.10}$$

$$\mu_r = \sum_{i=1}^{n_r} y_{ri}/n_r, \quad \mu = \sum_{i=1}^{n} y_i/n = \Sigma n_r \mu_r/n \tag{9.11}$$

$$p_r = n_r/n, \quad q_r = n_r \mu_r/n\mu, \quad r = 1, 2, \ldots, k, \tag{9.12}$$

where p_r is the r-th group population share and q_r is the r-th group income share. Their corresponding k-order vectors are:

$$p = (p_1, \ldots, p_r, \ldots, p_k), q = (q_1, \ldots, q_r, \ldots, q_k),$$

$$\Sigma p_r = \Sigma q_r = \sum_{r=1}^{k} \sum_{s=1}^{k} p_r q_s = 1, \tag{9.13}$$

where p and q are stochastic vectors, and $(p_r q_s)$ is a stochastic matrix; $F_r(y)$ and $f_r(y)$ stands for the r-th group CDF and PDF, respectively.

Definition 9.1 For notational simplicity and without loss of generality, the group income means are ordered by non-decreasing values, that is:

$$\mu_1 \leq \ldots \leq \mu_s \leq \ldots \leq \mu_r \leq \ldots \leq \mu_k. \tag{9.14}$$

Definition 9.2 Definition of average affluence: The r-th group is on average more affluent than the s-th group if $\mu_r > \mu_s$. When μ_r, μ_s, then they are on average equally affluent.

Definition 9.3 Gini's (1912, 1914, [2005]) definitions of the Gini mean difference (GMD) and the Gini ratio (G) for a population of n income units are:

$$\Delta = \int_0^\infty \left[\int_0^\infty |y - x| dF(x) \right] dF(y)/n^2,$$ (9.15)

$$G = \Delta/2\mu.$$ (9.16)

Definition 9.4 According to (9.10), (9.11), (9.15) and (9.16), and using the Riemann-Stieltjes integral to represent both continuous and discrete PDFs, the GMD and the ratio *within* the *r*-th income group are:

$$\Delta_{rr} = \int_0^\infty \left[\int_0^\infty |y - x| dF_r(x) \right] dF_r(y)$$ (9.17)

$$G_{rr} = \Delta_{rr}/2\,\mu_r, r = 1,2, \ldots, k.$$ (9.18)

Definition 9.5 Dagum (1980, 1987) defined the GMD and the Gini ratio *between* the *r*-th and *s*-th income distributions as:

$$\Delta_{rs} = \int_0^\infty \left[\int_0^\infty |y - x| dF_s(x) \right] dF_r(y),$$ (9.19)

$$G_{rs} = \Delta_{rs}/(\mu_r + \mu_s), r,s = 1,2, \ldots, k.$$ (9.20)

If $r = s$, we have the particular cases of the *r*-th group GMD (9.17) and Gini ratio (9.18), respectively.

Definition 9.6 Given $\mu_r > \mu_s$, the Dagum gross directional distance d_{rs} of the *r*-th with respect to the *s*-th income distributions is the weighted average of the *positive differences* $y_{rj} - y_{si}, j = 1, 2, \ldots, n_r$ and $i = 1, 2, \ldots, n_s$, that is:

$$d_{rs} = \int_0^\infty \left[\int_0^y (y - x) dF_s(x) \right] dF_r(y) > 0.$$ (9.21)

Introducing the indicator function:

$$I(y, x) = [0, \text{ if } y < x; 1, \text{ if } y > x; \text{ and } \frac{1}{2}, \text{ if } y = x],$$ (9.22)

we state (9.21) as follows:

$$d_{rs} = E[(Y - X)\, I(Y,X)] = \int_0^\infty \left[\int_0^\infty (y - x)\, I(y - x) dF_s(x) \right] dF_r(y).$$ (9.23)

Since (9.21) and (9.23) are Riemann-Stieltjes integrals, the case $I(y - x) = \frac{1}{2}$ is highly relevant when we work with observed income vectors and with observed income distributions presented by class intervals. In nonparametric analysis, to neglect this case would be a source of bias.

Equation (9.21), hence (9.23), have the dimension of income. We call them *gross directional distance* because they include the transvariation (overlapping) between income distributions (Gini 1916, 1959, Dagum 1960a, 1960b, 1961).

Definition 9.7 Given as in Definition 9.6 that $\mu_r > \mu_s$, the first-order moment of transvariation p_{rs} between the r-th and s-th income distributions is the weighted average of the positive differences $y_{si} - y_{rj}$, that is:

$$p_{rs} = \int_0^\infty \left[\int_0^y (y - x)dF_r(x) \right] dF_s(y). \tag{9.24}$$

Theorem 9.1 The gross directional distance d_{rs} and the first-order moment of transvariation p_{rs} are:

$$d_{rs} = E_r[YF_s(Y)] + E_s[YF_r(Y)] - E_s(Y), \tag{9.25}$$

$$p_{rs} = E_r[YF_s(Y)] + E_s[YF_r(Y)] - E_r(Y). \tag{9.26}$$

Proof. It follows from (9.20), see also Dagum (1960a, 1980, 1987), that:

$$d_{rs} = \int_0^\infty \left[yF_s(y) - \int_0^y xdF_s(x) \right] dF_r(y) = E_r[YF_s(Y)] - \mu_s \int_0^\infty L_s(y)dF_r(y) \tag{9.27}$$

Integrating the last term in (9.27) by parts, we prove (9.25).

Applying a similar approach to (9.24) we prove (9.26). In (9.25) and (9.26) we have

$$E_s(Y) = \mu_s \text{ and } E_r(Y) = \mu_r.$$

Corollary 9.1 The GMD between the r-th and s-th group income distributions is equal to the summation of the gross directional distance d_{rs} and the first-order moment of transvariation, that is:

$$\Delta_{rs} = d_{rs} + p_{rs} = 2E_r[YF_s(Y)] + 2E_s[YF_r(Y)] - \mu_s - \mu_r. \tag{9.28}$$

Proof. The first equality in (9.28) follows from the definitions (9.19), (9.21) and (9.24). The last member of the equality (9.28) follows from Theorem 9.1, hence from (9.25) and (9.26).

Corollary 9.2 For $\mu_s < \mu_r$ (the case of strict inequality in Definition 9.1), the following inequalities hold:

$$0 \le p_{rs} < d_{rs} \le \Delta_{rs} \tag{9.29}$$

Proof. For any non-degenerated random variable and by Definition 9.6 formalized in (9.21) and Definition 9.7 formalized in (9.24), it follows from Theorem 9.1, equations (9.25) and (9.26), that $p_{rs} \ge 0$, $d_{rs} > 0$ and $d_{rs} > p_{rs}$.

If the two distributions do not overlap, then the r-th distribution is completely to the right of the s-th distribution, hence $E_r[YF_s(Y)] = E_r(Y) = \mu_r$, $E_s[YF_r(Y)] = 0$, then as stated in (9.29), the upper limit of d_{rs} is equal to Δ_{rs}, otherwise, $d_{rs} < \Delta_{rs}$.

Corollary 9.3 If $\mu_r = \mu_s$, the following relationships hold:

$$0 < p_{rs} = d_{rs} = \Delta_{rs}/2. \tag{9.31}$$

Proof. For any two non-degenerated income variables, if $\mu_r = \mu_s$, there are some $X > Y$, hence, by Definition 9.7, eq. (9.24), $p_{rs} > 0$. Applying Theorem 9.1 and Corollary 9.1, the proof is completed.

Corollary 9.4 For $\mu_r > \mu_s$ and $\mu_r \ge \mu_s$, the following inequalities hold:

if $\mu_r > \mu_s$, then $0 \le p_{rs} < \Delta_{rs}/2 < d_{rs} \le \Delta_{rs}$, \hfill (9.32)

if $\mu_r \ge \mu_s$, then $0 \le p_{rs} \le \Delta_{rs}/2 \le d_{rs} \le \Delta_{rs}$. \hfill (9.33)

The proof of Corollary 9.4 follows from Theorem 9.1 and Corollaries 9.1 to 9.3.

Corollary 9.5 The GMD of the r-th group, that is, the GMD *within* the r-th income distribution is:

$$\Delta_{rr} = 2d_{rr} = 2p_{rr} = 4E_r[YF_r(Y)] - 2\mu_r. \tag{9.34}$$

Proof. In this case, $F_r(y)$ and $F_s(y)$ are identical CDFs, hence $\mu_r = \mu_s$. Applying Theorem 9.1, equations (9.25) and (9.26), and Corollaries 9.1 and 9.3, we prove (9.34).

Corollary 9.6 The GMD within the r-th income distribution is equal to four times the covariance between the income variable Y and its CDF $F_r(Y)$, that is:

$$\Delta_{rr} = 4cov\,[Y, F_r(Y)].$$

Proof. Since $E_r[F_r(Y)] = \frac{1}{2}$ and $E_r(Y) = \mu_r$, it follows from Corollary 9.5, equation (9.34), that :

$$\Delta_{rr} = 4\{E_r[F_r(Y)] - \mu_r/2\} = 4cov[Y, F_r(Y)], \tag{9.35}$$

$$d_{rr} = p_{rr} = 2cov[Y,F_r(Y)]. \tag{9.36}$$

For $\mu_r \geq \mu_s$, it follows from Corollary 9.4 that:

$$\Delta_{rs}/2 \leq d_{rs} \leq \Delta_{rs}, \tag{9.37}$$

hence the range of d_{rs} is $[\Delta_{rs}/2, \Delta_{rs}]$, therefore the origin of d_{rs} is $\Delta_{rs}/2$; that is why we call it *gross* directional distance between income distributions. To pass from the *gross* to the *net* directional distance, that is, to have zero as the origin of the *net* DD, we subtract $\Delta_{rs}/2$ from all the terms in (9.37) to obtain the support of the NDD, that is:

$$0 \leq d_{rs} - p_{rs} \leq \Delta_{rs}. \tag{9.38}$$

Therefore, to obtain the net DD we have to subtract from the gross DD d_{rs} the impact of the overlap (transvariation) p_{rs} between the r-th and the s-th distributions.

It follows from (9.38) that the NDD takes its maximum value Δ_{rs} when the two distributions do not overlap, hence, $p_{rs} = 0$; it takes the minimum value of zero when $d_{rs} = p_{rs}$, that is, when $\mu_r = \mu_s$.

It is important to observe that the null hypothesis of no directional affluence of the r-th with respect to the s-th distribution is:

$$H_0: d_{rs} = p_{rs} \Leftrightarrow H_0: \mu_r = \mu_s \tag{9.39}$$

and the alternative hypothesis, that might also include differences in their variances and asymmetries, which is the general case:

$$H_1: d_{rs} > p_{rs} \Leftrightarrow \mu_r > \mu_s. \tag{9.40}$$

If the null hypothesis H_0 is accepted, the preference between the r-th and the s-th income distributions is decided in favor of the one with the smaller Gini ratio. It implies that we choose the distribution presenting the smaller mathematical expectation of the Gini DF. The Gini DF has the exceptional feature that, after multiplying it by the average income, it takes the mathematical form of the second-order stochastic dominance.

If H_1 is accepted, to choose between the r-th and the s-th distributions, we have to take into account the directional distance ratio (DDR), to be introduced in Section 9.5, and the Gini ratio of both distributions, that is, the triplet (DDR, G_r, G_s).

Following Borch (1979), we state the following n-order stochastic dominance theorem.

Theorem 9.2 $F_r(y)$ is preferred to $F_s(y)$ by the principle of the n-order stochastic dominance if the following relation holds for all y, with strict inequality for some y:

$$F_{rn}(y) \leq F_{sn}(y).$$ (9.41)

For $n = 2$ we have the second-order stochastic dominance.

Proof. For any income variable with CDF $F(y)$, with support $(0, \infty)$:

$$F_n(y) = \int_0^y F_{n-1}(x)dx, \; n = 2, 3, \ldots \ldots;$$ (9.42)

$$F_1(y) = F(y), \text{ and } F(0) = 0.$$ (9.43)

Differentiating (9.42) for $n > 1$:

$$dF_n(y)/dy = F_{n-1}(y).$$ (9.44)

Integrating (9.42) by parts and applying (9.43) and (9.44):

$$F_n(y) = [1/(n-1)!] \int_0^y (y-x)^{n-1} dF(x)$$ (9.45)

For $n = 2$, it follows from (9.45):

$$F_2(y) = \int_0^y (y-x)dF(x) = yF(y) - \mu L(y).$$ (9.46)

Hence, the r-th income distribution $F_r(y)$ is preferred, by the second-order stochastic dominance, to the s-th, income distribution $F_s(y)$, if the following relation holds for all y, with strict inequality for some y:

$$F_{r2}(y) \leq F_{s2}(y)$$ (9.47)

Applying (9.46), $yF_r(y) - \mu_r L_r(y) \leq yF_s(y) - \mu_s L_s(y)$, we deduce:

$$F_{r2}(y) - F_{s2}(y) = y[F_r(y) - F_s(y)] - [\mu_r L_r(y) - \mu_s L_s(y)] \leq 0$$ (9.48)

for all y, with strict inequality for some y.

Corollary 9.7 The second-order stochastic dominance between the r-th and the s-th income distributions is a function of their corresponding average incomes μ_r and μ_s, and the Gini disutility functions $V_r[y, F_r(y)]$ and $V_s[y, F_s(y)]$.

Proof. The Gini ratio of the income distribution $F(y)$ is:

$$G = \Delta/(2\mu) = \int_0^\infty \left[\int_0^\infty |y - x| dF(x) \right] dF(y)/(2\mu) = \int_0^\infty \left[\int_0^y (y - x)dF(x) + \right.$$

$$\left. + \int_y^\infty (x - y)dF(x) \right] dF(y)/(2\mu) = \int_0^\infty \left[yF(y) - \mu L(y) \right] dF(y)/\mu$$

$$= \int_0^\infty \left[(y/\mu)F(y) - L(y) \right] dF(y) = E[(y/\mu)F(y) - L(y)] = E[F_2(y)]/\mu, \qquad (9.49)$$

hence:

$$V[y, F(y)] = (y/\mu)F(y) - L(y) = F_2(y)/\mu \qquad (9.50)$$

For the r-th and s-th income distributions, and applying (9.50) and the second-order stochastic dominance derived in (9.46), we obtain (9.48), proving Corollary 9.7.

Corollary 9.8 For the Gini ratio, the Dagum fundamental equation of income (9.1) becomes:

$$y = U[y, F(y)] + F_2(y) = U[y, F(y)] + yF(y) - \mu L(y) \qquad (9.51)$$

and the Gini utility function is:

$$U[y, F(y)] = y[1 - F(y)] + \mu L(y). \qquad (9.52)$$

Proof. Replacing the Gini DF (9.50) into the fundamental equation of income (9.1) we prove (9.51), and from it we derive (9.52).

Corollary 9.9 For any continuous and twice differentiable CDF $F(y)$, with support $[0, \infty)$, the disutility function corresponding to the Gini ratio is a non-negative monotonic increasing and convex function of income, and the Gini utility function is a non-negative monotonic increasing and concave function of income, both with support $[0, \infty)$.

Proof. It follows from (9.50) that:

$$dV/dy = F(y)/\mu > 0, y > 0; \qquad (9.53)$$

$$d^2V/dy^2 = f(y)/\mu > 0, y > 0; \qquad (9.54)$$

$$\lim_{y \to 0} V[y, F(y)] = 0, \quad \lim_{y \to \infty} V[y, F(y)] = \infty \qquad (9.55)$$

For the Gini UF, it follows from (9.52) that:

$$dU[y, F(y)]/dy = 1 - F(y) > 0, y > 0; \tag{9.56}$$

$$d^2U[y, F(y)]/dy^2 = -f(y) < 0, y > 0; \tag{9.57}$$

$$\lim_{y \to 0} U[y, F(y)] = 0, \text{ and } \lim_{y \to \infty} U[y, F(y)] = \infty, \tag{9.58}$$

and Corollary 9.9 is proven.

A popular misconception among econometricians, e.g., Atkinson (1970: 256) and Kakwani (1980, Lemma 5.6: 72) is to sustain that the Gini ratio is more sensitive to transfers to the middle-income classes. This is due to the fact that they ignore the true Gini disutility function (9.50) by considering a transformation of it by taking the ME of the LC in the last term of (9.49) that has destroyed its property. The following theorem demonstrates this erroneous belief.

Theorem 9.3 The Gini ratio is sensitive to all levels of transfers, and given the CDF $F(y)$, its sensitivity is an increasing function of the frequency of economic units between the transferor and the transferred economic units.

Proof. For any continuous and twice differentiable $F(y)$ (assumed only for expository simplification), we derive, (i) from Corollary 9.7, equations (9.49) and (9.50), that the Gini ratio is the mathematical expectation of the disutility function (9.50); and (ii) from Corollary 9.9, the Gini DF $V[y, F(y)]$ is a non-negative monotonic increasing and convex function of income y, therefore, a transfer Δy_j from an economic unit with income y_j to an economic unit with income y_i such that, $y_j - \Delta y_j > y_i$, gives a net decrease of the disutility function. At the limit, when $\Delta y \to 0$:

$$dV[y_i, F(y_i)]/dy_i - dV[y_j, F(y_j)]/dy_j < 0, y_j > y_i, \text{ and} \tag{9.59}$$

$$dG = (dG/dy_j)(-dy_j) + (dG/dy_i)dy_j < 0, \forall dy_j > 0, \tag{9.60}$$

satisfying propositions Proposition 9.1 and Proposition 9.2 advanced in Section 9.2, thus proving the first part of Theorem 9.3.

To prove the second part of Theorem 9.3, let $y_j = y$ and $y_i = y - h$, $h > 0$, and consider an infinitesimal transfer of income from an economic unit with income y to an economic unit with income $y - h$. Hence, it follows from (9.50), (9.53) and (9.59) that:

$$dV[y, F(y)]/dy - dV[y - h, F(y - h)]/dy = [F(y) - F(y - h)]/\mu > 0,$$

proving that the Gini ratio sensitivity is an increasing function of the frequency of economic units between the transferor and the transferred economic units. Furthermore, for any $F(y)$, the maximum sensitivity of G is reached when the transfer is done between the economic units having the largest and the smallest amount of income.

9.5 Directional distance ratio between income distributions

Contrary to the decomposition approach of IIMs, Dagum (1980, 1987) starts with the disaggregation of a population into k groups. He introduces a directional distance ratio (DDR) between each of the $k(k-1)/2$ binary combinations of income distributions *ordered* according to the non-decreasing values of the average income of the k groups (see Definition 9.1, equation (9.14)). The quantitative information of the k income distributions specified in (9.10) is completed with the estimation of the k Gini ratios. Since, in general, income distributions differ in mean, variance and asymmetry, hence in inequality, Dagum tests the null hypothesis that the DDR between a pair of income distributions is equal to zero. If the null is accepted, the preference is given to the group with the smaller Gini ratio; if rejected, the preference is decided as a function of DDR and the Gini ratios. For the case of the r-th and s-th income distributions, Dagum considers the triplet (DDR, G_r, G_s). This approach is highly informative to support the designs of relevant structural socioeconomic policies purporting to reduce income disparities between income distributions and inequalities within groups, for instance, between regions of a country and between genders.

In Section 9.4, Definition 9.5 introduced the *gross* DD d_{rs} between the r-th and s-th income distributions. It is mathematically formalized in (9.21) or (9.23) and solved in Theorem 9.1. Equation (9.38) introduced the *net* DD. Both *gross* and *net* directional distances have the dimension of income. It follows from (9.38) that the support of the *net* DD is the closed interval [0, Δ_{rs}]. To pass from the NDD to the DDR, we divide the NDD (9.38) by its maximum possible value. Hence, the DDR D_{rs} between the r-th and s-th income distributions is:

$$D_{rs} = (d_{rs} - p_{rs})/\Delta_{rs} = (d_{rs} - p_{rs})/(d_{rs} + p_{rs}), \quad D_{rs} \in [0,1] \tag{9.61}$$

It follows from (9.61) that D_{rs} is a dimensionless scalar and takes values in the closed unit interval [0, 1].

$D_{rs} = 0$ implies that $d_{rs} = p_{rs}$, hence $\mu_r = \mu_s$. If they are not mathematically equal to zero but the null hypothesis:

$$H_0: D_{rs} = 0 \tag{9.62}$$

is accepted, one concludes that from a statistical viewpoint both distributions are on average equally affluent. In principle, the preferred distribution is the one with the smaller Gini ratio. Furthermore, according to Corollary 9.7, the final choice should be done according to the second-order stochastic dominance criterion.

The alternative hypothesis is:

$$H_1: D_{rs} > 0. \tag{9.63}$$

A borderline case of H_1 is $D_{rs} = 1$. This limit value is taken when the r-th income distribution lies completely to the right of the s-th distribution, hence these two income distributions do not overlap. In this case, as proved in Corollary 9.2, there is no transvariation and $p_{rs} = 0$. If $D_{rs} \in (0, 1)$, that is, if D_{rs} is strictly positive and less than one for the $k(k-1)/2$ binary combinations of the k groups, the inequalities (9.14) and (9.32) become strict inequalities, therefore:

$$0 < D_{rs} < 1 \Leftrightarrow 0 < p_{rs} < \Delta_{rs}/2 < d_{rs} < \Delta_{rs}. \tag{9.64}$$

To test the null hypothesis (9.62), where the alternative is given by (9.63), Dagum proposes the one-sided Kolmogorov-Smirnov statistic:

$$D^+_{rs} = sup \ [F_s(y) - F_r(y)]. \tag{9.65}$$

Surveys of income and wealth distributions are based on large samples, hence it can be proved that the transformation:

$$4(D^+)^2 n_r n_s /(n_r + n_s) \xrightarrow{d} \chi^2(2) \tag{9.66}$$

converges to a chi-square distribution with two degrees of freedom.

9.6 Gini ratio decomposition

The decomposition of income inequality was first proposed by Theil (1967) who partitioned the total inequality T into: (i) the inequality within groups T_w, and (ii) the inequality between groups T_b. In the same year, Bhattacharya and Mahalanobis (B-M) (1967) proposed a similar two-term Gini ratio decomposition $G = G_w + G_b$.

Contrary to Theil, who mathematically derived the decomposition of total inequality T (although he made a wrong analogy with the one-way analysis of variance), B-M started defining G_b as the contribution to the total Gini ratio of the k groups, average income and derived G_w as the difference $G - G_b$. The limitations of this decomposition go beyond the one already admitted by the authors for the case where at least one pair of income distributions overlaps, which is in fact the norm. Sample surveys of income and wealth distributions have almost zero probability of not overlapping. In effect, what could be defined *ex-ante*, although it would not be a rigorous mathematical approach, is the inequality within the k income distributions; differently the gross inequality between the k groups is defined by the difference $G - G_w$. A very serious objection to both Theil's and B-M's decompositions is that, in order to obtain the contribution of the between-group inequalities, these authors use the *average* income of the k groups. This implies the counterfactual assumption that the k distributions have equal variance and asymmetry, and their shapes differ only in a displacement determined by the difference between their income means.

After B-M's contribution, several authors dealt with the decomposition of the Gini ratio, such as Rao (1969), Pyatt (1976), Silber (1989), Frosini (1990), and Deutsch and Silber (1999).

Dagum (1997a, 1997b, 1997c, 1998) mathematically derived a decomposition of the total Gini ratio G into three additive and properly weighted terms of all pair-wise income distributions under inquiry. Those are, (i) the *inequality within groups* G_w; (ii) the net contribution to G of the *inequality between groups* G_b; and (iii) the *transvariation or overlapping effect between income distributions* G_t. These three components have rigorous economic and statistical interpretations. Furthermore, G, as well as G_w, G_b and G_t are stated as weighted sums of the absolute differences between all binary combinations of incomes. When dealing with G and G_w, all the binary combinations are *within* each distribution, and for G_b and G_t, the binary combinations are *between* income distributions. Moreover, the sum of the weights of G_w, G_b and G_t is equal to one, according to (9.13). Starting with the observed income distribution (9.10) and its partition into k well defined income groups, the total Gini ratio (9.16) becomes:

$$G = \sum_{j=1}^{n} \sum_{i=1}^{n} |y_j - y_i| / (2n^2 \mu) = \sum_{r=1}^{k} \sum_{s=1}^{k} \sum_{j=1}^{n_r} \sum_{i=1}^{n_s} |y_{rj} - y_{si}| / (2n^2 \mu) \qquad (9.67)$$

Taking into account equations (9.11)–(9.13) and the definitions and theorems given in Section 9.4, we have (Dagum 1997a, Theorem 2):

$$G = \sum_{r=1}^{k} \sum_{s=1}^{k} G_{rs} p_r q_s = p(G_{rs}) q' = q(G_{rs}) p' \qquad (9.68)$$

where p' and q' are the transpose of the vectors p and q, and (G_{rs}) is the $k \times k$ symmetric matrix of the G_{rs}, for $r,s = 1, \ldots, k$. It follows from (9.68) that:

$$G = G_w + G_b + G_t, \qquad (9.69)$$

such that, when $r = s$, we have:

$$G_w = \sum_{r=1}^{k} p_r q_r G_{rr} \qquad (9.70)$$

In (9.70), the term $G_{rr} p_r q_r$ is the weighted contribution to G_w of the Gini ratio G_{rr} within the r-th distribution. When $r \ne s$:

$$G_b = \sum_{r=2}^{k} \sum_{s=1}^{r-1} (p_r q_s + p_s q_r)\, D_{rs} G_{rs} \tag{9.71}$$

$$G_t = \sum_{r=2}^{k} \sum_{s=1}^{r-1} (p_r q_s + p_s q_r)(1 - D_{rs}) G_{rs} \tag{9.72}$$

where D_{rs} is the DDR between the r-th and s-th distributions defined in (9.61). The factor $D_{rs} G_{rs}$ gives the net contribution of G_{rs} to G_b, that is, net of the transvariation between these two distributions, and the term $(p_r q_s + p_s q_r) D_{rs} G_{rs}$ is its weighted contribution. On the other hand, in (9.72), $(1 - D_{rs}) G_{rs}$ is the contribution to G_t of the transvariation between these two distributions, hence, $G_b + G_t$ gives the gross contribution to G of the inequality between the binary combinations of the k income distributions.

9.7 Decomposition of the generalized entropy ratio

The GEM, treated as a set of inequality measures, is the outcome of a formal, but not a substantial, analogy with the entropy measures introduced in thermodynamics and in information theory. It takes the form:

$$I_\beta = \int_0^\infty (y/\mu)\left[\left(y/\mu\right)^\beta - 1\right] dF(y)/[\beta(\beta + 1)],\ I_\beta \geq 0,\ \beta\ real \tag{9.73}$$

The inequality measure given in (9.73) is a dimensionless and non-normalized measure (Dagum 1993). In fact, it is the mathematical expectation of the disutility function:

$$V(y) = (y/\mu)[(y/\mu)^\beta - 1]/[\beta(\beta + 1)] \tag{9.74}$$

which depends only on y. Hence, applying (9.1), its corresponding utility function is strictly utilitarian; therefore, it excludes any interpersonal comparison of utilities. Working with a population of n economic units partitioned in k groups as in (9.10), the Riemann-Stieltjes integral (9.73) becomes:

$$I_\beta = (1/n) \sum_{i=1}^{n} (y/\mu)\left[\left(y/\mu\right)^\beta - 1\right]/[\beta(\beta + 1)] \tag{9.75}$$

Three well-known particular cases of (9.75) are:

(i) Theil (1967) inequality ratio:

$$T = \lim_{\beta \to 0} I_\beta = (1/n) \sum_{i=1}^{n} (y_i/\mu) \log(y_i/\mu) \tag{9.76}$$

(ii) Bourguignon (1979) inequality ratio, which was also considered by Theil (1967):

$$B = \lim_{\beta \to -1} I_\beta = -(1/n) \sum_{i=1}^{n} \log(y_i/\mu) = \log \mu - \log M_g \tag{9.77}$$

where M_g stands for the geometric mean.

(iii) Hirschman-Herfindahl (1945, 1950) ratio:

$$H = I_1 = CV(Y)/2 \tag{9.78}$$

where $CV(Y)$ is the Pearson coefficient of variation of the n-order vector given in (9.10). Considering the k groups, it follows from (9.10)–(9.12) and the GEM (9.75):

$$I_\beta = [1/\beta(\beta + 1)](1/n) \sum_{r=1}^{k} \sum_{i=1}^{n_r} (y_{ri}/\mu_r)\left[\left(y_{ri}/\mu_r\right)^\beta - 1\right] = I_{\beta w} + I_{\beta b} \tag{9.79}$$

where:

$$I_{\beta w} = \sum_{r=1}^{k} q_r(\mu_r/\mu)^\beta I_{\beta w_r} \tag{9.80}$$

$$I_{\beta b} = [1/\beta(\beta + 1)] \sum_{r=1}^{k} p_r(\mu_r/\mu)\left[\left(\mu_r/\mu\right)^\beta - 1\right] \tag{9.81}$$

being the $I_{\beta w_r}$ the GEM within the r-th group, that is:

$$I_{\beta w_r} = [1/n_r] \sum_{i=1}^{n_r} (y_{ri}/\mu_r)\left[\left(y_{ri}/\mu_r\right)^\beta - 1\right]/[\beta(\beta + 1)] \tag{9.82}$$

In (9.79), the two-term decomposition of the GEM are the contributions to the total GEM I_β of both inequalities, *within* ($I_{\beta w}$) and *between* ($I_{\beta b}$) the k groups. According to (9.81), the contribution to the total GEM I_β of the inequality between the k income distributions is only the inequality of the k income means ($\mu_1, \ldots, \mu_r, \ldots, \mu_k$). This decomposition is a wrong analogy with the one-way analysis of variance, where the null hypothesis H_0 is that the k income distributions are subsamples from a normal population with identical means and variances; while the alternative hypothesis H_1 is that the subsamples have equal variance but different means from the population.

Moreover, in the one-way analysis of variance, the deviations of the observed incomes with respect to their sample or subsample means are assumed to be normal i.i.d random errors with zero mean, constant variance and non-correlated. These probability distribution assumptions, uncritically adopted from genetic statistics and agricultural experiments, are totally inappropriate for income distributions which, by their own nature, are asymmetric and heavy tailed distributions. Furthermore, the incomes belonging to the poor and the upper one percentile of a population cannot be treated either as random normal deviations from the population mean or as outliers of the distribution.

Further objections to any member of the GEM of inequality are:

(i)   According to (9.74) and applying (9.1), the utility and disutility functions of the entropic set of IIMs are strictly utilitarian.
(ii) For Theil inequality, both utility and disutility functions are not monotonic increasing functions of income. Although the DF is convex, it starts decreasing, reaching a minimum at $y_m = \mu/e$ and then increases. As a consequence of this anomalous behavior, in the interval $(0, \mu/e)$ it contradicts the Pigou-Dalton principle of transfers. Moreover, it gives a wrong sensitivity outcome for any transfer of income from an economic unit with income $y > \mu/e$ to an economic unit with income $y < \mu/e$. For the other cases of the GEM of inequality, at least the DF is not monotonically increasing.
(iii) Although the proposed inequality ratios of entropic origin perform well as global measures of inequality, they lack statistic and socioeconomic foundations. They are the outcome of an unacceptable formal analogy with the concept of entropy as formalized in thermodynamics and information theory. In effect, perfect equality of income corresponds to perfect disorder (maximum entropy) and no information (in information theory). On the other hand, perfect inequality in the distribution of income corresponds to perfect order in entropy theory and to perfect information in information theory. What kind of perfect order is that where in a society of n economic units, one possesses the total mass of income and the remainder $n - 1$ has zero income?
(iv) The decomposition of any member of the GEM of inequality makes the wrong assumptions of the one-way analysis of variance. One consequence is the under-estimation of the between-groups inequality, hence an over-estimation of the within-groups inequality.

It follows from the GEM inequality decomposition (9.80)–(9.82) that:

(i)   The Theil inequality ratios (within and between groups) are the limits of (9.80)–(9.82) when $\beta \to 0$. Hence:

$$T_w = \lim_{\beta \to 0} I_{\beta w} = \sum_{r=1}^{k} q_r \, (1/n_r) \sum_{i=1}^{n_r} (y_{ri}/\mu_r) \log(y_{ri}/\mu_r) = \sum_{r=1}^{k} q_r T_{wr} \qquad (9.83)$$

$$T_{wr} = \lim_{\beta \to 0} I_{\beta wr} = (1/n_r) \sum_{i=1}^{n_r} (y_{ri}/\mu_r) \log(y_{ri}/\mu_r) \tag{9.84}$$

$$T_b = \lim_{\beta \to 0} I_{\beta b} = \sum_{r=1}^{k} p_r (\mu_r/\mu) \log(\mu_r/\mu) \tag{9.85}$$

(ii) The Bourguignon inequality ratios (within and between groups) are the limits of (9.80)–(9.82) when $\beta \to -1$. Therefore:

$$B_w = \lim_{\beta \to -1} I_{\beta w} = \sum_{r=1}^{k} (n_r/n) \log(\mu_r/M_{gr}) = \sum_{r=1}^{k} p_r B_{wr} \tag{9.86}$$

$$= \log M_g (\mu_1, \ldots, \mu_k) - \log M_g (M_{g1}, \ldots, M_{gk})$$

$$B_{wr} = \lim_{\beta \to -1} I_{\beta w_r} = \log \mu_r - \log M_{gr} \tag{9.87}$$

$$B_b = \lim_{\beta \to -1} I_{\beta b} = \sum_{r=1}^{k} p_r \log(\mu/\mu_r) = \log \mu - \log M_g (\mu_1, \ldots, \mu_k) \tag{9.88}$$

(iii) The Hirschman-Herfindahl inequality ratio within and between groups is obtained from (9.80)–(9.82) for $\beta = 1$. Hence:

$$H_w = I_{1w} = \sum_{r=1}^{k} q_r (\mu_r/\mu) H_{wr} \tag{9.89}$$

$$H_{wr} = I_{1wr} = (1/2) CV(Y_r) \tag{9.90}$$

$$H_b = I_{1b} = (1/2) CV(\mu_1, \ldots, \mu_k). \tag{9.91}$$

The symbols M_{gr}, $M_g(M_{g1}, \ldots, M_{gk})$ and $M_g(\mu_1, \ldots, \mu_k)$ in (9.86)–(9.88) stand for the geometric mean of the r-th group, and the geometric means of the k group geometric and arithmetic means, respectively; $CV(Y_r)$ in (9.90) denotes the coefficient of variation of the r-th income distribution, i.e., the coefficient of variation of the n_r-order vector $(y_{r1}, \ldots, y_{rn_r})$; and $CV(\mu_1, \ldots, \mu_k)$ in (9.91) stands for the coefficient of variation of the k income mean vector $(\mu_1, \ldots, \mu_k)$.

9.8 Metric distance and Gini dissimilarity measure

Another common erroneous belief among economists and econometricians is that metric distances have good properties to measure the inequality between income distributions. On the contrary, metric distances provide only a measure of dissimilarity between income distributions and lack informative content, in the sense that conclusions cannot be drawn on the stochastic dominance of one distribution relative to the other. As Chakravarty and

Dutta (1987) pointed out, metric distances do not have power to assess social welfare preferences.

Several attempts have been made in the literature to use metric distances to measure the inequality between income distributions under the conviction that they are more appropriate than the directional distance ratio introduced by Dagum (1980, 1987). The directional distance ratio, however, takes into account not only mean differences but also differences in variance and asymmetry, which are basic characteristics of the inequality between income distributions. The directional distance ratio measures the absolute and relative affluence between binary combinations of income distributions ordered by non-decreasing size of their respective average incomes.

Ebert (1984) proposed the following distance function between the income distributions $F_1(y)$ and $F_2(y)$:

$$d(r; F_1, F_2) = \left[\int_0^1 |y_1(p) - y_2(p)|^r \, dp\right]^{1/r}, r \geq 1 \tag{9.92}$$

The distance function (9.92) is Gini's (1915, 1965) r-order dissimilarity measure. It is the Gini mean of order r, $r \geq 1$, of the absolute values of the difference between the quantiles p, $0 \leq p \leq 1$, of the income distributions F_1 and F_2.

Given its symmetry property, the metric distance (9.92) cannot take into account the asymmetric relation stated in the Dagum directional distance ratio, the relation 'is on average more affluent than'. Indeed, for each quantile p, the integral in (9.92) is the addition of the absolute value $|y_1(p) - y_2(p)|^r$, independently of the affluence relations $y_1(p) > y_2(p)$, or $y_2(p) > y_1(p)$, or $y_1(p) = y_2(p)$.

For $r = 1$, equation (9.92) becomes:

$$d(1; F_1, F_2) = \int_0^1 |y_1(p) - y_2(p)| dp, \tag{9.93}$$

which is equal to the areas between the two CDFs F_1 and F_2, independently of whether F_1 intersects F_2 from above or from below. If they do not intersect, assuming that $F_2(y) \leq F_1(y)$, $y \in (0, \infty)$, with at least one strict inequality, then $F_2(y)$ is preferred to $F_1(y)$ by the first-order stochastic dominance, hence $y_2(p) \geq y_1(p)$, $0 < p < 1$. Furthermore, when $y_2(p) \geq y_1(p)$, we have $d(1; F_1, F_2) = E_2(Y) - E_1(Y) = \mu_2 - \mu_1$. In effect:

$$d(1; F_1, F_2) = \int_0^1 |y_1(p) - y_2(p)| dp = \int_0^\infty y dF_2(y) - \int_0^\infty y dF_1(y)$$

$$= \mu_2 - \mu_1 > 0 \tag{9.94}$$

Figure 9.1 illustrates a hypothetical case of two CDFs $F_1(y)$ and $F_2(y)$ with equal income mean and three intersecting points at $y(p_1)$, $y(p_2)$ and $y(p_3)$. In this case:

$$d(1; F_1, F_2, \mu_1 = \mu_2 = \mu) = 2\mu[L_2(p_1) - L_1(p_1) - L_2(p_2) + L_1(p_2) \\ + L_2(p_3) - L_1(p_3)] > 0 \tag{9.95}$$

which is the algebraic addition of twice the incomplete first-order moment distribution. Equation (9.95) is equal to the addition of the areas enclosed between the two distributions (see Figure 9.1) which is a proportion of the income mean μ. It is nothing but a measure of dissimilarity between F_1 and F_2.

For $\mu_2 \geq \mu_1$, it can be proved that $max\ d(1; F_1, F_2, \mu_2 \geq \mu_1) = \mu_2$, which occurs when the Gini ratio $G_1 = G[F_1(y)] = 1$, and $0 \leq G_2 < 1$.

9.9 A case study: Italian income distribution by regions for year 2000

Making use of the magnetic tape of the Italian Sample Survey of Income and Wealth for the year 2000, we partition the population of households into the following three regions: South (and Islands), Center, and North, to which we attach the subscript $r = 1, 2$, and 3, respectively. When it applies, we also estimate the values for the whole country.

Table 9.1 shows the values of the Dagum directional distance ratio jointly with those of the Gini, Theil, Bourguignon and Hirschman-Herfindahl inequality ratios, and their respective decompositions.

The first five rows present the following household information for each

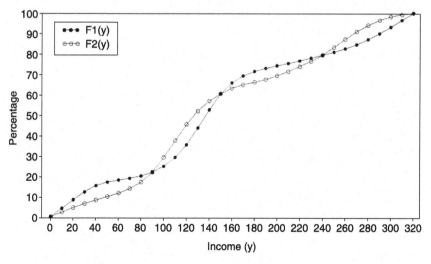

Figure 9.1 Two hypothetical CDFs with equal income mean and three intersection points

Table 9.1 2000 Italian household income distribution by region: directional distance ratio (DDR) between regions, and decomposition of Gini's, Theil's, Bourguignon's, and Hirschman-Herfindhal's indices

Directional distance ratio and decomposition	Region			Italy
	$r = 1$: *South*	$r = 2$: *Center*	$r = 3$: *North*	*Total*
1. Sample size: n_r	$n_1 = 2805$	$n_2 = 1618$	$n_3 = 3535$	$n = 7958$
2. Income mean: μ_r (in Euro)	$\mu_1 = 20984$	$\mu_2 = 28460$	$\mu_3 = 31871$	$\mu = 27340$
3. Population share: p_r	$p_1 = 0.353$	$p_2 = 0.203$	$p_3 = 0.444$	$\Sigma p_r = 1$
4. Income share: q_r	$q_1 = 0.270$	$q_2 = 0.212$	$q_3 = 0.518$	$\Sigma q_r = 1$
5. Goemetric mean: M_{gr} (in Euro)	$M_{g1} = 16459$	$M_{g2} = 23762$	$M_{g3} = 25927$	$M_g = 21702$
6. DDR: D_{rs}	$D_{12} = 0.416$	$D_{23} = 0.170$	$D_{13} = 0.532$	
7. Gini's ratio within: $G_{wr} = G_{rr}$	$G_{w1} = 0.368$	$G_{w2} = 0.319$	$G_{w3} = 0.339$	$G = 0.357$
8. Weighted Gini's ratio within: $p_r q_r G_{rr}$	0.035	0.014	0.078	$G_w = 0.127$
9. Gini's ratio between: G_{rs}	$G_{12} = 0.363$	$G_{23} = 0.332$	$G_{13} = 0.387$	
10. Net weighted contribution of row 9: $G_{brs} = (p_r q_s + p_s q_r) D_{rs} G_{rs}$	$G_{b12} = 0.011$	$G_{b23} = 0.020$	$G_{b13} = 0.062$	$G_b = 0.093$
11. Transvariation (between) G_{trs}	$G_{t12} = 0.027$	$G_{t23} = 0.055$	$G_{t13} = 0.055$	$G_t = 0.137$
12. Theil's ratio within: T_{wr}	$T_{w1} = 0.236$	$T_{w2} = 0.183$	$T_{w3} = 0.206$	$T = 0.225$
13. Weighted Theil's ratio within: $q_r T_{wr}$	0.064	0.039	0.106	$T_w = 0.209$
14. Unweighted Theil's ratio between: T_{br}	−0.204	0.039	0.178	
15. Weighted Theil's ratio between: $p_r(\mu_r/\mu)\log(\mu_r/\mu)$	−0.072	0.008	0.079	$T_b = 0.016$
16. Bourguignon's ratio within: $I_{-1wr} = \log(\mu_r/M_{gr})$	$I_{-1w1} = 0.243$	$I_{-1w2} = 0.180$	$I_{-1w3} = 0.206$	$I_{-1} = 0.231$
17. Weighted Bourguignon's ratio within: $p_r I_{-1wr} = p_r \log(\mu_r/M_{gr})$	0.085	0.037	0.092	$I_{-1w} = 0.214$
18. Unweighted Bourguignon's ratio between: $I_{-1br} = \log(\mu/\mu_r)$	0.265	−0.040	−0.153	
19. Weighted Bourguignon's ratio between: $p_r \log(\mu/\mu_r)$	0.093	−0.008	−0.068	$I_{-1b} = 0.017$
20. Hirshman-Herfindhal ratio within: $I_{1wr} = (1/2)CV(Y_r)$	$I_{1w1} = 0.320$	$I_{1w2} = 0.257$	$I_{1w3} = 0.291$	$I_1 = 0.315$
21. Weighted Hirshman-Herfindhal's ratio within: $q_r(\mu_r/\mu)I_{1wr}$	0.067	0.057	0.175	$I_{1w} = 0.299$
22. Unweighted Hirshman-Herfindhal's ratio between: $I_{1br} = [1/(2\mu^2)]\mu_r(\mu_r-\mu)$	−0.089	0.021	0.097	
23. Weighted Hirshman-Herfindhal's ratio between: $1/2q_r[(\mu_r/\mu) - 1)]$	−0.031	0.004	0.043	$I_{1b} = 0.016$

region and the total for Italy: (i) sample size (n_r), (ii) arithmetic mean (μ_r) in euro, (iii) population share (p_r), (iv) income share (q_r), and (v) geometric mean (M_{gr}) in euro. It follows from rows 1 to 7, 12, 16 and 20 that the South is the poorest region of Italy. Its relative poverty is compounded by having the highest income inequality.

Row 6 gives the estimates of the Dagum DDR between binary combinations of income distributions by regions. According to Definition 9.1, equation (9.14), these are ordered by increased values of the region income means.

It is apparent that, relative to the South, the Center (D_{12}) and the North (D_{13}) present statistically significant larger DDR's. Moreover, the income distribution of the South is more unequal than that of the other two regions. Considering jointly G_{rr}, G_{ss}, and D_{rs} we conclude that the income distributions of the North and the Central Regions dominate the one from the South. Although $D_{23} = 0.17$ between the Center and the North is rather small and $G_{22} < G_{33}$, it follows from the triplet $(G_{22}, G_{33}, D_{23}) = (0.319, 0.339, 0.17)$ that the North is more affluent and more unequal than the Center. In order to make a social welfare choice between the income distributions of the Center and the North further analysis is needed to assess whether this inequality difference by which the Center is to be preferred to the North really dominates or, in fact, is dominated by the difference in economic affluence that makes the North preferred to the Center.

The information provided by DDR and G (rows 6 and 7) enables the design of an economic policy of structural change with the scope of building a socioeconomic structure capable of generating processes of economic growth and social equity. On the contrary, the decomposition of the entropy measures of inequality does not offer any information to support this type of structural economic policy. Instead, the Dagum decomposition of the Gini ratio is much more informative, because it considers the relative economic affluence and the transvariation between each binary combination of income distributions. In fact, it follows from rows 7, 8, 10 and 11 of the last column of Table 1, that the total Gini ratio for Italy is $G = 0.357$, and the contribution to this total G of (i) the inequalities within regions is $G_w = 0.127$, (ii) the net inequality between regions is $G_b = 0.093$, and (iii) the transvariation is $G_t = 0.137$. It can be observed that the contributions of the inequality and transvariation of the binary combination of regions are positive and present very acceptable levels. The addition of these two contributions, that is, the gross contribution to the total G of the inequality between regions is $G_b + G_t = 0.230$, showing its weight.

Rows 12 to 15 give the Theil ratio for Italy and its decomposition by region; rows 16 to 19 give the same information for the Bourguignon ratio, and rows 20 to 23 for the Hirschman-Herfindahl ratio.

An unacceptable shortcoming of all the variants belonging to the generalized entropy measure of inequality between income distributions, as it can be verified by (9.81), and in Table 9.1, for Theil (row 14), Bourguignon (row 18) and Hirschman-Herfindahl (row 22), is that what is called the contribution between regions is a function only of the income means. To compound this shortcoming, equation (9.81) tells us that, when $\beta \geq 0$, as in the cases of Theil (row 14) and Hirschman-Herfindahl (row 22) ratios, the regions with mean incomes smaller than the mean income of the total population give negative values. This means that the poorer income groups contribute to reduce the inequality between income distributions (see the South region in Table 9.1). On the other hand, if $\beta < 0$, as for the Bourguignon ratio (row 18), unacceptable negative values are shown for the regions with mean incomes greater than the mean income of Italy.

9.10 Conclusion

This research introduced a fundamental equation of income specified and analyzed by Dagum (1990, 1993, 1998) and three propositions from which, given the mean income of a distribution, it is proved the dual relationship between SWF and IIM, and between UF and DF.

The fundamental equation of income derived for the Gini ratio proves that the Gini utility and disutility functions admit interpersonal comparisons of utilities and disutilities. On the other hand, all the members belonging to the GEM inequality are shown to have utility and disutility functions which are strictly utilitarian, hence they exclude any interpersonal comparisons of utilities and disutilities. Furthermore, the Gini UF and DF have a correct pattern for they are non-negative and strictly increasing functions (concave for the UF and convex for the DF). On the other hand, the DFs of all the members of GEM reveal a wrong depiction for they start decreasing, reach a minimum, and then increase. This wrong pattern of the DFs of entropic origin accounts for the misleading notion that the GEM inequality is more sensitivity to transfers of income to the poorest economic units. Conversely, the Gini ratio is sensitive to transfers to all levels of income. Moreover, we proved that the Gini ratio sensitivity is an increasing function of the frequency of economic units belonging to the income interval between the transferor and the transferred economic units, reaching its maximum when the transfer takes place between the richest and the poorest economic units.

This study also discussed in extent the Dagum DDR, and the decompositions of the Gini and GEM ratios. It is cogently argued that decomposing the Gini ratio into three terms provides excellent information on the contributions of the within-and between-group inequalities, and the transvariation of the pair-wise comparison of income distributions. On the other hand, the members of GEM as measures of inequality have very serious shortcomings, particularly when we derive the inequality between income distributions. Concerning the property of metric distances as substitutes of the directional distance ratio to measure the inequality between income distributions, we have shown that the former lack informative content and are simple dissimilarity measures. They do not have the power to assess the dominance of an income distribution relative to the other. Instead, the DDR and the Gini ratio decomposition contain useful information for the design of structural economic policies that will be able to generate socioeconomic processes of economic growth with social justice, while, for policy design, the GEM decomposition and the metric distances between income distributions are void of useful and relevant information. These observations are corroborated by the case study of the Italian income distribution by region, for year 2000, as discussed in Section 9.9 and summarized in Table 9.1.

References

Atkinson, A.B. (1970). 'On the measurement of inequality', *Journal of Economic Theory*, 2, 244–263.

Bentham, J. (1789). 'Introduction to the principles of morals and legislation', *The works of Jeremy Bentham*, 1, New York, Russel and Russel, Inc., 1962.

Bernoulli, D. (1738, [1954]). 'Exposition of a new theory of the measurement of risk', English translation, *Econometrica*, 1954, 22, 23–26.

Bhattacharya, N. and Mahalanobis, B. (1967). 'Regional disparities in household consumption in India', *Journal of the American Statistical Association*, 62, 143–161.

Borch, K. (1979). 'Utility and stochastic dominance', in *Expected Utility Hypotheses and the Allais Paradox,* M. Allais and O. Hagen, eds. Reidel Publishing, Dordrecht (Holland)–Boston (U.S.A.), 193–201.

Bourguignon, F. (1979). 'Decomposable income inequality measures', *Econometrica*, 47, 901–920.

Cantillon, R. (1755). *Essai sur la nature du commerce en général.* Reprinted for Harvard University, Boston, 1892.

Chakravarty, S.R. and Dutta, B. (1987). 'A note on measures of distance between income distributions', *Journal of Economic Theory*, 41, 185–188.

Dagum, C. (1960a). *Teoría de la Transvariación, sus Aplicaciones a la Economía,* Metron, University of Rome.

Dagum, C. (1960b). 'Transvariación entre más de dos distribuciones', *Studi in Onore di Corrado Gini,* Istituto di Statistica, Università di Roma, Vol. 1, Roma, 1960, 53–92.

Dagum, C. (1961). 'Transvariación en la hipotesis de variables alearorias normales multidimensionales', *Proceedings of the International Statistics Institute,* XXXVIII, Tokyo, 4, 473–486.

Dagum, C. (1977). 'A new model of personal income distribution: specification and estimation', *Economie Appliquée*, Paris, Tome XXX, (3), 413–437.

Dagum, C. (1978). 'A measure of inequality between income distributions', *Economie Appliquée*, XXX (3–4), 401–413.

Dagum, C. (1980). 'Inequality measures between income distributions', *Econometrica*, 48, 1971–1803.

Dagum, C. (1987). 'Measuring the economic affluence between populations of income receivers', *Journal of Business and Economic Statistics, American Statistical Association*, 5, 5–12.

Dagum, C. (1990). 'On the relationship between income inequality measures and social welfare functions', *Journal of Econometrics*, 43, 91–102.

Dagum, C. (1993). 'The social welfare bases of Gini and other income inequality measures', *Statistica*, LII, 3–30.

Dagum, C. (1994). 'Human capital, income and wealth distribution models with applications', *Proceedings of the Business and Economics Statistics Section, American Statistical Association*, 154th Meeting, 1994, 253–258.

Dagum, C. (1995). 'Income inequality measures and social welfare functions: a unified approach', in *Income Distribution, Social Welfare, Inequality and Poverty*, Vol. I, C. Dagum and A. Lemmi, eds. JAI Press, Greenwich (Connecticut), 177–199.

Dagum, C. (1997a). 'A new approach to the decomposition of the Gini income inequality ratio', *Empirical Economics*, 22, 515–531.

Dagum, C. (1997b). 'Scomposizione ed interpretazione delle misure di disuguaglianza di Gini e di entropia generalizzata', *Statistica*, LVII, 295–308.

Dagum, C. (1997c). 'Decomposition and interpretation of Gini and the generalized entropy inequality measures', *Proceedings of the American Statistical Association, Business and Economic Statistics Section*, 129–134.

Dagum, C. (1998). 'Fondements de bien-être social et décomposition des mesures d'inégalité dans la répartition du revenu', Tenth Invited Lecture in Memory of Françis Perroux, Collège de France, *Economie Appliquée*, LI, 151–202.

Dagum, C. (1999a). 'Linking the functional and personal distribution of income', in *Handbook of Income Inequality Measurement*, Jacques Silber, ed., Kluwer Academic Publishing, Hingham (MA), 1999, 101–128.

Dagum, C. (1999b). 'A study on the distributions of income, wealth, and human capital', Conférence Luigi Solari 1996, Département d'Econométrie, Université de Genève, *Revue européenne des sciences sociales*, Tome XXVII, n.113, 1999, 231–268.

Dagum, C. (2004). 'Specification and analysis of wealth distribution models with applications', paper presented at the American Statistical Association, Business and Economic Statistics Section, Toronto, August 8–12, 2004. *2004 Proceedings of the Joint Statistical Meetings – Business and Economic Statistics Section*, 1116–1123.

Dagum, C. (2005a). 'Income and wealth distributions, Dagum system of', in *Encyclopedia of Statistical Sciences*, Second edition, S. Kotz, N. Balakrishnan, C. Read and B. Vidakovic, Editors-in-Chief, J. Wiley, New York.

Dagum, C. (2005b). 'Income inequality measures', in *Encyclopedia of Statistical Sciences*, Second edition, S. Kotz, N. Balakrishnan, C. Read and B. Vidakovic, Editors-in-Chief, J. Wiley, New York.

Dagum, C. and Costa, M. (2004). 'Analysis and measurement of poverty. Univariate and multivariate approaches and their policy implications. A case study; Italy', in *Household Behaviour, Equivalence Scales, Welfare and Poverty*, C. Dagum and G. Ferrari, eds. Springer-Physica, Heidelberg and New York, 221–271.

Dagum, C. and Slottje, D.J. (2000): 'A new method to estimate the level and distribution of the household Human Capital with Applications', *Journal of Structural Change and Economic Dynamics*, Vol.11, 2000, 67–94.

Dagum, C. and Vittadini, G. (1996). 'Human capital measurement and distribution', *Proceedings of the Business and Economic Statistics Section, American Statistical Association*, 156th Meeting, 194–199.

Dagum, C., Gambassi, R. and Lemmi A. (1992). 'New approaches to the measurement of poverty', in *Poverty Measurement for Economies in Transition in Eastern European Countries*, Warsaw: Polish Statistical Association and Central Statistical Office, 1992, 201–225.

Dagum, C., Vittadini, G., Lovaglio, P.G. and Costa, M. (2003). 'A microeconomic recursive model of human capital, income and wealth determination: specification and estimation', paper presented at the American Statistical Association, Business and Economic Statistics Section, San Francisco, August 3–7, 2003. *2003 Proceedings of the American Statistical Association, Business and Economic Statistics Section*, 1119–1126.

Deutsch, J. and Silber, J. (1999). 'On some implications of Dagum's interpretation of the decomposition of the Gini index by population subgroups', in *Advances in Econometrics, Income Distribution and Scientific Methodology, Essays in Honor of Camilo Dagum*, D.J. Slottje, ed. Physica-Verlag, Berlin, New York, 269–291.

Ebert, U. (1984). 'Measures of distance between income distributions', *Journal of Economic Theory*, 32, 266–274.

Frosini, B.V. (1990). 'Ordinal decomposition of inequality measures in case of Dagum distributions', in *Income and Wealth Distribution, Inequality and Poverty*, C. Dagum and M. Zenga, eds. Springer-Verlag, Berlin and New York, 215–227.

Gini, C. (1909). 'Il diverso accrescimento delle classi sociali e la concentrazione della ricchezza', *Giornale degli Economisti*, XXXVIII, 69–83.

Gini, C. (1910). 'Indici di concentrazione e di dipendenza', *Atti della Riunione della Società Italiana per il Progresso delle Scienze*, and in C. Gini (1955), 3–120.

Gini, C. (1912). 'Variabilità e mutabilità', *Studio Economicogiuridici*, Università di Cagliari, Anno III, Parte 2°. In C. Gini (1955), 211–382.

Gini, C. (1914, [1955], [2005]). 'Sulla la misura della concentrazione e della variabilità dei caratteri', *Atti del R. Istituto Veneto di Scienze, Lettere e Arti*. Reprinted in C. Gini (1955), pp. 411–459. English version: 'On the measurement of concentration and variability of characters', *Metron*, Vol. LXIII(1), 2005, 3–38.

Gini, C. (1915). 'Di una misura della dissomiglianza tra due gruppi di quantità e delle sue applicazioni allo studio delle relazioni statistiche', *Atti R. Istituto Veneto di Scienze, Lettere ed Arti*, LXXIV.

Gini, C. (1916). 'Il concetto di transvariazione e le sue prime applicazioni', *Giornale degli Economisti e Rivista di Statistica*, and in C. Gini, ed. (1959), 21–44.

Gini, C. (1955). *Memorie di metodologia statistica, I, Variabilità e concentrazione*, Roma: Libreria Eredi Virgilio Veschi.

Gini, C. (1959). *Memorie di metodologia statistica, II, Transvariazione*, Roma: Libreria Goliardica.

Gini, C. (1965). 'La dissomiglianza', *Metron*, 24, 85–215.

Hirschman, A.O. (1945). *National Power and the Structure of Foreign Trade*. University of California Press, Berkeley, and Herfindahl, O.C. (1950), *Concentration in the Steel Industry*. Ph.D. Thesis, Columbia University, New York.

Kakwani, N.C. (1980). *Income Inequality and Poverty. Methods of Estimation and Policy Applications*. Oxford University Press, Oxford.

Pareto, V. (1895). 'La legge della domanda', *Giornale degli Economisti*, 59–68.

Pareto, V. (1896). *Ecrits sur la courbe de la répartition de la richesse*, Œuvres Complètes de Vilfredo Pareto publiées sous la direction de Giovanni Busino, Libraire Droz, 1965, Genève.

Pareto, V. (1897). *Cours d'Economie Politique*. Nouvelle édition publiée sous la direction de G.H. Bousquet et G. Busino, Librairie Droz, 1964, Genève.

Pyatt, G. (1976). 'On the interpretation and disaggregation of Gini coefficients', *The Economic Journal*, 86, 243–254.

Rao, V.M. (1969). 'Two decompositions of concentration ratio', *Journal of the Royal Statistical Society*, CXXXII. A, 418–425.

Ricardo, D. (1817). *Principles of political economy*, New edition by Piero Sraffa: Works and Correspondence of David Ricardo, Cambridge University Press, Cambridge, 1951.

Sen, A.K. (1976). 'Poverty: an ordinal approach to measurement', *Econometrica*, 44, 219–231.

Silber, J. (1989). 'Factor components, population subgroup, and the computation of the Gini index of inequality', *Review of Economics and Statistics*, 71, 107–115.

Theil, H. (1967). *Economics and Information Theory*. North-Holland, Amsterdam.

10 On the Shapley value and the decomposition of inequality by population subgroups with special emphasis on the Gini index

Joseph Deutsch and Jacques Silber

10.1 Introduction

More than twenty-five years ago Shorrocks (1980), analyzing the issue of decomposing inequality by population subgroups when the latter are defined by the age group to which the individuals belong, stressed the fact that 'one interpretation suggests a comparison of total inequality with the amount which would arise if inequality was zero within each age group, but the difference in mean income between age groups remained the same. . . .'. The second 'interpretation suggests a comparison of total inequality with the inequality value which would result if the mean incomes of the age groups were made identical, but inequality within each age group remained unchanged.' Deutsch and Silber (1999) compared these two approaches. Since the inequality index they used was the Gini index and given that the components of the latter (between- and within-groups inequality and over-lapping component) can have more than one definition, depending on how the individual incomes are ranked, Deutsch and Silber (1999) came up with a whole series of between- and within-groups components as well as overlapping terms, although they observed a relatively high correlation between the various definitions, at least on the basis of the data they used.

The purpose of this chapter is to come back to this issue of decomposing inequality by population subgroups but this time an approach is adopted, based on the concept of Shapley value, that allows combining in a systematic way the various possible definitions of the three components of the breakdown of inequality by population subgroups.

The chapter is organized as follows. Section 10.2 summarizes the concept of Shapley value and its application to the decomposition of any index. Section 10.3 applies this Shapley decomposition to the breakdown of the Gini index by population subgroups. Then Section 10.4 shows that the Shapley decomposition allows one also to take into account Shorrocks's (1980) ideas concerning the two possible ways of defining between- and within-groups inequalty. Section 10.5 combines the results of Sections 10.3 and 10.4 and offers a generalized breakdown of the Gini index by population subgroups. Section 10.6 gives an empirical illustration based on Israeli data for the years 1990 and 1998 while concluding comments are given in Section 10.7.

10.2 On the concept of Shapley decomposition[1]

Let an index I be a function of n variables and let I_{TOT} be the value of I when all the n variables are used to compute I. I could, for example, be the R-square of a regression using n explanatory variables, any inequality index depending on n income sources or on n population subgroups.

Now let $I_{I/k^k}(i)$ be the value of the index I when k variables have been dropped so that there are only $(n-k)$ explanatory variables and k is also the rank of variable i among the n possible ranks that variable i may have in the $n!$ sequences corresponding to the $n!$ possible ways of ordering n numbers. We will call $I_{I(k-1)^k}(i)$ the value of the index when only $(k-1)$ variables have been dropped and k is the rank of the variable (i).

Thus $I_{I/1^1}(i)$ gives the value of the index I when this variable is the first one to be dropped. Obviously there are $(n-1)!$ possibilities corresponding to such a case. $I_{I/1^0}(i)$ gives then the value of the index I, when the variable i has the first rank and no variable has been dropped. This is clearly the case when all the variables are included in the computation of the index I.

Similarly $I_{I/2^2}(i)$ corresponds to the $(n-1)$ (cases where the variable i is the second one to be dropped and two variables as a whole have been dropped. Clearly $I_{I/2^2}(i)$ can also take $(n-1)!$ possible values. $I_{I/2^1}(i)$ gives then the value of the index I, assuming only one variable was eliminated and the variable i has the second rank. Here also there are $(n-1)!$ possible cases.

Obviously $I_{I/(n-1)^n}(i)$ corresponds to the $(n-1)!$ cases where the variable i is dropped last and is the only one to be taken into account. If I is an inequality index, it will evidently be equal to zero in such a case. But if it is, for example, the R-square of a regression it would give us the R-square when there is only one explanatory variable, the variable i. Obviously $I_{I/n^n}(i)$ gives the value of the index I when variable i has rank n and n variables have been dropped, a case where I will always be equal to zero by definition since no variable is left.

Let us now compute the contribution $C_j(i)$ of variable i to the index I, assuming this variable i is dropped when it has rank j. Using the previous notations we define $C_j(i)$ as:

$$C_j(i) = (1/n!)\Sigma_{h=1 \text{ to } (n-1)!} [I_{I/(j-1)^j}(i) - I_{I/j^j}(i)]^h \tag{10.1}$$

where the superscript h refers to one of the $(n=1)!$ cases where the variable i has rank j. The overall contribution of variable i to the index I may then be defined as:

$$C(i) = (1/n!)\Sigma_{k=1 \text{ to } n} C_k(i) \tag{10.2}$$

It is then easy to prove that:

$$I = (1/n!)\Sigma_{i=1 \text{ to } n} C(i) \tag{10.3}$$

10.3 The Shapley decomposition and the respective contribution of ranks and income shares in the traditional decomposition of the Gini index

Numerous definitions of the Gini index have appeared in the literature (see Yitzhaki 1998) among which some clearly emphasize the fact that ranks play a role in the definition of the Gini Index. Such an approach has, for example, been proposed by Berrebi and Silber (1987) who defined the Gini index I_G as:

$$I_G = \Sigma_{i=1 \text{ to } n}((n - 2i + 1)/n)s_i \tag{10.4}$$

where s_i is the share of individual i who earns an income y_i in the total income of the population, assuming that $y_1 \geq \ldots y_i \geq \ldots \geq y_n$ and n is the size of the population.

Silber (1989) has however proven that equation (10.4) could also be expressed as:

$$I_G = e' G s \tag{10.5}$$

where e' is a row vector of individual population shares all equal to $(1/n)$, s is a column vector of individual income shares ranked by decreasing income values y_i while G is a square matrix called G-matrix whose typical element g_{hk} is equal to 1 if $h>k$, to -1 if $k>h$ and to 0 if $h=k$.

Let us now assume that the population is divided into population subgroups. More precisely we will suppose that each individual i among the n individuals belongs to a subgroup k. Let y_{ki} now be the income of such an individual i who belongs to a subgroup k. Assuming there are n_k individuals in each subgroup k, the overall Gini index I_G may be expressed as a function:

$$I_G = I_G(y_{1l}, \ldots, y_{l,nl}, \ldots, y_{kl}, \ldots, y_{k,nk}, \ldots, y_{Kl}, \ldots, y_{K,nK}) \tag{10.6}$$

where y_{hj} refers to the income of individual j who belongs to group h, n_h is the total size of group j and K is the total number of groups distinguished.

In computing this Gini index it is usually assumed that the mean average incomes y_{mk} of the various groups are different (though some of them may be equal) and that within each subgroup k the n_k individual incomes are different (though some of them may be equal).

To derive the respective contribution of ranks and income shares to the value of the Gini index we will assume that the states of reference, in applying the so-called Shapley decomposition (see Shorrocks 1999 and Sastre and Trannoy 2002 for more details), are as follows. For the impact of the rank, the rank a given individual i has when incomes are ranked by decreasing values, assuming one ignores that he/she belongs to a given group k, is compared with the rank he/she would have if the individuals were first classified by decreasing values of the average income of the group to which they belong, and second, within each group, by decreasing individual income (see Silber 1989 for more details on such a distinction). Similarly we compare the income share s_i of a given individual i with what would be his/her income share if he/she earned the average income of the group to which he/she belongs. Equations (10.4) to (10.6) that refer to the overall Gini index may therefore be also expressed as:

$$I_G = I_G(r_{\text{indiv}} \neq r_{\text{group}}; s_{\text{indiv}} \neq s_{\text{group}}) \tag{10.7}$$

where r and s refer to the rank and the income share of the individuals. Note that in equation (10.7) the indication $(r_{\text{indiv}} \neq r_{\text{group}}; s_{\text{indiv}} \neq s_{\text{group}})$ refers to the case where the computation of the Gini index is based only on the individual ranks and incomes and no account is taken of the group to which the individuals belong. On the contrary $(s_{\text{indiv}} = s_{\text{group}})$ would refer to the case where each individual is assumed to earn the average income of the group to which he/she belongs while $(r_{\text{indiv}} = r_{\text{group}})$ would refer to the case where individuals are first ranked by decreasing values of the average incomes of the groups, then within each group by decreasing individual income, as explained above.

Using the rules of the so-called Shapley decomposition, we may then express the respective contributions C_r of the ranks and C_s of the income shares as:

$$C_r = (1/2)\{[I_G(r_{\text{indiv}} \neq r_{\text{group}}; s_{\text{indiv}} \neq s_{\text{group}}) - I_G(r_{\text{indiv}} = r_{\text{group}}; s_{\text{indiv}} \neq s_{\text{group}})]$$
$$+ I_G(r_{\text{indiv}} \neq r_{\text{group}}; s_{\text{indiv}} = s_{\text{group}})\} \tag{10.8}$$

$$C_s = (1/2)\{[I_G(r_{\text{indiv}} \neq r_{\text{group}}; s_{\text{indiv}} \neq s_{\text{group}}) - I_G(r_{\text{indiv}} \neq r_{\text{group}}; s_{\text{indiv}} = s_{\text{group}})]$$
$$+ I_G(r_{\text{indiv}} = r_{\text{group}}; s_{\text{indiv}} \neq s_{\text{group}})\} \tag{10.9}$$

Note that in (10.8) and (10.9) the expression $I_G(r_{\text{indiv}} \neq r_{\text{group}}; s_{\text{indiv}} \neq s_{\text{group}})$ refers to the case where the Gini index is estimated on the basis of individual ranks and income shares. In other words, in such an expression the income shares in (10.5) are the individual income shares s_i ranked by decreasing values of the individual incomes y_i.

On the contrary $I_G(r_{\text{indiv}} \neq r_{\text{group}}; s_{\text{indiv}} = s_{\text{group}})$ corresponds to the case where the typical elements of the vector s in (10.5) are the income shares individuals would have if they earned the average income of the group to which they belong but these shares are ranked by decreasing individual incomes. In other words, the ranking of the individuals in computing $I_G(r_{\text{indiv}} \neq r_{\text{group}}; s_{\text{indiv}} =$

s_{group}) is the same as that used in computing the regular Gini index I_G ($r_{\text{indiv}} \neq r_{\text{group}}$; $s_{\text{indiv}} \neq s_{\text{group}}$). This index I_G ($r_{\text{indiv}} \neq r_{\text{group}}$; $s_{\text{indiv}} = s_{\text{group}}$) corresponds in fact to what Yitzhaki (1987) and Yitzhaki and Lerman (1991) have defined as the between-groups Gini index (see Deutsch and Silber 1999) and which will be henceforth labelled as $I_{\text{BETWEEN YITZHAKI}}$.

Finally I_G ($r_{\text{indiv}} = r_{\text{group}}$; $s_{\text{indiv}} \neq s_{\text{group}}$) corresponds to the sum of the between- and within-groups Gini indices as they are usually estimated (see Bhattacharya and Mahalanobis 1967 and Silber 1989), two expressions that will be henceforth labelled as $I_{\text{BETWEEN TRADITIONAL}}$ and $I_{\text{WITHIN TRADITIONAL}}$. Here the income shares defining the vector s in (10.5) are given by the individual incomes y_i and these shares s_i are ranked first by decreasing average incomes of the groups, and second within each group by decreasing individual income (see Silber 1989). We may therefore write (10.8) and (10.9) also as:

$$C_r = (1/2)\{[I_{\text{G, TOT}} - (I_{\text{G,BETWEEN TRADITIONAL}} + I_{\text{G,WITHIN TRADITIONAL}})]$$
$$+ I_{\text{G,BETWEEN YITZHAKI}}\} \qquad (10.10)$$

$$C_S = (1/2)\{[I_{\text{G,TOT}} - I_{\text{G,BETWEEN YITZHAKI}}] + [I_{\text{G,WITHIN TRADITIONAL}}$$
$$+ I_{\text{G,BETWEEN TRADITIONAL}}]\} \qquad (10.11)$$

But $[I_{\text{G,TOT}} - (I_{\text{G,BETWEEN TRADITIONAL}} + I_{\text{G,WITHIN TRADITIONAL}})]$ in (10.10) is by definition equal to the overlap $I_{\text{G, OVERLAP TRADITIONAL}}$ between the income distributions of the various groups (see Deutsch and Silber 1989) while $[I_{\text{G,TOT}} - I_{\text{G,BETWEEN YITZHAKI}}]$ in (10.11) corresponds to Yitzhaki and Lerman's (1991) within-groups Gini index denoted as $I_{\text{G,WITHIN YITZHAKI}}$. We may therefore also express the contribution C_r of the ranks as:

$$C_r = (1/2) \{I_{\text{G,OVERLAP TRADITIONAL}} + I_{\text{G,BETWEEN YITZHAKI}}\} \qquad (10.12)$$

Note that $I_{\text{G,BETWEEN YITZHAKI}}$ in expressions (10.11) to (10.12) reflects also the fact that there is overlap between the various income distributions.

Similarly the contribution C_S of the shares will be finally expressed as:

$$C_S = (1/2)\{[I_{\text{G,WITHIN YITZHAKI}}] + [I_{\text{G,WITHIN TRADITIONAL}}$$
$$+ I_{\text{G,BETWEEN TRADITIONAL}}]\} \qquad (10.13)$$

Finally note also that, in combining (10.12) and (10.13), we end up, as expected, with:

$$C_r + C_s = (1/2)[I_{\text{BETWEEN YITZHAKI}} + I_{\text{WITHIN YITZHAKI}}]$$
$$+ (1/2) [I_{\text{BETWEEN TRADITIONAL}} + I_{\text{WITHIN TRADITIONAL}} + I_{\text{G,OVERLAP TRADITIONAL}}]$$
$$C_r + C_s = (1/2)(I_{\text{G,TOTAL}} + I_{\text{G,TOTAL}}) = I_{\text{G,TOTAL}} \qquad (10.14)$$

10.4 The Shapley value and the decomposition of inequality by population subgroups

In the previous section we have shown that there are two possible decompositions by population subgroups of the Gini index, depending on how one ranks the individuals. In both cases, however, we have assumed that the between-groups decomposition is a residual, that is, it is the Gini index one obtains once the within inequality has disappeared. As emphasized by Shorrocks (1980) and analyzed at length by Deutsch and Silber (1999), it is, however, possible to imagine that the residual would be the within-groups inequality, the inequality that remains once the between-groups inequality has been eliminated. The present section will show that the Shapley decomposition allows one in fact to take both possibilities into account. For the sake of simplicity we present the results at this stage without referring to a specific inequality index.

Let us assume a population of N individuals where each individual i belongs to a given population subgroup k. Let y_{ki} be the income of such an individual i who belongs to a subgroup k. Assuming there are n_k individuals in each subgroup k, the overall income inequality I in this population may be expressed (see expression (10.6)) as:

$$I = I(y_{1,1}, \ldots, y_{l,nl}, \ldots, y_{k,1}, \ldots, y_{k,nk}, \ldots, y_{K,1}, \ldots, y_{K,nK}) \qquad (10.15)$$

In computing such an inequality we usually suppose that the mean average incomes y_{mk} of the various K groups are different (though some of them may be equal) and that within each subgroup k the n_k individual incomes are different (though some of them may be equal).

As mentioned previously and indicated in Shorrocks (1980) and Deutsch and Silber (1999), the breakdown of this overall inequality I may take two forms. Either we assume that the between-groups inequality is the one that is observed when there is no within-groups inequality or we suppose that the within-groups inequality is the inequality that remains when there is no between-groups inequality. It all depends, evidently, on which type of inequality is considered as a residual. The Shapley decomposition procedure allows one, however, to estimate the contribution of the between- and within-groups inequality to the overall inequality in a way that takes into account simultaneously both possibilities. To understand this we will assume that the terms of reference, in applying this Shapley decomposition, are as follows: for the between-groups inequality the groups' mean incomes are compared with the overall mean income in the population while for the within-groups inequality the individual incomes are compared with the mean income of the group to which they belong. Equation (10.15) which refers to the overall inequality may therefore also be expressed as:

$$I = I(y_{mk} \neq y_m; y_{ik} \neq y_{mk}) \qquad (10.16)$$

where y_m refers to the mean income in the total population.

The contribution C_{BET} of the between-groups inequality to the overall inequality I may therefore be expressed, applying the Shapley decomposition rules (see Section 10.2 above, as well as Shorrocks 1999 and Sastre and Trannoy 2002), as:

$$C_{BET} = (1/2) \{[I(y_{mk} \neq y_m; y_{ik} \neq y_{mk}) - I(y_{mk} = y_m; y_{ik} \neq y_{mk})] \tag{10.17}$$
$$+ I(y_{mk} \neq y_m; y_{ik} = y_{mk})\}$$

Similarly the contribution C_{WITH} of the within-groups inequality will be expressed as

$$C_{WITH} = (1/2)\{[I(y_{mk} \neq y_m; y_{ik} \neq y_{mk}) - I(y_{mk} \neq y_m; y_{ik} = y_{mk})]$$
$$+ I(y_{mk} = y_m; y_{ik} \neq y_{mk})\} \tag{10.18}$$

Note first that $I(y_{mk} \neq y_m; y_{ik} \neq y_{mk})$ refers in fact to the total inequality I_{TOT} computed on the basis of individual incomes and ignores the group to which the individuals belong. Second, one may observe that $I(y_{mk} \neq y_m; y_{ik} = y_{mk})$ refers to the traditional definition $I_{\text{Between, Between residual}}$ of the between-groups inequality that assumes that the between-groups inequality is the residual inequality, that is, the one that remains when there is no within-groups inequality.

Finally it is easy to understand that the inequality $I(y_{mk} = y_m; y_{ik} \neq y_{mk})$ corresponds to a definition $I_{\text{Within, Within residual}}$ of the within-groups inequality that assumes that the within-groups inequality is the one observed once the between-groups inequality has been eliminated. But the elimination of the latter assumes in fact that the mean incomes of all groups are identical, that is that all individual incomes have been multiplied by the ratio of the overall mean income in the population over the mean income of the group to which the individual belongs (see Deutsch and Silber 1999). In other words $I_{\text{Within, Within residual}}$ may be also expressed as:

$$I_{\text{Within, Within residual}} = I[y_{ll}(y_m/y_{ml}), \ldots, y_{l,nl}(y_m/y_{ml}),, y_{lk}\, (y_m/y_{mk}),, y_{l,nk}$$
$$(y_m/y_{mk}). .] \tag{10.19}$$

Note that the traditional within-groups inequality $I_{\text{Within, Between residual}}$ is expressed as:

$$I_{\text{Within, Between residual}} = I_{TOT} - I_{\text{Between, Between residual}} = I_{TOT} - I(y_{mk} \neq y_m; y_{ik}$$
$$= y_{mk}) \tag{10.20}$$

Finally the alternative and much less common definition of the between-groups inequality $I_{\text{Between, Within residual}}$ that assumes that the within-groups inequality is defined as a residual, will be expressed as:

$$I_{\text{Between, Within residual}} = I_{TOT} - I_{\text{Within, Within residual}} \tag{10.21}$$

$$= I_{\text{TOT}} - I[y_{1l}(y_m/y_{ml}), \ldots, y_{1,nl}(y_m/y_{ml}), \ldots, y_{1k}\,(y_m/y_{mk}), \ldots, y_{1,nk}\,(y_m/y_{mk}). \ldots]$$

Note that the decomposition of the overall inequality into two components C_{BET} and C_{WITH} given in (10.17) and (10.18) may evidently be applied to any inequality index.

10.5 Combining the two previous results: the Shapley value and the generalized decomposition of the Gini index by population subgroups

Let $G(y_{mk} \neq y_m; y_{ik} \neq y_{mk}; r_{ik} \neq r_{mk})$ refer to the traditional Gini index computed by assuming

- that the average incomes y_{mk} of the population subgroups k are different from the overall mean income y_m in the population
- that the individual incomes y_{ik} within population subgroup k are different from the mean income y_{mk} of this population subgroup
- that the individuals are ranked by decreasing individual income y_{ik}.

Let us also define s as the original vector of income shares $(y_{ik}/\Sigma_i\Sigma_k\,y_{ik})$ ordered by decreasing values and v as the vector of the income shares $(y_{ik}/\Sigma_i\Sigma_k\,y_{ik})$ multiplied by the ratio (y_m/y_{mk}) of the overall (in the whole population) average income over the average income of the group to which individual i belongs.

In other words s may be defined as:

$$s = (1/n)\{(y_{1,1}/y_m), \ldots, (y_{1,nl}/y_m), \ldots, (y_{1,k}/y_m), \ldots, (y_{nk,k}/y_m), \ldots,$$
$$(y_{1,K}/y_m), \ldots, (y_{nK,K}/y_m)\} \tag{10.22}$$

where n is the total number of individuals.

Similarly v is defined as:

$$v = (1/ny_m)\{(y_{1l}(y_m/y_{ml})), \ldots, (y_{nl,l}(y_m/y_{ml})), \ldots, (y_{1,K}(y_m/y_{mK})), \ldots,$$
$$(y_{nK,K}(y_m/y_{mK}))\} \tag{10.23}$$

Note that in (10.23) we have multiplied each income in (10.15) by the ratio (y_m/y_{mk}) of the overall mean income y_m in the population over the mean income y_{mk} of the group to which the individual belongs. Such a transformation will equalize all the mean incomes of the groups so that the between-groups inequality is now nil. In addition the within-groups inequality is not affected since each income in a given group is multiplied by a constant equal to the ratio of the overall mean income over the mean income of the group. It is easy to observe that (10.23) may also be written as:

$$v = (1/n)\{(y_{ll}/y_{ml}), \ldots,(y_{nl,l}/y_{ml}), \ldots,(y_{l,K}/y_{mK}), \ldots,(y_{nK,K}/y_{mK})\} \qquad (10.24)$$

Let us also give the following definitions:

$G_{\text{TOT}}(s)$ is the actual Gini inequality index based on the original income shares defined by the vector s.

$G_{\text{BETWEEN YITZHAKI}}(s)$ is the between-groups Gini index as defined by Yitzhaki, on the basis of the original vector s of income shares.

$G_{\text{WITHIN YITZHAKI}}(s)$ is the within-groups Gini index as defined by Yitzhaki, on the basis of the original vector s of income shares (see Section 10.3).

$G_{\text{BETWEEN TRADITIONAL}}(s)$ is the between-groups Gini index as it is defined traditionally in the literature (see Bhattacharya and Mahalanobis 1967; Deutsch and Silber 1999), on the basis of the original vector s of income shares.

$G_{\text{WITHIN TRADITIONAL}}(s)$ is the within-groups Gini index as it is defined traditionally in the literature (see Bhattacharya and Mahalanobis 1967; Deutsch and Silber 1999), on the basis of the original vector s of income shares.

$G_{\text{OVERLAP TRADITIONAL}}(s)$ is the residual of the traditional decomposition of the Gini index by population subgroup, called also overlap (see Bhattacharya and Mahalanobis 1967; Deutsch and Silber 1999), defined on the basis of the original vector s of income shares.

$G_{\text{TOT}}(v)$ is the value of the Gini inequality index based on the income shares defined by the vector v which was defined previously. Note that $I_{\text{TOT}}(v)$ is computed by assuming that the income shares defined by v are ranked by decreasing values. It should be clear that the ranking of the elements of v may be different from that of the elements of s.

$G_{\text{WITHIN TRADITIONAL}}(v)$ on the contrary is the value of the Gini inequality index based on the income shares defined by the vector v which was defined previously, assuming, however, that the income shares defined by v are ranked first by decreasing values of the original mean incomes y_{mk}, and second within each group by shares v.

We may then define the following Gini inequality indices:

$$G(y_{mk} \neq y_m; y_{ik} \neq y_{mk}; r_{ik} \neq r_{mk}) = G_{\text{TOT}}(s)$$

$$G(y_{mk} \neq y_m; y_{ik} = y_{mk}; r_{ik} \neq r_{mk}) = G_{\text{BETWEEN YITZHAKI}}(s)$$

$$G(y_{mk} \neq y_m; y_{ik} \neq y_{mk}; r_{ik} = r_{mk}) = G_{\text{BETWEEN TRADITIONAL}}(s)$$
$$+ G_{\text{WITHIN TRADITIONAL}}(s)$$

$$G(y_{mk} \neq y_m; y_{ik} = y_{mk}; r_{ik} = r_{mk}) = G_{\text{BETWEEN TRADITIONAL}}(s)$$

$$G(y_{mk} = y_m; y_{ik} \neq y_{mk}; r_{ik} \neq r_{mk}) = G_{\text{TOT}}(v) = G_{\text{WITHIN TRADITIONAL}}(v)$$
$$+ G_{\text{OVERLAP TRADITIONAL}}(v) = G_{\text{WITHIN YITZHAKI}}(v)$$

$$G(y_{mk} = y_m; y_{ik} \neq y_{mk}; r_{ik} = r_{mk}) = G_{\text{WITHIN TRADITIONAL}}(v)$$

$$G(y_{mk} = y_m; y_{ik} = y_{mk}; r_{ik} \neq r_{mk}) = 0$$

$$G(y_{mk} = y_m; y_{ik} = y_{mk}; r_{ik} = r_{mk}) = 0$$

We then observe that $G(y_{mk} = y_m; y_{ik} \neq y_{mk}; r_{ik} \neq r_{mk})$ which can be considered as the overall Gini index computed on the basis of vector v is in fact equal to the within-groups Gini index $G_{\text{WITHIN YITZHAKI}} (v)$ defined by Yitzhaki on the basis of the vector v since there is no between- groups inequality and the individuals are given their original rank. It is also equal to the sum of the $G_{\text{TRADITIONAL WITHIN}} (v)$ and of the $G_{\text{TRADITIONAL OVERLAP}} (v)$ since this sum is equal to the overall index $G_{\text{TOT}} (v)$ (there is here no between-groups inequality).

The index $G(y_{mk} \neq y_m; y_{ik} = y_{mk}; r_{ik} \neq r_{mk})$ refers to the between-groups inequality Gini index $G_{\text{BET, YITZHAKI}} (s)$ computed on the basis of the vector s of the original income shares defined in (10.22) since the within-groups inequality has been neutralized but the groups' income shares are ranked according to the ranking given by the original income shares given by s.

The index $G(y_{mk} = y_m; y_{ik} = y_{mk}; r_{ik} \neq r_{mk})$ is equal to zero since in this case every individual is given the average income of the overall population.

The index $G(y_{mk} \neq y_m; y_{ik} \neq y_{mk}; r_{ik} = r_{mk})$ corresponds clearly to the sum of the traditional within- and between-groups inequality defined by the Gini index computed on the basis of the vector s since each individual is given his original income and these incomes are ranked first by decreasing value of the mean income of the group to which they belong, and second within each group by decreasing individual income.

The index $G(y_{mk} = y_m; y_{ik} \neq y_{mk}; r_{ik} = r_{mk})$ corresponds to the case where the Gini index is computed on the basis of the vector v defined in (10.23) where each of these 'transformed incomes' (original incomes multiplied by the ratio of the overall mean income divided by the mean income of the group to which the individual belongs) is ranked first by decreasing values of the original mean incomes y_{mk}, and second within each group by decreasing values of the income shares defined by the vector v in (10.24). So this index $G(y_{mk} = y_m; y_{ik} \neq y_{mk}; r_{ik} = r_{mk})$ is clearly equal to the traditional within-groups Gini index, defined on the basis of the vector v.

The index $G(y_{mk} \neq y_m; y_{ik} = y_{mk}; r_{ik} = r_{mk})$ corresponds clearly to the traditional between-groups Gini index since the within-groups inequality has been neutralized and the individuals are ranked first by group, then within each group by decreasing individual original income.

Finally, it is easy to observe that the Gini index $G(y_{mk} = y_m; y_{ik} = y_{mk}; r_{ik} = r_{mk})$ is equal to zero since each individual is given the average income of the overall population.

We can now define the contribution to overall inequality of the between-groups inequality, that of the within-groups inequality and finally that of the ranks.

A) The contribution of the between-groups inequality

Using the Shapley decomposition approach (see Section 10.2) we derive that the contribution of the between-groups inequality C_{BET} may be expressed as:

$$C_{BET} = (2/6) \{[G(y_{mk} \neq y_m; y_{ik} \neq y_{mk}; r_{ik} \neq r_{mk})$$
$$- G(y_{mk} = y_m; y_{ik} \neq y_{mk}; r_{ik} \neq r_{mk})] \tag{10.25}$$
$$+ (1/6) [G(y_{mk} \neq y_m; y_{ik} = y_{mk}; r_{ik} \neq r_{mk}) - G(y_{mk} = y_m; y_{ik} = y_{mk}; r_{ik} \neq r_{mk})]$$
$$+ (1/6) [G(y_{mk} \neq y_m; y_{ik} \neq y_{mk}; r_{ik} = r_{mk}) - G(y_{mk} = y_m; y_{ik} \neq y_{mk}; r_{ik} = r_{mk})]$$
$$+ (2/6) [G(y_{mk} \neq y_m; y_{ik} = y_{mk}; r_{ik} = r_{mk}) - G(y_{mk} = y_m; y_{ik} = y_{mk}; r_{ik} = r_{mk})]\}$$

Using the previous definitions we then derive that:

$$C_{BET} = (2/6) [G_{TOT} (s) - G_{TOT} (v)] \tag{10.26}$$
$$+ (1/6) [G_{BET, YITZHAKI} (s) - 0]$$
$$+ (1/6) [G_{WITHIN\ TRADIT.} (s) + G_{BETWEEN\ TRADIT.} (s) - G_{WITHIN\ TRADIT.} (v)]$$
$$+ (2/6) [G_{BETWEEN\ TRADITIONAL} (s) - 0]$$
$$\Leftrightarrow C_{BET} = (2/6) [G_{TOT} (s) - G_{TOT} (v)] \tag{10.27}$$
$$+ (1/6) [G_{BET, YITZHAKI} (s)]$$
$$+ (1/6) [G_{WITHIN\ TRADITIONAL} (s) - G_{WITHIN\ TRADITIONAL} (v)]$$
$$+ (3/6) G_{BETWEEN\ TRADITIONAL} (s)$$

B) The contribution of the within-groups inequality

The contribution of the within-groups inequality, using again the Shapley decomposition presented in Section 10.2, may be expressed as:

$$C_{WITH} = (2/6) \{[G(y_{mk} \neq y_m; y_{ik} \neq y_{mk}; r_{ik} \neq r_{mk}) - G(y_{mk} \neq y_m; y_{ik} = y_{mk}; r_{ik} \neq r_{mk})] \tag{10.28}$$
$$+ (1/6) [G(y_{mk} = y_m; y_{ik} \neq y_{mk}; r_{ik} \neq r_{mk}) - G(y_{mk} = y_m; y_{ik} = y_{mk}; r_{ik} \neq r_{mk})]$$
$$+ (1/6) [G(y_{mk} \neq y_m; y_{ik} \neq y_{mk}; r_{ik} = r_{mk}) - G(y_{mk} \neq y_m; y_{ik} = y_{mk}; r_{ik} = r_{mk})]$$
$$+ (2/6) [G(y_{mk} = y_m; y_{ik} \neq y_{mk}; r_{ik} = r_{mk}) - G(y_{mk} = y_m; y_{ik} = y_{mk}; r_{ik} = r_{mk})]\}$$

Using the definitions previously given expression (10.28) may be also written as:

$$C_{WITH} = (2/6) [G_{TOT} (s) - G_{BETWEEN\ YITZHAKI} (s)] \tag{10.29}$$
$$+ (1/6) [G_{TOT} (v) - 0]$$

$+ (1/6) [G_{\text{WITHIN TRADIT.}} (s) + G_{\text{BETWEEN TRADIT.}} (s) - G_{\text{BETWEEN TRADIT.}} (s)]$

$+ (2/6) [G_{\text{WITHIN TRADITIONAL}} (v) - 0]$

$\Leftrightarrow C_{\text{WITH}} = (2/6) \, G_{\text{WITHIN YITZHAKI}} (s)$　　　　　　(10.30)

$+ (1/6) \, G_{\text{TOT}} (v)$

$+ (1/6) \, G_{\text{WITHIN TRADITIONAL}} (s)$

$+ (2/6) \, G_{\text{WITHIN TRADITIONAL}} (v)$

C) The contribution of the ranks to the overall inequality

The contribution of the ranks to the overall Gini index of inequality, using again the decomposition technique presented in Section 10.2, may be expressed as:

$C_{\text{RANKS}} = (2/6) \, \{[G(y_{mk} \neq y_m; y_{ik} \neq y_{mk}; r_{ik} \neq r_{mk}) - G(y_{mk} \neq y_m; y_{ik} \neq y_{mk}; r_{ik} = r_{mk})]$　　(10.31)

$+ (1/6) [G(y_{mk} = y_m; y_{ik} \neq y_{mk}; r_{ik} \neq r_{mk}) - G(y_{mk} = y_m; y_{ik} \neq y_{mk}; r_{ik} = r_{mk})]$

$+ (1/6) [G(y_{mk} \neq y_m; y_{ik} = y_{mk}; r_{ik} \neq r_{mk}) - G(y_{mk} \neq y_m; y_{ik} = y_{mk}; r_{ik} = r_{mk})]$

$+ (2/6) [G(y_{mk} = y_m; y_{ik} = y_{mk}; r_{ik} \neq r_{mk}) - G(y_{mk} = y_m; y_{ik} = y_{mk}; r_{ik} = r_{mk})]\}$

Using again the definitions given previously we may also write (10.31) as:

$C_{\text{RANKS}} = (2/6) [G_{\text{TOTAL}} (s) - G_{\text{BETWEEN TRADIT.}} (s) - G_{\text{WITHIN TRADIT.}} (s)]$　(10.32)

$+ (1/6) [G_{\text{TOT}} (v) - G_{\text{WITHIN TRADITIONAL}} (v)]$

$+ (1/6) [G_{\text{BETWEEN YITZHAKI}} (s) - G_{\text{BETWEEN TRADITIONAL}} (s)]$

$+ (2/6) [0 - 0]$

$\Leftrightarrow C_{\text{RANKS}} = (2/6) \, G_{\text{OVERLAP TRADITIONAL}} (s)$　　　　　　(10.33)

$+ (1/6) [G_{\text{OVERLAP TRADITIONAL}} (v)]$

$+ (1/6) \, G_{\text{BETWEEN YITZHAKI}} (s) - G_{\text{BETWEEN TRADITIONAL}} (s)]$

D) Summing the three contributions:

Combining (10.26), (10.30) and (10.33) we conclude that

$C_{\text{BET}} + C_{\text{WITH}} + C_{\text{RANKS}} =$

$\{(1/6) G_{\text{WITHIN TRADITIONAL}} (v) + (1/6) \, G_{\text{OVERLAP TRADITIONAL}} (v) - G_{\text{TOT}} (v)\}$

$+ \{(2/6) \, G_{\text{TOT}} (s)\}$

$+ \{(2/6)\ G_{\text{BETWEEN YITZHAKI}}\ (s) + (2/6)\ G_{\text{WITHIN YITZHAKI}}\ (s)\}$

$+ \{(2/6)\ G_{\text{WITHIN TRADITIONAL}}\ (s) + (2/6)\ G_{\text{BETWEEN TRADITIONAL}}\ (s)$

$+ (2/6)\ G_{\text{OVERLAP TRADITIONAL}}\ (s)\}$

$\Leftrightarrow C_{\text{BET}} + C_{\text{WITH}} + C_{\text{RANKS}} = 0 + (2/6)\ \{G_{\text{TOT}}\ (s) + G_{\text{TOT}}\ (s) + G_{\text{TOT}}\ (s)\}$

$$\Leftrightarrow C_{\text{BET}} + C_{\text{WITH}} + C_{\text{RANKS}} = G_{\text{TOT}}\ (s) \tag{10.34}$$

We have therefore been able to prove that the overall Gini index $G_{\text{TOT}}\ (s)$ may be decomposed into the sum of the respective contributions of the between-groups inequality $C_{\text{BETWEEN GROUPS}}$, the within-groups inequality $C_{\text{WITHIN GROUPS}}$ and that of the ranks C_{RANKS}, a contribution that is specific to the Gini index. Note that this contribution of the ranks goes beyond the overlap term or residual that has been emphasized hitherto in the literature but it still reflects the presence of overlap between the income distributions of the various subgroups.

10.6 An empirical illustration

We have applied the decomposition presented in Section 10.5 to the Israeli Income Surveys of 1990 and 1998. The two subpopulations that were distinguished are the Jewish and non-Jewish populations. Table 10.1 gives summary statistics for these two groups. The Jews represent the great majority of the households that were surveyed (95.4 percent in 1990 and

Table 10.1 Summary statistics for the two subpopulations

Summary statistics	1990 Income Survey	1998 Income Survey
Share of Jewish households	95.4	87.6
Share of non-Jewish households	4.6	12.4
Average total household income in the Jewish population (NIS)	3,068	10,041
Average total household income in the non-Jewish population (NIS)	2,246	7,033
Average per capita income in the Jewish population (NIS)	1,086	3,506
Average per capita income in the non-Jewish population (NIS)	552	1,530
Ratio of average total household income over square root of average size of household in Jewish population	1,753	5,715
Ratio of average total household income over square root of average size of household in non-Jewish population	1,053	3,179

Note
NIS refers to new Israeli shekels.

87.6 percent in 1998). The difference in incomes between the two groups is quite important. Thus in 1990 the average total household income in the non-Jewish population was equal to 73.2 percent of that in the Jewish population. The corresponding ratio for 1998 was 70.0 percent. If the comparison between the two subpopulations is based on per capita household income it appears that in 1990 the per capita household income in the non-Jewish population was equal to 50.8 percent of that in the Jewish population, the same ratio being equal to 43.6 percent in 1998. Finally, we have also used as measure of the welfare of household members the ratio of the total household income over the square root of the size of the household (see Buhman *et al.* 1988, for more details on this approach). In 1990 the value of this welfare indicator in the non-Jewish population was equal to 60.1 percent of that in the Jewish population, the corresponding ratio being equal to 55.6 percent in 1998.

Despite these important differences in the average welfare indicators of the two subpopulations distinguished, Table 10.2 indicates that the between-groups Gini index, whether computed as it is traditionally (see Silber 1989) or following Yitzhaki's approach (see Yitzhaki 1987), is extremely small (0.01 or even less). It is, however, very easy to prove that, for given average incomes of the two groups, the between-groups Gini index will be maximal when the two groups are of equal size and will be smaller the more different the population shares of the two groups are.[2]

The small value of the between-groups Gini index is therefore very easy to understand, given that the Jewish households represented in 1990 almost 88 percent of the total number of households and even more in 1998. This explains also why the overlapping component is relatively small in both years (between 0.01 and 0.09, depending on the approach and indicator used; see Table 10.2). Most of the inequality is therefore a within-groups inequality. Thus the within-groups Gini index varies between 0.33 and 0.44 (see Table 10.2), depending again on the approach and the welfare indicators that are selected.[3]

As far as the distinction between the various definitions of the components of the inequality breakdown is concerned, we observe, as expected, that the within-groups Gini index is higher when the Yitzhaki approach is used than when the traditional decomposition is applied. However, the relevant comparison to be made is really between the within groups computed on the basis of Yitzhaki's approach and the sum of the within-groups Gini index and overlapping component of the traditional approach and then the differences are much smaller.

One may also note that the within-groups Gini index is smaller when it is considered as a residual, that is once the between-groups inequality has been neutralized, than when the between-groups inequality is taken as the residual (after neutralizing the within-groups inequality). This appears clearly in Table 10.2 since, whatever the welfare indicator that is chosen, the within-groups Gini index computed on the basis of the vector v is smaller than that

Table 10.2 Value of various Gini indices in 1990 and 1998

Various Gini Indices	1990 Welfare indicator: total household income	1998 Welfare indicator: total household income	1990 Welfare indicator: per capita household income	1998 Welfare indicator: per capita household income	1990 Welfare indicator: household income divided by square root of size of household	1998 Welfare indicator: household income divided by square root of size of household
$G_{TOT}(s)$	0.42210	0.43837	0.39070	0.42946	0.38284	0.41366
$G_{BETWEEN\ TRADITIONAL}(s)$	0.01199	0.03384	0.02221	0.06591	0.01796	0.05109
$G_{WITHIN\ TRADITIONAL}(s)$	0.39061	0.35511	0.35989	0.34584	0.35408	0.33472
$G_{OVERLAP\ TRADITIONAL}(s)$	0.01950	0.04942	0.00861	0.01770	0.01079	0.02785
$G_{BETWEEN\ YITZHAKI}(s)$	0.00014	−0.00005	0.00019	0.00778	0.00063	0.00158
$G_{WITHIN\ YITZHAKI}(s)$	0.42196	0.43842	0.39050	0.42167	0.38221	0.41208
$G_{TOT}(v)$	0.42030	0.43283	0.38506	0.40939	0.37870	0.40104
$G_{WITHIN\ TRADITIONAL}(v)$	0.38597	0.34363	0.35208	0.32475	0.34780	0.31862
$G_{OVERLAP\ TRADITIONAL}(v)$	0.03434	0.08920	0.03299	0.08465	0.03089	0.08242
$G_{WITHIN\ YITZHAKI}(v)$	0.42030	0.43283	0.38506	0.40939	0.37870	0.40104

Note
The definitions of these various indices are given in Section 10.5.

computed on the basis of the vector s. This is true whether one uses the traditional definition of the within-groups inequality or that adopted by Yitzhaki, although in the latter case the differences are smaller. Such a result, though not striking, justifies certainly that one takes into account both ways of defining the between- and within-groups inequality. It is hence of interest to look at the contribution of the three components of the inequality breakdown, once all approaches have been incorporated, since this is exactly what the Shapley decomposition does, as was explained earlier. Table 10.3 summarizes these results.

It appears that even when all the possible decompositions are taken into account, the between-groups Gini index never represents more than 10.4 percent of the overall inequality. The highest relative contribution of the between-groups Gini index is observed in 1998 when the welfare indicator is the per capita household income and in this case its contribution is equal to

Table 10.3 Breakdown of the overall inequality (Gini index)

Different contributions	*1990 Welfare indicator: total household income*	*1998 Welfare indicator: total household income*	*1990 Welfare indicator: per capita household income*	*1998 Welfare indicator: per capita household income*	*1990 Welfare indicator: household income divided by square root of size of household*	*1998 Welfare indicator: household income divided by square root of size of household*
Contribution of between-groups inequality	0.00739	0.02067	0.01432	0.04446	0.01151	0.03270
Contribution of within-groups inequality	0.40446	0.39201	0.37168	0.37468	0.36547	0.36619
Contribution of ranks	0.01025	0.02569	0.00470	0.01032	0.00586	0.01477
Overall Gini index	0.42210	0.43837	0.39070	0.42946	0.38284	0.41366

0.044 for a Gini index equal to 0.429. This is also the case where the relative contribution of the within-groups inequality is the smallest (87.2 percent). Finally, one may note that the relative contribution of the ranks which reflects the overlapping of the distributions of the two subpopulations is highest in 1998 (this component represents therefore 11.3 percent of the overall inequality) when the welfare indicator is the total household income.

10.7 Conclusion

This chapter has proposed a more general approach to the decomposition of inequality by population subgroups. The idea first is to take into account the possibility that the between-groups inequality is the one that remains when the within-groups inequality has been neutralized but also the case where one defines the within-groups inequality only after having neutralized the between-groups inequality. We have also taken into account, when using the Gini index, the fact that there are various ways of defining the between- and within-groups inequality, depending on how the individual incomes are ranked. This inclusion of all the ways of defining the components of the breakdown of the overall inequality was made possible by applying the concept of Shapley value to the breakdown of income inequality by population subgroups.

The empirical illustration that followed the methodological sections gave the decomposition of inequality in Israel in 1990 and 1998 when two subpopulations were distinguished, the Jewish and the non-Jewish populations. Such a breakdown was repeated on the basis of three definitions of the welfare of individuals, that where the welfare indicator is equal to total household income, that where it is defined as the per capita household income and that where the two previous approaches are combined so that the welfare indicator is equal to the ratio of total household income over the square root of the size of the household.

Whatever the definition of welfare that was adopted it turned out that most of the inequality, at least when the Gini index is selected as a measure of inequality, is a within-groups inequality. The absolute as well as relative contribution of the between-groups inequality is small but this is a consequence of the fact that the two groups distinguished are of very unequal size. It is therefore clear that a way has to be found to neutralize at least partly this impact of the relative sizes of the groups. We hope, in future work, to be able to propose a solution to this important issue.

Notes

1 For more details see Shorrocks (1999).
2 This was in fact the idea behind the derivation of the Kuznets's curve in Robinson's (1976) note in the *American Economic Review*.
3 It is therefore not surprising that several economists (e.g., Kanbur 2003) have raised some doubts concerning the policy relevance of the traditional breakdown of income inequality by population subgroups.

References

Berrebi, Z. M. and Silber, J. (1987). 'Dispersion, asymmetry and the Gini index of inequality', *International Economic Review*, 28(2): 331–338.

Bhattacharya, N. and Mahalanobis, B. (1967). 'Regional disparities in consumption in India', *Journal of the American Statistical Association*, 62: 143–161.

Buhmann, B., Rainwater, R., Schmans, G. and Smeeding, T. (1988). 'Equivalent scales, well-being, inequality and poverty: sensitivity estimates across ten countries using the Luxembourg Income Study Database', *The Review of Income and Wealth*, 32: 115–142.

Deutsch, J. and Silber, J. (1999). 'Inequality decomposition by population subgroups and the analysis of interdistributional inequality', in J. Silber (ed.) *Handbook on Income Inequality Measurement*, Dordrecht and Boston: Kluwer Academic Press.

Kanbur, R. (2003). 'The policy significance of inequality decompositions', mimeo, Cornell University.

Robinson, S. (1976). 'A note on the U hypothesis relating inequality and economic development', *American Economic Review*, 66: 437–440.

Sastre, M. and Trannoy, A. (2002). 'Shapley inequality decomposition by factor components: some methodological issues', *Journal of Economics*, Supplement 9: 51–89.

Shorrocks, A. F. (1980). 'The class of additive decomposable inequality measures', *Econometrica*, 48: 613–625.

Shorrocks, A. F. (1999). 'Decomposition procedures for distributional analysis: a unified framework based on the Shapley value', mimeo, University of Essex.

Silber, J. (1989). 'Factors components, population subgroups and the computation of the Gini index of inequality', *The Review of Economics and Statistics*, 71: 107–115.

Yitzhaki, S. (1987). 'On stratification and inequality between ethnic groups in Israel', (in Hebrew) *Bank of Israel Survey*, 63: 31–41.

Yitzhaki, S. (1998). 'More than a dozen alternative ways of spelling Gini', *Research on Economic Inequality*, 8: 13–30.

Yitzhaki, S. and Lerman, R. I. (1991). 'Income stratification and income inequality', *Review of Income and Wealth*, 37: 313–329.

11 Analysis of the short-term impact of the Argentine social assistance program '*Plan Jefes y Jefas*' on income inequality applying the Dagum decomposition analysis of the Gini ratio

Héctor R. Gertel, Roberto F. Giuliodori and Alejandro Rodríguez

11.1 Introduction

Extreme poverty levels were seen in Argentina after the severe crisis unleashed at the end of 2001. This was worsened by a deep production stand-still, which made the national, provincial, and municipal governments face the need to generate programs for a comprehensive support of families, spe-cially in relation to all essential aspects, which would enable the eradication of the high levels of indigence, and favor social inclusion so as to mitigate, at least partly, the extreme household income inequality in an increasing polar-ized society. The '*Jefes y Jefas de Hogar*' Program (PJJH) is a social assistance program, focused on the unemployed heads of households with dependents under the age of 18 or with disabled individuals of any age, that the national government started out as of May 2002.[1] In order to achieve the social object-ives stated above, a cash transfer of US$45 ($150) (one-hundred and fifty Argentine pesos) per month is given to each beneficiary, which would corres-pond to the cost of the basic basket for adult equivalents at the end of 2001, a sum which by October 2002 was no longer up to date.[2] In consideration of this assistance, the program establishes that the plan recipients must be engaged in one of the following activities: enter into a training program (not clearly established), perform work for the community for up to 20 hours per week (which would be defined and verified locally through political mechanisms) or transform the assistance into an employment subsidy for the company hiring that person.

Among the positive aspects of the program cited, some reports[3] indicate that there is a higher degree of universalization in comparison to prior programs, such as the program *Joven*, focused on young people and on actions centered on labor training for low skilled workers; or the program *Trabajar*, scarcely transparent in the mechanisms used for granting and implementing it at the end of the 1990's. However, the program also has some design weaknesses, since the amount of the subsidy scarcely covers the cost, by mid-2002, of the basic subsistence basket for one person, and is, therefore, insufficient to grant dignity and to guarantee the objectives of the 'right to social inclusion' of the household as stated in the first paragraph of the executive act creating the program. The program also has some prognosis weaknesses as to its extension in time. It had been estimated that the potential number of eligible beneficiaries would amount to 1,750,000 recipients to be covered during the 2002 economic emergency, and that there would be a sustained decrease of this number in 2003 and 2004 when the World Bank contribution was to conclude. However, the number of recipients continued to be close to 1.6 million during the second semester of 2004, the national budget projected for 2005 provides for the continuity of the *Jefes* program, and poverty does not seem to have decreased in the country. Thus, it seems that the main research question today has to deal with the levels of social protection the Argentina's Plan *Jefes y Jefas* can provide to the indigents and the poor after the worst of the crisis is over. More specifically, in the chapter it is argued that a rigorous short-run measure of its contribution to enhance income distribution by reducing income inequality across regions and groups can be derived from a Gini coefficient decomposition procedure, such as the one introduced by Dagum (1997).

A first assessment recently performed for the World Bank by Galasso and Ravallion, (2004) including INDEC calculations, indicates that, all in all, the program reduced aggregate unemployment by up to five points. Notwithstanding the design weakness, this assessment reaches the conclusion that the program was effective since it compensated, at least partially, many households hit by the crisis and reduced extreme poverty. But a possible reduction in income inequality due to Program implementation was not included in the G&R assessment.

On the other hand, it is interesting to point out that one out of three plan recipients by October 2002 was reported as economically inactive in May of that year, which would be revealing an unexpected impact on the program, i.e. attracting a significant number of people who had previously been outside of the economically active population (see Table 11.A.1 of the Appendix).[4] This would also indicate that, in the case of those recipients, the legal requirements were not fully fulfilled,[5] i.e., they were ineligible. It is then possible to conclude from the program's own characteristics and from its implementation that it is a subsidy given to people who were not always eligible, and that the recipients' counterpart work requirement was not always duly controlled. Besides, the impact on employment is uncertain, since it is not clear whether it generated new jobs in spite of the fact that the plans granted are sometimes computed as new job positions. Under these conditions, the main result of the program should be considered through the short-term impact it had on income distribution and the possible containment of social unrest.[6] That is why it is the purpose of this work to analyze two related issues which were not incorporated in the abovementioned assessments, namely, if the distribution of the plans has been neutral in relation to the regional distribution of income; and to what extent the decrease in aggregate unemployment reflects an improvement of the Gini coefficient. This chapter attempts to answer these questions mainly through the use of the information provided by the *Encuesta Permanente de Hogares* (EPH) (Permanent Household Survey) published by the INDEC (the Argentine Government's Statistics Institute), and is organized as follows: Section 11.2 provides the characteristics of the '*Jefes y Jefas de Hogar*' Program recipients, while Section 11.3 compares the income distribution functions for the subpopulations considered in this work, which result from including, on the one hand, the income derived from the plans, and on the other, from excluding this income. Section 11.4 describes the procedure for the decomposition analysis of the applied income inequality Gini coefficient, while Section 11.5 presents the results obtained. Finally, Section 11.6 contains a summary of the main conclusions.

11.2 Characteristics of the population and PJJH recipients

Table 11.1 shows the distribution of population and the PJJH recipients in the urban areas included in the EPH, grouped under two regions, namely: Extended Greater Buenos Aires Area (GBAA), including the City of Buenos Aires, Greater Buenos Aires, and La Plata in this study, on the one hand, and the inland (INT) which includes the rest of the large urban conglomerates considered in the EPH, in October 2002.

According to the data corresponding to October 2002, the proportion of recipients in relation to the total population was 3.7 percent of the whole country, 3.8 percent inland, and 3.6 percent in the GBAA area. If these rates are instead calculated in relation to the Economically Active Population (EAP), the results are 7.8 percent for the country, 8.9 percent for inland, and 7.1 percent for the GBAA area. As may be observed, the inland cities received slightly more assistance.

Table 11.A.1 in the Appendix summarizes the demographics of the individuals and households receiving social plans and of the individuals and households for the total population in each one of the regions. It is possible to observe that both in the GBAA as well as in the INT areas about 70 percent of the plan recipients are female, and about half of them are single. The plan recipients belong to households larger than the mean. It may also be observed that about 23 percent of the plan recipients declared to be unemployed the last time they were included in the survey before October 2002 (prior status = unemployed). Besides, about 33 percent had declared themselves to be inactive, while approximately 43 percent claimed to be employed.

Table 11.1 Total EPH urban population and PJyJH recipients by region. October 2002

Population	GBAA*		INT**		Country	
	PJyJH recipients	Total	PJyJH recipients	Total	PJyJH recipients	Total
Total	411283	11412179	382636	9954103	793919	21366282
Relative weight (%)		53.4		46.6		100
PJyJH recipients (% of the region)	3.6		3.8		3.7	
Distribution of PJyJH recipients (%)	51.8	100	48.2	100	100	100

* GBAA includes the city of Buenos Aires, Greater Buenos Aires and La Plata.
** INT includes the rest of the urban areas in the EPH
Source: EPH, October 2002

An aspect to be borne in mind is that the plan recipients, both in the GBAA as well as in the INT area, are older than the mean. Also, in the inland area, the recipients are slightly younger and have more schooling than a similar population in the GBAA area. Table 11.A.1 in the Appendix provides further information of help in identifying population profile.

11.3 The income distribution functions including and excluding the plans

For the purposes of this work, the total household income per capita per adult equivalent was used. It is considered that the application of this concept makes it possible to better visualize the impact of the fixed sum given through the plans, according to the household size, and it responds to the program's own statements when it indicates that it is intended to benefit household by supporting their heads so as to promote a greater social inclusion.

Table 11.2 shows the proportion of the population below the poverty and indigence lines, including and excluding income of the PJJH. It is possible to observe that the plan impact was mainly focused on the reduction in the proportion of the indigent population and that, instead, its incidence as an instrument to reduce poverty was very scarce. This characteristic is seen both in the GBAA and the INT area.

Besides, a visual comparison of the income density functions obtained from including and excluding the income of the plans would confirm that the impact of the plans on the income of the indigent is the strongest. Figure 11.1 for GBAA and Figure 11.2 for INT have been designed to show how the relevant sections in the density functions have moved in each region after the application of the program.

First, it is possible to observe that both in the GBAA and INT areas the changes concentrate mainly in the lower part of the distribution, below US$90 ($300). The kurtosis increases in both distributions due to the

Table 11.2 Population below the poverty and the indigence lines in two scenarios. (Percentage)

Region	Scenarios		
	Income from PJyJH excluded	*Income from PJyJH included*	*Change*
GBAA			
Poverty	53.4	52.6	−1.4
Indigence	28.0	25.1	−10.3
INT			
Poverty	61.3	60.5	−1.4
Indigence	34.2	30.5	−10.9

Source: EPH October 2002

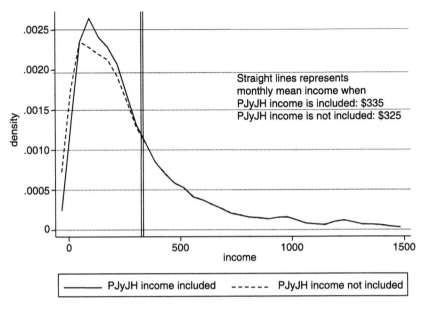

Figure 11.1 The GBAA per capita family income distributions

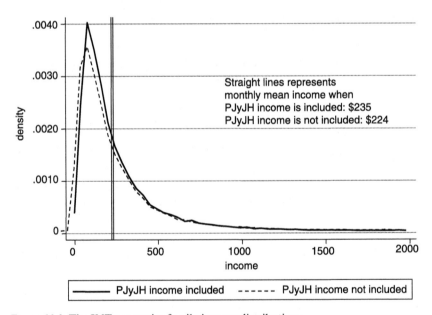

Figure 11.2 The INT per capita family income distributions

introduction of the plan, confirming that it produces a shift of individuals with no income or with very low income towards the US$45 region, approximately. More specifically, the estimates made indicate that the most significant change takes place in the first decile of the household income per capita per adult equivalent, where in the GBAA area it changes from US$8.6 ($28.66) before the plans to US$15.26 ($50.85) after their inclusion as of October 2002.

In the inland area, that decile shifts from US$7.64 ($25.45) to US$13.16 ($43.86). At the level of the quartiles, the change is relatively less significant since in the GBAA area, there is an increase from US$27.49 ($91.62) to US$31.68 ($105.26), and in the inland area from US$20.27 ($67.57) to US$24.00 ($80.00). All this is in agreement with what has been stated above in the sense that the greatest impact of the program is on the reduction of the proportion of indigent population, with a tiny effect on poverty reduction.

11.4 Decomposition of the income inequality Gini coefficient

After the description given above, it is important to see how the application of the *Plan Jefes y Jefas de Hogar* has modified the total population income distribution, approximately six months after its application. To that end, an analysis of the Gini coefficient was made applying the Dagum decomposition method which proposes the breakdown explained below.[7]

The starting point is the total Gini coefficient (G), computed as:

$$G = \frac{\sum_{j=1}^{n} \sum_{i=1}^{n} |v_i - y_j|}{2n^2 Y} \qquad (11.1)$$

where 'n' is the population size to be analyzed and 'Y' is the mean income of the total population. The decomposition of G is as follows:

$$G = G_w + G_{nb} + G_t \qquad (11.2)$$

being G_w the inequality measure within the subpopulations, G_{nb}, the inequality measure between subpopulations weighted for relative affluence, and G_t, the transvariation contribution between populations. At the same time:

$$G_w = \sum_{j=1}^{k} G_j s_j p_j \qquad (11.3)$$

where G_j is the Gini coefficient of the population in region j_{th} and 'k' is the number of subpopulations (regions) into which the original population is divided, s_j is the proportion the j_{th} subpopulation holds of the total income and p_j is the proportion of the global population represented by the j_{th} subpopulation.

$$G_{nb} = \sum_{j=2}^{k} \sum_{h=1}^{j-1} G_{jh} (p_j s_h + p_h s_j) D_{jh} \tag{11.4}$$

where G_{jh} is the Gini coefficient to measure inequality between the j_{th} and h_{th} populations calculated as:

$$G_{jh} = \frac{\sum_{j=1}^{nr} \sum_{i=1}^{ng} |y_{ig} - y_{jr}|}{(nr)(ng)(Y_r + Y_g)} \tag{11.5}$$

D_{jh} is the relative affluence existing between subpopulations as defined in Dagum (1997), s_h is the proportion the h subpopulation holds of the total income and p_h is the proportion of the global population represented by the h subpopulation. Finally:

$$G_t = \sum_{j=2}^{k} \sum_{h=1}^{j-1} G_{jh} (p_j s_h + p_h s_j)(1 - D_{jh}) \tag{11.6}$$

The decomposition proposed was applied to the global population according to income and region criteria. For the income, as it was previously defined, results are presented: (i) without including the sum from the PJJH plans and (ii) including income from the PJJH. With respect to regions, a distinction was made between: (iii) Extended Greater Buenos Aires Area (GBAA), and (iv) the rest of the large urban conglomerates considered in the sample (INT). For each decomposition, the G_w, G_{nb}, and G_t were calculated.

The impact of the plans in each one of the Gini components arises from the comparison of both decompositions. After generalizing, and naming the effect of the application of the plans to the Gini coefficient as *EG*, then:

$$EG = [Gw_p - Gw_{sp}] + [Gnb_p - Gnb_{sp}] + [Gt_p - Gt_{sp}] \tag{11.7}$$

where the *p* and *sp* subscripts indicate that the corresponding components refer to the income including and excluding the sum from the plans, respectively.

The first addend of the second term of (11.7) reflects within-group contribution of the plans to inequality; the second addend, the between-groups contribution to inequality; and the last term, the impact on the transvariation zone, i.e., the density overlap region. These calculations were made both for the Extended Buenos Aires area as well as for the inland of the country so as to examine separately the impact of the plans on the income distribution of each one of these populations, and to make a comparison of the results. For further details of the calculations made, see Tables 11.A.3–11.A.6 in the Appendix.

11.5 Results

The two initial concerns of this chapter, related to the possible regional neutrality of the program and to its impact on income inequality if universalized, were addressed through the application of the decomposition model of the Gini coefficient described in the previous section. Thus it was possible to provide an answer to the following questions: Which was the impact on the Gini coefficient of the application of the program as executed until October 2002 in the two regions considered in this work? Which would have been the impact of the program on the Gini coefficient if the recipients who did not fulfill their counterpart work had been discharged from the program? Which would have been the impact of the program on the Gini coefficient if a sufficient number of plans had been granted so as to cover all those unemployed in October 2002? Each one of these scenarios is examined separately below.

Impact of the plans granted as of October 2002

In order to analyze the impact of the plans granted as of October 2002, a comparison was made between the Gini coefficient resulting from a calculation of the per capita income per adult equivalent, in which the $150 cash transfer was included for each one of the 831,155 plans valid as of that date, and the Gini coefficient which would have resulted from a hypothetical situation in which no PJJH plan existed. For the latter, the sum received from the plan by the plan recipients who were in the EPH was subtracted from the income. The results are shown in Table 11.3 that was constructed using information about *Gw*, *Gnb* and *Gt* provided by Tables 11.A.3 and 11.A.4.

Table 11.3 PJyJH impact on the Gini coefficient decomposition. October 2002 All recipients are included

Concept			*Gw*				*Gnb*	*Gt*
Population included	*PJyJH income is:*	*G**	*INT*	*GBAA*	*Total*			
All cases	Not included	0.5559	0.0926	0.1874	0.2800	0.1270	0.1488
All cases	Included	0.5299	0.0878	0.1791	0.2669	0.1229	0.1400
PJyJH impact							
Gini coeffcent reduction		0.026	0.0048	0.0083	0.0131	0.0041	0.0088
Change in Gini (%)		4.7	5.2	4.4	4.7	3.2	5.9
Relative composition (%)		100	18.5	31.9	50.4	15.8	33.8

* of per capita family income per adult equivalents
Source: Own calculation based on EPH

Table 11.3 shows that there is a 0.026 reduction in the value of the total Gini coefficient – equivalent to 4.7 percent – with the addition of the plans, which represents a decrease in the extent of income inequality. The G_w component, which reflects inequality within each one of the populations, represents 50.4 percent of total reduction. This means that half the impact of the introduction of the plan is seen in the internal inequality reduction in each region. This reduction was not uniform since in the INT area it amounted to 5.2 percent, while in GBAA it was of 4.4 percent. The rest of the impact is seen in the net inequality between distributions, related to the degree of separation of the curves (G_{nb}), and in the inequality in the transvariation zone (G_t), corresponding to the overlap of both distributions. The G_{nb} coefficient experienced a reduction in the 3.2 percent range, and G_t experienced the greatest relative improvement (5.9 percent).

Figure 11.3 helps to further visualize how the income curves in each one of the above described subpopulations shifted after the $150 cash transfer was introduced, even when it is necessary to point out that the truncation of the graphs does not allow a true appreciation of the size of the economic distance existing among the distributions. The figure has two parts: (a) illustrates the income curves of GBAA and INT with PJJH income not included while (b) shows GBAA and INT income curves with PJJH income included. The economic distance[8] between regions is only slightly modified after the application of the PJJH program, which is coherent with the fact that the cash subsidies were introduced in the two regions with similar intensity. After applying the plan, there is, in both distributions, a shift of individuals who had no income or whose income is close to zero towards the region of the corresponding modal values. This movement caused the increase in the observed kurtosis values, in GBAA risen from 33.6 to 34.2 and in INT from 74.9 to 77.6. The income gap between regions, also called affluence, had a value close to 0.46 before the program application, indicating that the separation between curves was slightly less than half of the possible path, and has remain practically unaltered after the implementation of the PJJH program, as seen in Tables 11.A.3–11.A.4 of the Appendix. This could indicate that, after the implementation of the PJJH program, the separation between the income density functions of the two regions has not experienced a significant change.

Impact of the plans granted as of October 2002 if the recipients who did not fulfill their counterpart work were excluded

There is debate about the number of plans allocated during the period herein analyzed and on the criteria applied for their granting. As stated in the introduction, the guidelines for the implementation of the PJJH are provided for in the executive decree No. 505/02. However, when analyzing Table 11.A.1 of the Appendix, under 'position in household', in the GBAA area, 43 percent of the recipients are heads of household; therefore there is compliance with the current legislation. The remaining 57 percent corresponds to

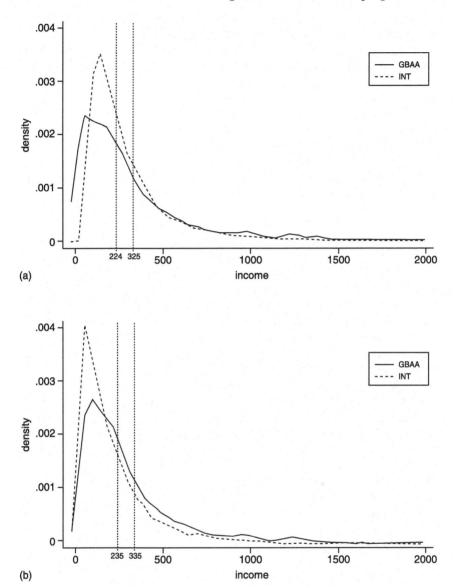

Figure 11.3 The income distributions of GBAA and INT (a) PJyJH income excluded;
(b) PJyJH income included Total household income, per capita, per adult
equivalent

spouses, children, and other members of the household who are not included within the recipients eligible for this plan. Besides, when analyzing in this same table the prior status of the recipients, still in the GBAA area, one notices that about 33 percent of the plan recipients in October 2002 were inactive in the prior EPH survey of May 2002. The situation is similar in the inland area. These two simple observations suggest that, when granting the plans, the legislation may not have been strictly observed.

Additionally, Table 11.4 shows that 26.3 percent of the recipients in the GBAA area did not fulfill the counterpart work requirement, while 21.9 percent did not in the INT area.

In the face of this, it was considered convenient to further study this latter situation, hence extending the analysis to the impact of the application of the PJJH plans on the inequality of income distribution, to the hypothetical situation in which the plans corresponding to recipients not fulfilling their counterpart work requirement were eliminated. Thus, for the purpose of this simulation, the $150 cash transfer received by these individuals was not calculated so as to quantify the net impact of the program on the Gini coefficient of income inequality.

Table 11.5 is based on Tables 11.A.3 and 11.A.5 and shows the results obtained when calculating the impact of the PJJH corresponding to the scenario described in the prior paragraph, i.e., when excluding a total of 200,775 recipients in October 2002 who declared that they were not doing any counterpart work in return for the $150 they received. The impact was determined by comparing the Gini coefficient obtained for this latter situation with the Gini coefficient resulting from the consideration of the hypothetical situation in which there was no PJJH plan, as used in the calculations of Table 11.3. The comparison of both decompositions yields the net impact attributed to each one of the components.

It is possible to observe that when the recipients who did not provide any counterpart work are excluded from the total number of plans considered, the improvement in the Gini coefficient due to the impact of the program is of 0.0201 (equivalent to 3.6 percent), which is less than the reduction of 4.7 percent observed in Table 11.3. The participation of each component in the total coefficient is within values similar to those observed in said Table 11.3. This means that the exclusion of the plans corresponding to the population who did not comply with the counterpart work requirement would not have modified the internal structure of the income distribution among the regions herein considered.

Table 11.4 PJyJH recipients by counterpart work requirements declared. October 2002. (Percentage)

	Region	
Counterpart work requirements	*GBAA*	*INT*
Principal job declared	71.8	74.1
Subsidiary job declared	1.9	4.0
No counterpart work declared	26.3	21.9
Total	100	100

Source: Own calculation based on EPH

Table 11.5 PJyJH impact on the Gini coefficient decomposition. October 2002. Recipients with no counterpart work declared are not included

Concept		G^*	G_w			G_{nb};	G_t
Population included	PJyJH income is:		INT	GBAA	Total		
All cases	Not included	0.5559	0.0926	0.1874	0.2800	0.1270	0.1488
All cases, except PJyJH recipients with no counterpart work declared	Included	0.5358	0.0889	0.1810	0.2700	0.1236	0.1422
PJyJH impact							
Gini coefficient reduction		0.0201	0.0037	0.0064	0.0100	0.0034	0.0066
Change in Gini (%)		3.6	4.0	3.4	3.6	2.7	4.4
Relative composition (%)		100	18.4	31.8	49.8	16.9	32.8

* of per capita family income per adult equivalents
Source: Own calculation based on EPH

Towards universality: the impact of granting 1.8 million plans

As already pointed out, one of the explicit objectives of the PJJH program is to universalize it in order to reach all individuals meeting the requirements established. As also indicated, in May 2002, it was estimated that there were approximately 1,863,000 unemployed in the area covered by the EPH, as observed in Table 11.A1. In order to make an approximation to the measurement of the short-term impact of universalizing the program, the number of recipients was then extended to 1.8 million by simulation, obtaining as a result the Gini coefficient and the decomposition shown in Table 11.6, based on information obtained from Tables 11.A.3 and 11.A.6.

It is possible to observe that the Gini coefficient decreases by 0.00385 in comparison to the situation resulting from the consideration of the income as of October 2002 without including the $150 cash transfer of the plan recipients. This variation is equivalent to a 6.9 percent improvement in the income inequality coefficient attributable to the universalized program, and is certainly the one with largest magnitude if compared with the impact calculated for the two scenarios previously considered. If the cost of the program for this number of recipients were US$1,080 million per annum, then each percentage point reduction in the Gini coefficient has an approximate associate cost of US$156 million per year.

As regards the relative participation of each one of the regions, this is not substantially modified, but with the expansion of the number of recipients, there is an increase in Gb, the Gini coefficient component that reflects the net differences in income between regions (from 15.8 percent, in Table 11.3, to 20.8 percent), also decreasing the relative significance of the income overlap area.

11.6 Conclusions

By using the Gini coefficient, the work analyzed the short-term impact on income inequality attributed to the PJJH program for three alternative scenarios and according to the regional division adopted to capture possible differences between the area of the capital of the country and the inland. The first scenario considered all plans granted, the second estimated only the recipients who complied with the counterpart work requirement, and the third was expanded to include 1.8 million recipients in order to consider universalizing the program.

The three scenarios show that the Gini coefficient improves in relation to the hypothetical situation in which there is no PJJH program. When considering all plans granted as of October 2002, the coefficient decreases by 4.7 percent indicating that there was a relative improvement in the personal income inequality, which somehow explains the decrease in social unrest for that time.[9]

If the plans received by individuals whose situation does not fulfill the legal

Table 11.6 PIyJH impact on the Gini coefficient decomposition. October 2002. Simulation for 1.8 million recipients

Concept		G^*	Gw			Gnb	Gt
Population included	PIyJH income is:		INT	GBAA	Total		
All cases	Not included	0.5559	0.0926	0.1874	0.2800	0.1270	0.1488
All cases	Included (simulation for 1.8 million recipients)	0.5174	0.0861	0.1745	0.2606	0.1190	0.1378
PIyJH impact							
Gini coefficient reduction		0.0385	0.0065	0.0129	0.0194	0.0080	0.0110
Change in Gini (%)		6.9	7.0	6.9	6.9	6.3	7.4
Relative composition (%)		100	16.9	33.5	50.4	20.8	28.6

* of per capita family income per adult equivalents
Source: Own calculation based on EPH

requirements (they do not fulfill the counterpart work requirement) are excluded, the Gini coefficient improves less, with a 3.6 percent relative reduction.

Finally, when universalizing was introduced as a possible scenario, the greatest impact is obtained, of about 6.9 percent in the example, equivalent to a 0.0385 (3.85 percentage points) reduction in the coefficient.

Thus, the granting of a fixed $150 monthly cash transfer, even when there is consensus that is lower than the requirements of a typical family to emerge from poverty, improves, in the short term, the income inequality indicator. In this sense, the 3.85 percent point reduction which would be obtained in the Gini coefficient in this third scenario would be associated with a US$1,080 million annual cost; thus, in general terms for this program, each percentage point improvement in the Gini coefficient represents a US$156 million cost.

As regards the structure of the decomposition of the Gini coefficient in the scenario which covers all plans, half of the impact produced by their incorporation is seen in the reduction of the internal inequality in each region, i.e., the capital city and the inland area. However, the reduction was not uniform since it amounted to 5.2 percent in the inland, and to 4.4 percent in the capital of the country. The rest of the impact was observed through the net inequality between distributions as well as in the inequality in the overlap area, although the economic distance is not significantly modified.

When the recipients who did not perform their counterpart work are excluded from the total number of plans, the share of each one of the components in the total coefficient does not record either significant change, indicating that the income distribution inequality between regions is not affected by this anomaly in the execution of the program. In the last scenario considered, again, the relative participation of each one of the components is not substantially modified, reasserting the neutral character of the plan in relation to the regional distribution of the pre-existing income to its application.

Finally, although the program seems to have a significant and positive short-term impact on income distribution inequality, as measured with the Gini coefficient, and besides being neutral in relation to the pre-existing regional distribution, there is still doubt as to whether this program is a mechanism sustainable through time, mainly due to the incognita on other effects not included in this analysis and to the possibilities of long-term financing.

Appendix

Table 11.A.1 Main characteristics of the population

	Population of GBAA				Population of INT			
Characteristics	*With plans*	*%*	*Total*	*%*	*With plans*	*%*	*Total*	*%*
Total	411283	100	11412179	100	382636	100	9954103	100
Sex								
Male	136286	33.1	5392509	47.3	112197	29.3	4706583	47.3
Female	274997	66.9	6019670	52.7	270439	70.7	5247520	52.7
Average age	36.1		32.2		35.3		30.4	
Marital status								
Married/Unmarried couples	186805	45.4	6718350	58.9	198397	51.9	6297961	63.3
Single	224478	54.6	4693829	41.1	184239	48.1	3656142	36.7
Home position								
Head of the family	178269	43.3	3402165	29.8	166234	43.4	2764510	27.8
Spouse	161109	39.2	2216906	19.4	114955	30.0	1673401	16.8
Children	52701	12.8	4596247	40.3	71881	18.8	4353954	43.7
Other	19204	4.7	1196861	10.5	29566	7.7	1162238	11.7
Average years of schooling	7.7		8.1		8.2		8.0	
Actual State*								
Employed	339089	82.4	3345425	29.3	325750	85.1	3119081	31.3
Unemployed	32035	7.8	997060	8.7	17452	4.6	670472	6.7
Inactive	40158	9.8	7069694	61.9	39434	10.3	6164550	61.9
Previous State**								
Employed	177839	43.2	3852752	33.8	167901	43.9	3021070	30.3
Unemployed	98790	24.0	1073886	9.4	85634	22.4	789360	7.9
Inactive	134654	32.7	6485541	56.8	129101	33.7	6143672	61.7
Home Size	5.3		4.4		5.5		4.8	

* October 2002; ** Reported state in May 2002 by people participating in both measurements (October and May)
Source: Own calculation based on EPH and INDEC data

Table 11.A.2 Basic basket of foodstuffs and poverty line in pesos per month

Month	Equivalent adult		Standard home	
	BBF	*PL*	*BBF*	*PL*
Jun 01	61.76	151.93	190.84	469.46
Jul 01	61.59	151.51	190.31	468.17
Aug 01	61.37	150.97	189.63	466.50
Sep 01	61.02	150.11	188.55	463.84
Oct 01	60.50	150.04	186.95	463.62
Nov 01	60.75	150.05	187.72	463.66
Dec 01	60.46	149.34	186.82	461.45
Jan 02	62.41	154.15	192.85	476.33
Feb 02	65.82	161.26	203.38	498.29
Mar 02	69.83	169.69	215.77	524.33
Apr 02	81.76	193.77	252.64	598.75
May 02	86.20	202.57	266.36	625.94
Jun 02	90.67	210.35	280.17	650.00
Jul 02	94.93	218.34	293.33	674.67
Aug 02	100.94	227.12	311.90	701.79
Sep 02	104.87	231.76	324.05	716.15
Oct 02	103.74	230.31	320.56	711.66
Nov 02	105.08	232.23	324.70	717.59
Dec 02	105.72	232.59	326.67	718.70
Jan 03	106.92	235.22	330.38	726.83
Feb 03	107.56	235.56	332.36	727.88
Mar 03	107.83	233.99	333.19	723.03
Apr 03	106.55	232.28	329.24	717.75
May 03	104.60	229.07	323.21	707.83
Jun 03	103.13	227.92	318.67	704.27
Jul 03	102.31	227.13	316.14	701.83
Aug 03	102.08	225.60	315.43	697.10
Sep 03	101.99	224.38	315.15	693.33
Oct 03	104.12	228.02	321.73	704.58
Nov 03	105.24	229.42	325.19	708.91
Dec 03	105.76	231.61	326.80	715.67
Jan 04	105.81	231.72	326.95	716.01
Feb 04	106.17	232.51	328.07	718.46
Mar 04	106.02	232.18	327.60	717.44
Apr 04	106.52	233.29	329.15	720.87
May 04	106.66	233.58	329.58	721.76
Jun 04	106.88	234.08	330.26	723.31
Jul 04	106.14	234.57	327.97	724.82
Aug 04	107.90	236.30	333.41	730.17

Source: INDEC

Table 11.A.3 Gini decomposition for income distribution of total urban population. October 2002. Simulation does not include income from PJyJH

	Gw INT	GBAA	Total	Gmb	Gt	Total
	0.0926	0.1874	0.2800	0.1270	0.1488	0.5559
	16.66%	33.71%	50.37%	22.85%	26.77%	100%
Gini / Between Gini	0.5329	0.5597		0.5615	0.5615	
Affluence				0.4605	0.4605	
pi	0.4659	0.4659		0.4659	0.4659	0.4659
si	0.3731	0.3731		0.3731	0.3731	0.3731
pc	0.5341	0.5341		0.5341	0.5341	0.5341
sc	0.6269	0.6269		0.6269	0.6269	0.6269

Source: Own calculation based on EPH

Table 11.A.4 Gini decomposition for income distribution of total urban population. October 2002. Simulation includes income from all PJyJH

	Gw INT	GBAA	Total	Gmb	Gt	Total
	0.0878	0.1791	0.2669	0.1229	0.1400	0.5299
	16.58%	33.79%	50.37%	23.19%	26.43%	100%
Gini / Between Gini	0.5017	0.5371		0.5349	0.5349	
Affluence				0.4674	0.4674	
pi	0.4659	0.4659		0.4659	0.4659	0.4659
si	0.3758	0.3758		0.3758	0.3758	0.3758
pc	0.5341	0.5341		0.5341	0.5341	0.5341
sc	0.6242	0.6242		0.6242	0.6242	0.6242

Source: Own calculation based on EPH

Table 11.A.5 Gini decomposition for income distribution of total urban population. October 2002. Simulation includes income from PJyJH whose recipients keep their counterpart work requirements

	Gw INT	GBAA	Gnb	Gt	Total
Value	0.0889	0.1810	Total 0.27 / 0.1236	0.1422	0.5358
%	16.59%	33.79%	50.38% / 23.07%	26.54%	100%
Gini	0.5084	0.5427	Between Gini 0.5409	Between Gini 0.5409	
			Affluence 0.4650	Affluence 0.4650	
pi	0.4659	0.4662	0.4659	0.4659	
si	0.3754	0.3754	0.3754	0.3754	
pc	0.5341	0.5341	0.5341	0.5341	
sc	0.6246	0.6246	0.6246	0.6246	

Note
Includes about 601,000 recipients in this category

Table 11.A.6 Gini decomposition for income distribution of total urban population. October 2002. Simulation includes total number of PJyJH recipients expanded to 1.8 million

	Gw INT	GBAA	Gnb	Gt	Total
Value	0.0861	0.1746	Total 0.2606 / 0.1190	0.1378	0.5174
%	16.64%	33.74%	50.37% / 23.00%	26.62%	100%
Gini	0.4869	0.5268	Between Gini 0.5221	Between Gini 0.5221	
			Affluence 0.4635	Affluence 0.4635	
pi	0.4662	0.4662	0.4662	0.4662	
si	0.3792	0.3792	0.3792	0.3792	
pc	0.5338	0.5338	0.5338	0.5338	
sc	0.6208	0.6208	0.6208	0.6208	

Source: Own calculation based on EPH
Note
Through a simulation, plans' recipients have been expanded to 1.8 million

Notes

1 Act 25.561 and Regulatory Decree 165/2002 declare the national emergency until December 31, 2002. Within this framework, on January 22, 2002 a bill within the guidelines of the Jefes Program begins to be considered, and is finally enacted under Executive Act 565 dated April 3. Under this act, the Treasury Department shall be responsible for reallocating the resources of the national budget necessary for the program's implementation (sect.15). The program was then extended (and was still in force in 2004), and in 2003, the World Bank approved a loan for US$600 million to be allocated, together with the national state-owned resources, to the expansion of the program so as to cover 1,750,000 recipients. According to the estimates, this number has been rapidly exceeded, being by mid-2004 close to 2 million recipients. For an assessment of the program according to its value as social safety net, see, for example, Galasso and Ravallion (2004).
2 See Table 11.A.2 in the Appendix.
3 See Di Lorenzo *et al*, www.losocial.com.ar/plantillas/ima6.htm, page1.
4 Approximately 74 percent of the recipients who were economically inactive in May 2002 declared to be employed in October of that same year.
5 Act N° 25561.
6 The economic effects of social tensions derived from income inequality have been recently studied by Esteban and Ray (1994) and Duclos, Esteban and Ray (2002) through the conceptualization and measurement of polarization, which are based on the notions of identification and alienation between groups of individuals.
7 See Dagum (1997).
8 The concept of directional economic distance, also called 'affluence' was proposed by Dagum (1980) and its calculation appears in Tables 11.A3 to 11.A6 in the Appendix. This is closely linked to the notion of polarization, as developed by Esteban, Gradin and Ray (1999).
9 An additional calculation of a polarization measure, as proposed in Duclos, Esteban and Ray (2002) to capture the changes in social tensions, was performed by the authors of this chapter using information of per capita family income per adult equivalents for EPH, October 2002. Results, given $a = 1$, indicated that polarization in Argentina decreased from 0.25 under a situation where incomes from PJJH were not computed, to 0.241 when income of PJJH for 1.8 million recipients were considered, showing a positive effect of the program. These results are fairly consistent with those obtained in Horenstein and Olivieri (2004). However, it should be remarked that this improvement in the polarization measure associated to the implementation of the PJJH is not big enough to restore the observed value of 0.2285 obtained by Horrenstein and Olivieri for 1998. A slight modification of example 4 and Figure 4b (Esteban and Ray 1994: 827) can help in providing an interpretation for the improvement. Let the population be divided into three groups: the indigent, the poor and middle class, and the rich. The indigents and poor are far from the rich and the rich are a tiny fraction of the whole population. Any movement in the mass of indigents to the right of the distribution (i.e., due to the perception of the $150 of the PJJH) causes a reduction in the polarization measure.

References

Dagum, C. (1980). 'Inequality Measures between Income Distributions with Applications', *Econometrica,* 48 (7): 1791–1803.
Dagum, C. (1997). 'A New Approach to the Decomposition of the Gini Income Inequality Ratio', *Empirical Economics*, 22: 515–531.

Duclos, J. Y., Esteban J. and Ray, D. (2002). 'Polarization: Concepts, Measurement, Estimation', Maxwell School of Citizenship and Public Affairs, Syracuse University, New York, Working Paper 335.

Esteban, J. M. and Ray, D. (1994). 'On the Measurement of Polarization', *Econometrica*, 62 (4): 819–851.

Esteban, J. M., Gradin, C. and. Ray, D (1999). 'Extensions of a Measure of Polarization with an Application to the Income Distribution of Five OECD Countries', Instituto de Estudios Económicos de Galicia, Spain, Working Paper 24.

Galasso, E. and Ravallion, M. (2004). 'Social Protection in a Crisis: Argentina's Plan *Jefes y Jefas*', Development Research Group, World Bank, Washington, D.C.

Horenstein, M. and Olivieri, S. (2004). 'Polarización del Ingreso en la Argentina: Teoría y Aplicación de la Polarización Pura del Ingreso', CEDLAS, Universidad Nacional de La Plata, Documento de Trabajo 15.

12 The Gini unbound

Analyzing class inequality with model-based clustering

Tim F. Liao

12.1 Introduction

Economic inequality has long captured researchers' interest, and the most widely used measure of inequality is the Gini index (or Gini inequality ratio) pioneered by the Italian statistician Corrado Gini (1912) and often presented together with its associated Lorenz curve, attributed to Lorenz (1905). The measure has become popular for measuring not only economic but other types of inequality as well in recent years, such as education and health inequality. As such the Gini index is an immensely useful measure. However, how much can the statistic really measure in terms of the shape and form of inequality, be it income, education, or health? This chapter sets out to answer the question.

To motivate the research, let us examine three simulated income distributions (Figure 12.1). All the three distributions in the figure have an equal amount of inequality of about 0.30 according to the Gini index, despite the different shapes of Samples A, B, and C. Sample A has a symmetrical distribution while Samples B and C both possess a distribution skewed to the right, resembling an income distribution found in many of today's societies.

To anticipate the conclusion, the three samples are simulated by rather different strategies. Sample A is generated by a normal distribution, Sample B has two distributions mixed together, one normal and the other lognormal, and Sample C contains a mixture of three distributions, two normal and one lognormal. In other words, we may consider distribution A consists of just one income class, distribution B of two classes, and distribution C of three classes.

The current chapter focuses on a method that relies on Gini decomposition and uses exploratory means to obtain latent classes or clusters that in turn serve as the basis for group membership for the decomposition (Liao 2006). Much research has been done on the decomposition of the Gini in recent years (Dagum 1997a, 1997b, 1998; Milanovic and Yitzhaki 2002; Mussard, Terraza and Seyte 2003; Yao and Liu 1996; Yao 1999; Yitzhaki 1994). This chapter utilizes the contributions of some of these authors.

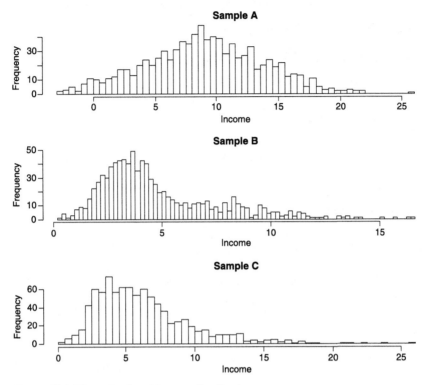

Figure 12.1 Three simulated income distributions

The Gini index, while extremely useful, has a limitation in measuring inequality: it is less sensitive to how the distribution is stratified than to how individual values differ. To illustrate, this chapter presents two kinds of inequality – individual and class inequality, and employs a model-based method – latent class/clustering analysis to extend the Gini index for understanding and measuring stratified inequality.

The three income distributions presented earlier already demonstrated the ambivalence of the Gini index and its inability in distinguishing samples with very different shapes of stratification. How do we get at the underlying stratification, if we are given the data, as is most often the case, without knowing the generating mechanism? In the section to follow I present a form of latent class or cluster analysis that can be used to estimate memberships of classification or stratification. Next, a real-world example of income data from the Philippines is examined to illustrate the estimation method and to apply Gini decomposition by using cluster classification schemes suggested by the model-based method. The decomposition results are further used to form three stratification indices for measuring the amount of stratification or class inequality relative to the total amount of inequality in terms of the Gini, in terms of the number of pairwise comparisons or relationship ties, and in terms of the Gini adjusted with the proportion of comparison pairs. The same method and treatments are applied as well to the three samples of simulated data presented earlier before some summary remarks.

12.2 Model-based cluster analysis

Let y_i indicate a random distribution such as income, and let us imagine that there are an unknown K number of classes or clusters in the distribution. We use the concept of clustering in everyday life. For example, in supermarkets, different types (or clusters) of drinks, meat, and produce are grouped and displayed in the same or nearby locations. In statistical modeling, the same principle is applied in cluster analysis – similar items (in terms of a preset criterion) are grouped together.

Briefly, cluster analysis can be viewed as a way to group similar objects, with unknown number of groups whose forms (i.e., cluster parameters) are also unknown (Kaufman and Rousseuw 1990). Another view is given by Everitt (1993), who considered cluster analysis as obtaining a useful division of objects into classes, whose numbers and properties are to be determined. In essence, these ideas can be carried on to the analysis of social inequality, where the researcher seeks an understanding of the groups or social or economic classes within which individuals are more similar than across these classes, judged by certain attributes such as income.

A recent development takes the approach of model-based clustering, which specifies a statistical model for the population from which the sample under study is assumed to have come. Model-based clustering has a number of advantages (Vermunt and Magidson 2002): First, the choice of the cluster criterion that is used to minimize the within-cluster variation and maximize the between-cluster variation is less arbitrary in model-based clustering than in conventional cluster analysis; second, model-based clustering is flexible in allowing various simple and complex distributional forms of the observed variables within the clusters; furthermore, no scaling decisions have to be made about the observed variables in model-based clustering while in conventional cluster analysis scaling is always an issue.

Model-based clustering also allows the observed variables to be continuous or categorical (i.e., nominal or ordinal) because clusters can be treated as latent classes; therefore the method can be seen as latent class analysis. Here we consider only continuous observed variables in our model specification because our concern in this chapter is income. The basic model-based clustering specification takes the form:

$$f(\mathbf{y}_i \mid \theta) = \sum_{k=1}^{K} \pi_k f_k (\mathbf{y}_i \mid \theta_k), \tag{12.1}$$

where $\mathbf{y}_i$ represents an individual's scores on a set of observed variables, K denotes the number of clusters (to be estimated), π_k designates the prior probability of a case's belonging to cluster k (or the size of cluster k), and θ defines the model parameters (Vermunt and Magidson 2002). Equation (12.1) specifies the distribution of $\mathbf{y}_i$ given the model parameter θ as a mixture of cluster-specific densities, $f(\mathbf{y}_i \mid \theta_k)$.

Equivalently, we may express the model in (12.1) in its likelihood form (Fraley and Raftery 2002):

$$L(\theta_k, \pi_k \mid \mathbf{y}_i) = \prod_{i=1}^{n} \sum_{k=1}^{K} \pi_k f_k(\mathbf{y}_i \mid \theta_k), \tag{12.2}$$

where most commonly $f(\mathbf{y}_i \mid \theta_k)$ is the multivariate normal (Gaussian) density ϕ_k, parameterized by its mean μ_k and covariance matrix Σ_k. Banfield and Raftery (1993) proposed parameterizing the cluster-specific covariance matrices Σ_k by eigenvalue decomposition:

$$\Sigma_k = \lambda_k D_k A_k D_k^T, \tag{12.3}$$

where D_k is the orthogonal matrix of eigenvectors, A_k is a diagonal matrix whose elements are proportional to the eigenvalues, λ_k is an associated scalar of proportionality. More specifically, $\lambda_k = |\Sigma_k|^{1/d}$, where d is the number of indicators, and $A_k = \text{diag}\{a_{1k}, \ldots, a_{pk}\}$ and $1 = a_{1k} \geq a_{2k} \geq \ldots \geq a_{pk} > 0$. The three parameters offer a nice interpretation: D_k describes the orientation of the kth cluster in the mixture, A_k its shape, and λ_k its volume. Put differently, if a latent class or cluster is viewed as a group or cluster of points in a multidimensional space, the volume is the size of the cluster, and the orientation and shape parameters indicate whether the cluster mixture is spherical, diagonal, or ellipsoidal. For example, the kth cluster will be roughly spherical if the largest and the smallest eigenvalues of Σ_k are of the same magnitude.

The combination of these parameter specifications determines the specific statistical model to fit. For example, for one-dimensional data such income distributions, there are only two models to estimate, E for equal variance and V for varying variance. For multidimensional data that involve multiple variables, things are more complex. For example, VEI denotes a model in which the volumes of the clusters are varying (V), the shapes of all the clusters are equal (E), and the orientation is of the identity (I). For details on multidimensional models, see Fraley and Raftery (1999).

In conventional cluster analysis, the data analyst must deal with the issue of selection of the clustering method and that of determining the number of clusters. In model-based clustering, the two issues reduce to a single concern of model selection. In Fraley and Raftery's (2002) approach, Bayesian-model selection via Bayes factors and posterior probabilities is preferred. This in practice is evaluated by way of the Bayesian Information Criterion (BIC), which is implemented in MCLUST, a contributed R package (Fraley and Raftery 1999, 2002).

Estimating the number of clusters and individuals' memberships in the clusters is probably the major purpose of model-based clustering methods. However, it is also possible to obtain density estimation, in which the value of mixture likelihood at individual points is of interest. Roeder and Wasserman (1997) used normal mixtures for univariate density estimation and BIC to decide the number of components. Fraley and Raftery's (1999, 2002) method can be viewed as a multivariate extension because the parameter estimates for the best model describes a multivariate mixture density for the data. The MCLUST package also computes a quantity known as uncertainty, which is defined by subtracting the probability of the most likely group or cluster for each observation from 1. A descriptive analysis of uncertainty can indicate how well the observations are classified. Uncertainty plots can be produced for single or multidimensional data.

12.3 Analyzing income inequality with model-based clustering

Before we apply the Gini index to the income data from the Philippines, let us first review how the Gini is calculated. The Gini index is related to the Lorenz curve as twice the area between the 45-degree line and the Lorenz curve, and can be formally written as below (see, for example, Chotikapanich and Griffiths 2001).

Let $\pi = F(y_i)$ indicate the distribution for y_i, and let $\eta = F_1(y_i)$ represent the corresponding first-moment distribution function. The relation between η and π, defined for $0 \leq y_i < \infty$, is the Lorenz curve, and relation can be denoted by $\eta = L(\pi)$. The Gini index can then be defined accordingly:

$$G = 1 - 2 \int_0^1 L(\pi)d\pi \tag{12.4}$$

And it can also be written as:

$$G = -1 + \frac{2}{\mu_y} \int_0^\infty yF(y)f(y)dy \tag{12.5}$$

There exist numerous computational formulae for implementing the Gini calculation. Perhaps the most revealing one is that used by Dagum (1997a, 1997b, 1998) and Mussard, Terraza and Seyte (2003):

$$G = \frac{\sum_{i=1}^n \sum_{j=1}^n |y_i - y_j|}{2n^2 \mu} \tag{12.6}$$

All the various computation formulae will give you the same results. However, (12.6) demonstrates that what is really measured by the Gini index is a weighted average of pairwise differences between the individual cases in the sample. It is the overall individual mean differences that matter, whether or not these individuals may fall into classes or clusters. Although recent research has shown that Gini's mean difference is a superior measure of variability for non-normal distribution (Yitzhaki 2003), the Gini index does not capture well the clustering nature of the data, a more important point for studying social and economic stratification.

When our concern is only with the shape of inequality, such analysis is relatively simple because there are only two possible models to consider – equal variance (E) or varying variance (V). For an empirical example, we apply Fraley and Raftery's (1999, 2002) model-based clustering to household income data of the Ilocos region in the Philippines. The data come from the 1997 Family and Income and Expenditure Survey and the 1998 Annual Poverty Indicators Survey (APIS), conducted by the National Statistics Office of the Philippines. There are four provinces covered in the data: Ilocos Norte, Ilocos Sur, Pangasinan, and La Union, and the data set is available as megadata accompanying the R ineq package for inequality analysis which produces statistics such as the Gini coefficient and some generalized entropy measures.

As recent research has shown, income inequality may vary spatially because of the local development policy there (Balisacan and Fuwa 2003). This necessitates analyzing patterns of income inequality separately for the regions or provinces. Using the same 1997 survey data, Balisacan (2001) showed that Ilocos Norte (poverty line = 7,084 pesos per capita or ppc) and Ilocos Sur (poverty line = 7,906 ppc) were among the 10 provinces with the lowest poverty incidence while the other two provinces, La Union (poverty line = 7,669 ppc) and Pangasinan (poverty line = 7,542 ppc) were neither among the highest nor the lowest 10 provinces, all with lower poverty lines lower than Metro Manila (poverty line = 10,577 ppc). The cost-of-living index in these four provinces of the Ilocos region ranged from 67.0 to 74.7 (Metro Manila = 100).

First, let us analyze the issue of income inequality by using the Gini index and the Lorenz curve. Figure 12.2 presents the Lorenz curves for the four provinces of Pangasinan, La Union, Ilocos Norte, and Ilocos Sur, with corresponding Gini indices listed below the panels. It is rather difficult to see much difference among the four Lorenz curves, except that the one for La Union may indicate a slightly greater amount of inequality than the others. The Gini indices for the four sets of data can be lined up from low to high inequality: Pangasinan, Ilocos Norte, Ilocos Sur, and La Union. The greatest pairwise comparison is between La Union and Pangasinan, with a mere difference about 0.06. For the sake of comparison, the empirical distributions of income in the four provinces are presented in Figure 12.3.

However, the issue of stratification is entirely ignored by such analysis.

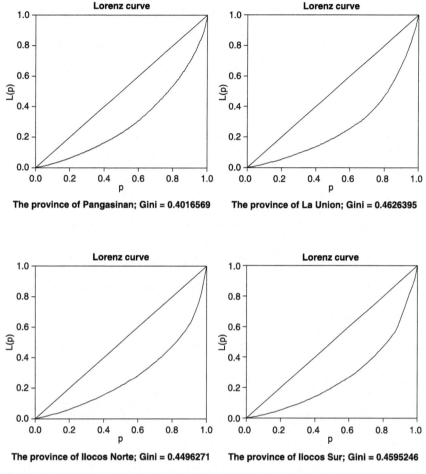

Figure 12.2 Gini indices and Lorenz curves for the four Filipino provinces

Next, we move on to analyzing the same data with model-based clustering by using the MCLUST program. For the province of Pangasinan, the province with the lowest inequality among the four, the model assuming unequal variances fits better than the one assuming equal variances at most number of possible clusters, and suggests the model with four latent classes as the best-fitting (Figure 12.4). The uncertainty plot clearly indicates three uncertain regions although the density plot gives only three obvious peaks and a long tail with a slightly elevated end region.

For the province of La Union, however, the two-cluster unequal-variance model fits the best (Figure 12.5). Judging by the uncertainty and the density plots, there appear to be two classes, even though the second cluster is rather spread out.

For the province of Ilocos Norte, the two-cluster unequal-variance model

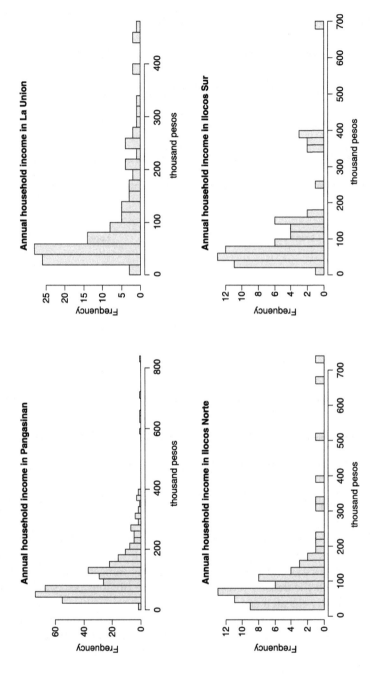

Figure 12.3 Empirical income distributions of the four provinces

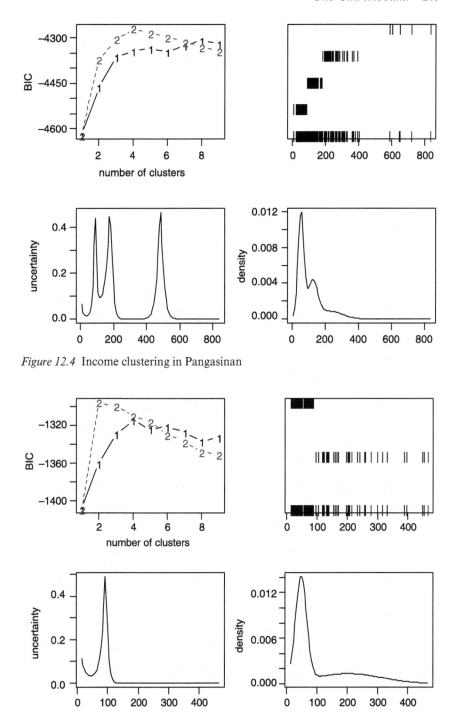

Figure 12.4 Income clustering in Pangasinan

Figure 12.5 Income clustering in La Union

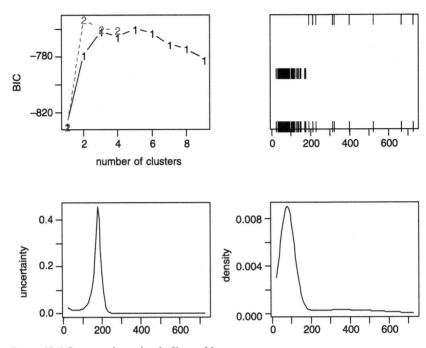

Figure 12.6 Income clustering in Ilocos Norte

also fits the best (Figure 12.6). The uncertainty and the density plots indicate a similar pattern of clustering to that existing in the La Union data, with perhaps less elevated second cluster in the Ilocos Norte data.

For the province of Ilocos Sur, it is the four-cluster equal-variance model that fits the data the best (Figure 12.7). The three major clusters or latent classes for the province are clearly shown by either the density plot or the uncertainty plot, indicated by the three peak uncertainty regions between the four clusters, with the last cluster being an elevated right tail, caused by an outlier.

Finally, Figure 12.8 summarizes the overall income distribution in the entire Ilocos region. For the region as a whole, the unequal variance model with four latent classes fits the best, supported by any of the panels in the graph. When data from subregions are combined, it is likely that the maximum number of clusters from a subregion is maintained, unless the data, when combined, happen to smooth out the troughs.

Interestingly, the model-based clustering method allows us to see much greater detail in how the provinces differ in their patterns of stratification. Such detail is ignored by the Gini index or the Lorenz curve because these measures of inequality focus on only one kind of inequality.

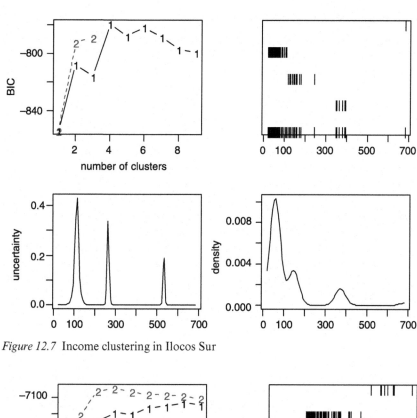

Figure 12.7 Income clustering in Ilocos Sur

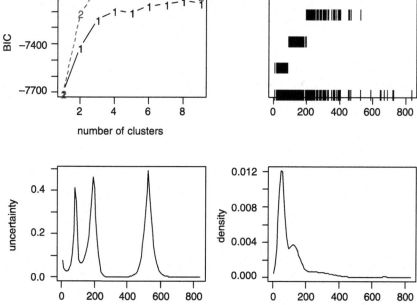

Figure 12.8 Income clustering in the Ilocos Region

12.4 Individual versus class inequality

Inequality may exist in two forms: Individuals differ in their income (or other attributes), and this form can be called 'individual inequality'. Groups of individuals differ in their income (or other attributes) from other groups in the population (or sample), and this form can be called 'class inequality'. The first kind is measured by methods including pairwise differences between individuals. The second type, 'class inequality', broadly conceived as whether there exist classes or clusters of individuals in the sample (or population), can only be partially captured by the absolute distances between individuals of the classes. The number of classes can serve as an indicator of such inequality. However, is a population with two classes more stratified than one with three? A more informative measure is desirable. One may use the decomposition of Gini indices into the between-class and within-class components when the classes are ordered as a means to partition income inequality for the purpose of measuring stratification. We follow the decomposition methods presented in Dagum (1997a, 1997b). The overall Gini is computed as (12.6), and the within and between components of inequality are computed respectively as:

$$
G_w = \sum_{k=1}^{K} \frac{\displaystyle\sum_{i=1}^{n_k} \sum_{j=1}^{n_k} |y_i - y_j|}{2n^2 \mu} \tag{12.7}
$$

where n_j is the size of each j class or cluster, and K, the number of estimated classes or clusters, and:

$$
G_b = \sum_{k=2}^{K} \sum_{h=1}^{k-1} \frac{\displaystyle\sum_{i=1}^{n_k} \sum_{j=1}^{n_h} |y_i - y_j|}{n^2 \mu} \tag{12.8}
$$

Alternatively, the components of the Gini index can also be expressed as weighted averages of population shares and incomes shares. For the within-group component, we have:

$$
G_w = \sum_{k=1}^{K} \frac{p_k \, s_k \displaystyle\sum_{i=1}^{n_k} \sum_{j=1}^{n_k} |y_i - y_j|}{2n^2 \mu} \tag{12.9}
$$

where $p_k = \dfrac{n_k}{n}$ and $s_k = \dfrac{n_k \mu_k}{n \mu}$ representing the population share and income for the kth group. Similarly, for the between-group component, we obtain:

$$G_b = \sum_{k=2}^{K} \sum_{h=1}^{k-1} \frac{(p_k s_r + p_r s_k) \sum_{i=1}^{n_k} \sum_{j=1}^{n_h} |y_i - y_j|}{(\mu_k + \mu_r) n_k n_h} \tag{12.10}$$

where income shares and populations shares are again used in the weighting. However, either (12.7) or (12.9), or (12.8) or (12.10), should lead to the same within-class or between-class component results.

I have shown two useful ways of measuring stratification (Liao 2006), once class membership is estimated with the model-based latent class method for ordered (income) classes. Here we consider two straightforward extensions, a Gini decomposition obtained from an adjustment using the proportion of between-class pairs of comparisons and a similarly obtained stratification index. When the total amount of inequality is allocated into the individual (or within) and class (or between) components, the first index of relative stratification can be simply computed as:

$$S_1 = \frac{G_b}{G} = \frac{G - G_w}{G} \tag{12.11}$$

where G_b is the net or total between-class component because all classes are ordered and there is no transvariation. This measure ranges from 0, where all inequality is individual-based and there is no stratification in the population to 1, where all inequality is contributed by stratification and there is no variation within classes. The measure is relative because it is the amount of class inequality expressed as a proportion of total inequality in terms of the Gini index.

A shortcoming of (12.11) is its overemphasis of the between-group differences because G_b is calculated using ordered population groups, which by their very ordered nature will have greater differences between members of different groups than those within the same groups. To have a stratification index that is immune to this overemphasis, we can use the index that focuses on pairwise individual comparison ties or relationships instead of values of (income) differences:

$$S_2 = \frac{\sum_{k=2}^{K} \sum_{h=1}^{k-1} \sum_{i=1}^{n_k} \sum_{j=1}^{n_h} d}{(n^2 - n)/2} \tag{12.12}$$

where d is the number of unique (income) differences existing between any pairs of members i and j belonging to group k and group h, respectively, and the denominator gives the total number of (income) differences between any pairs of the members in a population, simplified from the usual combinatorial formula, $\binom{n}{2}$, the number of combinations of taking two members at a time out of population sized n. For most practical considerations, $d = 1$ because there exists only one unique comparison between two members in a pair. The measure of S_2 is based on the number of stratified members in a population. Whereas S_1 represents the proportion of the Gini index explained by between-group differences in (income) values, S_2 represents the proportion of the number of difference comparison between members in a population that exists between members of stratified groups (or paired population shares). The value range of S_2 is also (0, 1).

Although stratification index S_2 is immune to the overemphasis of between-class (income) value differences, it does not reflect inequality in terms of the Gini. I present below a simple extension of the Gini components and of S_1 by the information gained from S_2. Because S_2 measures the proportion of paired population shares that is between the classes, the Gini index can be directly allocated into the proportion of the Gini that is responsible by the between-group comparisons:

$$G_{b.relative} = S_2 G \tag{12.13}$$

The within-group counterpart can be worked out similarly from (12.12) and (12.13). This measures the proportion of the Gini that is responsible by the between-class comparisons, assuming that all between-class comparisons and within-class comparisons have equal weights regardless of their actual location on the (income) scale. In an almost equal society where only one class can be found but people's income does differ, $G_{b.relative}$ as well as G_b is equal to 0, with $G_{w.relative}$ equal to G as well as G_w. When there is stratification, however, $G_{b.relative}$ tends to be penalized because $G_{w.relative}$ does not reduce to zero when G_w is zero. Because S_1 is dominated by the between-class component, we further adjust it by S_2, obtaining:

$$S_3 = S_2 S_1 \tag{12.14}$$

The measure of S_1 is made relative to the proportion of paired comparisons. S_2 can be interpreted with 0 being no stratification and 1 being full stratification, with 0.5 as a halfway point. However, unlike S_2, which is in terms paired comparisons only, S_3 gives us the proportion of the Gini that is between classes *and* responsible by paired comparisons between classes. It is always lower than S_1 and S_2 unless for the two extreme values of 0 and 1 (for S_1 or S_2).

To illustrate, I present in Table 12.1 the three inequality measures – the Gini, the within- and between-class components of the Gini, and the indices of relative stratification, S_1, S_2, and S_3 – for the four provinces of the Ilocos region (Table 12.1). The model-suggested classification schemes were used to obtain the ordering of the classes in the income distributions before computing decompositions. According to the Gini, Pangasinan has the

Table 12.1 Comparing the Gini, its components, and relative stratification, the Filipino income data

Province	Gini	$Gini_{within}$	$Gini_{between}$	$Gini_{w.relative}$	$Gini_{b.relative}$	S_1	S_2	S_3
Pangasinan	0.401657	0.042992	0.358665	0.163440	0.238217	0.892964	0.593086	0.529604
La Union	0.462640	0.102090	0.360550	0.257053	0.205587	0.779332	0.444378	0.346318
Ilocos Norte	0.449627	0.142308	0.307319	0.340679	0.108948	0.683498	0.242308	0.165617
Ilocos Sur	0.459525	0.058951	0.400574	0.231376	0.228149	0.871713	0.496488	0.432795
The Ilocos Region	0.426951	0.046137	0.380813	0.179057	0.247893	0.891938	0.580614	0.517871

lowest individual inequality while La Union the highest. However, Pangasinan actually has a much higher level of relative stratification according to the relative stratification indices when compared with La Union (0.89 versus 0.78, 0.59 versus 0.44, and 0.53 versus 0.35). Their between-class components (G_b) are quite similar; it is the difference in their within-class components (G_w) that determines the difference in the index of relative stratification of S_1, the number of such differences S_2, and the summary S_3. It is also revealing to contrast Ilocos Norte and Ilocos Sur: The two provinces have about the same amount of total inequality as measured by Gini, 0.45, but Ilocos Norte has a higher amount of individual inequality while Ilocos Sur has a higher mount of class inequality. The former province has an S_1 of 0.68, an S_2 of 0.24 and an S_3 of 0.17 while the latter has an S_1 of 0.87, an S_2 of 0.50 and an S_3 of 0.43, indicating about double amount of stratification in the southern province when compared to the northern counterpart. Compared with Ilocos Norte, Ilocos Sur has 0.19 of the Gini index more generated by stratification according to S_1, or twice as many of the pairwise relations explained by stratification as suggested by S_2, and more than twice as much Gini explained by pair-based contrasts between classes as indicated by S_3.

To further demonstrate the issue of stratification in (income) distributions, we consider below three simulated samples presented at the outset of the chapter, each of which has 900 cases, generated as a random normal (or a normal and a lognormal) variate:

Sample A: $\mathcal{N}$ ($\ln\mu = 2.2$, $\ln\sigma = 1.5$, $n = 900$)
Sample B: ($\mathcal{N}(\ln\mu = 1.2$, $\ln\sigma = 0.1$, $n = 600$) & $\mathcal{LN}(\ln\mu = 2.0$, $\ln\sigma = 0.3$, $n = 300$)
Sample C: $\mathcal{N}(\ln\mu = 1.2$, $\ln\sigma = 0.1$, $n = 350$), $\mathcal{N}$ ($\ln\mu = 1.8$, $\ln\sigma = 0.1$, $n = 300$) & $\mathcal{LN}$ ($\ln\mu = 2.3$, $\ln\sigma = 0.3$, $n = 250$)

By design, the first sample has no stratification; the second sample has two classes; the third sample contains three classes. For the first simulated sample, there can be only one cluster identified, as it should because of the condition under which the data are generated. Since the model is estimated with the minimum number of classes (i.e., 1), no plots are produced. The BIC, classification, uncertainty, and density plots for the second and third samples are presented in Figures 12.9 and 12.10 (the first is a trivial point, thus not reported in a figure).

For Sample B, a two-class model provides the best fit, as it should, according to the varying-variance model. The density and uncertainty plots further confirm the choice. Similarly, a three-class model is the one with the best fit for Sample C, according to the varying-variance assumption. Again, that choice is confirmed by the uncertainty and density plots. All the results should come as no surprise because the data are simulated with one, two, and three clusters for the three samples respectively.

Next, we compare the Gini and the class inequality measures for the three

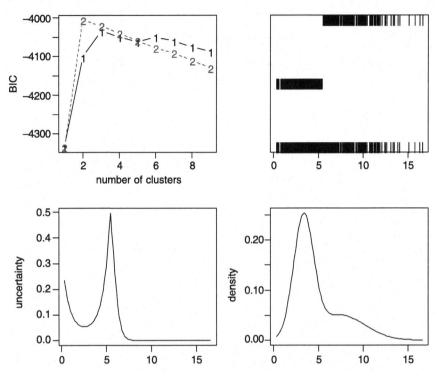

Figure 12.9 Simulated income data (Sample B) according to the mixture distribution of $\mathcal{N}(\ln\mu = 1.2,\ \ln\sigma = 0.1,\ n = 600)$ & $\mathcal{LN}(\ln\mu = 2.0,\ \ln\sigma = 0.3,\ n = 300)$; Gini: 0.296517

samples (Table 12.2). For the sake of comparison, we also include the Gini component decomposition results for the three hypothetical samples. The comparison of the simulated data should shed further light on the within- and between-class measures and the relative stratification indices because of the simulated, controlled nature of the three datasets.

For the three simulated samples, the comparison is informative. According to the Gini index, there is no discernable difference between the three samples, all yielding a coefficient of around 30 per cent. According to the model-based latent class analysis, Sample A has only one stratum, and thus has no class inequality, with a G_b of 0, G_w equal to G, and the stratification indices of 0. Sample B and Sample C both have a relatively high degree of class inequality because of the obvious stratification in the data. Sample B has a higher level of individual inequality than Sample C because of the greater total cluster-specific variances due to few clusters. The difference in stratification between the two samples is 13 per cent when using the relative stratification index 1 as the gauge but 20 per cent or greater if the other two indices are used, with Sample C having a higher amount of between-class inequality. Note that S_1 measures the amount of inequality between classes relative to

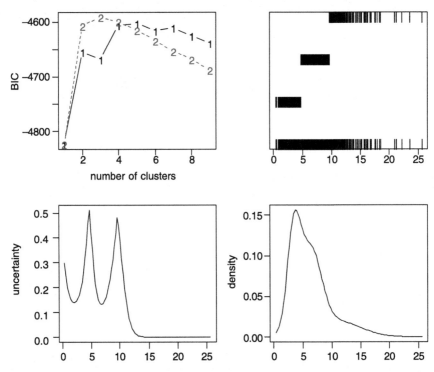

Figure 12.10 Simulated income data (Sample C) according to the mixture distribution of $\mathcal{N}$ ($\ln\mu = 1.2$, $\ln\sigma = 0.1$, $n = 350$), $\mathcal{N}$ ($\ln\mu = 1.8$, $\ln\sigma = 0.1$, $n = 300$) & $\mathcal{LN}$ ($\ln\mu = 2.3$, $\ln\sigma = 0.3$, $n = 250$); Gini: 0.297532

the total amount of inequality measured in Gini anywhere in the sample. A high value may be found even though the total amount inequality is low. For a more complete understanding of the patterns of stratification, we now consider S_2, which shows that about 41 per cent of pairwise comparative differences in Sample B are attributable to stratification whereas the amount is 61 per cent in Sample C. Index S_3 shows that 29 per cent of the between-class proportion of the Gini is due to the paired comparisons between classes in Sample B, and that percentage is 52 for Sample C. In the last two simulated samples, the amount of inequality is moderate although the majority of which, especially in the case of Sample C, is found in stratified inequality. For a measure of class inequality, the between-class components of the Gini index can be consulted with. Either the G_b or the $G_{b.relative}$ gives a greater amount of between-class component of the Gini than its within-class counterpart for Sample C; the same is not true for Sample B because the 'relative' between-class component accounts for less than half of the Gini when adjusted by the proportion of between-class comparisons though the 'absolute' between-class component has a much higher value than the 'absolute' within-class component. The 'absolute' (in the sense that absolute differences

Table 12.2 Comparing Gini decomposition and relative stratification, three simulated income samples

Sample	Gini	$Gini_w$	$Gini_b$	$Gini_{w,relative}$	$Gini_{b,relative}$	S_1	S_2	S_3
A: N ($\ln\mu = 2.2$, $\ln\sigma = 1.5$, $n = 900$)	0.299843	0.299843	0.000000	0.299843	0.000000	0.000000	0.000000	0.000000
B: $N(\ln\mu = 1.2$, $\ln\sigma = 0.1$, $n = 600$) & $LN(\ln\mu = 2.0$, $\ln\sigma = 0.3$, $n = 300$)	0.296517	0.084951	0.211567	0.175396	0.121122	0.713505	0.408481	0.291453
C: N ($\ln\mu = 1.2$, $\ln\sigma = 0.1$, $n = 350$), N ($\ln\mu = 1.8$, $\ln\sigma = 0.1$, $n = 300$) & LN ($\ln\mu = 2.3$, $\ln\sigma = 0.3$, $n = 250$)	0.297532	0.044741	0.252791	0.116074	0.181457	0.849626	0.609875	0.518166

are computed) Gini index and its components and the 'relative' (in the sense that the amount of stratified differences are made relative to a total amount or further relative to paired comparison portions) components and indices can be used together to assess inequality in a population to offer a better, more insightful understanding.

12.5 Summary

In this chapter I identified that for studying (income) inequality the Gini index is sensitive to individual-based differences and rather insensitive to class-based stratification. I demonstrated a model-based latent class method for estimating ordered classes within a distribution, whose membership is further used to decompose the Gini index into the within- and between-class components of inequality. The components are then used to form a Gini-based index, a comparison-based index, and a Gini-based paired comparison-adjusted index of relative stratification.

Both the empirical income data from the Philippines and the simulated data illustrate that the Gini may be misleading in understanding stratification when only the overall amount of inequality is considered. Using the method presented, the researcher can better understand and analyze inequality by separating the individual-based from the class-based inequality. The true power of the Gini index is released when we tease out the distinction between the two types of inequality by assessing Gini components and the relative stratification indices. The Gini index – when extended and informed by the model-based latent cluster analysis – can not only shed light on the amount of inequality that is individual-based but also the amount of inequality that is class-based. The Gini, as the unbound Prometheus, has potentially more power, and possesses much potency for the study of economic and social stratification.

References

Balisacan, A. M. (2001). 'Poverty Comparison in the Philippines: Is What We Know about the Poor Robust?' Asian and Pacific Forum on Poverty: Reforming Policies and Institutions for Poverty Reduction, Asian Development Bank, Manila, February 5–9, 2001.

Balisacan, A. M. and N. Fuwa. (2003). 'Is Spatial Income Inequality Increasing in the Philippines?' The United Nations University/World Institute for Development Economic Research Project Conference on Spatial Inequality in Asia, United Nations University Centre, Tokyo, March 28–29, 2003.

Banfield, J. D. and A. E. Raftery. (1993). 'Model-Based Gaussian and Non-Gaussian Clustering.' *Biometrics* 49: 803–821.

Chotikapanich, D. and W. Griffiths. (2001). 'On Calculation of the Extended Gini Coefficient.' *Review of Income and Wealth* 47 (4): 541–547.

Dagum, C. (1997a). 'A New Approach to the Decomposition of the Gini Income Inequality Ratio.' *Empirical Economics* 22 (4): 515–531.

Dagum, C. (1997b). 'Decomposition and Interpretation of Gini and the Generalized Entropy Measures.' *Proceedings of the American Statistical Association, Business and Economic Statistics Section, 157th Meeting*: 200–205.

Dagum, C. (1998). 'Fondements de bien-être social et décomposition des mesures d'inégalité dans la répartition du revenu.' *Economie Appliquée*: 151–202.

Everitt, B. S. (1993). *Cluster Analysis*. London: Edward Arnold.

Fraley, C. and A. E. Raftery. (1999). 'MCLUST: Software for Model-Based Cluster Analysis.' *Journal of Classification* 16: 297–306.

Fraley, C. and A. E. Raftery. (2002). 'Model-Based Clustering, Discriminant Analysis, and Density Estimation.' *Journal of American Statistical Association* 97: 611–631.

Gini, C. (1912). 'Variabilitá e mutabilitá: Contributo allo studio delle distribuzioni e delle relazioni statistiche. In *Studi Economico-giuridici della Regia Facoltà Giurisprudenza*, anno III, parte II. Bologna: Cuppini.

Kaufman, L and P. J. Rousseuw. (1990). *Finding Groups in Data*. New York: Wiley.

Liao, T. F. (2006). 'Measuring and Analyzing Class Inequality with the Gini Index Informed by Model-Based Clustering.' *Sociological Methodology* 36: 201–224.

Lorenz, M. O. (1905). 'Methods of Measuring Concentration of Wealth', *Journal of the American Statistical Association*, 9: 209–219.

Milanovic, B. and S. Yitzhaki. (2002). 'Decomposing World Income Distribution: Does the World Have a Middle Class?' *Review of Income and Wealth* 48: 155–178.

Mussard, S., M. Terraza, and F. Seyte. (2003). 'Decomposition of Gini and the Generalized Entropy Inequality Measures.' *Economics Bulletin* 4: 1–5.

Roeder, K. and L. Wasserman. (1997). 'Practical Bayesian Density Estimation Using Mixtures of Normals.' *Journal of American Statistical Association* 92: 894–902.

Vermunt, J. and J. Magidson. (2002). 'Latent Class Cluster Analysis.' In Applied Latent Class Analysis, edited by J. A. Hagenaars and A. L. McCutchen, pp. 89–106. Cambridge, UK: Cambridge University Press.

Yao, S. (1999). 'On the Decomposition of Gini Coefficients by Population Class and Income Source: A Spreadsheet Approach and Application.' *Applied Economics* 31: 1249–1264.

Yao, S. and J. Liu. (1996). 'Decomposition of Gini Coefficients by Class: A New Approach. *Applied Economics Letters* 3: 115–119.

Yitzhaki, S. (1994). 'Economic Distance and Overlapping of Distributions.' *Journal of Econometrics* 61: 147–159.

Yitzhaki, S. (2003). 'Gini's Mean Difference: A Superior Measure of Variability for Non-Normal Distribution.' *Metron* 61: 285–316.

Part IV

Lorenz curve and Gini measures in applied economics

13 The Lorenz curve in economics and econometrics

Christian Kleiber

13.1 Introduction

One hundred years ago, in June 1905, a short article entitled Methods of Measuring the Concentration of Wealth appeared in the *Publications of the American Statistical Association* (the forerunner of the *Journal of the American Statistical Association*), proposing a simple method, subsequently called the Lorenz curve, for visualizing distributions of income or wealth with respect to their inherent 'inequality' or 'concentration.' Its author, Max Otto Lorenz, was about to complete his Ph.D. dissertation at the University of Wisconsin. This article apparently remained his only publication in a scientific journal, and it made him famous. A short biography of M.O. Lorenz is available in Kleiber and Kotz (2003, pp. 263–265).

According to Derobert and Thieriot (2003), the term 'Lorenz curve' occurs for the first time in King (1912), a statistics textbook written for economists and social scientists. However, it was not until the early 1970s that interest in the Lorenz curve increased substantially, at least in the English-language statistical and economic literature, triggered by the seminal papers of Atkinson (1970) and Gastwirth (1971). They presented the welfare-economic implications of Lorenz-curve comparisons (Atkinson) and a simple definition of the Lorenz curve for fairly general distributions (Gastwirth). It did not hurt that both were published in highly regarded journals. Among the first contributions of this new wave were Sen's (1973) Radcliffe lectures at the University of Warwick, Fellman's (1976) analysis of transformations, and Jakobsson's (1976) and Kakwani's (1977) studies of progressive taxation.

In the statistical literature, an important paper is due to Goldie (1977) who studied the asymptotics of the Lorenz curve in what nowadays would be called an empirical-process framework. At about the same time, the Lorenz ordering found a multitude of applications in theoretical statistics, often in the form of the more restrictive majorization ordering, among them inequalities for power functions in multivariate analysis. See Marshall and Olkin (1979) and Tong (1988, 1994). The monographs of Arnold (1987) and Csörgö, Csörgö and Horvath (1986) further popularized the concept among statisticians, leading to numerous applications, notably in reliability theory.

The *Current Index of Statistics*, for the year 2004, provides some 140 papers with the keywords 'Lorenz curve' or 'Lorenz order,' while the 2004 version of *EconLit*, the American Economic Association's electronic database, provides some 200 hits just for the years 1969–present. Presumably more than 500 methodological papers have been written in the last 50 years in statistical and econometric journals, not to mention numerous publications of an applied nature that do not list 'Lorenz curve' as a keyword.

In view of this large number of publications it appears impossible to provide a comprehensive view in a short chapter such as the present one. Instead, this chapter tries to survey selected applications of the Lorenz curve and of the closely connected Lorenz and majorization orderings in economics and econometrics. My survey is somewhat biased towards statistical distribution theory. In particular, the two classical topics related to the Lorenz curve are not covered at all: economic disparity measures and taxation problems. For surveys of these I refer to Mosler (1994) and to Arnold (1990) and Lambert (2001), respectively.

13.2 Lorenz curves and the Lorenz order

To draw the Lorenz curve of an *n*-point empirical distribution $\mathbf{x} = (x_1, \ldots, x_n)$, $x_i \geq 0$, $\sum_{i=1}^{n} x_i > 0$, say of household income, one plots the share $L(k/n)$ of total income received by the $k/n \cdot 100\%$ of the poorest households, $k = 0, 1, 2, \ldots, n$, and interpolates linearly. In the discrete (or empirical) case the Lorenz curve is therefore defined in terms of the $n + 1$ points

$$L\left(\frac{k}{n}\right) = \frac{\sum_{i=1}^{k} x_{i:n}}{\sum_{i=1}^{n} x_{i:n}}, \quad k = 0, 1, \ldots, n, \tag{13.1}$$

where $x_{i:n}$ denotes the *i*th smallest income, and a continuous curve $L(u)$, $u \in [0, 1]$, is given by

$$L(u) = \frac{1}{n\bar{x}} \left\{ \sum_{i=1}^{\lfloor un \rfloor} x_{i:n} + (un - \lfloor un \rfloor) x_{\lfloor un \rfloor + 1:n} \right\}, \quad 0 \leq u \leq 1,$$

where $\lfloor un \rfloor$ denotes the largest integer not exceeding un.

The appropriate definition of the Lorenz curve for a general distribution follows easily by recognizing the expression (13.1) as a sequence of standardized empirical incomplete first moments. In view of $E(X) = \int_0^1 F_X^{-1}(t) \, dt$, where the quantile function F_X^{-1} is defined as the pseudoinverse of the cumulative distribution function (CDF), F_X,

$$F_X^{-1}(t) = \sup\{x \mid F_X(x) \le t\}, \quad t \in [0, 1],$$ (13.2)

equation (13.1) may be rewritten in the form

$$L_X(u) = \frac{1}{E(X)} \int_0^u F_X^{-1}(t)\, dt, \quad u \in [0, 1].$$ (13.3)

Hence any distribution supported on the non-negative halfline with a finite and positive first moment admits a Lorenz curve. Following Arnold (1987), I shall occasionally denote the set of all random variables with distributions satisfying these conditions by $\mathcal{L}$. It is a direct consequence of (13.3) that the Lorenz curve has the following properties:

- L is continuous on $[0, 1]$, with $L(0) = 0$ and $L(1) = 1$
- L is increasing
- L is convex.

Conversely, any function possessing these properties is the Lorenz curve of a certain statistical distribution (Thompson, 1976). It is also worth noting that the Lorenz curve itself may be considered a CDF on the unit interval. By construction, the quantile function associated with this 'Lorenz-curve distribution' is also a CDF. It is sometimes referred to as the Goldie curve, after Goldie (1977) who studied its asymptotic properties.

Among Italian statisticians, the representation (13.3) in terms of the quantile function was used as early as 1915 by Pietra who was not aware of Lorenz's contribution. It has later been popularized by Piesch (1967, 1971) in the German-language literature. However, it was not until Gastwirth's 1971 *Econometrica* article that interest increased substantially in the English-language economic and statistical literature.

Incidentally, the definition given above is not Lorenz's original definition. Obviously, there are four variants of the basic idea (see Figure 13.1): Lorenz used the graph $(L(u), u)$, an increasing but concave function. Chatelain (1907), in what would seem to be an independent discovery of the Lorenz curve, employed, up to some scaling, $(u, L(1 - u))$. King (1912) also used Chatelain's version, while Chatelain (1910) himself soon switched to $(u, 1 - L(1 - u))$, without mentioning Lorenz's pioneering work. On combinatorial grounds, it would be of some interest to determine a source proposing the form $(u, 1 - L(u))$, but I have been unable to locate such work. However, this variant coincides, under certain conditions, with the common version of a tool known as the receiver-operating-characteristic (ROC) curve

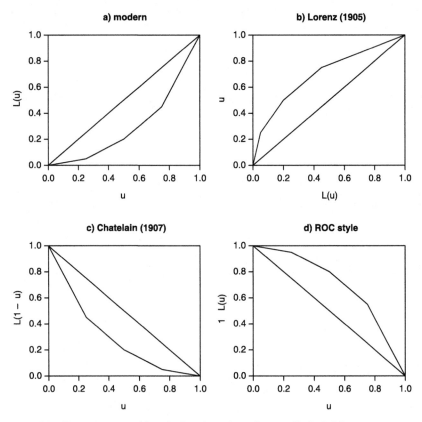

Figure 13.1 Lorenz curves, historical and modern, for **x** = (1, 3, 5, 11).

in biostatistics. Further information on the history of the Lorenz curve may be found in Derobert and Thieriot (2003).

The definition of the Lorenz curve suggests we compare entire distributions by comparing the corresponding Lorenz curves. By construction, the diagonal of the unit square corresponds to the Lorenz curve of a society in which everybody receives the same income and hence serves as a benchmark case against which actual income distributions may be measured. Indeed, virtually every software package that provides this graphical display by default also plots the diagonal of the unit square.

There are several variants of this idea: For two vectors **x** = $(x_1, \ldots, x_n)$, **y** = $(y_1, \ldots, y_n)$ of identical length n satisfying $\sum_{i=1}^{n} x_i = \sum_{i=1}^{n} y_i$, one may define

$$\mathbf{x} \geq_M \mathbf{y} :\Leftrightarrow \sum_{i=n-j}^{n} x_{i:n} \geq \sum_{i=n-j}^{n} y_{i:n}, \quad j = 0, 1, \ldots, n.$$

This is the majorization ordering introduced by Hardy, Littlewood and Pólya (1929). It has found a multitude of applications in statistics and applied mathematics; see the famous text by Marshall and Olkin (1979) for a comprehensive survey. If $\sum_{i=1}^{n} x_i \neq \sum_{i=1}^{n} y_i$ there are several options. The Lorenz curve proceeds via rescaling of the data, i.e. the transformation $(x_1, \ldots, x_n) \mapsto (x_1/\sum_{i=1}^{n} x_i, \ldots, x_n/\sum_{i=1}^{n} x_i)$, thereby extending majorization in two directions, permitting (i) scale-free comparisons – in economic terms, currencies or inflation play no role – and (ii) comparisons of populations of different sizes (the 'population principle' of economic inequality measurement). Finally, a general definition based on (13.3) permits comparisons of fairly arbitrary distributions, provided the corresponding random variables are non-negative with positive expectations:

Definition 13.1 *For $X_1, X_2 \in \mathcal{L}$, the random variable X_1 is said to be at least as unequal (or variable) as X_2 in the Lorenz sense if $L_1(u) \leq L_2(u)$ for all $u \in [0, 1]$. That is,*

$$X_1 \geq_L X_2 :\Leftrightarrow L_1 \leq L_2. \tag{13.4}$$

It is convenient to use the notations $X_1 \geq_L X_2$ and $F_1 \geq_L F_2$ simultaneously. Economists usually prefer to denote the situation where $L_1 \leq L_2$ as $X_2 \geq_L X_1$, because the distribution F_2 is, in a certain sense, associated with a higher level of economic welfare (Atkinson, 1970). Here I shall use the form (13.4) which appears to be the common one in the statistical literature.

It is clear from (13.4) that the Lorenz order is a partial order; it is scale free in the sense that

$$X_1 \geq_L X_2 \Leftrightarrow a \cdot X_1 \geq_L b \cdot X_2, \quad \text{for all } a, b > 0.$$

13.3 Characterizations

Since any distribution is characterized by its quantile function it follows from (13.3) that the Lorenz curve characterizes a distribution in $\mathcal{L}$ up to a scale parameter (e.g. Iritani and Kuga, 1983). As mentioned above, the Lorenz curve itself may be considered a CDF on the unit interval. This implies, inter alia, that this 'Lorenz-curve distribution' – having bounded support – can be characterized by the sequence of its moments. Furthermore, these 'Lorenz-curve moments' characterize the underlying distribution up to a scale parameter. This characterization is due to Aaberge (2000). Below I present a slightly different account, following Kleiber and Kotz (2002), which relates the problem to the moment problem of order statistics.

What are the moments of the 'Lorenz-curve distribution'? Denote by X_L a random variable supported on $[0, 1]$ with CDF L. Then

$$E(X_L^k) = k \int_0^1 u^{k-1} \{1 - L(u)\} du.$$

It is not difficult to see that

$$E(X_L) = \frac{G}{2} + \frac{1}{2},$$

where

$$G = 2 \int_0^1 (u - L(u)) du = 1 - 2 \int_0^1 L(u) du \qquad (13.5)$$

is the Gini coefficient, perhaps the most widely used measure of income inequality (Gini, 1914). The Gini index is a relative measure of income inequality since it depends only on income shares. A sizable number of alternative representations are available. For the characterizations of interest here, the expression

$$G = 1 - \frac{\int_0^\infty \{1 - F(x)\}^2 dx}{E(X)} = 1 - \frac{E(X_{1:2})}{E(X)}, \qquad (13.6)$$

presumably due to Arnold and Laguna (1977), is the most appropriate. Here the order statistics $X_{i:n}$ are deined in the ascending order, i.e. $X_{1:n} \le X_{2:n} \le \ldots \le X_{n:n}$. Kakwani (1980) proposed a one-parameter family of generalized Gini indices by introducing different weighting functions for the area under the Lorenz curve,

$$G_n = 1 - n(n-1) \int_0^1 L(u)(1-u)^{n-2} du,$$

here n is a non-negative integer. The traditional Gini coefficient is obtained for $n = 2$. Donaldson and Weymark (1980, 1983) and Yitzhaki (1983) have arrived at the same family from different considerations. These authors also defined a family of 'equally-distributed-equivalent-income functions' of the form

$$\Xi_n = -\int_0^\infty x \, d\{(1 - F(x))^n\},$$

which may be rewritten as $\Xi_n = \int_0^\infty \{1 - F(x)\}^n \, dx$. Muliere and Scarsini (1989) observed that Ξ_n equals $E(X_{1:n})$ and that

$$G_n = 1 - \frac{\Xi_n}{E(X)} = 1 - \frac{E(X_{1:n})}{E(X)}. \tag{13.7}$$

Equation (13.7) is a direct generalization of (13.6).

This shows that the Lorenz-curve moments are closely related to moments of order statistics. Furthermore, it suggests to reduce the characterization in terms of Lorenz-curve moments to the well-known moment problem of order statistics.

The moment problem of order statistics inquires to what extent the CDF F is uniquely determined by (a subset of) the first moments of all of its order statistics

$$\{E(X_{i:n}) \mid i = 1, 2, \ldots, n; n = 1, 2, 3, \ldots\}. \tag{13.8}$$

It follows from

$$E(X_{i:n}) = i\binom{n}{i} \int_0^1 F^{-1}(u) \, u^{i-1}(1 - u)^{n-i} \, du$$

that $E|X_{i:n}| \le c \cdot E|X|$, for some $c > 0$; thus a finite mean of the parent distribution assures the existence of the first moment of any order statistic. This implies that characterizations in terms of the moments of order statistics are of interest for heavy-tailed distributions of the Pareto type, for which only a few moments exist and, consequently, no characterization in terms of (ordinary) moments is feasible. Many parametric models for the size distribution of personal income are of this type; see Kleiber and Kotz (2003) for a recent survey. In view of the familiar recurrence relation (David, 1981, p. 46)

$$(n - i) E(X_{i:n}) + i E(X_{i+1:n}) = n E(X_{i:n-1})$$

it is not necessary to know the whole array (13.8); one merely requires one moment for each sample size, e.g. the sequence of expectations of minima $E(X_{1:n})$ will suffice. The basic characterization result is thus as follows:

Lemma 13.1 *Let* $E|X| < \infty$. *For* $n = 1, 2, 3, \ldots$, *let* $i(n)$ *be an integer with* $1 \le i(n) \le n$. *Then,* F *is uniquely determined by the sequence* $\{E(X_{i(n):n}) \mid n = 1, 2, 3, \ldots\}$.

The most natural choices for $i(n)$ are either 1 or n. Many refinements of this fundamental result are available in the literature; see, for example, Kamps (1998) for further details. Lemma 13.1 yields the following characterization via the moment problem of order statistics:

Theorem 13.1 *Any* $F \in \mathcal{L}$ *is characterized, up to a scale, by its sequence of generalized Gini indices,* $\{G_n\}$.

Various extensions of this theorem are discussed by Kleiber and Kotz (2002).

As an example, consider the exponential distribution with scale parameter λ. Its CDF is $F(x) = 1 - e^{-\lambda x}$, $x \ge 0$, $\lambda > 0$, and therefore $E(X_{1:n}) = \lambda/n$, hence the sequence $\{G_n \mid G_n = 1 - 1/n\}$ characterizes the family of exponential distributions up to a scale.

13.4 The Lorenz order within parametric families of income distributions

Parametric models for the size distribution of personal income have been of interest to econometricians and applied statisticians for more than a hundred years. An income distribution has the property that its CDF F is supported on the positive halfline, i.e. $\mathrm{supp}(F) \subseteq [0, \infty)$. Atkinson's (1970) classic paper has created much interest in stochastic orders for the comparison of income distributions such as the Lorenz order. It is therefore quite surprising that only fairly recently attempts have been made to characterize the Lorenz order within common parametric families of income distributions.

For one- and two-parameter models this is straightforward, and it is well known that the Lorenz order is linear within the Pareto and lognormal families. Indeed, for the Pareto distribution, with CDF $F(x) = 1 - (x/x_0)^{-a}$, $x \ge x_0 > 0$, quantile function $F^{-1}(u) = x_0(1 - u)^{-1/a}$, $0 < u < 1$, and mean $E(X) = ax_0/(a - 1)$ (which exists if and only if $a > 1$), it follows that

$$L(u) = 1 - (1 - u)^{1 - 1/a}, \quad 0 < u < 1. \tag{13.9}$$

Hence Lorenz curves from Pareto distributions with a different a never intersect. Specifically,

$$X_1 \ge_L X_2 \Leftrightarrow a_1 \le a_2.$$

For the lognormal distribution, with CDF $\Phi((\log x - \mu)/\sigma)$, where $x > 0$, $\mu \in \mathbb{R}$, $\sigma > 0$, and Φ is the CDF of the standard normal distribution, the Lorenz curve is given by

$$L(u) = \Phi(\Phi^{-1}(u) - \sigma^2), \quad 0 < u < 1.$$

It follows that $X_1 \geq_L X_2$ if and only if $\sigma_1^2 \geq \sigma_2^2$.

Within three- and four-parameter families the Lorenz order is no longer linear, however. The first results for a three-parameter family are due to Taillie (1981), who studied the generalized gamma distribution. More than a decade later, Wilfling and Krämer (1993) obtained results for the popular Singh-Maddala (1976) family, and Kleiber (1996) considered the even closer-fitting Dagum (1977) distributions. These distributions are special cases of a four-parameter distribution, the generalized beta distribution of the second kind (hereafter: GB2) introduced by McDonald (1984) and Venter (1983) in econometrics and actuarial science, respectively. In empirical applications, the GB2 distribution has been found to outperform its competitors, sometimes by wide margins; see Bordley, McDonald and Mantrala (1996) for a comparative study including some 15 distributions. The GB2 distribution has the density

$$f_{GB2}(x) = \frac{a \, x^{ap-1}}{b^{ap} \, B(p, q) \, [1 + (x/b)^a]^{p+q}}, \quad x > 0, \tag{13.10}$$

where $B(\cdot, \cdot)$ is the beta function and all four parameters a, b, p, q are positive. The parameter b is a scale parameter, the others are shape parameters. Note that a GB2 distribution has finite mean – and, therefore, admits a Lorenz curve – if and only if $aq > 1$. For further details and more than twenty other distributions related to the GB2, see Kleiber and Kotz (2003).

As of early 2005, a complete characterization of the Lorenz ordering within the GB2 family of distributions is still unavailable. The most general result is as follows (Kleiber, 1999):

Theorem 13.2 *Let X_1, X_2 be in $\mathscr{L}$, with $X_i \sim GB2(a_i, b_i, p_i, q_i)$, $i = 1, 2$. Then*

(a) $a_1 \leq a_2, a_1 p_1 \leq a_2 p_2$, and $a_1 q_1 \leq a_2 q_2$ imply $X_1 \geq_L X_2$.
(b) $X_1 \geq_L X_2$ implies $a_1 p_1 \leq a_2 p_2$ and $a_1 q_1 \leq a_2 q_2$.

This leaves open constellations of the type $a_1 \leq a_2$, $p_1 \geq p_2$, and $q_1 \geq q_2$, but $a_1 p_1 \geq a_2 p_2$ and $a_1 q_1 \geq a_2 q_2$. However, Theorem 13.2 encompasses complete characterizations for all subfamilies of the GB2, thereby providing a unified approach to most commonly considered income distribution functions. Specifically, for the Singh-Maddala distribution, with $SM(a, b, q) \equiv GB2(a, b, 1, q)$, Theorem 13.2 yields

$$X_1 \geq_L X_2 \Leftrightarrow a_1 \leq a_2 \text{ and } a_1 q_1 \leq a_2 q_2,$$

for the Dagum distribution with $D(a, b, p) \equiv GB2(a, b, p, 1)$, it implies

$$X_1 \geq_L X_2 \Leftrightarrow a_1 \leq a_2 \text{ and } a_1 p_1 \leq a_2 p_2,$$

for the beta distribution of the second kind, with $B2(b, p, q) \equiv GB2(1, b, p, q)$, we have

$$X_1 \geq_L X_2 \Leftrightarrow p_1 \leq p_2 \text{ and } q_1 \leq q_2,$$

whereas for the log-logistic distribution with $LL(a, b) \equiv GB2(a, b, 1, 1)$ the condition is

$$X_1 \geq_L X_2 \Leftrightarrow a_1 \leq a_2.$$

The proof of part (a) of Theorem 13.2 utilizes a representation of the GB2 distribution as the distribution of the ratio of two independent generalized gamma variates and Taillie's (1981) Lorenz ordering results for that distribution. Necessity is proved via properties of regularly varying functions; see Kleiber (2000, 2002) for further details. Indeed, a comparison of (13.10) and Theorem 13.2 (b) reveals that aq determines the rate of decrease of the density in the upper tail, while ap does likewise for the lower tail. Figure 13.2 provides an illustration for two Dagum distributions: the more unequal distribution is associated with heavier tails, as is to be expected from Theorem 13.2 (b).

13.5 Some probability inequalities in econometrics

A problem in statistical distribution theory that is of considerable interest in econometrics is the distribution of quadratic forms in normal random variables. Suppose x is multivariate standard normal, $x \sim \mathcal{N}(0, I_n)$, A is a real $n \times n$

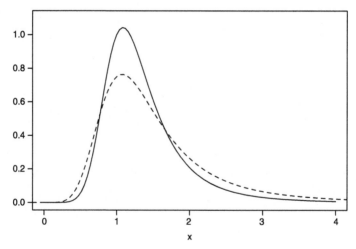

Figure 13.2 Two Dagum distributions: $X_1 \sim D(3, 1, 2)$ (dashed), $X_2 \sim D(4, 1, 2)$ (solid), hence $X_1 \geq_L X_2$

matrix, and consider the quadratic form $Q(x) := x^T A x$. What is the distribution of Q? From the theory of linear models it is well known that

$$A^T = A \text{ and } A^2 = A \Leftrightarrow Q(x) \sim \chi^2(rk(A)).$$

where $rk(A)$ denotes the rank of A. What if A is not an idempotent matrix? This occurs, inter alia, in connection with the Durbin-Watson test, where A is the difference of two positive semidefinite matrices.

The problem may be rewritten in the form

$$Q(x) = \sum_{j=1}^{n} \lambda_j x_j^2$$

where the $x_j \sim \mathcal{N}(0, 1)$ are i.i.d.and the λ_j are the eigenvalues of A. If these eigenvalues are distinct, the distribution of Q is not available in closed form and must be determined numerically. However, it is possible to obtain qualitative results using the Lorenz curve, or rather the majorization ordering.

Suppose now that A is p.s.d., hence $\lambda_j \geq 0$, $j = 1, \ldots, n$. A classical inequality due to Okamoto (1960) states that

Theorem 13.3 *Suppose $X_j \sim \mathcal{N}(0, 1)$ are i.i.d. and $\lambda_j \geq 0$. Then*

$$P\left(\sum_{j=1}^{n} \lambda_j X_j^2 \leq x\right) \leq P(Y \leq x/\tilde{\lambda}), \tag{13.11}$$

where $Y \sim \chi_n^2$ and $\tilde{\lambda} := (\prod_{j=1}^{n} \lambda_j)^{1/n}$ is the geometric mean of the λ_j.

Note that the RHS of (13.11) is a chi-square probability and therefore easily computed. In view of $\tilde{\lambda} = \exp(\frac{1}{n} \sum_{j=1}^{n} \log \lambda_j)$ and the basic majorization inequality $(\log \lambda_1, \ldots, \log \lambda_n) \geq_M (\log \tilde{\lambda}, \ldots, \log \tilde{\lambda})$, the inequality (13.11) suggests that a generalization of Okamoto's inequality in terms of majorization might be available. The following result is due to Marshall and Olkin (1979, p. 303):

Theorem 13.4 *Suppose $X_j \sim \mathcal{N}(0, 1)$, i.i.d., and $a_j, b_j > 0$. Suppose further $(\log a_1, \ldots, \log a_n) \geq_M (\log b_1, \ldots, \log b_n)$. Then*

$$P\left(\sum_{j=1}^{n} a_j X_j^2 \leq x\right) \leq P\left(\sum_{j=1}^{n} b_j X_j^2 \leq x\right).$$

This theorem says that the probability $P\left(\sum_{j=1}^{n} a_j X_j^2 \leq x\right)$ is decreasing in $(\log a_1, \ldots, \log a_n)$, in the sense of majorization, hence the more variable the vector of logarithms of the eigenvalues of A is, the more likely is Q to take on extreme values. Further majorization inequalities and bounds in terms of the harmonic mean of the λ_j are discussed by Tong (1988).

13.6 Condorcet jury theorems

A further problem in statistical distribution theory involving the Lorenz curve, or rather the Lorenz order, is concerned with bounds for the CDF of the sum of heterogeneous Bernoulli variables. This has an interesting application in the theory of social choice. Consider a panel of jurors facing a binary choice. One of the alternatives is assumed to be correct. Being experts, the jurors are able to do better than a fair coin, that is, they are able to identify the correct alternative with a probability exceeding 1/2.

In his *Essai sur l'application de l'analyse à la probabilité des décisions rendues à la pluralité des voix*, Condorcet (1785) expressed the belief that these jurors, utilizing a simple majority rule, would be likely to make the correct decision. Mathematical formulations substantiating this belief have become known as Condorcet jury theorems (CJTs) in social choice and (theoretical) political science; see Grofman and Owen (1989) and Boland (1989) for surveys and further references.

Suppose the random variable X_i indicates whether the ith expert makes the correct decision, where $p_i = P(X_i = 1)$, for $i = 1, \ldots, n$. Define $S := \sum_{i=1}^{n} X_i$, the random variable indicating the number of correct decisions. Clearly, if $p_i \equiv p$ for all i and the experts decide independently,

$$h_k(p) := P(S \geq k) = \sum_{i=k}^{n} \binom{n}{i} p^i (1-p)^{n-i}.$$

In order to avoid ties, it is convenient to suppose that the jury size is odd, $n = 2m + 1$. Hence the majority rule corresponds to $k = m + 1$, and the quantity of interest is

$$h_{m+2}(p) := P(S \geq m + 1) = \sum_{i=m+1}^{2m+1} \binom{2m+1}{i} p^i (1-p)^{2m+1-i}.$$

The classical form of the CJT is as follows:

$h_{m+1}(p) > p$, i.e. with a majority voting system, we are more likely to arrive at the correct decision with a panel of experts of equal competence p than with a single individual of competence p.

This is the simplest and most popular form of the CJT. At least two generalizations would seem to be of interest: the first replaces homogeneity with varying competence, the second allows for correlation. I shall confine myself to the first.

The experts now have different abilities to identify the correct alternative, that is, p_i does not necessarily equal p_j, $i \neq j$. The p_is are collected in a vector, $\mathbf{p} := (p_1, \ldots, p_n)$. A convenient reference point is provided by the average expert competence, $\bar{p}$.

Perhaps surprisingly, this setting invokes the following classical inequality due to Hoeffding (1956):

Lemma 13.2 *Let $k > 0$ be an integer and suppose $\bar{p} \geq k/n$. Then*

$$P(S \geq k) \geq \sum_{i=k}^{n} \binom{n}{i} p^{-i} (1 - \bar{p})^{n-i}.$$

With $k = m + 1$ this yields Boland's (1989) generalization of the CJT:

Theorem 13.5 *Suppose $n \geq 3$, $\bar{p} \geq 1/2 + 1/(2n)$. Then*

$$h_{m+1}(\mathbf{p}) := h_{m+1}(p_1, \ldots, p_n) > \bar{p}.$$

A panel of experts with average competence $\bar{p}$ will therefore do better than a single expert with competence $\bar{p}$.

How is all this related to the Lorenz order? The preceding theorem suggests that, in view of the basic majorization inequality $\mathbf{p} = (p_1, \ldots, p_n) \geq_M (\bar{p}, \ldots, \bar{p})$, it might be true that $\mathbf{p}_1 \geq_M \mathbf{p}_2$ implies $h_{m+1}(\mathbf{p}_1) \geq h_{m+1}(\mathbf{p}_2)$. Indeed there exists a result along these lines, but the details are more involved. A more general version depends on a refinement of Hoeffding's inequality due to Gleser (1975):

Lemma 13.3 *Suppose $\mathbf{p}_1 \geq_M \mathbf{p}_2$. Then*

$$P(S \leq k|\mathbf{p}_1) \leq P(S \leq k|\mathbf{p}_2), \quad k \leq \lfloor n\bar{p} - 2 \rfloor,$$

Note that, for $\mathbf{p}_2 = (\bar{p}, \ldots, \bar{p})$, the lemma yields Hoeffding's result. As discussed by Gleser, the more stringent condition $k \leq \lfloor n\bar{p} - 2 \rfloor$ cannot be removed in the general case. Lemma 13.3 yields

Theorem 13.6 *Suppose $n \geq 7$ and $\bar{p} \geq 1/2 + 5/(2n)$. Then $\mathbf{p}_1 \geq_M \mathbf{p}_2$ implies*

$$h_{m+1}(\mathbf{p}_1) \geq h_{m+1}(\mathbf{p}_2).$$

The majorization approach yields further insights for CJTs, among them results for super-majority voting rules; see Kleiber (2005) for further discussion.

13.7 Generalized Lorenz curves

The Lorenz curve is only a partial order, so what does one do if two Lorenz curves intersect? The most widely used alternative to the Lorenz order is the generalized Lorenz order, due to Shorrocks (1983) and Kakwani (1984). It is defined in terms of the generalized Lorenz curve, GL_X, where

$$GL_X(u) = E(X) \cdot L_X(u) = \int_0^u F_X^{-1}(t)dt, \quad 0 \leq u \leq 1, \tag{13.12}$$

and suggests preferring a distribution F over another distribution G if its generalized Lorenz curve is nowhere below the generalized Lorenz curve of G. This is denoted as $F \geq_{GL} G$. (Note that this definition represents a reversal of the inequality defining the Lorenz order in section 13.2. For the purposes of this section, this is more convenient than the standard version.) Generalized Lorenz curves are nondecreasing, continuous and convex, with $GL_X(0) = 0$ and $GL_X(1) = E(X) =: \mu_X < \infty$. Thistle (1989a) shows that a distribution is uniquely determined by its generalized Lorenz curve. Also, from, for example, Thistle (1989b), generalized Lorenz dominance is equivalent to second-order stochastic dominance, denoted here as $SD(2)$, where $F \geq_{SD(2)} G$ if and only if

$$\int_0^x F(t)\, dt \leq \int_0^x G(t)\, dt \text{ for all } x \in \mathbb{R}_+.$$

Being defined in terms of the Lorenz curve, the generalized Lorenz order encompasses inequality (equity) aspects, being scaled by $E(x)$, it also encompasses size (efficiency) aspects. It is therefore of interest to pursue decompositions of the generalized Lorenz order into these equity and efficiency aspects. The Lorenz curve provides a natural tool for measuring equity. One way to study efficiency, in a global sense, is to consider the classical stochastic order (more familiar as first-order stochastic dominance, or $SD(1)$, in economics), where $F \geq_{SD(1)} G$ if $F(x) \leq G(x)$ for all x. In the terminology of welfare economics, $F \geq_{SD(1)} G$ means that the distribution F is ranked higher than G by all social welfare functions with increasing utility, while $F \geq_{SD(2)} G$ means that F is ranked higher than G by all social welfare functions with increasing and concave utility.

Kleiber and Krämer (2003) provide the following result:

Theorem 13.7 *Suppose F, G are income distributions supported on the positive halfline with finite expectations. Then the following are equivalent:*

(a) $F \geq_{GL} G$.

(b) There exists an income distribution H_1, with $\mu_{H_1} = \mu_G$, such that $F \geq_{SD(1)} H_1 \geq_L G$.

(c) There exists an income distribution H_2, with $\mu_{H_2} = \mu_F$, such that $F \geq_L H_2 \geq_{SD(1)} G$.

As an illustration, consider the gamma distribution, with density

$$f(x) = \frac{\lambda^a}{\Gamma(a)} x^{a-1} e^{-\lambda x}, \quad x > 0,$$

where $\lambda > 0$, $a > 0$. Suppose $F \sim Ga(a, \lambda)$ and $G \sim Ga(\beta, v)$, respectively. Taillie (1981) shows that $F \geq_L G$ if and only if $a \geq \beta$. From, for example, Ramos, Ollero and Sordo (2000, pp. 290–291) we moreover have that $\lambda > v$ and $a/\lambda \geq \beta/v$ imply $F \geq_{GL} G$, whereas $\lambda \leq v$ and $a \geq \beta$ imply $F \geq_{SD(1)} G$. Now suppose $F \sim Ga(20,5)$ and $G \sim Ga(10,4)$, hence $F \geq_{GL} G$. Then H_1 may be chosen as $Ga(15,6)$, whereas H_2 could be $Ga(12,3)$, for example. The generalized Lorenz curves of all these distributions are depicted in Figure 13.3.

13.8 Conclusion

Evidently, the Lorenz curve and the associated Lorenz order have considerable further potential in theoretical and applied economics. On the

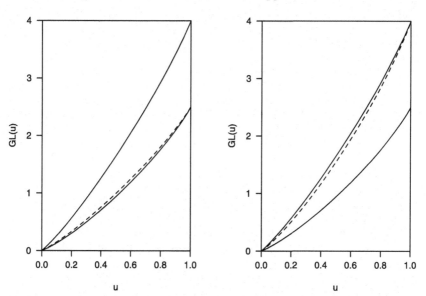

Figure 13.3 Generalized Lorenz curves for two gamma distributions: Ga(20,5) (top) and Ga(10,4) (bottom). Two intermediate generalized Lorenz curves (dashed) as described in Theorem 13.7: $H_1 \sim Ga(15,6)$ (left panel), $H_2 \sim Ga(12,3)$ (right panel).

theoretical side, it would be interesting to explore generalizations of majorization inequalities to the Lorenz case, for example in the context of Condorcet jury theorems.

On the practical side, what appears to be lacking is a suite of tools for distributional analysis in a major statistical software package. As of early 2005, there are several stand-alone tools for distributional analyses that require the use of an additional statistics package for more standard tasks. I am currently working on an add-on package for the R language (R Development Core Team, 2005) that provides functions for the analysis of income data, including Lorenz curves and the fitting of size distributions, while at the same time giving access to a large number of standard tools via the comprehensive R system.

References

Aaberge, R. (2000). Characterizations of Lorenz curves and income distributions. *Social Choice and Welfare*, 17, 639–653.

Arnold, B.C. (1983). *Pareto Distributions*. Fairland, MD: International Co-operative Publishing House.

Arnold, B.C. (1987). *Majorization and the Lorenz Order*. Lecture Notes in Statistics 43, Berlin and New York: Springer.

Arnold, B.C. (1990). The Lorenz order and the effects of taxation policies. *Bulletin of Economic Research*, 42, 249–264.

Arnold, B.C. and Laguna, L. (1977). On generalized Pareto distributions with applications to income data. International Studies in Economics No. 10, Dept. of Economics, Iowa State University, Ames, Iowa.

Atkinson, A.B. (1970). On the measurement of inequality. *Journal of Economic Theory*, 2, 244–263.

Boland, P.J. (1989). Majority systems and the Condorcet jury theorem. The *Statistician*, 38, 181–189.

Bordley, R.F., McDonald, J.B., and Mantrala, A. (1996). Something new, something old: Parametric models for the size distribution of income. *Journal of Income Distribution*, 6, 91–103.

Chatelain, É. (1907). Les successions déclarées en 1905. *Revue d'Économie politique*, 160–170.

Chatelain, É. (1910). Le tracé de la courbe des successions en France. *Journal de la Société Statistique de Paris*, 51, 352–356.

Condorcet, N. (1785). Essai sur l'application de l'analyse à la probabilité des décisions rendues à la pluralité des voix. Paris: Imprimerie Royale.

Csörgö, M., Csörgö, S., and Horvath, L. (1986). *An Asymptotic Theory for Empirical Reliability and Concentration Processes*. Lecture Notes in Statistics 33, Berlin and New York: Springer.

Dagum, C. (1977). A new model of personal income distribution: Specification and estimation. *Economie Appliquée*, 30, 413–437.

David, H.A. (1981). *Order Statistics*, 2nd ed. New York: John Wiley.

Derobert, L. and Thieriot, G. (2003). The Lorenz curve as an archetype: A historico-epistemological study. *European Journal of the History of Economic Thought*, 10, 573–585.

Donaldson, D. and Weymark, J.A. (1980). A single-parameter generalization of the Gini index of inequality. *Journal of Economic Theory*, 22, 67–86.

Donaldson, D. and Weymark, J.A. (1983). Ethically flexible Gini indices for income distributions in the continuum. *Journal of Economic Theory*, 29, 353–358.

Fellman, J. (1976). The effect of transformations on Lorenz curves. *Econometrica*, 44, 823–824.

Gastwirth, J.L. (1971). A general definition of the Lorenz curve. *Econometrica*, 39, 1037–1039.

Gini, C. (1914). Sulla misura della concentrazione e della variabilità dei caratteri. *Atti del Reale Istituto Veneto di Scienze, Lettere ed Arti*, 73, 1203–1248. English translation (2005) in *Metron*, 63, 3–38.

Gleser, L.J. (1975). On the distribution of the number of successes in independent trials. *Annals of Probability*, 3, 182–188.

Goldie, C. (1977). Convergence theorems for empirical Lorenz curves and their inverses. *Advances in Applied Probability*, 9, 765–791.

Grofman, B. and Owen, G. (1989). Condorcet models, avenues for future research. In: B. Grofman and G. Owen: *Information Pooling and Group Decision Making*, Greenwich, CT: JAI Press, 93–102.

Hardy, G.H., Littlewood, J.E., and Pólya, G. (1929). Some simple inequalities satisfied by convex functions. *Messenger of Mathematics*, 58, 145–152.

Hoeffding, W. (1956). On the distribution of the number of successes in independent trials. *Annals of Mathematical Statistics*, 27, 713–721.

Iritani, J. and Kuga, K. (1983). Duality between the Lorenz curves and the income distribution functions. *Economic Studies Quarterly*, 34, 9–21.

Jakobsson, U. (1976). On the measurement of the degree of progression. *Journal of Public Economics*, 5, 161–168.

Kakwani, N. (1977). Applications of Lorenz curves in economic analysis. *Econometrica*, 45, 719–727.

Kakwani, N. (1980). On a class of poverty measures. *Econometrica*, 48, 437–446.

Kakwani, N. (1984). Welfare ranking of income distributions. *Advances in Econometrics*, 3, 191–213.

Kamps, U. (1998). Characterizations of distributions by recurrence relations and identities for moments of order statistics. In: Balakrishnan, N., and Rao, C.R. (eds.): *Handbook of Statistics*, Vol. 16. Amsterdam: Elsevier.

King, W.I. (1912). *The Elements of Statistical Method*. New York: Macmillan.

Kleiber, C. (1996). Dagum vs. Singh-Maddala income distributions. *Economics Letters*, 53, 265–268.

Kleiber, C. (1999). On the Lorenz order within parametric families of income distributions. *Sankhyā*, B 61, 514–517.

Kleiber, C. (2000). *Halbordnungen von Einkommensverteilungen*. Angewandte Statistik und Ökonometrie, Vol. 47. Göttingen: Vandenhoeck & Ruprecht.

Kleiber, C. (2002). Variability ordering of heavy-tailed distributions with applications to order statistics. *Statistics & Probability Letters*, 58, 381–388.

Kleiber, C. (2005). A majorization approach to Condorcet jury theorems. Working paper, Universität Dortmund.

Kleiber, C. and Kotz, S. (2002). A characterization of income distributions in terms of generalized Gini coefficients. *Social Choice and Welfare*, 19, 789–794.

Kleiber, C. and Kotz, S. (2003). *Statistical Size Distributions in Economics and Actuarial Sciences*. Hoboken, NJ: John Wiley.

Kleiber, C. and Krämer, W. (2003). Efficiency, equity, and generalized Lorenz dominance. *Estadística*, 55 (Special Issue on Income Distribution, Inequality and Poverty, ed. C. Dagum), 173–186.

Lambert, P.J. (2001). *The Distribution and Redistribution of Income*, 3rd ed. Manchester: Manchester University Press.

Lorenz, M.O. (1905). Methods of measuring the concentration of wealth. *Quarterly Publications of the American Statistical Association*, 9 (New Series, No. 70), 209–219.

McDonald, J.B. (1984). Some generalized functions for the size distribution of income. *Econometrica*, 52, 647–663.

Marshall, A.W. and Olkin, I. (1979). *Inequalities: Theory of Majorization and Its Applications*. Orlando, FL: Academic Press.

Mosler, K. (1994). Majorization in economic disparity measures. *Linear Algebra and Its Applications*, 199, 91–114.

Muliere, P. and Scarsini, M. (1989). A note on stochastic dominance and inequality measures. *Journal of Economic Theory*, 49, 314–323.

Piesch, W. (1967). Konzentrationsmasse von aggregierten Verteilungen. In: A.E. Ott (ed.): *Theoretische und empirische Beiträge: zur Wirtschaftsforschung*. Tübingen: J.C.B. Mohr (Paul Siebeck), 269–280.

Piesch, W. (1971). Lorenzkurve und inverse Verteilungsfunktion. *Jahrbücher für Nationalökonomie und Statistik*, 185, 209–234.

Piesch, W. (1975). *Statistische Konzentrationsmasse*. Tübingen: J.C.B. Mohr (Paul Siebeck).

Pietra, G. (1915). Delle relazioni fra indici di variabilità, note I e II. *Atti del Reale Istituto Veneto di Scienze, Lettere ed Arti*, 74, 775–804.

R Development Core Team (2005). R: *A Language and Environment for Statistical Computing*. R Foundation for Statistical Computing, Vienna, Austria. URL http://www.r-project.org/

Ramos, H.M., Ollero, J., and Sordo, M.A. (2000). A sufficient condition for generalized Lorenz order. *Journal of Economic Theory*, 90, 286–292.

Sen, A.K. (1973). *On Economic Inequality*. Oxford: Clarendon Press.

Shorrocks, A.F. (1983). Ranking income distributions. *Economica*, 50, 3–17.

Singh, S.K. and Maddala, G.S. (1976). A function for the size distribution of incomes. *Econometrica*, 44, 963–970.

Taillie, C. (1981). Lorenz ordering within the generalized gamma family of income distributions. *Statistical Distributions in Scientific Work*, 6, 181–192.

Thistle, P.D. (1989a). Duality between generalized Lorenz curves and distribution functions. *Economic Studies Quarterly*, 40, 183–187.

Thistle, P.D. (1989b). Ranking distributions with generalized Lorenz curves. *Southern Economic Journal*, 56, 1–12.

Thompson, W.A., Jr. (1976). Fisherman's luck. *Biometrics*, 32, 265–271.

Tong, Y.L. (1988). Some majorization inequalities in multivariate statistical analysis. *SIAM Review*, 30, 602–622.

Tong, Y.L. (1994). Some recent developments on majorization inequalities in probability and statistics. *Linear Algebra and Its Applications*, 199, 69–90.

Venter, G. (1983). Transformed beta and gamma distributions and aggregate losses. *Proceedings of the Casualty Actuarial Society*, 70, 156–193.

Wilfling, B. and Krämer, W. (1993). Lorenz ordering of Singh-Maddala income distributions. *Economics Letters*, 43, 53–57.

Yitzhaki, S. (1983). On an extension of the Gini inequality index. *International Economic Review*, 24, 617–628.

14 Income inequality and the economic position of women in Norway 1970–2002

Hilde Bojer

14.1 Introduction

This chapter studies individual income inequality in Norway during the period when the majority of Norwegian women acquired some degree of economic independence. In the 1950s and 1960s, the labor force participation of Norwegian women was fairly low. It increased dramatically during the 1970s, and is now in line with the other Nordic countries, and among the highest in the world.

The labor force participation of highly educated women in the Nordic countries is broadly similar to that of other European countries. It is the women with little or no education that are more active in paid work in Nordic countries (Rubery *et al.* 1999: 92–93). Here, I shall not discuss the reason for this difference but study some results of the extensive labor force participation of Norwegian women. One notable result is that economic inequality among women has strongly diminished in the period studied. As the increase in labor force participation stagnated during the 1990s, so has the decrease in women's internal inequality.

14.2 Individual income and distributional policy

Traditionally, income is regarded as a measure of possible consumption. Consumption, in its turn, determines the welfare of the individual. Hence, a welfarist approach to income distribution concentrates on household income per equivalent adult as the best empirical approximation to a measure of welfare. Several weaknesses of this approach are well known. From a consumption/welfarist point of view the two most important are that leisure is not included in consumption, and that there may be inequalities in the distribution within the household. But income is more than a means to acquire consumption goods. Income is power, prestige, status and – above all, from a woman's point of view – economic independence. Writing 'from a woman's point of view' does not imply that economic independence is assumed to be of no importance to men. On the contrary, most men take as a matter of course the independence that follows from earning their own income. For women, on the other hand, even the legal right to economic autonomy is historically quite recent in modern economies, and is far from being acquired globally. The universal increase in all industrialized countries of women's participation in paid work may be due to several causes, but one cause is certainly women's universal desire for freedom from economic dependence on parents or spouse.

In fact, if we take modern ethical individualism seriously, the only variable of interest for distributional policy is individual income as far as adults are concerned. In modern, advanced economies, marriage and cohabiting are free choices for both women and men. Children are another matter. Studies of children's welfare have to include the income of the household they live in since they do not have a free choice of parents, and neither can nor ought to provide for themselves.

14.3 Data sources, income concept and inequality measure

The data are collected from income tax returns supplemented by information from register data. Details are given in Section 14.6. The income concept used is individual gross income, which equals all taxable income before deductions and before taxes. It consists of the components capital income, entrepreneurial income, wage income and transfers. This income concept broadened to a certain extent during the 1980s as more transfers became taxable and fringe benefits were included in taxable income. After a tax reform in 1992, both registration and definition of capital income changed with fairly noticeable effects, as we shall see. Therefore, I have made some analyses using gross income less capital income (GILC) as well as gross income (GI).[1] The inequality measure used is the generalized entropy measure with parameters 0.5 and 2.

$$I(a) = \frac{1}{a(a-1)} \left[\frac{1}{n} \sum_j \left(\frac{Y_j}{m} \right)^a - 1 \right] \tag{14.1}$$

Here, Y_j stands for the income of person j, while m is the mean income. $I(2)$ is ordinally equivalent to the coefficient of variation, v: the measure shown in the figures is $v/2$. $I(0.5)$ weights the lower/middle end of the distribution while $v/2$ weights the top of the distribution to an extreme degree. As will be seen, in several cases the two measures give different orderings of distributions.

The generalized entropy measure is additively decomposable by group, (Shorrocks 1984). Let the population consist of groups such that m_g is the mean income of group g, p_g is its share of the population and $\mu_g = m_g/m$. Then:

$$I(a) = \sum_g p_g \mu_g^a I_g(a) + I_B(a) \tag{14.2}$$

$I_g(a)$ is the within-group inequality of group g. $I_B(a)$ is the between-groups inequality, calculated as if all individuals in a group had the same income:

$$I_B(a) = \frac{1}{a(a-1)}\left[\sum_g p_g \left(\frac{m_g}{m}\right)^a - 1\right] \qquad (14.3)$$

An advantage of using the additively decomposable inequality measures is the transparency of the relationship between trends in inequality in each group and relative mean incomes on the one hand, and total inequality on the other hand. As it turned out, the chief influence on overall inequality has been the size of the groups, in particular for women.

Equation (14.2) can also be used to calculate the 'contribution to inequality' of each group as:

$$C_g(a) = p_g \mu_g^a I_g(a) \qquad (14.4)$$

14.4 Structure

The population is divided into eight groups, by sex and occupational status. I have computed inequality for each group, and between-group inequalities. Ideally, the grouping by occupational status should have been according to employment and hours worked, as in labor market surveys. No such information is, however, obtainable from income tax returns. Statistics Norway instead groups individuals according to size and composition of income. Persons with entrepreneurial income, work income and/or taxable transfers above a certain limit are grouped as self-employed, employees or pensioners according to the dominant income component. Others are grouped as others. The majority of these have very low incomes, but may still be economically active. Quite a few women with short part-time work belong to this group. The income limit is set equal to the minimum old-age pension each year.

The occupational status groups show great internal stability. This is obviously true with respect to the size and composition of their income. But there are characteristic and stable differences between the groups also with regard to internal inequality (see Figure 14.1).

The structural changes with respect to occupational groups in the period are shown in Table 14.2. The structure of the adult population has changed

Table 14.1 Relative income by sex and occupational status 2002. Overall mean = 1

Self-employed		Employees		Pensioners		Others	
Men	*Women*	*Men*	*Women*	*Men*	*Women*	*Men*	*Women*
1.95	1.36	1.52	1.00	0.80	0.55	0.25	0.17

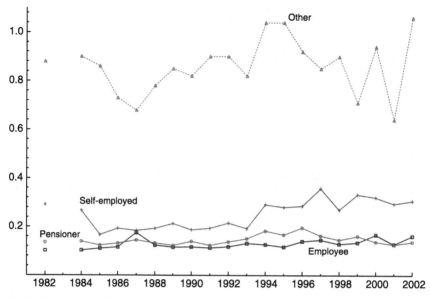

Figure 14.1 Inequality by occupational status

Table 14.2 Men and women by occupational status 1970–2002. (Per cent)

	1970	1982	1992	2002
Men				
Self-emp.	14*	10	8	6
Employee	64*	64	58	60
Pensioner	15*	17	22	24
Other	7*	8	12	9
All	100	100	100	100
Women				
Self-emp.	1*	2	3	2
Employee	25*	41	46	51
Pensioner	17*	25	33	33
Other	57*	32	19	14
All	100	100	100	100

* rough estimates in 1970
Note
Persons 18 years and over

very little as far as men are concerned, while the structural changes have been dramatic for women.

Among men, there has been a steady decrease in the share of self-employed and increase in that of pensioners. The increase in pensioners is mostly demographic, reflecting an ageing population. The percentage of other first increased, and then started decreasing, the increase probably reflecting lengthening periods of education.

For women, there is a dramatic decrease in the share of other, increasing the share of pensioners as well as employees. Again, the increase in pensioners is mainly demographic. But it is worth noting that for many women in the 1970s and beginning of the 1980s, income increased when they became old-age pensioners.[2] The minimum old-age pension is fixed by the Norwegian Parliament (Storting) every year, and may therefore be regarded as an unofficial, administratively fixed poverty line. With this interpretation, the proportion of women earning less than the poverty line has shrunk from around 57 per cent in 1970 to 14 per cent in 2002, not all that different from the corresponding proportion for men, 9 per cent.

This fact alone marks a social revolution in the economic position of women, and has more than doubled their income relative to men. (See Figure 14.2.)

14.5 Results

The main results are presented in the figures below.[3] The data from the 1970s are sparser and less reliable than those from later years. Therefore, only a few of the graphs cover the whole period. The two inequality measures used give the same ordering of years and groups in many cases. I therefore show computations with both only when there are what I judge to be interesting differences.

14.5.1 Women's relative incomes

Figure 14.2 shows women's average income as a percentage of men's average income, overall and for the two large occupational status groups. With some fluctuations, the group relative incomes have been fairly constant in the period, with no discernible long-term trend. Note that pensioners are better off relative to men than employees. Overall, women's relative average income has more than doubled: from 27 per cent in 1970 to 60 per cent in 2002. The increase is entirely due to changes in occupational status.

The apparent stability in the 1990s hides two different developments. Relative wage income increased slowly but steadily, while relative capital income decreased.[4] Women's relative income reflects both differences in wage rates and differences in labor force participation and working hours. The average wage rate of women is about 20 per cent that of men's (Barth and Dahle-Olsen 2004). The rest of the difference in wage income is due to women working part-time to a much greater extent than men.

14.5.2 Inequality

Figure 14.3 shows total individual inequality 1982 to 2002 using both inequality measures. They show roughly the same development up to the end of the 1980s. After 1992, however, they diverge, with $v/2$ showing a marked

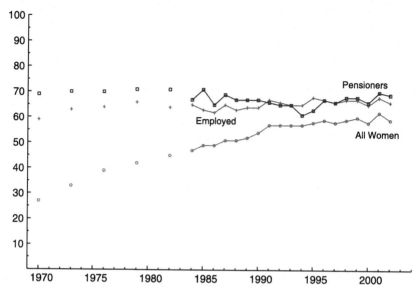

Figure 14.2 Women's relative income 1970–2002, gross income

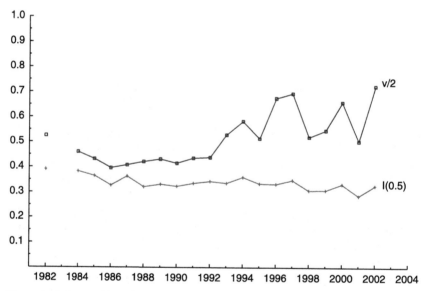

Figure 14.3 Inequality 1982–2002. All adults, gross income

increase in inequality in the 1990s. This increase in inequality is due to an increase in capital income, which accrues mainly to men with high incomes, and therefore strongly influences $v/2$. The measure $I(0.5)$ shows stability, or a slight decrease, if anything.

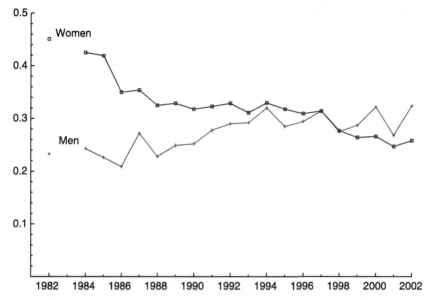

Figure 14.4 Inequality 1982–2002. Women and men, gross income. Inequality measure $I(0.5)$

Figure 14.4 shows that the development in total inequality measured by $I(0.5)$ is the net result of two very different trends. Women's internal inequality consistently decreases, apart from a few small fluctuations. Men's internal inequality increases after about 1985, and fluctuations during the 1990s are larger than in the 1980s. Also, women's internal inequality was greater than men's until the late 1990s, but is now smaller. But here, the situation is depicted differently by the coefficient of variation, as seen in Figure 14.5.

When inequality is measured by the coefficient of variation, men's internal inequality is larger than women's for most of the period. Also, women's inequality seems to increase in 1995 and then reach a permanently higher level than in the preceding ten years. The reason for the change in ordering of women and men is clear: women's inequality is dominated by many very small incomes. Men's inequality is more influenced by a few very high incomes (Lorenz curves supporting this statement are found in Bojer 2003).

14.5.3 Decomposition of inequality

Figure 14.6 clearly demonstrates the structural reasons for women's decreasing inequality. Internal inequality, like relative income in Figure 14.2, has been stable in both the two large occupational groups, with pensioners' inequality slightly larger than that of employees during the whole period. The steady disappearance, year after year, of women with incomes below the poverty line has diminished income inequalities among women;

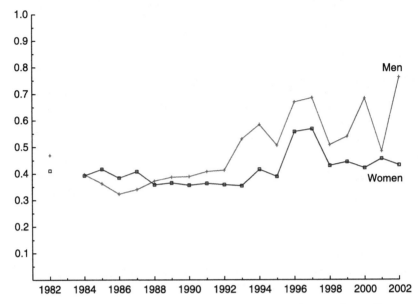

Figure 14.5 Inequality 1982–2002. Women and men, gross income. Inequality measure *v*/2

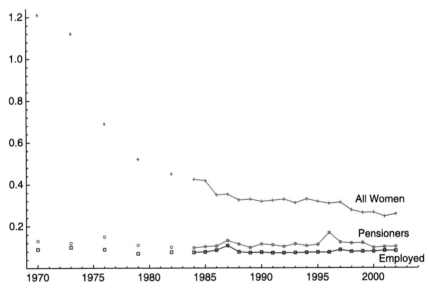

Figure 14.6 Inequality 1970–2002. All women, by occupational status, gross income. Inequality measure *I*(0.5)

unambiguously up to the beginning of the 1990s, less certainly for the last ten years. This internal equalizing of women's income may be specific to Norway, or to the Nordic countries, as explained in the Introduction.

Figure 14.7 shows contributions to inequality for men, women and between-group inequality as described by equations (14.2) and (14.4). The lowest line shows between-group inequality I_B. The contributions to inequality of men and women respectively are written:

$$C_g = p_g \mu_g^{0.5} I_g \text{ for } g = M, W.$$

We see that between-group inequality and the contribution from women's internal inequality steadily diminish, while the contribution from men's inequality increases.

In Figure 14.8 the groups are numbered as follow: Self-employed = 1, Employees = 2, Pensioners = 3 and Other = 4. The decomposition in Figure 14.8 again shows that women's decreased internal inequality is due to decreases in the contribution from others and, above all, to decreasing between-group inequality. Both decreases stem from the diminishing numbers of others.

We see no such clear pattern in the equivalent curves for men's inequality.[5]

14.5.4 Impact of capital income

The last four figures demonstrate the impact of increased capital incomes during the 1990s. The increase has two very different causes. One is a tax

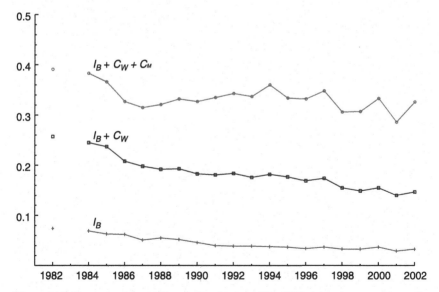

Figure 14.7 Decomposition of inequality by sex 1982–2002, gross income. Inequality measure $I(0.5)$

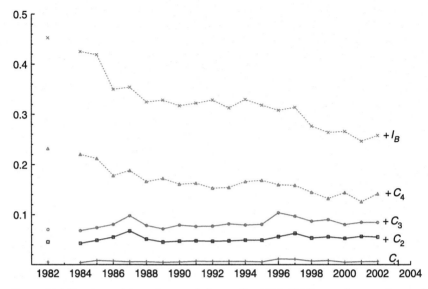

Figure 14.8 Decomposition of women's inequality 1982–2002, gross income. Inequality measure $I(0.5)$

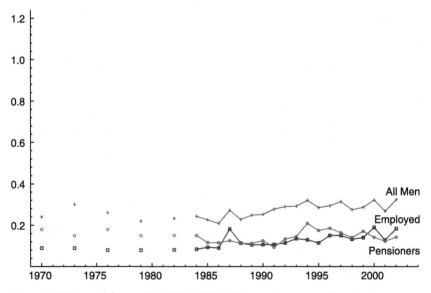

Figure 14.9 Internal inequality 1970–2002. All men, by occupational status, gross income. Inequality measure $I(0.5)$

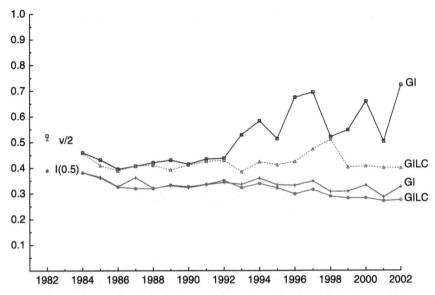

Figure 14.10 Inequality 1982–2002. All adults, gross income (GI) and gross income less capital income (LCI). Inequality measure *I*(0.5)

reform in 1992 which made more types of capital income taxable, and is therefore purely a matter of better registration. The other cause is an economic boom which increased capital income in reality. Figures 14.11 and 14.12 show that capital income makes a considerably larger difference to men than to women.

Of particular interest, I think, is Figure 14.13 which shows that internal inequality of employees has been as good as constant for the last 20 years when capital income is cleansed out. It should be stressed, perhaps, that capital income here and in the following is *gross* capital income, that is, losses and capital expenditures are not deducted.

We see that the internal inequality of women employees is smaller than that of men, and also more stable, even when capital income is removed. This result is not obviously to be expected. True, wage dispersal is smaller for women due to Norway's strongly segregated labor market, with women concentrated in a few service sectors. But, on the other hand, the dispersion of women's working hours is much greater than that of men.

14.6 Data

The data are from Surveys of Income and Wealth produced by Statistics Norway. There are two different types of data. In 1970, 1973, 1976 and 1979 they were samples from income tax returns, so persons without taxable income were not included. I have made rough estimates of the number of

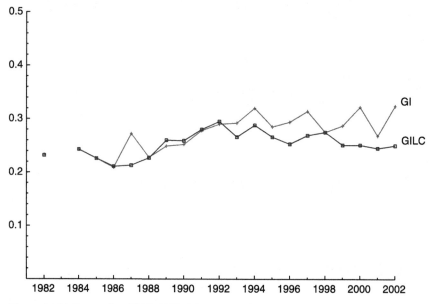

Figure 14.11 Inequality 1982–2002. Men, gross income (GI) and gross income less capital income (GILC). Inequality measure $I(0.5)$

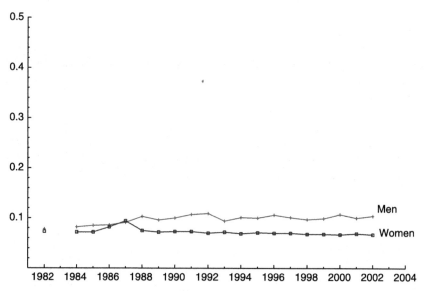

Figure 14.13 Inequality of employees 1982–2002. Women and men, gross income less capital income (GILC). Inequality measure $I(0.5)$

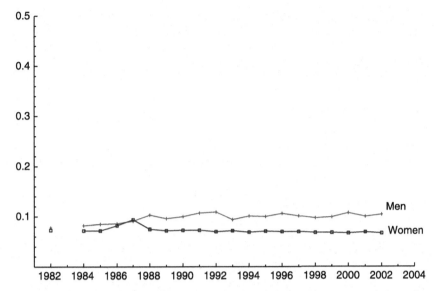

Figure 14.13 Inequality of employees 1982–2002. Women and men, gross income less capital income (GILC). Inequality measure *I*(0.5)

men and women without income by comparing income survey estimates of persons with income with population statistics.

From 1982 on, the Surveys are stratified probability samples of Norwegian households, organized with both households and individuals as units, and comprising the whole population, adults as well as children. I have retained adults 18 years and over only.

From 1984 on, the Surveys are annual. The sample sizes are varying: 18,000 adults in 1982, 5,000 in 1984 and 1985, 7,000 in 1986, 1987, 1988 and 1989, 12,000 in 1990 and from then on increasing every year up to over 50,000 in 2002, except for 1993, when the sample was 7,000 adults.

Notes

1 For further details about data and income concepts see SSB 2004.
2 In Norway, every person is entitled to a minimum old-age pension at 67 years.
3 Detailed numerical results and figures for 2003 and 2004 are found in Bojer (2005a). Data for 2003 and 2004 were not available when this chapter was written. A quick check revealed that figures for these years are substantially the same as for 2001 and 2002.
4 The sharp fluctuations in 2001 and 2002 are due to dividends being retained in 2001 for taxation purposes.
5 Decomposition of men's internal inequality can be found in Bojer (2005b).

References

Barth, E. and H. Dahle-Olsen (2004), 'Lønnsforskjeller mellom kvinner og menn i et tredveårs perspektiv (Wage differences between men and women in a thirty years' perspective)', *Søkelys på arbeidsmarkedet* 21(1): 65–74.

Bojer, H. (2003), *Distributional Justice. Theory and Measurement*, Routledge.

Bojer, H. (2005a), 'Individuell inntektsfordeling 1970–2002', (Individual income distribution 1970–2002), www.folk.uio.no/hbojer.

Bojer, H. (2005b), *Income inequality and the economic position of women in Norway 1970–2002*, Memorandum 07/2005, Department of Economics, University of Oslo.

Rubery, J., M. Smith and C. Fagan (1999), *Women's Employment in Europe. Trends and Prospects*, Routledge.

Shorrocks, A. F. (1984), 'Inequality decomposition by population subgroups', *Econometrica* (52): 1369–1385.

SSB 2004, *Inntekts–og formuesstatistikk for husholdningene 2002*, (Statistics on income and wealth of private households), NOS D310, Statistisk sentralbyrå (Statistics, Norway).

15 Technological choices under institutional constraints

Measuring the impact on earnings dispersion

Elisabetta Croci Angelini and Francesco Farina

15.1 Introduction

The performance of a country is more often evaluated in terms of too high an unemployment rate than too high earnings[1] inequality. The technological decisions of the firms in developed countries have been held responsible for the employment rate, but their impact on earnings dispersion is much less debated. By the same token, labour market regulation is alleged to move the economic system away from the macroeconomic equilibrium, as the minimum wage and the employment protection legislation (EPL) reduce labour demand and slow down the flow of the younger labour force towards employment; nevertheless, the focus is on the target for the employment rate more than on how wide earnings inequality should be tolerated. Recently, wages as well as earnings inequality has gained momentum – almost to the same extent of employment and unemployment rates – not only on equity but also on efficiency grounds, as the firms' production process is considered a co-determining factor in the evolution of pay disparities.[2]

It is apparent that wage dispersion is strictly interwoven with employment rates across skill levels, as they are jointly determined by the trajectories followed by firms in choosing their productive techniques, as well as by labour market institutions providing insurance to risk-averse workers against unemployment and low wages. In addition, the competitive pressure of imports from the developing countries is part of the explanation of the switch to labour-saving techniques.[3]

Very scant research work has been carried on so far to provide empirical evidence on the technological patterns determined by restrictions placed by labour market regulation on the employers' production decisions. We aim at contributing to fill this gap by studying the impact of technological choices on earnings dispersion when institutional constraints narrow the capacity of the firm to decide on the employment level and on the productive techniques combining high-skill and low-skill workers.

Our empirical investigation concerns the European economies after the recession of the early 1990s. In Section 15.2, we compare different approaches to the analysis of the interaction between technology and institutions. In Section 15.3, for each country under scrutiny and for each sector the skill premium (SP) and the high-skill ratio (HR) are related to the index of earning dispersion (EDI) (Gini 1914) we use in order to disentangle the combined effect of earnings and employment percentages of high-, intermediate-, and low-skill workers. In Section 15.4, evidence is presented to account for the evolution of wages and employment at the sectoral level and a Theil decomposition (Theil 1972) is accomplished so to analyse the trends in earnings and wage dispersion between-sectors and within-sectors. Section 15.5 concludes.

15.2 The impact of technologies and institutions on employment and wage levels

The opinion about the trends of employment rates and earnings inequality in the European Union is sharply divided. The empirical investigation indicates that in the past decades bargaining institutions have been compressing the wage distribution, thus causing lower employment of the less educated male workers while female employment has been rising along with an increase in the participation rate (Blau and Kahn 2000). According to the view recently proposed by the OECD, by compressing wages, labour market regulation hampers labour demand. The clue is that those European countries where earnings inequality has risen more than average during the 1990s also appear to have experienced a relative increase in employment (and a relative decrease in unemployment).[4] Other studies contend this interpretation by showing that the sign of the correlation between the employment rate and the earnings inequality turns out to be negative when reference is made to the household level,[5] and for jobs in traditional sectors.[6]

The OECD view relies upon a well-known approach to wage inequality in Europe, which interprets the labour market performances of European countries as a result of the degree of labour market regulation (Krugman 1994). According to the Krugman hypothesis, a downward shift in the relative labour demand for low-skill workers is expected to result in a higher wage inequality in countries characterized by a flexible labour market and in a higher unemployment rate in countries characterized by a rigid labour market. In fact, the tenet is widely shared that starting from the end of the 1970s in many European countries labour market institutions have increasingly protected the wages of the *insiders*, at the cost of a lift in structural unemployment in the two subsequent decades. Under wage compression, employment and participation rates of the low-skill labour force were stuck, especially in those sectors more exposed to harsher international competition.

The Krugman hypothesis was anticipating that in Europe – differently from what was happening in the US where a flexible labour market exists – wage inequality would have decreased, as a consequence of persistent unemployment causing a much lower proportion of low-pay workers at the bottom of the wage distribution.[7] Yet, data for the 1980s and the early 1990s seem to indicate a fall in labour demand not only for the low-skill but also for the high-skill workers; in addition, in the second half of the 1990s labour market deregulation is alleged to have improved the overall employment rate in most EU countries, due to an increasing number of low-skill workers in low-pay jobs, albeit at the cost of widening the wage inequality.[8] While the implementation of active labour market programmes (ALMP) was expected to raise workers' skills and capabilities, and cause an upgrading in wage levels, with possible reduction in wage and/or earnings disparities (Agell 1999 and 2002), other labour market reforms have favoured the expansion of jobs for low-skill workers with temporary labour contracts (Layard and Nickell 1999).

Empirical evidence also indicates that economic growth has remained sluggish in Europe, a possible reason being an interaction between institutions and technological choices which determines an inverse correlation between productivity and employment (van Ark *et al.* 2003). During the first half of the 1990s, productivity gains largely came from the expulsion of low-skill workers; later on, in the period 1996–2001, a rising labour input caused the slowdown in labour productivity and in wage levels at the bottom of the wage distribution (Blanchard 2004 and 2006). Wage levels for every skill level seem to be influenced in Europe by investment decisions made by firms driven by the need to cope with productivity of workers at a constant employment level (Pischke 2005).

These studies suggest that an alternative to the Krugman's view can be envisaged. The influence of institutions does not absolutely orient firms towards the choice of labour-saving techniques, thus compressing the wage distribution and enlarging the unemployment rate. Technological patterns differ, depending on sectoral characteristics, the skill distribution of the labour force, and a varying degree of labour market regulation.

The two main technological strategies conceived by Acemoglu (1999, 2002) respond to different combinations of these factors. The first strategy is the skill-biased technical change (SBTC) driven by the ICT-intensive producing and using sectors. The incentive of high profits stemming from investment in innovation determined in the United States a strong labour demand for highly educated workers, well above the rising supply of new entrants in the labour market with university degrees, thus widening the wage distance between high-skill and low-skill workers (the so-called skill premium). Empirical evidence confirms that wider wage dispersion across skill levels in the US manufacturing was a result of skill-biased organizational changes both within and across plants (Dunne *et al.* 2004).

Acemoglu presents a production function with constant elasticity of substitution (CES):

$$Y(t) = [(A_L(t) L(t))^\rho + (A_H(t) H(t))^\rho]^{1/\rho}$$

where $\rho \leq 1$, and its implicit relative labour demand function, expressing the skill premium, is:

$$\frac{W_H}{W_L} = \frac{A_H/A_L}{(H/L)^{-(1-\rho)}} = \frac{(A_H/A_L)^{(\sigma-1)}}{(H/L)^{-1/\sigma}}$$

The skill premium depends on A_H and A_L, the factor-augmenting technological terms, and on the elasticity of substitution – $\sigma \equiv 1/(1-\rho)$ – between the high-skill (H) and the low-skill (L) workers. The condition for the implementation of SBTC is labour market flexibility. The productivity gaps created by SBTC between the high-skill and the low-skill workers through A_H and A_L respectively should be reflected by the wage and employment gaps between these two groups of workers. Under the condition of $\sigma > 1$, a rising wage inequality is explained by an increase in the A_H/A_L ratio higher than the H/L ratio, which raises the relative wage rate for the more educated and more productive high-skill workers.

In many European countries the SBTC could not develop, as firms have been suffering from an opportunity set of production techniques restrained by labour market institutions, with job protection and minimum wage playing a very relevant role (Acemoglu 2003). To equalize the low-skill workers productivity to their wage above the equilibrium level, employers would have been compelled to resort to 'complementary technologies', whereby low-skill workers share functions and mansions with high-skill workers so raising their labour performances. Differently from the Krugman interpretation, the company facing a rigid labour market does not remain passive, but adjusts its productive technology in order to cope with possible inefficiencies connected to labour market regulation.

To understand why labour market regulation may have prevented Europe from following the skill-biased technological trajectories which characterized the US economy during the 1990s, we construct an example, inspired by Acemoglu (2003), to describe an institutionally-constrained technological decision. Suppose labour market regulation consists of a minimum wage equal to 6 and an EPL causing high firing costs. Assume that in a firm one high-skill worker and one low-skill worker are employed, and the bargaining makes the wage to be equal to ¾ and ½ of productivity for the high skill and the low skill respectively. The high-skill worker's productivity is equal to 24, so that her wage level is 18, while the low-skill worker productivity is equal to 8, but must be paid the minimum wage 6 instead of 4, thus exceeding the ½ of productivity. Total production is 32, total wages are 24, and profits are 8. Now suppose a switch to SBTC, through an innovative investment which costs 1 to the firm. As a second high-skill worker substitutes the low-skill worker, the two high-skill workers are paid, as before, ¾ of productivity. Total production rises to 48, so that the minimum wage would no longer be binding and profits increase to 11 (= 48 − 36 − 1). Alternatively, in order to avoid possibly prohibitive firing costs, but still escape the minimum-wage constraint, the firm could lay out an investment in a 'complementary technology', whereby the low-skill worker shares mansions with the high-skill worker. The employer could consider an investment, assumed to cost 2 and allowing the low-skill worker's productivity to rise from 8 to 12, while the high-skill worker's productivity stays at 24. Since total production would be 36, the minimum wage would not be binding, and profits would increase to 10 (= 36 – 24 – 2).

While profits appear to be higher with the SBTC, we did not quantify yet the firing costs. Under the SBTC the low-skill worker could not be substituted, but must be paid even if he does not take part in production, until the legal dispute is settled. Hence, whether or not the SBTC dominates the 'complementary technology' depends on the effect of the second institutional factor – the EPL – combining with the minimum wage. If the job protection legislation is such to determine a firing cost higher than 1, the higher profitability warranted by the SBTC vanishes.

The rationale conveyed by the numerical example is that when the higher profits permitted by SBTC cannot be obtained, as litigation costs discourage firing the low-skill workers, a 'complementary technology' may be chosen, allowing the low-skill workers' productivity to match the minimum wage. By pointing to the adjustment of technology to institutions, this view may explain the Acemoglu guess that SBTC has spread in Europe to a much lesser extent than in the US. Yet, a comprehensive analysis considering different labour market institutions across the European countries constraining the employers' technological decisions, and their fall-out on labour demand and the wage level for different skill groups, is still lacking.[9]

This interpretative impasse over interactions between technology and institutions as the determinant of earnings dispersion is confirmed by simple calculations. On the basis of the information provided by the ECHP dataset, covering the 15 EU countries (hereafter, EU-15) in the years 1994–2001, we have computed for each country a Gini index for wages net of taxes as well as the ratio of working (with an employer in paid job for at least 15 hours per week) to total population. Since the ECHP dataset only surveys the population aged at least 16, this 'working ratio' is meant to be more informative of both (1) the employment rate,[10] as it focuses on the self-declared employed, while keeping information about the population structure like the activity rate does; and (2) the activity rate,[11] as it provides information on the working population net of the unemployed and of children under 16. The picture is uplifted, but does not change substantially, when the working ratio is referred to all employed persons including the self-employed and those with unpaid work in family enterprise.

Figure 15.1 shows the scatter diagram of the Gini indices and the working ratio for the waves 1 (1994), 4 (1997) and 8 (2001). The Scandinavian countries (Denmark, Finland and Sweden) tend to show higher-than-average working ratios and lower-than-average net wage inequality, so are to be found in the upper left section of the diagram. The Anglo-Saxon countries (Ireland

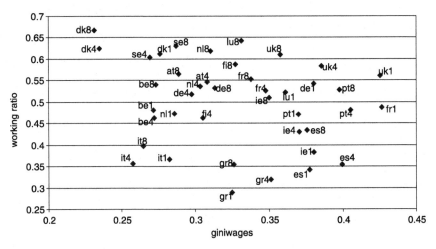

Figure 15.1 Working ratios and Gini net wages in the EU-15 (1994, 1997, 2001)

and the United Kingdom) tend to occupy the upper right section, presenting on the whole higher-than-average levels both for employment (Ireland moves from lower- to higher-than-average working ratios during the eight years of the survey) and for net wage inequality. The Continental countries (Austria, Belgium, France, Germany, Luxembourg and the Netherlands) are positioned in the middle of the picture and the Mediterranean countries (Italy, Greece, Portugal and Spain) in general show the lowest employment rates and, with the exception of Portugal, are found at the bottom of the diagram.

Therefore, no evidence of a unified pattern for employment and wage dispersion emerges in the eight-year period throughout the EU-15, let alone when focusing on the evolution across countries, as the role institutions play in each country is unclear. On the one hand, the wage distribution of European economies was certainly affected by the large movements in employment rates of the 1990s. After the sharp fall in unemployment had caused the 1990–93 recession in the whole EU except Germany (whose cycle was overheated by the inflationary consequences of reunification), the recovery in growth rates in the second half of the decade boosted an Europe-wide increase in the employment rates, also signalled by a structural break in econometric estimates (Mourre 2004; Arpaia and Mourre 2005). On the other hand, in many econometric estimates '(c)ountry dummies explain a larger proportion of the relation between wage inequality and unemployment' (Bertola, Blau and Kahn 2002: 18). Hence, differing 'initial conditions' across countries – such as technological gaps in the productive structure and the impact of the educational system on the skill distribution of the labour force[12] – could have differently impinged both on the employment performance and earnings disparities. The EU-15 widespread heterogeneity in the relationship between employment and earnings dispersion may conceal the presence of more profound regularities beneath aggregate data. In the following, we exploit the availability of microdata directly observing the human capital of the employed workers through matching between skills and working positions.

15.3 The evolution of employment rates and earnings inequality in Europe

Research and empirical evidence about employment growth and wage dispersion across skill levels is very scant. A recent IMF investigation far from conveys the real picture, as 'due to available data, (. . .) results relate to income shares of workers in skilled and un-skilled sectors, rather than to income shares of skilled and un-skilled workers themselves' (IMF 2007: 168). To find out how interactions between institutions and technology impact on earnings distribution, we enquire how the rise in ICT investment relates both to the skill premium and the larger utilization of low-skill and low-pay workers permitted by the relaxation of employment and wage rigidities. In fact, a measure of earnings inequality is needed whereby in measuring earnings dispersion changes in employment across skill levels are taken into account. For instance, in the event of recourse to the strategy of SBTC, due to the decrease induced by labour-saving techniques in the number of low-skill workers, the widening of wage disparities could have been underestimated by the computation of earnings dispersion.

The ECHP dataset permits the breakdown of earnings distribution across 18 economic sectors and 20 working positions, shown in Appendix 15.1 and 15.2, respectively. All information was re-aggregated in three macro-sectors according to their link with information and communication technologies (ICT)[13]: ICT producing (A), intensively ICT users (B), and less intensive ICT utilizing sectors (C), both for manufacturing (1) and Services (2), while working positions were aggregated into three skill levels: high (H), intermediate (I) and low (L). Our investigation covers seven European countries – Belgium, Denmark, France, Italy, Germany, the Netherlands, United Kingdom – whose sectoral structure in terms of employment is shown in Appendix 15.3 for wave 1 (1994) and wave 8 (2001). The reason behind this selection is to refer our analysis to clusters of countries characterized by similar labour markets institutions, so as to compare the cluster of the so-called Continental countries to a representative country from each cluster, namely the United Kingdom for the Anglo-Saxon, Denmark for the Scandinavian and Italy for the Mediterranean cluster.

Variations in the skill premium (SP) – the wedge across wages: $SP = w_H / w_L$ – are contrasted with variations in the 'high-skill ratio' (HR), the fraction of high-to-lower skill workers, where $HR = H / (I + L)$. While the SP signals how the employees' bargaining power interacts with the firm's choice of techniques, the HR signals how the relative proportions of workers across skill categories evolve over time by following this choice.

To better characterize this empirical background, we devise four patterns of technological choices, depending on a varying combination of techno-logical choices and institutions: (1) SBTC; (2) Complementary Technology; (3) Restructuring; (4) Downsizing.

(1) In case regulation does not constrain the substitution of capital and high-skill workers to low-skill workers, firms may find it profitable to intro-duce labour-saving techniques. The presence of SBTC manifests in an increase of both SP and HR, as the high skill-intensive techniques implying the expulsion of low-skill workers push up the share of high-skill workers *vis-à-vis* the low-skill and low-pay workers; (2) In case regulation constrains, firms realize complementary technologies by investing in low-skill workers when EPL inhibits their dismissal due to high firing costs (i.e. too high litiga-tion costs in the courts) and their productivity has to be raised to the level of the minimum wage (legally imposed or defended by unions). The choice of a 'complementary technology' entails a decrease both in the SP and in the HR, through the reduction of minimum wage and/or the relaxation of EPL enlarging the relative number of intermediate and low-skill workers. Firms might also choose intermediate strategies resulting from the influence of add-itional variables, such as the country's productive structure and the peculiar skill characteristics of the labour force; (3) the restructuring strategy, whereby the retrenchment of the low-skill traditional productions under the com-petitiveness pressure of developing economies causes the loss (or the out-sourcing) of low-pay jobs, so that in spite of deregulation wage compression remains (or SP even falls) and the high-skill to low-skill workers ratio (HR) increases; (4) the downsizing strategy, whereby labour market deregulation prompts the structural change towards small-size firms, with a higher per-centage of low-skill workers in the presence of lowering wage rates, so caus-ing an increase in SP and a fall in HR.

The four patterns of technological choices, reflecting different decisions about product and process innovation taken by firms under institutional con-straints, are reflected by the measure of earnings dispersion. Figure 15.2 shows the construction of the earnings dispersion index (EDI) where workers are ranked on the basis of their average wages (and corresponding skill level).

Unlike the more usual Gini index, where percentiles are equally numerous, the population on the X axis has been partitioned into three groups ($k = 3$) denoted by a, β and γ, where $a + \beta + \gamma = 1$, corresponding to the three skill levels, from lowest to highest; while on the Y axis s_a, s_β and s_γ, where, again, $s_a + s_\beta + s_\gamma = 1$, indicate their respective earnings shares. The EDI is calcu-lated as the ratio between the area (λ) limited by the diagonal and the Lorenz curve, and the whole triangle area. Were we unable to measure the separate influence of skill premium and wage distance between high-skill and low-skill workers, it would have been difficult to go back to the cause of variation of the EDI. However, by construction, it is apparent that EDI varies depending on the relative strength of the variation in SP and HR. As we will now see, the computation of the EDI reveals that earnings dispersion augments in many macro-sectors. No clear evidence results for 13 cases only (over the 42 cases

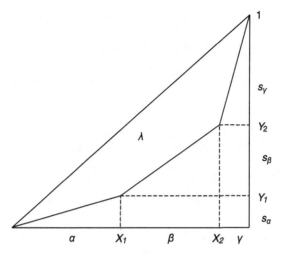

Figure 15.2 Earnings dispersion index (EDI)

examined), since the lines for the initial (1994) and the final (2001) year cross each other.

In Figure 15.3, manufacturing and services have been re-aggregated into six macro-sectors (ICT producing, ICT intensive using, and ICT less intensive using, both for manufacturing and services) as described above. Wage disparities are computed by using average wage levels for each sector and category of high-intermediate- and low-skill workers, and allowing for a varying number of workers in each category.

Table 15.1 classifies the variations of SP and HR between 1994 and 2001 by attributing – for each country – the macro-sectors to one of the four strategies on the basis of the sign of their variation and also specifying whether the EDI would increase or decrease. Upward movements of both SP and HR hint to SBTC and result in a rising EDI, because the enlarging wage distance between skill levels happens to be more relevant than the expulsion of low-skill workers. Complementary technology, which corresponds to both SP and HR moving downwards, is found in a minority of cases and mainly in Continental countries. An SP increase (probably due to a lowering of low-skill wages) larger than the HR reduction (a clue to a modest improvement in job creation) suggests the evolution towards a downsizing strategy, which is mainly chosen by firms not involved in the ICT revolution with an high percentage of low-skill workers.

The most frequent strategy in Europe seems to be the restructuring strategy, as a decreasing SP and an increasing HR point to the prevalence of reduction of low-skill jobs in the presence of wage compression, both in manufacturing and in service sectors. All Denmark macro-sectors manifest SP and HR variations indicating restructuring; the Netherlands and Germany follow, with three macro-sectors each. However, due to the crossing of

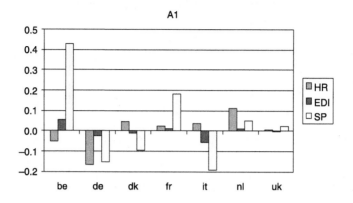

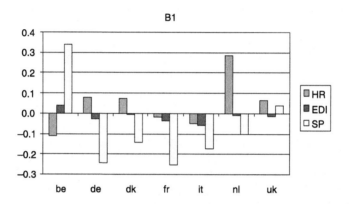

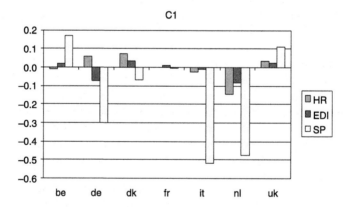

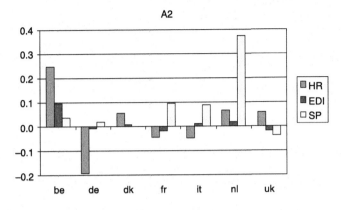

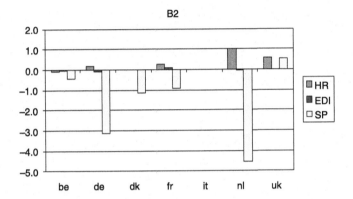

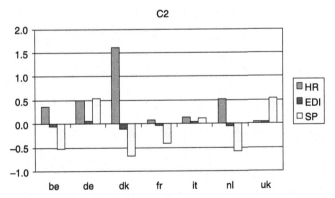

Figure 15.3 EDI, SP and HR. First differences for 7 EU countries (1994–2001)

Table 15.1 Summary results for the 4 strategies in the 6 macro-sectors and frequencies of strategies for the 7 EU countries

	SBTC			Complementary technology			Restructuring			Downsizing		
	EDI up	EDI down	crossing	EDI up	EDI down	crossing	EDI up	EDI down	crossing	EDI up	EDI down	crossing
A1	F, NL	–	UK	–	–	D	–	I, DK	–	B	–	–
B1	–	–	UK	–	F, I	–	–	–	D, DK, NL	B	–	–
C1	UK	–	–	F	–	I, NL	DK	D	–	B	F	D
A2	B, NL	–	–	–	–	–	DK	UK	–	I	–	–
B2	I, UK	–	–	–	–	B	F	D	DK, NL	–	F	–
C2	D, I, UK	–	–	–	–	–	B, DK, F	–	NL	–	–	–

the initial and final lines, the computation of EDI does not offer a clear interpretation for the complementary technology and the restructuring strategy.

The United Kingdom is the only country where all macro-sectors (except the producing ICT service sectors[14]) present the sign of variations of SP and HR corresponding to the choice of SBTC. Only a few countries – in particular France and Italy, both in intensive and less intensive ICT using manufacturing – present SP and HR variations corresponding to complementary technologies. Finally, the downsizing strategy is confirmed by the EDI increasing in four over six cases. This technological choice, which is shown by earnings dispersion varying as an effect of rising low-skill employment levels more than of the wage wedge, seems to be followed essentially by Belgium (where low-skill employment increases concern in two out of six macro-sectors), and by the ICT-producing service sectors of Germany, France and Italy.

15.4 Theil decomposition of earnings dispersion between and within sectors

Whatever the direction of the SP and HR values, the above picture could be distorted by movements in the earnings inequality indicators occurring between sectors rather than within sectors. The values of the earnings inequality computed by the EDI could therefore conceal a compositional effect.

The strong increase in the EU-15 employment during the second half of the 1990s stems mostly from the creation of new jobs in market-related services, which experienced a very strong value-added growth (Marimon and Zilibotti 1998). In fact, labour market flexibility fuelled the process of job shifting from the more capital-intensive manufacturing sectors to low-productivity and low-pay service sectors. In the period 1997–2001, job intensity of growth (the ratio of employment growth to value-added growth) reached very high values in financial, real estate renting and business services. Also in sectors like trade, repairs, hotels and restaurant, transport and communication, characterized by a large percentage of self-employment and temporary positions, employment has grown at a faster pace than in manufacturing and the relative price of labour has fallen accordingly.

The employment expansion in the EU-15 services sector has concerned both high-skill researchers, engineers and managers in the ICT-producing and -using sectors, and low-skill workers in technology extension and provision of software service either to firms or directly to consumers. In the labour-intensive service sectors the employment increases have instead involved the utilisation of intermediate-skill workers, in operations which cannot be informatized by firms in manufacturing (for instance, the outsourcing of non-routine occupations by computer-using companies). Finally, in more recent years the production and use of ICT has started increasing also in the EU-15, with investment in ICT reaching 18 per cent over total investment and contributing 42 per cent of labour productivity growth; in the US these percentages were 29 per cent and 80 per cent, respectively (Denis *et al.* 2005).

These structural changes legitimate the suspicion that a compositional effect might play a part in explaining developments in employment growth. The 'Baumol disease' hypothesis predicts that productivity growth rates are lower in the service sectors characterized by routine occupations than in manufacturing. Since labour market deregulation should translate differential productivity growth into wider wage differentials, low-skill workers are expected to move from manufacturing to service occupations. In increasing the employment levels, the expansion of the service sectors could have been a more important factor than the interaction between technology and institutions.

Consequently, the variation in wage inequality in the period 1994–2001 could have been different from the variation in earnings inequality. Due to a varying speed of relaxation of constraints posed by labour market institutions on employment growth in services across European countries, the measurement of within-sectors earnings inequality could have been affected by a shift of workers towards self-employment and/or by a rising share of temporary contracts in services' jobs. These two phenomena artificially reduce the breadth of earnings inequality, thus underestimating the gap between earnings inequality and wage inequality.

To get an idea of this possible bias, we computed the Theil decomposition, both for the earnings and the wage distributions. By separating out the between-sectors *vis-à-vis* the within-sectors inequality, we aim to assess the relative expansion of the service sector. It is also worth noticing that the between-sector component refers to reallocation of resources across industries due to market share reshuffling among sectors, as well as entry and exit. A rising market contestability encourages firms to invest in innovation mainly when the sector and/or the country is close to the technological frontier, and the incumbents are under the threat of a Schumpeterian process of imitation (Aghion *et al.* 2005). Hence, a stimulus to technical change as an effect of deregulation also depends on how far from the technological frontier in the middle of the 1990s the manufacturing and service sectors of the EU-15 economies were.

The Theil decomposition in the within-sectors and the between-sectors variation of the earnings and the wage inequality described in Figure 15.4 was conducted on the ECHP dataset over the whole 18 sectors of the seven EU countries for the period 1994–2001. Self-employed workers and temporary contracts are the main source of divergence between the earnings and wage measures of dispersion, as well as across employment rates. Hence, evidence showing that the same variations happen within and between sectors and for both measures (wages of employees as well as total remunerations) will be taken as an indicator that the expansion of service sectors does not

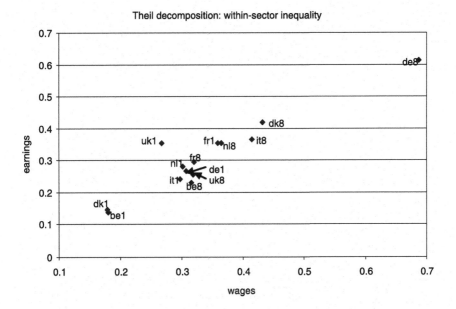

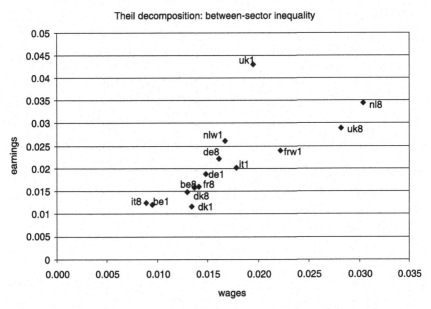

Figure 15.4 Sectoral earnings dispersion within and between sectors: 1994 (1) and 2001 (8)

significantly affect the wage and earnings trends, so that the measurement of the EDI should not be biased by a composition effect. On the contrary, where the evolution of earnings inequality between sectors does not find confirmation for wages – or the change in between-sectors inequality indices significantly differs from the change for the within-sectors indices – the composition effect consisting of a disproportionate rise in self-employment and/or temporary positions in the expanding service sectors is likely to be at work.

Since in most countries the sign of variation of the inequality indices replicates both for wages and earnings as well as for the within- and the between-sectors components, the Theil decomposition seems to signal that the evidence of a composition effect is not impressive. The earnings and wage inequality appear to increase in most Continental countries (Belgium, Germany, the Netherlands), while is decreasing in France both for the within and between indices.

However, the United Kingdom presents a higher inequality for earnings and a lower inequality for wages, both within and between sectors (see Table 15.2). This is a clear indicator of an upward trend of the earnings of self-employed workers, to a larger extent in the technology-based services, whereas the wage wedge among the dependent workers is shrinking in both the Theil components. In other words, the contemporaneous increase of the two indices of earnings dispersion signals that the income gap of self-employed workers (and, possibly, also some mistaken reporting of the pay of temporary contracts) widens both in terms of average wage across sectors and in terms of within-sectors dispersion, possibly increasing the gap of the upper portion of the earnings distribution due to the relative expansion of the ICT service companies.

Two countries show uneven results across Theil decomposition. Italy shows a tendency towards widening disparities within sectors and shrinking disparities across sectors both for wages and earnings. Since sectors characterized by a lower-than-average wage level appear to be approaching the high-average wage sectors, the expansion of the services does not seem to concern the technology-based sectors. Contrary to the overall trend, a composition effect – wherever present – is perhaps driving the earnings distribution towards compression. Denmark appears to join the Continental countries as for the within-sector inequality indices, while the between-sectors earnings dispersion decreases. The change in the sign of variations for the between sectors inequality index *vis-à-vis* the within sectors one – which occurs in both the wages and the earnings measures for Italy, and only in the earnings one for Denmark – clearly deserves closer scrutiny.

Table 15.2 First differences in wages and earnings inequality within and between sectors (1994–2001)

within inequality				between inequality			
		earnings				earnings	
		+	–			+	–
wages	+	B, D, DK, I, NL		wages	+	B, D, NL	DK
	–	UK	F		–	UK	F, I

15.5 Concluding remarks

Our aim in this chapter was to show that European firms, in contrast to the hypothesis put forward by Krugman, do not stay passive in the face of institutional constraints but their technological choices are meant to combine productive strategies with labour-market conditions.

During the 1990s, a wide range of productive strategies were implemented in European countries, as witnessed by the variety of variations experienced by the skill premium and by the high-skill ratio. The earnings dispersion index suggests that the most frequent technological decisions taken by European firms in the second half of the 1990s can be regarded as a restructuring strategy. The recourse to complementary technology has not been practised much by firms. The likely explanation is that institutional reforms implemented during the 1990s in the EU-15 labour markets have introduced wage flexibility – and also the abatement of job protection, though to a lesser extent – which enlarged the opportunity set of technological choices with respect to the previous period (to which the Acemoglu hypothesis refers).

To the question whether rising earnings dispersion in European countries during the 1990s stemmed from SBTC, the computation of the EDI analysis provides a negative answer, except in the case of the United Kingdom.[15] Hence, our computation confirms that the United Kingdom largely differentiates from the other EU countries as the only productive structure where the presence of skill-biased techniques is pervasive. The UK is also a country for which the computation of the Theil decomposition clearly shows a composition effect. The expansion of the technology-based service sectors drifts the evolution of the earnings dispersion away from the wage dispersion, due to the increasing number of high-income high-skill workers disproportionately widening the earnings distribution.

Notes

1 In the following, earnings disparities (i.e. all workers: employees and self-employed) are analysed; when labour is limited to the sub-set of employees only, reference will be made to wage disparities (which include wages and salaries).

2 Huge difficulties both on theoretical and on empirical grounds arise when labour needs be precisely separated from capital (for the self-employed) and in particular from human capital (for the skilled labour). Although some corrections have been proposed and extensively relied upon (Guscina 2006), so far they have been mainly regarded as rules of thumb. The empirical flair of this chapter, based on microdata supplied by ECHP, makes the debate about the definition of labour somewhat unnecessary: 'total net personal income' (PI100) is broken down into 'total net income from work' (PI110), 'non-work private income' (PI120) and 'total social insurance receipts' (PI130); in turn, code PI110 is broken down into 'wage and salary earnings' (PI111) and 'self-employment income' (PI112), while 'capital income' is coded PI121. Data availability has induced the choice of the variable PI110, and the inclusion of the warning.

3 Globalization and trade openness also propose an explanation for recent developments, such as a rising ratio of temporary over long-term labour contracts and

a rising earnings inequality (Feenstra 2007). We do not directly deal with international trade, but its impact on earnings dispersion is at least partially embodied in the way technological and institutional factors interact in the determination of jobs and pays.

4 'Employment and unemployment developments – in particular, the relative employment of youths and older persons of working age – tended to be less favourable in countries in which earnings inequality rose more slowly since 1970 (or fell), than in countries where the earnings inequality rose more rapidly. Furthermore, the apparent trade-off between a strong employment performance and a more equal distribution of earnings appears to have worsened, consistent with relative labour demand having shifted towards high-skill workers' (OECD 2004: 129).

5 'Unlike for earnings inequality among full-time employed individuals, for pretax-pretransfer income among households we observe sizeable increases over time in most countries. This development appears to have been driven to an important extent by changes in employment. In countries with better employment performance, low-earning households benefited relative to high-earning ones; in nations with poor employment performance, low-earning households fared worse.' (Kenworthy and Pontusson 2005: 21–2).

6 'In sum, our examination of the wage compression hypothesis (like that of the other empirical researchers) finds little support for the belief that lack of jobs in the EU is due to the effect of the compression of wages on employment in low skill industries' (Freeman and Schettkat 2001: 25).

7 Atkinson and Brandolini (2006) have drawn attention to the unemployment rate as a major cause of variation of wage and salaries inequality by taking into account the differences between skilled and unskilled workers.

8 In the year 2000 temporary contracts were 13.4 per cent in the EU-15, ranging from over 33 per cent in the 'outlier' Spain, to 6.7 per cent in the United Kingdom and below 5 per cent in Ireland and Luxembourg (Eurostat).

9 Additional factors are likely to be involved in the evolution of technological choices, first of all the conditions of competitiveness of the market structure, as studied by the rapidly developing literature on the negative impact on growth and employment of rigid goods and labour markets (Bassanini, Hemmings and Scarpetta 2001; Blanchard and Giavazzi 2003).

10 While the employment rate refers to the percentage of workers who actually have jobs, different definitions co-exist: Eurostat refers to the employed persons aged 15–64 as a percentage of the same age population; the UK Office for National Statistics (ONS) refers to the proportion of the working age population who are in employment: aged 16–64 if men, 16–59 if women. In addition the definitions of both workers and jobs may differ, for example, as to whether the job is paid and the weekly hours are at least 15.

11 Similarly, the activity rate refers to the percentage of working population; however, Eurostat defines activity rate of the labour force as a percentage of the population of working age (15–64), the Italian ISTAT refers to the ratio between labour force and the population over 15, while the UK ONS refers to the population over 16. Since these definitions differ, a cross-country comparison is more easily referred to the first differences than in terms of absolute values.

12 However, the measurement of the technological level of workers through the general educational attainment of the population leads to inconsistency problems (Croci Angelini and Farina 2007).

13 The six macro-sectors are formed by re-aggregating the 18 ECHP manufacturing and service sectors according to the classification used by the European Commission services (see Denis *et al.* 2005).

14 Among the most important sub-sectors of the producing ICT service sectors,

computer services are lacking, as the ECHP does not classify them in a separate category. Hence, the measurement of the EDI for this sub-sector is likely to be biased.
15 These findings are confirmed by recent studies comparing the growth perform-ances of the EU and the US economies. During the 1990s, for the first time in the last two decades, both the capital deepening and the TFP presented growth rates lower in the EU than in the US. While the declining capital investment in Europe might be partially explained by the end of the capital-for-labour substitution which followed the rise in the wage/profit rate, the second indicator definitely points to lower rate of innovation and ICT investment in the EU *vis-à-vis* the US (O'Mahony and van Ark 2003). Moreover, in the EU a productivity growth in the ICT-producing manufacturing industries much lower than the US one was only partially counteracted by the relatively better productivity performance in ICT-using manufacturing and ICT-producing services in the first half of the 1990s (van Ark *et al.* 2003).

References

Acemoglu, D. (1999), 'Changes in Unemployment and Wage Inequality: An Alterna-tive Theory and Some Evidence', in *American Economic Review*, 89: 1259–78.

Acemoglu, D. (2002), 'Technical Change, Inequality, and the Labour Market', *Journal of Economic Literature*, 40: 7–72.

Acemoglu, D. (2003), 'Cross-Country Inequality Trends', *Economic Journal*, 113: F121–F149.

Agell, J. (1999), 'On the Benefits from Rigid Labour Markets: Norms, Market Failures and Social Insurance', *Economic Journal*, 109: F143–F164.

Agell, J. (2002), 'On the Determinants of Labour Market Institutions: Rent Seeking versus Social Insurance', *German Economic Review*, 3: 107–135.

Aghion, P., N. Bloom, R. Blundell, R. Griffith, and P. Howitt (2005), 'Competition and Innovation: An Inverted-U Relationship,' *Quarterly Journal of Economics*, 120: 701–28.

von Ark, B., R. Inklaar, R. McGuckin, and M. Trimmer (2003), 'The Employment Effects of the "New Economy". A comparison of the European Union and the United States', *National Institute Economic Review*, 184.

Arpaia, A. and G. Mourre (2005), 'Labour Market Institutions and Labour Market per-formance: A Survey of the Literature', *European Economy*, Economic Papers, n.235.

Atkinson, A.B. and A. Brandolini (2006), 'From Earnings Inequality to Income Inequality in European and U.S. Labour Markets', in F. Farina and E. Savaglio (eds.), *Inequality and Economic Integration*, Routledge, London.

Bassanini, A., P. Hemmings, and S. Scarpetta (2001), 'Economic Growth: The Role of Policies and Institutions. Panel Data Evidence from OECD Countries', OECD Economic Department Working Paper n. 283.

Bertola, G., F.D. Blau, and L.M. Kahn (2002), 'Comparative Analysis of Labour Market Outcomes: Lessons for the US from International Long-run Evidence', in A. Kruger and R. Solow (eds.), *The Roaring Nineties: Can full Employment be Sustained?*, Russell Sage and Century Foundations.

Blanchard, O. (2004), 'The Economic Future of Europe', *Journal of Economic Perspectives*, 18: 3–26

Blanchard, O. (2006), 'European Unemployment: The Evolution of Facts and Ideas', *Economic Policy*, 16: 5–59

Blanchard, O. and F. Giavazzi (2003), 'Macroeconomic Effects of Regulation and Deregulation in Goods and Labour Markets', *Quarterly Journal of Economics*, 118: 879–907.

Blau, F.D. and L.M. Kahn (2000). ' "Gender Differences in Pay" ', *Journal of Economic Perspectives*, 14: 75–99.

Croci, Angelini E. and F. Farina (2007), 'Wage Inequality in Europe: The Role of Labour Market and Welfare Institutions', in N. Acocella and R. Leoni (eds.), *Social Pacts, Employment and Growth: A Reappraisal of Ezio Tarantelli's Thought*, Physica-Verlag, Berlin.

Denis, C., K. McMorrow, W. Roger, and R. Veugelers (2005), 'The Lisbon Strategy and the EU's Structural Productivity Problem', European Economy, Economic Papers, n. 221.

Dunne, T., L. Foster, J. Haltiwanger, and K.R. Troske (2004), 'Wage and Productivity Dispersion in United States Manufacturing: The Role of Computer Investment', *Journal of Labour Economics*, 22: 397–429.

Feenstra, R.C. (2007), 'Globalization and its Impact on Labor', Global Economy Lecture 2007, Vienna Institute for International Economic Studies.

Freeman, R. and R. Schettkat (2001), *Differentials in Service Industry Employment Growth: Germany and the US in the Comparable German-American Structural Database*, Brussels, European Commission, DG Employment and Social Affairs.

Gini, C. (1914), 'Sulla misura della concentrazione e della variabilità dei caratteri', in *Atti del Reale Istituto Veneto di Scienze, Lettere e Arti*, Vol. LXXIII: 1203–48 (English translation: 'On the Measurement of Concentration and Variability Characters', *Metron* (2005), LXIII: 3–38).

Guscina, (2006), *Effects of Globalization on Labour's Share in National Income*, IMF Working Paper No. 06/294, the International Monetary Fund.

IMF (2007), *World Employment Outlook*, Washington.

Kenworthy, L. and J. Pontusson (2005), 'Rising Inequality and the Politics of Redistribution in Affluent Countries', *Perspectives on Politics*, 1: 1–44.

Krugman, P. (1994), 'Past and Prospective Causes of High Unemployment', in *Reducing Unemployment: Current Issues and Policy Options*, Kansas City, Federal Reserve Bank of Kansas City.

Layard, R. and S.J. Nickell (1999), 'Labour Market Institutions and Economic Performance' in O. Ashenfelter and D. Card (eds.), *Handbook of Labor Economics*, North-Holland, Amsterdam.

Marimon, R. and M. Zilibotti (1998), 'Actual versus Virtual Employment in Europe: Is Spain Different?', *European Economic Review*, 42: 123–53.

Mourre, G. (2004), 'Did the Pattern of Aggregate Employment Growth Change in the Euro Area in the late 1990s?', *Applied Economics*, 38: 1783–1807.

O'Mahony, M. and B. van Ark (2003), 'EU Productivity and Competitiveness: An Industry Perspective – Can Europe Resume the Catching-up?', Enterprise Directorate-General, European Commission, Brussels.

OECD (2004), *Employment Outlook 2004*, Paris.

Pischke, J.-S. (2005), 'Labour Market Institutions, Wages and Investment: Review and Implications', *CESifo Economic Studies*, 5: 47–75.

Theil, H. (1972), *Statistical Decomposition Analysis: With Applications in the Social and Administrative Sciences*, Amsterdam-London, North Holland Publishing Company.

Appendix 15.1

Table 15.A.1 Sectoral breakdown

Codes	Labels	Sectors
A + B	Agriculture, hunting and forestry + Fishing	Other
C	Mining and quarrying	C1
DA	Manufacture of food products, beverages and tobacco	C1
DB + DC	Manufacture of textiles, clothing and leather products	C1
DD + DE	Manufacture of wood and paper products; publishing and printing	B1
DF – DI	Manufacture of coke, refined petroleum/chemicals/rubber and plastic/products etc.	B1
DJ + DK	Manufacture of metal products, machinery and equipment n.e.c.	A1
DL – DN	Other manufacturing	A1
E	Electricity, gas and water supply	C2
F	Construction	Other
G	Wholesale and retail trade; repair of motor vehicles, motorcycles and personal/household goods	Other
H	Hotels and restaurants	Other
I	Transport, storage and communication	A2
J	Financial intermediation	B2
K	Real estate, renting and business activities	C2
L	Public administration and defense; compulsory social security	Other
M	Education	Other
N	Health and social work	Other
O – Q	Other community, social and personal service activities; private households with employed persons; extra-territorial organizations and bodies	Other
–8	not applicable	
–9	missing	

Appendix 15.2

Table 15.A.2 Occupational breakdown

Codes	Labels	Class
1112	Legislators, senior officials + Corporate managers	H
1300	Managers of small enterprises	H
2122	Physical, mathematical and engineering science professionals + Life science and health professionals	H
2300	Teaching professionals	H
2400	Other professionals	H
3132	Physical and engineering science professionals + Life science and health associate professionals	H
3334	Teaching associate professionals + Other associate professionals	H
4142	Office clerks + Customer services clerks	I
5100	Personal and protective services workers	I
5200	Models, salespersons and demonstrators	I
6100	Skilled agricultural and fishery workers	L
7174	Extraction and building trades workers + Other craft and related trades workers	L
7273	Metal, machinery and related trades workers + Precision, handicraft, printing and related trades workers	L
8183	Stationary-plant and related operators + Drivers and mobile-plant operators	L
8200	Machine operators and assemblers	L
8400	8 – Miscellaneous (ECHP-specific code)	L
9100	Sales and services elementary occupations	L
9200	Agricultural, fishery and related laborers	L
9300	Laborers in mining, construction, manufacturing and transport	L
9400	9 – Miscellaneous (ECHP-specific code)	L
–8	not applicable	–8
–9	missing, armed forces, 5 – Miscellaneous (ECHP-specific code)	–9

Appendix 15.3

Table 15.A.3 Employment structure by country

	wave 1	wave 1	wave 1	wave 1	wave 8	wave 8	wave 8	wave 8
Belgium	H	I	L	total	H	I	L	total
A1	0,02	0,02	0,06	0,10	0,02	0,01	0,06	0,09
B1	0,02	0,01	0,03	0,07	0,02	0,02	0,03	0,06
C1	0,01	0,02	0,03	0,06	0,01	0,01	0,02	0,04
A2	0,01	0,02	0,02	0,05	0,02	0,02	0,02	0,07
B2	0,02	0,02	0,00	0,05	0,03	0,03	0,00	0,06
C2	0,04	0,03	0,02	0,10	0,04	0,02	0,01	0,07
other	0,26	0,17	0,14	0,57	0,29	0,20	0,13	0,62
total	0,40	0,30	0,31	1,00	0,42	0,32	0,26	1,00
Germany	H	I	L	total	H	I	L	total
A1	0,05	0,02	0,08	0,15	0,05	0,01	0,11	0,18
B1	0,02	0,01	0,04	0,07	0,03	0,01	0,04	0,07
C1	0,01	0,02	0,02	0,05	0,01	0,00	0,02	0,03
A2	0,01	0,01	0,02	0,04	0,01	0,01	0,03	0,05
B2	0,02	0,03	0,00	0,05	0,02	0,02	0,00	0,04
C2	0,03	0,01	0,02	0,06	0,05	0,02	0,02	0,09
other	0,28	0,14	0,16	0,57	0,27	0,14	0,14	0,54
total	0,43	0,24	0,34	1,00	0,43	0,22	0,35	1,00
Denmark	H	I	L	total	H	I	L	total
A1	0,02	0,01	0,07	0,10	0,03	0,01	0,09	0,13
B1	0,02	0,00	0,02	0,04	0,01	0,00	0,01	0,02
C1	0,01	0,01	0,03	0,05	0,00	0,00	0,02	0,03
A2	0,02	0,02	0,03	0,07	0,01	0,02	0,02	0,05
B2	0,02	0,02	0,00	0,03	0,01	0,01	0,00	0,02
C2	0,05	0,01	0,02	0,08	0,06	0,01	0,01	0,08
other	0,25	0,20	0,18	0,63	0,31	0,21	0,15	0,67
total	0,38	0,27	0,36	1,00	0,44	0,27	0,29	1,00
France	H	I	L	total	H	I	L	total
A1	0,03	0,01	0,06	0,10	0,03	0,01	0,05	0,09
B1	0,02	0,01	0,03	0,06	0,02	0,00	0,03	0,05
C1	0,01	0,01	0,03	0,05	0,01	0,01	0,03	0,04
A2	0,02	0,02	0,02	0,06	0,02	0,02	0,03	0,06
B2	0,02	0,02	0,00	0,04	0,02	0,01	0,00	0,03
C2	0,05	0,02	0,03	0,10	0,06	0,03	0,03	0,11
other	0,23	0,19	0,19	0,61	0,23	0,20	0,17	6,00
total	0,37	0,27	0,37	1,00	0,38	0,28	0,34	1,00
Italy	H	I	L	total	H	I	L	total
A1	0,01	0,02	0,08	0,12	0,02	0,01	0,07	0,10
B1	0,01	0,01	0,03	0,05	0,01	0,01	0,03	0,05
C1	0,01	0,01	0,05	0,07	0,01	0,01	0,04	0,06
A2	0,01	0,02	0,03	0,05	0,01	0,02	0,03	0,06
B2	0,01	0,02	0,00	0,03	0,01	0,02	0,00	0,03
C2	0,03	0,02	0,02	0,06	0,04	0,03	0,02	0,09
other	0,16	0,20	0,26	0,62	0,17	0,24	0,21	0,62
total	0,24	0,30	0,46	1,00	0,26	0,34	0,40	1,00

Table 15.A.3 continued

	wave 1	wave 1	wave 1	wave 1	wave 8	wave 8	wave 8	wave 8
Netherlands	H	I	L	total	H	I	L	total
A1	0,02	0,00	0,03	0,05	0,02	0,00	0,02	0,05
B1	0,02	0,01	0,03	0,06	0,02	0,00	0,02	0,04
C1	0,01	0,00	0,02	0,04	0,01	0,00	0,02	0,03
A2	0,01	0,03	0,03	0,07	0,01	0,02	0,02	0,06
B2	0,03	0,01	0,00	0,04	0,03	0,01	0,00	0,04
C2	0,07	0,02	0,03	0,11	0,08	0,02	0,02	0,12
other	0,32	0,19	0,13	0,64	0,35	0,20	0,11	0,66
total	0,47	0,26	0,26	1,00	0,52	0,27	0,21	1,00
UK	H	I	L	total	H	I	L	total
A1	0,03	0,02	0,05	0,10	0,02	0,01	0,02	0,05
B1	0,02	0,01	0,03	0,06	0,01	0,00	0,01	0,03
C1	0,01	0,01	0,04	0,06	0,00	0,00	0,01	0,01
A2	0,01	0,02	0,03	0,06	0,01	0,01	0,02	0,04
B2	0,03	0,02	0,00	0,05	0,01	0,01	0,00	0,02
C2	0,06	0,02	0,02	0,10	0,04	0,02	0,01	0,06
other	0,24	0,21	0,12	0,57	0,33	0,27	0,19	0,79
total	0,41	0,31	0,29	1,00	0,42	0,32	0,26	1,00

16 Redistributing global income to benefit the poor

Yuri Dikhanov and Michael Ward

16.1 Introduction

In this chapter the authors use previously derived distributions that were originally disseminated in approximate form in 1999 (Annual Conference of the Australian Academy of Social Sciences, Canberra) and later refined to incorporate more detailed and extensive data on national income distributions drawn from a much wider range of countries. The updated distributions were presented to the ISI Congress in Korea in July 2001. In this latest version, greater resort has been made to the WIDER database. The quasi-exact methodology (Dikhanov 1999), originally applied because of the lack of suitable data, has been further developed in order to use the results to refine global measures of poverty as well as to monitor shifts in global inequality over time.

Beyond the data and methodological questions, the authors highlight the inadequacy of conventional policies currently being advocated to reduce and eventually eliminate the scourge of permanent poverty. These policies concentrate on ways not only to stimulate economic growth but also to make it more pro-poor. The strategies in place assume that, to generate the increased money incomes necessary to resolve the problem of poverty and to halve the percentage of the population who are poor, renewed growth can be achieved using the traditional instruments of trade and the promotion of domestic and foreign investment. Raising, to the extent of doubling, the present level of aid disbursements from donors is expected to increase household receipts and increase the flow of non-market goods and services. A lot of hope is also pinned on public debt forgiveness and that this will prove relevant and adequate in bringing about an improvement in the flow of public social services. All these strategies are necessary but they are far from sufficient as solutions to the fundamental and apparently systemic problems that are now confronting the majority of low-income countries that are trying to assert their place in the international economy.

It is explicitly suggested that a more fundamental approach involving the redistribution of incomes from the rich to the poor *at a global level* is the only solution that really makes a difference. In principle, the argument could be even more forcibly applied to a redistribution of the productive wealth owned by the richest people in the world. Economic theory postulates that the current change in national wealth basically determines whether the present value of expected future changes in consumption is positive or negative; that is, whether future consumption will lie above or below current consumption. What has yet to be explored thoroughly is whether the nature and composition of that wealth, defined in terms of the physical productive capital, natural resources and human capital, that also includes technical skills, each country possesses, affect the distribution of net disposable income and, hence, consumption and well-being of people. Decisions in this area, however, inevitably come up against the familiar dilemma between the goose and golden egg; specifically, whether redistribution undermines the willingness to invest and thus the capacity to generate new income.

Nevertheless, many of the reasons for the ineffectiveness of traditional policy approaches can be found embedded in the overall national and global distribution of wealth among and between institutions and households. The social, economic and institutional power associated with high incomes has a strong tendency to influence decisions and support the observed distribution of income and existing status of societies.

16.2 Global poverty: a review of current policies to reduce it

For the time being, information on wealth holdings, particularly along global lines, is sparse. The following table summarizes the estimated global distribution of income by major regions.

Table 16.1 shows how the rate of poverty has changed over the past 30 years. There is evidence to suggest that the earlier picture for 1960 would tell a very similar story on inequality and show, perhaps, an even higher incidence of poverty. It is evident that economic growth for a large part of the globe has not worked to reduce the incidence of poverty or its severity among the lowest income groups. This is partly because, except in countries like China,

Table 16.1 Total number in absolute poverty, 1970–2015 (Below $700 p.a. in 1999 PPP terms)

	1970	*1980*	*1990*	*2000*	*2015 (est)*
WORLD	**1.41**	**1.54**	**1.36**	**1.17**	**0.80**
Latin America	0.04	0.03	0.04	0.04	0.04
East Asia	0.78	0.80	0.53	0.38	0.10
South Asia	0.42	0.52	0.49	0.33	0.14
	1.20	*1.32*	*1.02*	*0.71*	*0.24*
Africa	0.16	0.20	0.29	0.42	0.51

Note
In billions of people
Source: Dikhanov and Ward (2001); Dikhanov (2005)

growth has not been effectively 'pro-poor' and partly because, in many areas of the world, real per capita incomes have been undermined by rapid population growth.

But it also may be because trade is not as 'free' – or indeed as fair – to developing countries as most international policymakers would like to believe and because what investment has taken place has sometimes been inappropriate and misdirected. In part this is because a lot of public investment has been misdirected as a consequence of the ineptitude of official decision-makers or as an inevitable result of possible corruption (as The World Bank has suggested in their extensive discussion of the role of 'governance'). An equally likely explanation, however, seems to lie in the inadequate capacity of the entire supporting and inter-related development environment to ensure and, in addition, encourage the desired 'trickle down' effects and to make sure these 'trickled through' to households most vulnerable and at risk. It is well known that increases in income are not representative of improved welfare but, simply from a technical statistical point of view, increases in arithmetic mean income (GDP or GNP per capita) provide a poor marker of improvements in individual material well-being. This is because this measure is driven, in national accounts terms, by what happens at the upper end of a characteristically skewed income distribution.

The level of official aid is so low (see the UNDP Human Development Report 2003 for a review of aid levels by donors and recipients over the past decade) that raising aid to the 'acceptable' and internationally recommended standard target of 0.7 per cent of donor countries' GNP is unlikely to have any significant effect. In any case, it is well recognized that much of present aid funding is still spent by agencies that mostly operate within an international context and much of the ultimate income flows return to the developed countries. This is despite the overwhelming evidence coming out of the ICP relating to the purchasing power parities for low-income countries that, for most of the goods and services they require, aid is most effective, dollar for (local) 'dollar', if it is spent entirely within the aid recipient country.

The issue of debt forgiveness is quite complex and has many dimensions that impinge, potentially, on a country's perceived creditworthiness in the international capital markets and how debt is taken up. The real value of debt forgiveness to governments is the release of regular obligations for debt servicing that bite into other crucial budgetary expenditures that support current public services. The issue is subject to considerable controversy but, in many cases, forgiveness merely takes a country back to square one and an initial basic starting point of development. For some countries, the question under discussion is not about debt forgiveness but rather one of the temporary postponements of existing debt obligations of government.

The trace of global inequality over the 30-year period from 1970 to 2000 shows clearly that the overall shape of the underlying distributions of incomes in various regions of the world has not changed significantly. If some recent trends continue, however, the situation may improve over the next 10 to

15 years. But this also depends on certain more optimistic assumptions about the economic performance of the former Soviet Union and that both China and India will continue to make real progress at their present fast rate. The evidence suggests, however, that for most areas of the globe, the general pattern of inequality will not alter fundamentally and those who are poor now will remain poor in the future. This belies the assertion that the poor benefit equally from growth. Measures of the 'within' and 'between' inequality that go to make up aggregate inequality and changing decile ratios provide evidence to show a widening disparity between rich and poor at the extremes. Cornia (2005) shows that inequality worsened in 70 per cent of 73 developing countries analysed.

Even if the whole distribution moves to the right to reflect average income increases, relative poverty tends to increase along with widening inequality. Although the issue is not revealed by the diagrams, it is also recognized that the problem of both poverty and national inequality, while slowly shifting, is one related dominantly to those households living in the rural areas who mostly remain dependent directly on agriculture for their livelihood.

16.3 The income redistribution option

As already indicated above, the observed pattern and structure of incomes offers a hint of a potential solution to reducing future poverty. A joint policy initiative at the international level, going beyond the political rhetoric that has been engendered by the MDGs could bring about a redistribution of incomes from the richest to the poorest.

Unfortunately, this requires a degree of global governance that currently remains non-existent. A new strategic approach needs to be developed and implemented at a global level by an agency that is not simply a collection of independent nation states each with its own separate or combined agenda. In other words, the world needs a truly global body with independent authority and not an organization that is yet another 'inter-national' agency with nation states sitting on the governing council. While controversial, it is worth recalling that the introduction of income tax, and of progressive taxation structures in particular, in the nineteenth and twentieth centuries in most of Europe, recognized the important responsibility of governments to bring about a fairer distribution of available incomes in the name of social justice. There is no reason why such a fundamental principle, which touches on the nature of basic human rights, should not be observed in a similar quest to strengthen the 'équité mondiale'.

16.4 Defining the global distribution of income

The technical statistical creation of the accompanying distributional diagrams has been fully described (Dikhanov and Ward 2001). The Figures

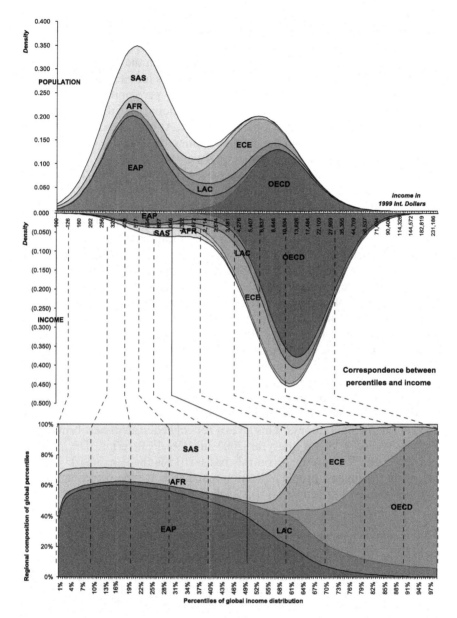

Figure 16.1 World income distribution, 1970

16.1–16.3 of world income are based on ranking individual incomes and a household approach to derive estimates of the global income distribution. This draws on reported national household survey data to define the 'within-country inequality' and a national accounting framework to generate purchasing power parity (PPP) estimates to convert GNP per capita numbers

– adjusted to an approximate disposable income basis – to define the 'between-countries inequality'.

The results for each country are adjusted to fit the year in question by taking account of price and population changes from the stated benchmark. The data are then aggregated by region, the results for each country having been first arrayed in ascending order of income per capita in log income terms. The process is intuitively logical; the regional distributions are subsequently aggregated into the global framework. At each stage, first the countries and then the corresponding regional entities are respectively weighted by the appropriate national and regional GDPs in PPP terms.

The linking across all countries is achieved by extending the 'quasi-exact' estimation method of polynomial interpolation to allow information that is not necessarily uni-modal to be presented as it is observed. For every region, the largest eight countries (by GDP) are taken to represent their respective region and to determine the overall shape and location of the regional distribution. This estimate is then grossed up according to World Bank and IMF estimates of the overall GNP in PPP terms covering all countries in each region. This core country selection procedure generally results in a total income coverage of around 80 per cent for most regions.

The latest benchmark figures (in practice, 1999, but re-centered to 2000) are used to update the findings to 2015, the crucial year of reckoning for MDG achievement and policy performance evaluation. The widely recognized World Bank low income policy threshold criterion for poverty of one dollar per head per day in 1985 PPP prices (i.e. $365 a year) is adjusted to take into account inflation, growth and updates in the PPP estimates, as well as differences between household consumption in national accounts and household expenditure/income surveys. This gives a roughly equivalent new benchmark for poverty of $799 for the year 2000 in 1999 PPP terms. The regional projections to 2015 are made on this basis. 2015 is the benchmark year for achieving the highest profile millennium goal to halve the percentage (note, not total number) of people who, globally, are living in poverty.

16.5 Exercises to simulate the effects of redistribution

In the first scenario, a fixed share of those incomes accruing to the richest people in the world, taken globally, is reallocated to those living below the internationally recognized poverty line. This line is, in effect, the 1985 one dollar per head per day 'absolute' poverty measure, $365 p.a., adjusted upwards to $799 a year in 2000. In a second simulation (not shown), the exercise was repeated but conducted on a separate region-by-region basis. To provide a baseline reference, the exercise could be readily reworked on an individual country basis using similar low 'tax' transfer rates and then grouped into their respective regions. The point of this exercise would be to show the incidence of these transfers if they were to fall on those people within each country who are best able to afford it. This procedure recognizes

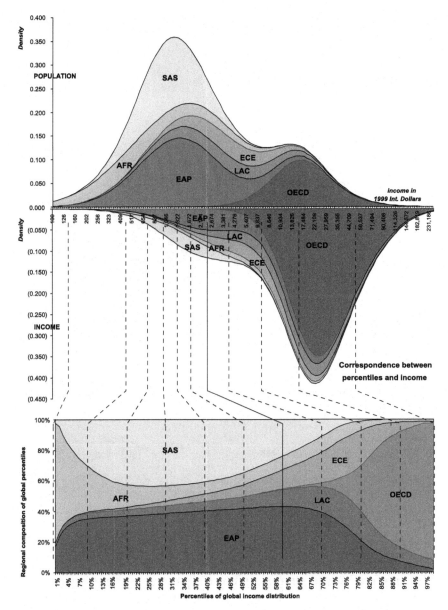

Figure 16.2 World income distribution, 2000

that not only is it inappropriate to regard all countries with low average incomes per head as housing just poor people but also that it is the level of jurisdiction at which such redistributive transfers are potentially feasible. The issue is of growing importance as the 'within-country' inequality extends and becomes increasingly significant. In many cases, however, the lack of good

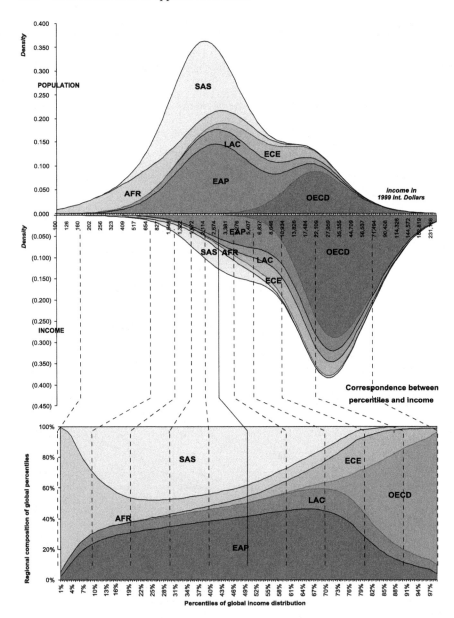

Figure 16.3 World income distribution, 2015

governance renders such a policy of internal redistribution politically unworkable, despite the worsening of inequality.

An evident outcome of the main simulation reveals that the shape of the global distribution is significantly disturbed by the proposed measure. The derived redistribution indicates that greater 'fairness' can only be properly achieved through the application of progressive marginal rates of tax and not lump sum transfers. These rates, ideally, should be variably applied over the whole income range, even where the 'taxation' of only the highest decile (or even percentile) income group is contemplated. The conclusion, evident from the graphs, is that the impact of even a small percentage of the richest incomes transferred to the lowest income groups results in a dramatic reduction in the total number of poor in absolute terms. This is because it pushes so many across the minimum income threshold defining poverty. Nevertheless, such a simple measure leaves many who were only just above the line no better off than before.

Any intuitive assessment of the three alternatives outlined above – and other choices are also possible – would reveal that the redistribution impact is greatest when the transfer is effected at the global level rather than across regions or within states. This is because most inequality (around 70 to 73 per cent on average) is explained by 'between-country' differences in income. In other words, the conclusion must be – not unexpectedly – that the greatest impact is achieved by transferring income from the richest (individuals) in the richest (countries) to the poorest in the poorest countries.

16.6 Implications for policy change

The above result underlines the importance of not relying on economic mechanisms alone, despite the experience of China, and now India, to bring about a lasting, significant and speedy improvement in the global distribution of income. The performance of these countries shows that a big reduction in poverty is feasible based on economic growth and employment creation. There is a corresponding need, however, for a new international consensus to organize relatively marginal but regular redistributive transfers to bring about a fairer distribution of consumption and corresponding reduction in absolute poverty. The above simulated outcome raises political awareness and should persuade the global community of the relevance of implementing an agreement to levy an international 'tithe' on the highest global incomes.

Since a direct tax would not prove popular among governments and there is not, as yet, any appropriate global governance arrangement to bring into effect what would appear to those affected to be a 'smash and grab' policy to redistribute individual incomes across national borders without consent, a more realistic and acceptable approach is clearly called for. One suggestion is to bring into force a scheme to encourage the temporary postponement of present consumption and use the resulting 'surplus' to raise the levels of investment in poorer countries. The conventional economic basis of such an argument rests on an assumption of entropy implying a dollar saved, or not spent, by a rich person involves less of a loss to them than the gain obtained by poor people from the same dollar invested, or even consumed, in a low income country. Increasing personal savings, specifically among the richer people in the global community, either voluntarily or compulsorily, would be

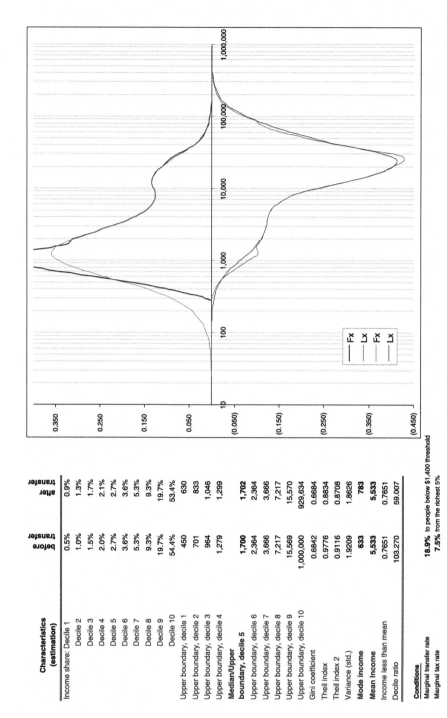

Characteristics (estimation)	before transfer	after transfer
Income share: Decile 1	0.5%	0.9%
Decile 2	1.0%	1.3%
Decile 3	1.5%	1.7%
Decile 4	2.0%	2.1%
Decile 5	2.7%	2.7%
Decile 6	3.6%	3.6%
Decile 7	5.3%	5.3%
Decile 8	9.3%	9.3%
Decile 9	19.7%	19.7%
Decile 10	54.4%	53.4%
Upper boundary, decile 1	450	630
Upper boundary, decile 2	701	833
Upper boundary, decile 3	964	1,046
Upper boundary, decile 4	1,279	1,299
Median/Upper boundary, decile 5	**1,700**	**1,702**
Upper boundary, decile 6	2,364	2,364
Upper boundary, decile 7	3,666	3,666
Upper boundary, decile 8	7,217	7,217
Upper boundary, decile 9	15,569	15,570
Upper boundary, decile 10	1,000,000	929,634
Gini coefficient	0.6842	0.6684
Theil index	0.9776	0.8834
Theil index 2	0.9116	0.8708
Variance (std.)	1.9209	1.8626
Mode Income	**633**	**783**
Mean Income	**5,533**	**5,533**
Income less than mean	0.7651	0.7651
Decile ratio	103.270	59.007

Conditions

Marginal transfer rate	**18.9%** to people below $1,400 threshold
Marginal tax rate	**7.5%** from the richest 5%

Figure 16.4 World income distribution, 2000, before and after a hypothetical wealth transfer

a simple way to achieve this beneficial transfer. The temporary holding of compulsory personal savings certificates, that might be better known as 'Individual Development Credits', would follow much along the same lines as Keynes' famous 'post-war credits'. They would need to be personally guaranteed by all host governments, in the same way as any entitlement in an unfounded pension scheme. In addition, just as with charitable contributions, special tax concessions could be devised to provide incentives to encourage even greater savings than the minimum required. The consequent availability of such a growing and substantial development fund would then facilitate the reallocation of resources to poorer countries for development purposes. The proposal serves a very similar purpose to straight 'taxation' but imposes less pain on certificate holders, all of whom would eventually be able, after a predefined number of years, to reclaim their money. This would be held nominally in trust on behalf of the subscribers by their respective governments, not by the recipient countries.

A savings scheme based on the official collection of a standard compulsory savings trance, or a tithe that is varied according to the level of each income group, would be the simplest means to achieve the desired objective. While most of the richest residents will be found in the high-income countries, it would be more internationally equitable to draw up a global list of all the richest people in every country in the world who could enter into such a scheme of compulsory savings or the compulsory acquisition of development credits. The details of who would collect the savings funds and how this would be done, the length of time certificates would need to be held before credits could be redeemed, whether any nominal interest would be paid on them, and how the funds collected would be redistributed, and so on, all still need to be worked out. (The authors would favour an allocation mechanism similar to that adopted by the UK Camelot Lottery Fund in distributing proceeds to worthy causes and deserving charities. They would also prefer to use a local NGO channel rather than an official transmission mechanism for deciding how exactly the funds available should be spent).

Clearly, a simple once-and-for all transfer would not be sufficient to significantly reduce the extent of poverty on a sustainable basis. The framework employed here relates to annual flows and so a small transfer, as described, would have to occur each year to ensure the immediate poverty reduction targets for 2015 are achieved. The example shows that even at a very low compulsory annual 'savings rate', the internationally agreed 2015 poverty goals could be easily reached. Any additional income raised over and above this specific objective could go to improve the scope of the collective public non-market goods and services in health, education, social security and community facilities that local poor communities significantly rely on. The absence of these services, or the otherwise lack of access to them, not only adds other key dimensions of poverty but exposes vulnerable groups to greater risks while enforcing a reduction in the general well-being of the community. The better provision of non-market services should be perceived as an important investment that enhances the quality of the human capital needed to secure a more sustainable development trajectory. Equally, government services contribute to improving individual life chances and enhance the status of poor people and their ability to participate in society.

For the rich countries, a policy of postponing consumption would have desirable and beneficial environmental externalities, reducing waste and restricting the potential scope for excessive consumerism. It could support shifts to non-monetary social values and contribute to correcting the many output distortions that result from the extreme skewness of incomes. In general, therefore, the policy would clearly lend considerable support to any longer term political intention to establish a more desirable and balanced social production order and a more equitable society, a goal clearly implicit in the thinking behind the work of both Gini and Lorenz.

16.7 Concluding observations

This chapter has used a number of intuitive procedures and innovative statistical techniques to reconstruct the gradual evolvement and complex nature of the global income distribution over the latter part of the twentieth century. Given that the distribution of wealth is known to be considerably more skewed than income (but far more difficult to quantify), and that such a legacy tends to get passed down institutionally through the same families and social orders over time and is thus not spread more equitably across society, what has been argued above for redistributing the marginal top end of incomes has even greater relevance to the holding of wealth.

The basic approach and the essential parametric forms that emerge from the analysis of income distribution within countries and movements over time have been used to recreate evidence, over the same period, of the existing politically and administratively defined regional composition of that global income distribution. The procedure was conducted in a way that maintained the overall consistency of the original nationally reported figures with the numbers associated with the collection of countries forming a well-defined region. The regions were then aggregated to generate a consistent and coherent global set of estimates pertaining to all levels of income per head. This allowed a greater in-depth investigation into how the nature of income poverty could be affected by various aid and income transfers as well as economic growth in each region.

The authors, while acknowledging the significance of other early research in this area of global income measurement (Bourguignon 2001, for example), have taken a different methodological approach that is justified by its greater precision and ability to generate meaningful and empirically observed conditions. The creation of the component distributions uses a distinct but robust polynomial interpolation and aggregation procedure. It draws attention to several important issues not always fully taken into account in other work in this area and reveals, in particular, the bi-modal characteristics of the global income distribution in a way that underlines the relative importance of the 'between' factors and thus makes the distinction between 'north' and 'south' stand out more clearly. In so doing, it suggests some important aspects of this core and periphery relationship that have to do with the growth of global output, the distribution of productive wealth (that is, the ownership of economic assets), and the pattern and control of international trade associated with this situation.

Technical Addendum

1. The distribution functions generated are continuous rather than discrete.
2. Incomes are ranked across all individuals in the world in ascending order of magnitude and matched to the overall income estimates. The corresponding distributions are thus based on individual and household micro-data bounded by macro-estimates derived from the national accounts, particularly relating to disposable income and personal consumption.
3. Distributions are standardized to the same income per capita scale (in logarithmic terms).
4. The beginning and end points that set the outer limits to these distributions are fixed and kept constant each year to facilitate comparisons over time and across space. The lower bound is set at zero income. This does not recognize explicitly the role of transfers.
5. The income and associated population distributions are normalized. On the same graph, the area under each respective curve is the same. This is equal to one (a particularly useful feature when implementing different simulations).
6. A unique graphical presentation that utilizes the areas both above and below the x-axis, referred to as a 'Dikhanov' diagram, has been devised to fully illustrate the imbalances between the geographical provenance of aggregate incomes and the respective shares accruing to income receivers. This enables observers to see at a glance how total income is actually distributed across the world.
7. The graphs bring out, very clearly, the bi-modal nature of the 'conventional' perspective of the individual distribution of global income, a feature that appears to have remained constant for the last half-century at least. The result indicates some imperfections in an assumed international market equalization mechanism.

Traditionally, the distribution of individual income, when ranked and accumulated in ascending order – at least by community or household enquiry groups – up to the national level was presumed to follow a standard pattern. From empirical observations drawn from different country studies, the distribution of income was assumed to be log normal and uni-modal in nature. Indeed, in all the widely used quadratic methods applied to raw data that have been previously used to estimate the pattern of income distribution, it has always been accepted this is so; to be anything else would disturb the significance and relevance of both Gini and Lorenz formulations. The above diagrams show that, whilst uni-modal at the national level, the global distribution of income and some regional distributions are not because of the dominance of between-country income differences over the within-country differences. The global distribution is distinctly bi-modal in character and this highlights the evident 'economic gap' that exists between the developed and developing countries.

References

Bourguignon, F. (2001), 'The Pace of Economic Growth and Poverty Reduction', LACEA 2001, Montevideo, Uruguay.

Cornia, G.A. (2005), 'Inequality, Growth and Poverty in an Era of Liberalisation and Globalization', WIDER Studies in Development Economics, Oxford University Press, UK.

Dikhanov, Y. (1999), 'The Quasi-Exact Distribution of Global Income', World Bank Policy and Research Bulletin, vol. 10, no. 3, September.

Dikhanov, Y. (2005), 'Trends in Global Income Distribution, 1970–2000 and Scenarios for 2015', Third Forum on Human Development; *Cultural Identity Democracy and Global Equity*, Jointly organized by UNDP and French Ministry of Foreign Affairs, Paris, France, January 17–19.

Dikhanov, Y. and Ward, M. (2001), 'The Evolution of Global Inequality', Proceedings of the ISI General Congress, Seoul, Korea, August 2001.

UNDP (2003), 'Human Development Report 2003, Millennium Development Goals: A Compact among Nations to end Human Poverty', UNDP and Oxford University Press.

17 Inequality aversion, income inequality, and social policy in the US

1947–1998

Daniel L. Millimet, Daniel J. Slottje and Peter J. Lambert

17.1 Introduction

Researchers have long been interested in the determinants of within-country income redistribution. Persson and Tabellini (1994), Saint-Paul and Verdier (1993), and others, relying on the median voter hypothesis, predict greater redistribution in less equal societies. Perotti (1996), however, rejects this claim empirically, finding no increased propensity to redistribute income in countries with greater levels of inequality (as measured by the income share of the middle class). Milanovic (1999) examines redistributive effects in 17 democracies in terms of Lorenz shifts. Consistent with Perotti's findings, the author finds the median voter hypothesis unable to explain differences in redistribution across these countries. Ravallion and Lokshin (2000) (building on the model of Bénabou and Ok (2001) and Hirshman's (1973) theory of a 'tunnel effect') argue that preferences for redistribution depend not just on the median voter's current position in the income distribution but also his/her expectations of future income mobility. Gradstein and Milanovic (2004) present evidence suggesting that democracies (specifically countries with greater voting participation by the general population) – except for the recent experiences in Eastern Europe – tend to favor redistribution. In conclusion, Milanovic (1999) calls for 'a totally different mechanism to explain redistribution.'

The goal of this paper is to answer Milanovic's call by building on previous work in Lambert *et al.* (2003). Specifically, we seek to analyze inequality aversion in the United States over the last half of the twentieth century. To do so, we focus on two of the most common measures of inequality: the Gini coefficient, G, and the Atkinson index, $I(e)$.[1] The Atkinson index is a function of the underlying distribution of income and the inequality aversion parameter, e, of the decision-maker or society. The index measures the fraction of total income that could be sacrificed with no loss of social welfare if the remainder were equally distributed. The Gini coefficient is based on an alternative representation of the underlying income distribution.

Many studies have compared the level of 'objective' inequality both across countries as well as within a particular country over time. This is typically accomplished through the use of the Gini coefficient.[2] Others have compared the level of subjective inequality by utilizing the Atkinson index and arbitrarily setting the aversion parameter at a variety of values. In this chapter, however, we build on the hypothesis of a 'natural rate' of subjective inequality (hereafter referred to as NRSI) originally conceived in Lambert *et al.* (2003). In that study, the authors suppose that the level of subjective inequality is identical across all countries. In other words, given certain country-specific preferences for inequality, every country arranges its affairs such that the perceived level of inequality is identical. Contrary to previous research utilizing the Atkinson index, under such a hypothesis inequality aversion is country-specific, not the level of subjective inequality. The authors then confirm at least the possibility of an equilibrium level of subjective inequality by documenting that countries with high (low) aversion to inequality have low (high) levels of objective inequality. Finally, the authors explore the political and socio-economic factors associated with the observed cross-country inequality aversion differentials.

In the present analysis, we explore the applicability of the NRSI hypothesis to the US. Specifically, we suppose that decision-makers in the US implicitly structure social policies to result in the same degree of annual subjective inequality. Under this hypothesis, the level of perceived inequality is constant over time, but inequality aversion and the underlying income distribution are time-specific. According to this framework, annual differences in objective inequality – as measured by the Gini coefficient – are accounted for by aversion differentials over time. In other words, inequality aversion should be greater (less) during periods of lower (higher) objective inequality. This forms the basis for the current test of the NRSI hypothesis.

Besides lending insight into historical preferences for inequality in the US, the present analysis is a necessary complement to the previous cross-sectional work in Lambert *et al.* (2003). As described in Li *et al.* (1998), the majority of world inequality is between countries; within-country inequality is relatively stable and accounts for less than 10 percent of overall world inequality from 1947 to 1994. Consequently, if the NRSI hypothesis is valid, inequality aversion should also be relatively stable (volatile) within (between) countries. This chapter is a first step in testing the time-series implication of the NRSI hypothesis.

In particular, we seek to address the four fundamental questions posed in Lambert *et al.* (2003) with respect to historical changes in the US. First, what time-specific values of the inequality aversion parameter *e* would account for the historical differences in objective inequality, and yet still be compatible with the hypothesis that common political and economic forces are operating such that US policymakers perceive the same degree of subjective inequality, call it φ, each year? Second, given the annual level of inequality aversion that renders subjective inequality equal to φ, what empirical factors account for its variation over time? Third, given that φ, the assumed 'natural rate' of inequality, is unobserved, how do the values of the aversion parameter – as well as the predictive ability of the empirical factors examined – depend on the choice of φ? Finally, what can we infer about the adjustment process needed to maintain subjective inequality at the natural rate φ? Specifically, we address this final point by turning to the future and forecasting the likely effects of the upcoming US presidential election on inequality aversion and objective income inequality.

Our data are from the US and span the years 1947–1998. The factors we examine under the 'natural rate' hypothesis as potential determinants of annual inequality aversion include political and socio-economic indicators such as a given president's political affiliation, the number of democrats in the House of Representatives and the Senate, real GDP per capita, the annual growth rate in real GDP, the unemployment rate, unionization rates, education levels of men and women, female labor force participation rates, the male-female wage ratio, expenditures by the federal government, crime rates, among others.

After examining the potential determinants of inequality aversion, we throw the process into reverse. What if one of the determining factors of inequality aversion is altered; for example, through the election of a new president? The resultant change in inequality aversion, while leaving the actual income distribution unaltered, will throw subjective inequality into disequilibrium, away from the value φ. What adjustments in the observed objective income distribution should we expect to see in order to return the level of subjective inequality to the natural rate φ?

Finally, we use our data on the annual level of inequality aversion to shift the debate over the effect of inequality on economic growth in a new direction. Specifically, we examine the effect of lagged objective inequality and inequality aversion on short-run economic growth, controlling for the potential endogeneity of inequality aversion and other potential determinants of economic growth. Consistent with the recent findings in Forbes (2000), the results indicate that higher lagged objective inequality raises short-run economic growth. However, we also find that lower lagged inequality aversion accelerates economic growth. Thus, it is unclear which is the driving force. It is plausible that lower inequality aversion is the culprit, if inequality aversion leads to policy outcomes aimed at long-run redistribution versus immediate growth. As a result, empirical studies focusing on income inequality may actually be capturing the underlying effect of the inequality aversion differentials documented in this chapter as well as in Lambert *et al.* (2003).

The chapter unfolds as follows. Section 17.2 briefly introduces Atkinson's (1970) measure of inequality, describes the NRSI hypothesis, and presents the data and estimation strategy. In section 17.3, we analyze the factors that account for differences in inequality aversion over time and link these differences to changes in observed objective inequality. Section 17.4 examines the relationship between inequality aversion, objective inequality, and short-run economic growth. Section 17.5 provides some concluding remarks.

17.2 Model

17.2.1 Preliminaries

As elucidated in Lambert *et al.* (2003) and elsewhere, for the case of a discrete income distribution $F = \{y_1, y_2, \ldots, y_N\}$, the Atkinson index is given by:

$$I_F(e) = 1 - \left[\frac{1}{N} \sum_{i=1}^{N} \left(\frac{y_i}{\mu_F}\right)^{1-e}\right]^{1/(1-e)} \tag{17.1}$$

for $e \neq 1$, whilst for $e = 1$ the index takes the value:

$$I_F(1) = 1 - \frac{\tilde{\mu}_F}{\mu_F} \tag{17.2}$$

where μ_F is mean income and $\tilde{\mu}_F$ is geometric mean income. The parameter e measures inequality aversion.[3]

For data partitioned into k equal-sized groups (e.g., quintiles), where q_j is the share of aggregate income belonging to group j, the Atkinson index for $e \neq 1$ can be estimated as:

$$I_F(e) = 1 - \left[\frac{1}{K} \sum_{j} (kq_j)^{1-e}\right]^{1/(1-e)} \tag{17.3}$$

For $e = 1$ we have $I_F(1) = 1 - kq_F$, where q_F is the geometric mean income share.

$I_F(e)$ has a clear interpretation; it represents the fraction of national income that is socially 'redundant.' In other words, it is the share of total income that can be discarded if the remainder is equally distributed among all individuals. As $e \to 0$, we have the polar case of inequality neutrality; utility becomes linear in individual incomes. Consequently, no loss of total income would be accepted in exchange for complete equality (i.e., $I_F(e) \to 0$ as $e \to 0$ for all F). At the other end of the spectrum, as $e \to \infty$, the welfare ranking of income distributions approaches the Rawlsian leximin. For further details, the reader is referred to Atkinson (1970), Lambert (2001, Chapter 4), and Lambert *et al.* (2003).

The Atkinson index $I_F(e)$ differs from the Gini coefficient and other summary statistics-based inequality indices in its explicitly ethical foundation. It embodies the inequality aversion parameter of a decision-maker, and captures the amount the social decision-maker would pay to eliminate inequality; thus, it is referred to as 'subjective' in contrast to the Gini coefficient. Although the ethical underpinnings of the Gini coefficient have been well documented (see, for example, Slottje *et al.* 1989), the index is regarded as authoritative by many; we call it 'objective' for the present study.[4]

According to the Atkinson index, two entirely different income distributions F_1 and F_2 could be attributed the same level of inequality by two different decision-makers:

$$I_{F_1}(e_1) = I_{F_2}(e_2) \tag{17.4}$$

where $e_1 \neq e_2$. Also, $\partial I_F(e)/\partial e > 0$ for all F. These facts are at the crux of the NRSI hypothesis.

17.2.2 The Natural Rate of Subjective Inequality

To analyze historical differences in inequality aversion in the US, let F_t be the income distribution function at time t ($t = 1947, \ldots, 1998$). Given the natural rate of subjective inequality, φ, we first identify the inequality aversion parameter, e_t, such that the subjective inequality in distribution F_t equals φ for all t:

$$I_{F_t}(e_t) = \varphi \text{ for all } t \tag{17.5}$$

We then analyze the determinants of the inequality aversion parameters e_{1947}, $e_{1948}, \ldots, e_{1998}$, identifying the empirical factors associated with the changing degree of aversion. If x is a vector of possible explanatory variables and x_j the jth component, we wish to estimate a function $\psi(x)$ such that

$$e_t \approx \psi(x^t) \tag{17.6}$$

where x^t indicates the values of x at time t; or, at least, to sign the partial derivatives $\partial \psi/\partial x_j$.

With the explanatory variables in x and function $\psi(x)$ determined, new political or social conditions in the US that alter one of the explanatory variables, say x_j^t, will cause the level of subjective inequality to diverge from the historical natural rate of inequality φ. For example, suppose $\partial \psi/\partial x_j > 0$ and that x_j^t increases to $x_j^t + \Delta x_j^t$. Then e_t increases to $e_t + \Delta e_t$, where $\Delta e_t = (\partial \psi/\partial x_j)\Delta x_j^t > 0$. This causes the level of subjective inequality to increase since the decision-maker is now more inequality averse and would be willing to sacrifice more 'distributive income' to eliminate the inequality in the given income distribution, F_t:

$$I_{F_t}(e_t + \Delta e_t) = \varphi + \left[\left(\frac{\partial I_{F_t}(e_t)}{\partial e_t}\right)\Delta e_t\right] > \varphi \tag{17.7}$$

Given the new degree of inequality aversion $e_t + \Delta e_t$ at time t, can the natural rate of inequality φ be restored? Yes, if redistributive policies (e.g., directly through the tax system or indirectly through increased expenditures on education, government sponsored training programs, raising the minimum wage, improved child care benefits, etc.) are undertaken that alter the income distribution from F_t to H_t, say, where:

$$I_{H_t}(e_t + \Delta e_t) = I_{F_t}(e_t) = \varphi < I_{F_t}(e_t + \Delta e_t) \tag{17.8}$$

The condition in (17.8) requires H_t to be objectively more equal than F_t (so that a decision-maker with inequality aversion $e_t + \Delta e_t$ would pay less to eliminate inequality in H_t than in F_t). Taking the Gini as our measure of objective inequality, then H_t has a lower Gini coefficient than F_t (i.e., $G_{H_t} < G_{F_t}$).

If this is the mechanism whereby the natural rate φ is restored, then, according to the NRSI, the Gini coefficient should be inversely related to the same set of explanatory variables, x. In other words, we can express the Gini coefficient at time t as:

$$G_{F_t} = \omega(x^t) \tag{17.9}$$

and if $\partial\psi/\partial x_j > 0$ (as assumed previously), then $\partial\omega/\partial x_j < 0$. This constitutes the testable implication of the NRSI.

Lambert *et al.* (2003) verified the validity of the NRSI through the use of cross-country data. Here, we test its validity over time in the US. Since it perhaps seems more reasonable that a particular country tolerates the same level of perceived inequality over time – as opposed to a diverse cross-section of countries – one would a priori expect the NRSI to hold for the US over time as well.

17.2.3 Data

To test the NRSI hypothesis, we have gathered data on quintile shares and other political, social, and economic variables from the US over the period 1947–1998. Table 17.A1 (see the data appendix) contains the income shares by quintile for these years and the Gini coefficient. We then use the data on income shares, along with the Atkinson index for partitioned data in (17.3) and the formula for $I_F(1)$, to find the value of e that achieves a given level of subjective inequality, φ. Because equation (17.3) and the formula for $I_F(1)$ cannot be solved explicitly for e, we conduct a grid search over potential values of e until we find the value that yields the desired level of subjective inequality. To do this, we compute the value of (17.3) for e between zero and ten, $e \neq 1$, (and the value of $I_F(1)$) with a step size of $1.0*10^{-5}$.

As in Lambert *et al.* (2003), we perform this exercise for several possible values of φ since we do not presume to know the 'true' value of φ. Table 17.A2 (see the data appendix) reports the values of e that yield an Atkinson index value of 0.10, 0.15, 0.20, 0.25, 0.30, 0.35, and 0.40.[5] Recall, the value of the Atkinson index reports the percentage of income which could be discarded with no loss in social welfare if the remainder is equally divided; thus, these values span a wide range. Finally, to ensure a consistent measure of objective inequality, we calculate the Gini coefficient over this time period based on the formula for partitioned data given in Basmann and Slottje (1999). Table 17.1 contains the summary statistics. Variable definitions and sources are relegated to the appendix.

17.3 Results

17.3.1 Preliminaries

To analyze those factors associated with the level of inequality aversion in the US, we first must ensure our analysis is robust to the choice of φ. Thus, we use several values for φ, ranging from 0.10 to 0.40. Table 17.2 presents the correlation matrix between the time-specific inequality aversion parameters for each value of φ. For notation, $e_{0.10}$ refers to the value of e such that I_F (e) = 0.10, etc. For all values of φ the correlations are extremely close to unity, implying that over a wide range of φ, the arbitrary choice of φ does not appear to be problematic. Also included in Table 17.2 are the correlations between the time-specific aversion parameters and the Gini coefficient. In all cases, the correlations between the e's and the Gini coefficient are negative and close to unity in absolute value. Consequently, periods of higher

Table 17.1 Summary statistics

Variable	Years	Mean	Std. dev.	Minimum	Maximum
President (1 = Democrat)	1947–1998	0.46	0.50	0	1
Senate (# Democrats)	1947–1998	54.56	7.27	45	68
Representatives (# Democrats)	1947–1998	252.13	25.63	188	295
Per capita GDP (1000s, 96 US$)	1947–1998	19.12	6.17	10.37	31.51
Growth rate (GDP per capita)	1948–1998	0.02	0.02	–0.03	0.06
Female LFPR	1947–1997	0.46	0.09	0.32	0.60
Female-male wage ratio	1951–1998	0.63	0.05	0.57	0.74
Gov't spending (% GDP)	1947–1998	0.12	0.04	0.06	0.23
Total public education expenditures (% GDP)	1965–1998	0.21	0.12	0.08	0.41
Immigration (1000s)	1947–1994	477.79	330.43	147.29	1827.17
% Foreign-Born	1947–1998	0.06	0.01	0.05	0.09
Poverty threshold (96 US$)	1959–1998	5064.71	28.12	5013.63	5101.84
Unemployment rate	1947–1997	0.06	0.02	0.03	0.10
% HS+, males	1947–1998	0.57	0.18	0.30	0.83
% HS+, females	1947–1998	0.58	0.16	0.33	0.83
% 4 yrs. college+, males	1947–1998	0.16	0.07	0.07	0.27
% 4 yrs. college+, females	1947–1998	0.11	0.06	0.05	0.22
Union share	1947–1998	0.26	0.10	0.10	0.37
Union membership (1000s)	1947–1998	14361.71	3115.28	9306	18295
Crime index	1960–1998	4523.69	1304.15	1887.21	5950.01
Minimum wage (96 US$)	1947–1997	3.37	0.65	1.66	4.60

Table 17.2 Inequality aversion: correlation matrix, 1947–1998

	$e_{0.10}$	$e_{0.15}$	$e_{0.20}$	$e_{0.25}$	$e_{0.30}$	$e_{0.35}$	$e_{0.40}$	*Gini*
$e_{0.10}$	1.0000							
$e_{0.15}$	0.9995	1.0000						
$e_{0.20}$	0.9980	0.9995	1.0000					
$e_{0.25}$	0.9952	0.9977	0.9994	1.0000				
$e_{0.30}$	0.9908	0.9944	0.9973	0.9993	1.0000			
$e_{0.35}$	0.9846	0.9894	0.9836	0.9969	0.9992	1.0000		
$e_{0.40}$	0.9762	0.9822	0.9878	0.9927	0.9965	0.9991	1.0000	
Gini	−0.9909	−0.9870	−0.9818	−0.9748	−0.9660	−0.9550	−0.9415	1.0000

objective inequality are characterized by less inequality averse decision-makers in the US, as the NRSI theory predicts.

To further illustrate these points, Figure 17.1 plots the value of the natural logarithm of $e_{0.10}$, $e_{0.20}$, $e_{0.30}$, and $e_{0.40}$ versus the natural log of the Gini coefficient. The relationships are virtually monotonically downward-sloping and the four cases are nearly parallel to one another. Finally, Figure 17.2 plots the level of aversion over time. Panel A plots $e_{0.10}$, $e_{0.20}$, $e_{0.30}$, and $e_{0.40}$, marking times of presidential changes. As in Figure 17.1, the four cases yield similar insights into relative changes in the degree of inequality aversion over this period. Panel B re-plots $e_{0.10}$ and $e_{0.40}$ against time, but re-scales the axes to

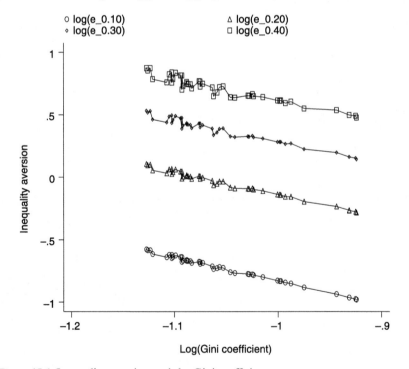

Figure 17.1 Inequality aversion and the Gini coefficient

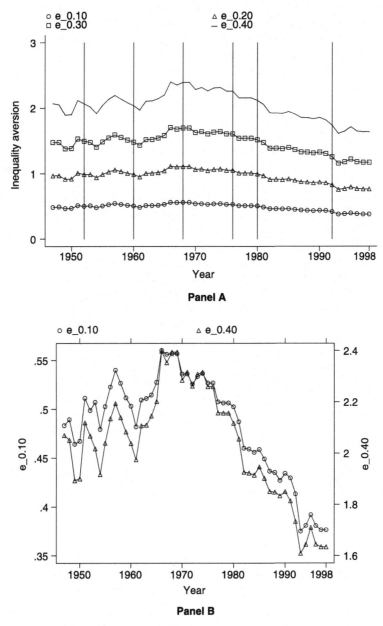

Figure 17.2 Inequality aversion in the US: 1947–1998

illustrate how each measure yields virtually identical inferences concerning changes in relative inequality aversion. Consequently, our lack of knowledge of the actual NRSI is not problematic.

Our next robustness check concerns the use of the Gini coefficient as our measure of objective inequality. To ensure that the conclusions suggested by Table 17.2 and Figure 17.1 are not due to the underlying assumptions (or preferences) of the Gini coefficient, Tables 17.3 and 17.4 present the correlations between $e_{0.10}$ and the quintile shares (Table 17.3) as well as the cumulative quintile shares, or Lorenz ordinates (Table 17.4).[6] We find that increases in inequality aversion are associated with significantly higher income shares for the four lowest quintiles, examined either individually or cumulatively. Thus, the inference that periods of greater inequality aversion have lower levels of objective inequality is robust across these choices of objective inequality measures. This finding is consistent with the model in Bénabou (2000) used to explain why the US is characterized by high objective inequality and low redistribution.

Finally, it is interesting to compare the values of the inequality aversion parameter obtained here and those estimated in Gouveia and Strauss (1994) and Young (1990) using the equal-sacrifice model.[7] Gouveia and Strauss (1994) fit the equal-sacrifice model to effective federal US income taxes between 1979 and 1989, finding implied e-values between 1.72 and 1.94. Young (1990) performs a similar exercise, finding $e = 1.63$ for 1957, $e = 1.53$ for 1967, $e = 1.79$ for 1977, and $e = 1.37$ for 1987 using the nominal tax schedules in those years. He finds slightly lower values using the effective tax schedule for 1957, 1967, and 1977. In comparison, if we take $\varphi = 0.30$, then the NRSI hypothesis yields e-values of 1.59, 1.68, 1.54, and 1.33 for 1957, 1967, 1977, and 1987, respectively. The values are *not* overly distinct.

17.3.2 Factors impacting inequality aversion

We now turn our focus to exploring the determinants of inequality aversion over time.[8] To proceed, Figures 17.3 and 17.4 present several time plots of

Table 17.3 Inequality aversion and quintile shares: correlation matrix, 1947–1998

	$e_{0.10}$	q_1	q_2	q_3	q_4	q_5
$e_{0.10}$	1.0000					
q_1	0.9468	1.0000				
q_2	0.9046	0.7277	1.0000			
q_3	0.9142	0.7500	0.9589	1.0000		
q_4	0.3909	0.3912	0.2284	0.4685	1.0000	
q_5	−0.9598	−0.8416	−0.9381	−0.9844	−0.5230	1.0000

Table 17.4 Inequality aversion and Lorenz ordinates: correlation matrix, 1947–1998

	$e_{0.10}$	q_1	$q_1 + q_2$	$q_1 + q_2 + q_3$	$q_1 + q_2 + q_3 + q_4$
$e_{0.10}$	1.0000				
q_1	0.9468	1.0000			
$q_1 + q_2$	0.9805	0.8744	1.0000		
$q_1 + q_2 + q_3$	0.9679	0.8389	0.9930	1.0000	
$q_1 + q_2 + q_3 + q_4$	0.9598	0.8416	0.9663	0.9850	1.0000

various US attributes and social policy choices and inequality aversion. Several interesting correlations emerge. First, the number of Congressional representatives and senators affiliated with the democratic party is correlated with inequality aversion. The correlation coefficients are 0.28 and 0.42,

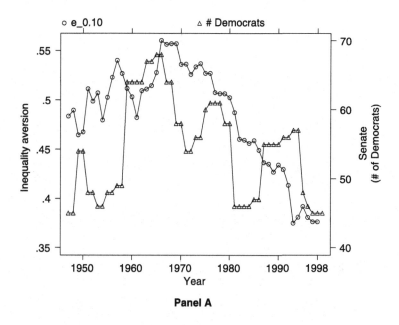

Panel A

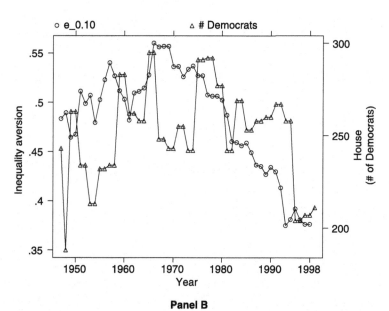

Panel B

Figure 17.3 Inequality aversion and select US attributes: 1947–1998

respectively. Second, the female-male earnings ratio is highly negatively correlated with inequality aversion; yielding a correlation coefficient of –0.91.
Third, union membership and union share are positively correlated with
inequality aversion. The correlation coefficients are 0.94 and 0.86, respectively. Finally, in terms of policy outcomes, we find significant correlations

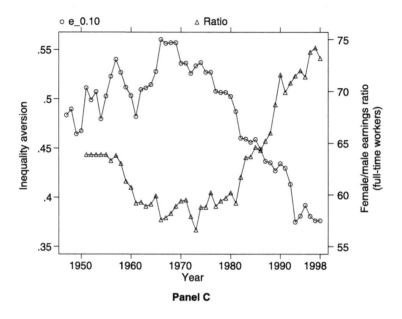

Panel C

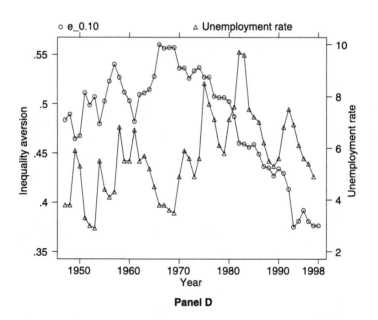

Panel D

between inequality aversion and minimum wage (correlation coefficient of 0.89), the poverty threshold (−0.83), and government expenditure on education as a fraction of GDP (0.90).

To test the NRSI hypothesis and better analyze the determinants of inequality aversion in the US, Table 17.5 presents the results of some simple

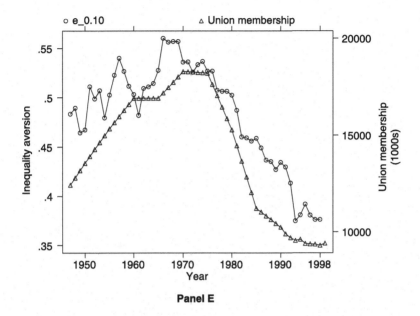

Panel E

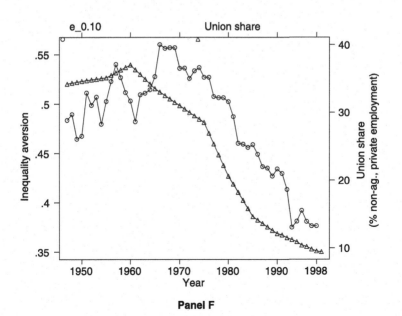

Panel F

AR(1) regressions using $\ln(e_{0.10})$ and $\ln(G)$, the natural logarithm of the Gini coefficient, as the dependent variables.[9] We estimate two different specifications (Models I and II) to vary the treatment of the GDP growth rate. The most important result to examine – that which is the basis for the NRSI

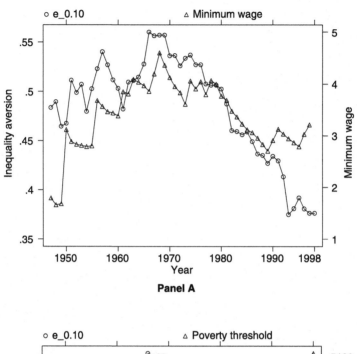

Panel A

Panel B

Figure 17.4 Inequality aversion and select US policy outcomes: 1947–1998

hypothesis – is whether changes in the socio-political climate, thereby altering the inequality aversion of decision-makers, result in alterations of the observed income distribution such that the natural rate of inequality is restored. Thus, attributes associated with greater inequality aversion must also be associated with lower levels of objective inequality, if subjective inequality is to remain equal to φ. Examining Table 17.5 verifies that this is

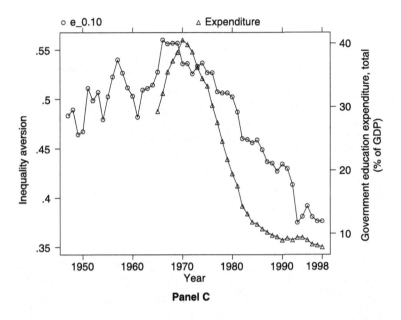

Panel C

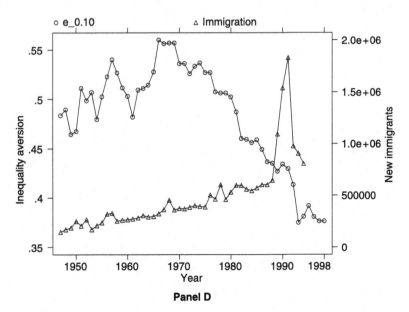

Panel D

Table 17.5 Determinants of inequality aversion ($e_{0.10}$) and objective inequality (Gini): semi-log AR(1) specification†

Variable	Model I $e_{0.10}$		Model I Gini		Model II $e_{0.10}$		Model II Gini	
President (1 = Democrat)	0.02	(2.82)	-0.01	(-2.50)	0.02	(2.89)	-0.01	(-2.55)
Senate (# Democrats)	-0.01	(-4.60)	$2.80*10^{-03}$	(4.38)	-0.01	(-4.24)	$2.90*10^{-03}$	(4.17)
House of Reps. (# Democrats)	$1.21*10^{-03}$	(4.18)	$-6.00*10^{-04}$	(-4.20)	$1.26*10^{-03}$	(4.15)	$-6.19*10^{-04}$	(-4.11)
ln (Per capita GDP)	0.73	(2.44)	-0.35	(2.34)	0.65	(1.97)	-0.32	(-1.87)
Unemployment rate	-0.02	(-2.48)	0.01	(2.38)	-0.02	(-2.48)	0.01	(2.27)
Growth rate	-0.01	(-4.85)	$3.30*10^{-03}$	(2.94)				
Growth rate* [I = 1 | Growth < 0]					-0.01	(-1.65)	0.01	(1.62)
Growth rate* [I = 1 | Growth > 0]					-0.01	(-3.09)	$2.97*10^{-03}$	(3.15)
Female LFPR	-0.06	(-11.51)	0.03	(10.47)	-0.05	(-11.15)	0.03	(9.91)
Female-male wage ratio	$1.74*10^{-03}$	(0.70)	$-9.93*10^{-04}$	(-0.79)	$1.56*10^{-03}$	(0.62)	$-9.28*10^{-04}$	(-0.73)
Union share	0.01	(2.05)	$-3.66*10^{-03}$	(-1.66)	0.01	(2.01)	$-3.77*10^{-03}$	(-1.64)
Crime index	0.27	(3.73)	-0.13	(-3.46)	0.29	(3.75)	-0.13	(-3.41)
% HS+, males	-0.03	(-1.81)	0.01	(1.17)	-0.04	(-1.94)	0.01	(1.27)
% HS+, females	0.01	(0.42)	$1.78*10^{-03}$	(0.16)	0.01	(0.60)	$6.24*10^{-05}$	(0.00)
% 4 yrs. college+, males	0.13	(9.17)	-0.06	(-8.36)	0.13	(9.22)	-0.06	(-8.38)
% 4 yrs. college+, females	-0.04	(-3.68)	0.02	(3.40)	-0.04	(-3.55)	0.02	(2.87)
Gov't spending (%GDP)	2.67	(9.05)	-1.33	(-9.02)	2.68	(8.62)	-1.33	(-8.62)
ρ	-0.70		-0.65		-0.71		-0.66	

† N=37. Robust t-statistics in parenthesis. Refer to the text and/or appendix for variable definitions.

the case. In almost every case, the sign (and significance) of the coefficient is identical, but of the opposite sign, across the model using $e_{0.10}$ as the dependent variable and the model using the Gini coefficient.

Examining the specific point estimates, several intriguing findings emerge. First, inequality aversion and objective inequality are significantly associated with the political composition of policymakers in the federal government. As one might expect, a Democrat-controlled White House and House of Representatives is associated with periods of greater (lower) inequality aversion (objective inequality). On the other hand, Democratic senators are associated with lower (greater) inequality aversion (objective inequality). One possible explanation may be that Democratic senators have grander political aspirations and consequently may act more conservative while members of the Senate. Second, during periods of greater economic prosperity, inequality aversion (objective inequality) is higher (lower). A 10% increase in per capita GDP is associated with a 7.3% increase in inequality aversion and with a 3.5% decrease in the Gini coefficient. Similarly, a one percentage point drop in the unemployment rate is connected with a 2% increase in inequality aversion and a 1% decrease in objective inequality. An increase in inequality aversion during times of relative prosperity is consistent with the finding that charitable giving increases with incomes.

Third, we find significant effects of education levels. An increase in the share of males (females) with at least four years of college is associated with a rise (fall) in inequality aversion; conversely for objective inequality. High school completion rates for males have at best a marginal negative impact on inequality aversion and no effect for females. Fourth, while there is no effect of the female–male wage ratio, greater female labor force participation is associated with lower inequality aversion and greater objective inequality. As one might expect greater female empowerment to raise inequality aversion – given the literature on women being more risk-averse than men (see, for example Jianakoplos and Bernasek (1998) and findings by Ravallion and Lokshin (2000) that women tend to favor redistribution) – this result may appear striking. However, the results may indicate that while women are more risk-averse, as they enjoy greater success (in terms of education levels and labor market participation), policymakers become less concerned over inequality. Alternatively, the results may reflect some degree of reverse causation. In particular, the greater labor force participation of women may stem from the growing degree of objective inequality in the US and the inability of single-earner households to enjoy a comfortable standard of living. Fifth, a greater union presence, more widespread crime, and higher total government expenditure as a share of GDP are associated with greater inequality aversion and a lower Gini coefficient.

Finally, we find a significant negative effect of the annual growth rate of GDP on inequality aversion (Model I). In Model II, we allow for differential effects of growth depending on whether the growth rate is positive or negative. The more flexible spline model yields little new information; the point estimates are very similar and the difference in standard errors is attributable to the infrequency of observations with negative growth rates. The fact that periods of higher growth are associated with greater objective inequality and lower inequality aversion is consistent with Quadrini (1999) who argues that growing economies are characterized by higher income inequality and less redistribution. An alternative explanation may be due to reverse causation. According to Forbes (2000), greater objective inequality enhances economic growth. This is in stark contrast with previous findings by Persson and Tabellini (1994) and Perotti (1996). Thus, the fact that objective inequality (inequality aversion) is high (low) during periods of low or negative growth may reflect this fact. We will return to this in the next section.

17.4 Aversion, objective inequality, and economic growth

Besides examining the empirical factors influencing inequality aversion in the US, we can also use the level of aversion to explain economic outcomes. For example, improved understanding of the connection between income distribution and growth has been the impetus behind many recent studies (see, for example, Bénabou 2000, Forbes 2000, Perotti 1996, Alesina and Rodrik 1994, Persson and Tabellini 1994, Saint-Paul and Verdier 1993). If one accepts the NRSI hypothesis, then one must recognize that the level of objective inequality embodied in a nation's income distribution at any point in time is determined by the level of country- and time-specific inequality aversion. Thus, any correlation between economic growth and income inequality may be spurious and in actuality reflect the linkage between inequality aversion and growth rates.

To explore such a possibility, Panel A in Figure 17.5 plots inequality aversion and per capita GDP by year. Panels B, C, and D plot inequality aversion and the annual, 3-year moving average, and 5-year moving average growth rate of per capita GDP, respectively. While there does not appear to be a strong unconditional relationship between the growth rate and inequality aversion, we do note that the correlation coefficient between one-year lagged inequality aversion and short-run per capita economic growth is -0.14, -0.12, and -0.10 in Panels B, C, and D, respectively.

To analyze these relationships in a regression framework, we build on the recent work in Forbes (2000). Applying her panel data model to the present time series context, we begin with the following estimating equation:

$$growth_t = a_G + x_{t-1}\beta_G + \gamma_G \ln(y_{t-1}) + \delta_G G_{t-1} + \varepsilon_t^G \qquad (17.10)$$

where $growth_t$ is the growth rate of per capita income at time t, x_{t-1} is a vector of lagged control variables, y_{t-1} is lagged per capita income, G_{t-1} is the lagged Gini coefficient, and ε_t^G is a well-behaved normally distributed error term. δ_G is the typical parameter of interest. Recognizing that $growth_t \cong \ln(y_t) - \ln(y_{t-1})$, we may re-write (17.10) as

$$\ln(y_t) = a_G + x_{t-1}\beta_G + \gamma_G^* \ln(y_{t-1}) + \delta_G G_{t-1} + \varepsilon_t^G \qquad (17.11)$$

where $\gamma_G^* = \gamma_G + 1$.

Equation (17.11) constitutes the first portion of our analysis. In line with the NRSI hypothesis, we also replace the Gini coefficient in (17.11) with our measure of inequality aversion, $e_{0.10}$. Thus, we also estimate:

$$\ln(y_t) = a_A + x_{t-1}\beta_A + \gamma_A^* \ln(y_{t-1}) + \delta_A e_{0.10, t-1} + \varepsilon_t^A \qquad (17.12)$$

where $\gamma_A^* = \gamma_A + 1$ and everything else is previously defined.

Two issues arise prior to the estimation of (17.11) and (17.12). First, we must decide on the variables to be included in x. In addition to the usual controls for educational attainment (percentage of males and females with a high school diploma and the percentage with at least four years of college), we include measures of total government spending as a share of GDP, unionization rates, the unemployment rate, and the female labor force participation rate. In addition, for forecast purposes surrounding the approaching presidential election, we also include a dummy variable for the political affiliation of the president as well as the number of Democratic senators and representatives.

Second, under the NRSI hypothesis, inequality aversion and, consequently, the level of objective inequality are endogenous. The failure to control for the potential endogeneity of inequality in previous empirical analysis of the inequality-growth relationship is problematic (Forbes 2000). However, based on the results presented in Table 17.5, we assume that the level of criminal activity affects inequality aversion and objective inequality, but has no effect on the growth rate in the US. Thus, this represents a valid instrument for the Gini coefficient in (17.11) and inequality aversion in (17.12). Finally, we note that treating lagged per capita income as exogenous is not problematic – unlike in Forbes (2000) – since we are not including fixed or random effects in the present analysis; we focus only on the US.[10] Moreover, by focusing solely on the US, we also minimize concerns surrounding measurement error bias since there is presumably greater continuity in the data collection methods from a single country.

Table 17.6 presents estimates of (17.11) and (17.12). Model I is estimated via OLS. Model II instruments for inequality aversion and the Gini coefficient. The IV results are consistent with the findings in Forbes (2000). Specifically, we find a significant, positive effect of objective inequality on the growth rate in the following period. In particular, a one point increase in the Gini coefficient leads to a 1.8 percent increase in the growth rate of per capita income. This is approximately a one standard deviation increase; thus, the effect is not inconsequential.[11] However, if we replace the Gini coefficient with our measure of inequality aversion, the coefficient is significant and negative in the IV model. Therefore, greater inequality aversion has an adverse effect on economic growth. A one standard deviation increase in

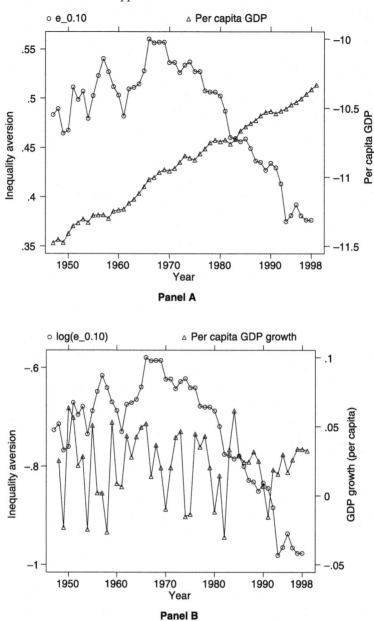

Figure 17.5 Inequality aversion and economic growth: 1947–1998

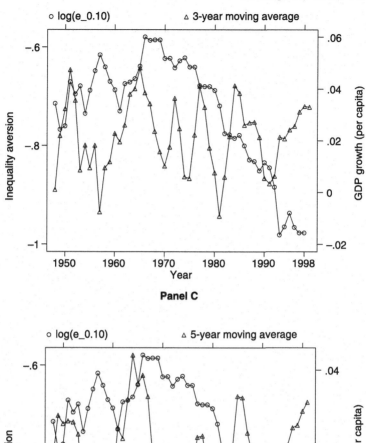

Panel C

Panel D

inequality aversion (corresponding to a 0.05 increase in $e_{0.10}$) causes the growth rate to fall by roughly 7.6 percent, or more than three standard deviations.

Taking these results at face value, it is not possible to know if the positive correlation between objective inequality and economic growth estimated by Forbes (2000) is merely picking up the effect of inequality aversion. If greater

Table 17.6. Determinants of economic growth in the US: 1947–1998†

Variable	OLS		Instrumental variable (IV)	
$e_{0.10}$	-0.17 [p = 0.56]		-1.47 [p = 0.03]	
Gini coefficient		0.61 [p = 0.47]		1.77 [p = 0.03]
ln (per capita GDP)‡	0.40 [p = 0.17]	0.42 [p = 0.15]	0.73 [p = 0.05]	0.61 [p = 0.07]
% HS+, males	0.02 [p = 0.36]	0.02 [p = 0.35]	0.04 [p = 0.06]	0.03 [p = 0.18]
% HS+, females	-0.01 [p = 0.52]	-0.02 [p = 0.48]	-0.05 [p = 0.04]	-0.03 [p = 0.10]
% 4 yrs. college+, males	-0.04 [p = 0.09]	-0.03 [p = 0.13]	0.04 [p = 0.28]	0.01 [p = 0.70]
% 4 yrs. college+, females	0.01 [p = 0.28]	0.01 [p = 0.36]	0.01 [p = 0.69]	0.01 [p = 0.46]
President (1 = Democrat)	0.01 [p = 0.28]	0.01 [p = 0.44]	$-1.97*10^{-03}$ [p = 0.82]	$3.21*10^{-04}$ [p = 0.97]
Senate (# Democrat)	$3.98*10^{-04}$ [p = 0.72]	$3.99*10^{-04}$ [p = 0.72]	$-8.48*10^{-04}$ [p = 0.57]	$1.90*10^{-04}$ [p = 0.88]
House of Reps. (# Democrat)	$1.41*10^{-04}$ [p = 0.60]	$1.46*10^{-04}$ [p = 0.58]	$5.03*10^{-04}$ [p = 0.20]	$1.86*10^{-04}$ [p = 0.54]
Gov't spending (% GDP)	0.10 [p = 0.68]	0.12 [p = 0.63]	2.50 [p = 0.04]	1.15 [p = 0.12]
Union share	$-4.92*10^{-03}$ [p = 0.19]	$-4.85*10^{-03}$ [p = 0.18]	0.01 [p = 0.26]	$1.66*10^{-04}$ [p = 0.98]
Unemployment rate	0.02 [p = 0.02]	0.02 [p = 0.01]	0.01 [p = 0.53]	0.02 [p = 0.10]
Female labor force participation	-0.01 [p = 0.23]	-0.01 [p = 0.25]	-0.03 [p = 0.00]	-0.02 [p = 0.01]
Observations	52		39	

† All independent variables are lagged on year. Refer to the text and/or appendix for variable definitions. IV results use the lagged crime index to instrument for inequality aversion and the Gini coefficient. P-values associated with the hypothesis that the coefficient is zero are presented in brackets.

‡ Coefficient corresponds to γ in equation (10); not $\gamma*$.

inequality aversion diverts resources and the focus of decision-makers away from unconstrained growth, then social policies that sacrifice short-run growth for the sake of equality may receive greater support. However, given the high degree of correlation between inequality aversion and objective inequality, it is not possible to include both measures in a single growth regression and test this claim. Thus, while Forbes (p. 871) states that 'further careful assessment of the numerous linkages between inequality, growth, and their determinants is necessary,' the present analysis strengthens this claim.

17.5 Conclusion

The goal of the present study is two-fold. First, we set out to further test the natural rate of subjective inequality hypothesis of Lambert *et al.* (2003) using time-series data from the US. Finding the data to be consistent with this hypothesis, we find a significant correlation between the level of inequality aversion and attributes such as political affiliation, education, government spending, unemployment, unionization, economic growth, per capita income, female labor force participation, among others. In addition, we document a strong association between inequality aversion and social policies such as the minimum wage, government spending on education, and government-established poverty thresholds. These policies may represent the mechanism by which the observed income distribution is altered such that the natural rate of subjective inequality is maintained.

Second, we use variation over time in the level of inequality aversion in the US to shed new light on the debate surrounding the effect of current inequality on short-run economic growth. Specifically, we show that the recent finding in Forbes (2000) that income inequality is positively correlated with short-run economic growth within countries holds using time-series data from the US as well. Moreover, our result is robust to the treatment of inequality as endogenous. However, we also suggest that the coefficient on inequality may actually be capturing the effect of inequality aversion – not objective inequality – on economic growth. Given that greater inequality aversion may lead to implementation of social and economic policies designed to diminish the level of objective inequality (as opposed to improving prospects of future growth), future research on the ties between inequality aversion, the natural rate of subjective inequality hypothesis, and economic growth could prove quite fruitful.

Finally, we note the relevance of the present study to the 2008 US presidential election. A victorious Democratic presidential candidate in the race implies a 2 percent expected increase in inequality aversion, a 1 percent decrease in objective inequality, and a subsequent 1.1 percent decrease in future economic growth ceteris paribus. A successful Republican candidate will maintain the status quo ceteris paribus.

Notes

1 It is important to note up front that our emphasis on the Atkinson and Gini indices is a choice. Other measures could have been examined. See also note 4.

2 Obviously the Gini coefficient – especially when used as opposed to an extended Gini coefficient – entails some preferences for inequality. Thus, in actuality it is no more objective perhaps than other measures of inequality. However, in the spirit of common (mis)perceptions, we refer to the Gini coefficient throughout our analysis as reflecting objective inequality (see also Lambert *et al.* 2003).

3 As stated in Atkinson (1970), inequality aversion is assumed to be constant relative to ensure the measurement of inequality is invariant to equiproportionate changes in income. In the remainder of the analysis we maintain this assumption.

4 To emphasize, we use the Gini coefficient to approximate 'objective' inequality given its historical as well as current importance in the study of inequality. Clearly other indices could have been used (e.g., section 17.3 also utilizes the Lorenz ordinates). In particular, use of the Gini coefficient as opposed to an extended Gini entails some implicit preferences regarding inequality.

5 The corresponding values of $I_F(e)$ are not presented in the table, but in all cases except one we are able to find a value of e that brings $I_F(e)$ to exactly the desired value. For the lone exception, $I_F(e)$ only deviates from the desired value by $-1.4*10^{-4}$.

6 Hereafter, we present results only for $e_{0.10}$. We have confirmed that the inferences are invariant to the choices of φ we tried.

7 The equal-sacrifice model assumes that income taxes are set such that (for some particular utility function) the loss in individual utility is equated across all income levels. Given a sufficiently diminishing marginal utility of income, the equal-sacrifice tax is progressive (see, for example, Young 1994). Ok (1995) and Mitra and Ok (1996, 1997) have studied intensively the question whether a given tax schedule $t(y)$, where y is income, can be rationalized as an equal-absolute sacrifice tax for some plausible (increasing and concave) utility function $U(y)$. They show that tax schedules $t(y)$ satisfying $t'(y) > 0$ and $t''(y) > 0$ for all y are equal-absolute sacrifice taxes (Ok 1995, Theorem 2); that among increasing piecewise-linear tax schedules, essentially only the convex ones are equal-absolute sacrifice taxes (Mitra and Ok 1996, Corollary 3.10); and that more generally some non-convex progressive tax schedules are, and some are not, equal absolute-sacrifice taxes (Mitra and Ok 1997, Theorem 1 and examples). Mitra and Ok were able to demonstrate, in particular, that the statutory personal income tax codes in Turkey between 1981 and 1985 and in the USA between 1988 and 1990, though progressive, were not equal-absolute sacrifice taxes.

8 We use the word "determinants" loosely as we do no attempt to deal with issues of endogeneity.

9 One must be careful to not to dismiss the validity of considering inequality aversion and the Gini coefficient as separate variables. As stressed in our opening remarks, the Atkinson index is a function of the underlying income distribution and inequality aversion and the Gini coefficient is a different function of the underlying income distribution. Therefore, while related, the Gini coefficient and the Atkinson index (for a given level of inequality aversion) offer distinct representations of the underlying income distribution and the relationship between the Gini coefficient and inequality aversion is not clear a priori (as seen in that Figure 17.1 is not a straight line). See also Lambert *et al.* (2003) and Harvey (2005).

10 If the error term is serially correlated, then lagged per capita income will no longer be exogenous. However, Forbes (2000) ignores such a possibility in her analysis (conditional on the inclusion of country fixed effects). Thus, we continue with this assumption.

11 Not only is the effect of an extremely large magnitude, it is also of the order of ten times larger than the coefficient reported in Forbes (2000). One possibile explanation for the larger effect found here is that our dependent variable is the growth rate in the following year, whereas Forbes examines the average growth rate over the subsequent five years. When we tried lags longer than one year (specifically, two-, three-, four-, and five-year lags), the results were not significant. Thus, the effect of inequality on economic growth appears to diminish rapidly over time. Another possible explanation is that inequality is treated as exogenous in Forbes. Finally, Forbes uses panel data on 45 countries, whereas the present analysis is restricted to the US.

References

Alesina, A. and D. Rodrik (1994). 'Distributive politics and economic growth', *Quarterly Journal of Economics* 109: 465–90.

Atkinson, A.B. (1970). 'On the measurement of inequality', *Journal of Economic Theory* 2: 244–63.

Basmann, R.L. and D.J. Slottje (1999). 'A note on the Gini measure for discrete distributions', in D.J. Slottje (ed.) *Advances in Econometrics, Income Distribution, and Scientific Methodology*, Heidelberg: Physica-Verlag.

Bénabou, R. (2000). 'Unequal societies: income distribution and the social contract', *American Economic Review* 90: 96–129.

Bénabou, R. and E.A. Ok (2001). 'Social mobility and the demand for redistribution: the POUM hypothesis', *Quarterly Journal of Economics* 116: 447–87.

Forbes, K.J. (2000). 'A reassessment of the relationship between inequality and growth', *American Economic Review* 90: 869–87.

Gouveia, M. and R.P. Strauss (1994). 'Effective federal individual income tax functions: an exploratory empirical analysis', *National Tax Journal* 47: 317–38.

Gradstein, M. and B. Milanovic (2004). 'Does liberté = égalité? A survey on the empirical evidence on the links between democracy and inequality with some evidence on the transition economies', *Journal of Economic Surveys* 18: 515–37.

Harvey, J. (2005). 'A note on the "natural rate of subjective inequality" hypothesis and the approximate relationship between the Gini coefficient and the Atkinson index', *Journal of Public Economics* 89: 1021–25.

Hirschman, A.O. and M. Rothschild (1973). 'The changing tolerance for income inequality in the course of economic development', *Quarterly Journal of Economics* 87: 544–66.

Jianakoplos, N.A. and A. Bernasek (1998). 'Are women more risk-averse?', *Economic Inquiry* 36: 620–30.

Lambert, P.J. (2001). *The Distribution and Redistribution of Income*, 3rd Edition, Manchester: Manchester University Press.

Lambert, P.J., D.L. Millimet, and D.J. Slottje (2003). 'Inequality aversion and the natural rate of subjective inequality', *Journal of Public Economics* 87: 1061–90.

Li, H., L. Squire, and H. Zou (1998). 'Explaining international and intertemporal variations in income inequality', *Economic Journal* 108: 26–43.

Milanovic, B. (1999). 'Do more unequal countries redistribute more? Does the median voter hypothesis hold?', mimeo, The World Bank.

Mitra, T. and E. Ok (1996). 'Personal income taxation and the principle of equal sacrifice revisited', *International Economic Review* 37: 925–48.

Mitra, T. and E. Ok (1997). 'On the equitability of progressive taxation', *Journal of Economic Theory* 73: 316–34.

Ok, E. (1995). 'On the principle of equal sacrifice in income taxation', *Journal of Public Economics* 58: 453–67.

Perotti, R. (1996). 'Growth, income distribution, and democracy: what the data say', *Journal of Economic Growth* 1: 149–87.

Persson, T. and G. Tabellini (1994). 'Is inequality harmful for growth?', *American Economic Review* 84: 600–21.

Quadrini, V. (1999). 'Growth, learning and redistributive politics', *Journal of Public Economics* 74: 263–97.

Ravallion, M. and M. Lokshin (2000). 'Who wants to redistribute? The tunnel effect in 1990s Russia', *Journal of Public Economics* 76: 87–104.

Saint-Paul, G. and T. Verdier (1993). 'Education, democracy, and growth', *Journal of Development Economics* 42: 399–407.

Slottje, D.J., R.L. Basmann, and M. Nieswiadomy (1989). 'On the empirical relationship between several well-known inequality measures', *Journal of Econometrics* 42: 49–66.

Young, H.P. (1990). 'Progressive taxation and equal sacrifice', *American Economic Review*, 80: 253–66.

Young, H.P. (1994). *Equity*, Princeton, N.J.: Princeton University Press.

Data appendix

Variables and sources:

- Quintile shares are obtained from the US Census Bureau historical tables (http:\\www.census.gov\hhes\income\histinc\f02.html).
- Politicala affiliation of Congressional members are obtained from http:\\www.policsci.com\almanac\history\polidivs.htm.
- Gross domestic product and total government spending are obtained from the US Bureau of Economic Analysis (http:\\www.bea.doc.gov).
- Population is available from the US Census Bureau (http:\\www.census.gov).
- Poverty thresholds are also available through the US Census Bureau.
- Unionization membership and labor market shares (defined as the percentage of covered non-agricultural, private sector employment) are obtained from http:\\www.demographia.com.
- The percentage of the US population that is foreign-born is available through the US Census Bureau.
- The number of newly admitted immigrants is obtained from the US Immigration and Naturalization Service (INS), *Statistical Yearbook of the Immigration and Naturalization Service, 1994*, Washington, DC: US Government Printing Office, 1996.
- The female-male wage ratio is available through the US Department of Labor Women's Bureau (http:\\www.dol.gov).
- Education attainment levels are obtained from the US Department of Education (http:\\nces.ed.gov).

- The annual minimum wage is found at http:\\epinet.org\datazone\ minimumwage.html.
- The crime index is defined as the number of crimes per 100,000 individuals and is available through the US Department of Justice (http:\\www.doj.gov).

Table 17.A1 Annual income distribution

Year	Gini Index	Income Share by Quintile				
		Lowest 20%	Second 20%	Third 20%	Fourth 20%	Highest 20%
1947	0.378	5.0	11.9	17.0	23.1	43.0
1948	0.369	4.9	12.1	17.3	23.2	42.5
1949	0.379	4.5	11.9	17.3	23.5	42.8
1950	0.375	4.5	12.0	17.4	23.4	42.7
1951	0.361	5.0	12.4	17.6	23.4	41.6
1952	0.374	4.9	12.3	17.4	23.4	42.0
1953	0.360	4.7	12.5	18.0	23.9	40.9
1954	0.373	4.5	12.1	17.7	23.9	41.8
1955	0.366	4.8	12.3	17.8	23.7	41.4
1956	0.355	5.0	12.5	17.9	23.7	40.9
1957	0.351	5.1	12.7	18.1	23.8	40.3
1958	0.354	5.0	12.5	18.0	23.9	40.6
1959	0.366	4.9	12.3	17.9	23.8	41.1
1960	0.369	4.8	12.2	17.8	24.0	41.2
1961	0.376	4.7	11.9	17.5	23.8	42.1
1962	0.365	5.0	12.1	17.6	24.0	41.3
1963	0.360	5.0	12.1	17.7	24.0	41.2
1964	0.352	5.1	12.0	17.7	24.0	41.2
1965	0.357	5.2	12.2	17.8	23.9	40.9
1966	0.348	5.6	12.4	17.8	23.8	40.4
1967	0.399	5.5	12.4	17.9	23.9	40.3
1968	0.388	5.6	12.4	17.7	23.7	40.6
1969	0.391	5.6	12.4	17.7	23.7	40.6
1970	0.394	5.4	12.2	17.6	23.8	41.0
1971	0.396	5.5	12.0	17.6	23.8	41.1
1972	0.401	5.4	11.9	17.5	23.9	41.3
1973	0.397	5.5	11.9	17.5	24.0	41.1
1974	0.395	5.5	12.0	17.5	24.0	41.0
1975	0.397	5.4	11.8	17.6	24.1	41.1
1976	0.398	5.4	11.8	17.6	24.1	41.1
1977	0.402	5.2	11.6	17.5	24.2	41.5
1978	0.402	5.2	11.6	17.5	24.1	41.6
1979	0.404	5.2	11.6	17.5	24.1	41.6
1980	0.403	5.1	11.6	17.5	24.3	41.5
1981	0.406	5.0	11.3	17.4	24.4	41.9
1982	0.412	4.7	11.2	17.0	24.3	42.8
1983	0.414	4.7	11.1	17.1	24.3	42.8
1984	0.415	4.7	11.0	17.0	24.4	42.9
1985	0.419	4.8	11.0	16.9	24.3	43.0
1986	0.425	4.7	10.9	16.9	24.1	43.4
1987	0.426	4.6	10.7	16.8	24.0	43.9
1988	0.427	4.6	10.7	16.7	24.0	44.0
1989	0.431	4.6	10.6	16.5	23.7	44.6
1990	0.428	4.6	10.8	16.6	23.8	44.2
1991	0.428	4.5	10.7	16.6	24.1	44.1
1992	0.434	4.3	10.5	16.5	24.0	44.7
1993	0.454	4.1	9.9	15.7	23.3	47.0
1994	0.456	4.2	10.0	15.7	23.3	46.8
1995	0.450	4.4	10.1	15.8	23.2	46.5
1996	0.455	4.2	10.0	15.8	23.1	46.9
1997	0.459	4.2	9.9	15.7	23.0	47.2
1998	0.456	4.2	9.9	15.7	23.0	47.2

Table 17.A2 Annual inequality aversion

Country	Gini index	$e_{0.10}$	$e_{0.15}$	$e_{0.20}$	$e_{0.25}$	$e_{0.30}$	$e_{0.35}$	$e_{0.40}$
1947	0.378	0.483	0.724	0.967	1.216	1.478	1.759	2.069
1948	0.369	0.489	0.730	0.972	1.219	1.476	1.750	2.051
1949	0.379	0.464	0.690	0.915	1.143	1.378	1.626	1.893
1950	0.375	0.467	0.694	0.920	1.149	1.384	1.632	1.900
1951	0.361	0.511	0.761	1.010	1.264	1.528	1.809	2.118
1952	0.374	0.499	0.742	0.986	1.235	1.493	1.767	2.067
1953	0.360	0.507	0.750	0.989	1.230	1.477	1.736	2.018
1954	0.373	0.479	0.710	0.938	1.168	1.403	1.650	1.916
1955	0.366	0.503	0.745	0.987	1.231	1.483	1.750	2.040
1956	0.355	0.523	0.776	1.027	1.282	1.546	1.827	2.134
1957	0.351	0.540	0.800	1.058	1.319	1.590	1.877	2.193
1958	0.354	0.527	0.781	1.033	1.288	1.552	1.831	2.138
1959	0.366	0.512	0.759	1.005	1.254	1.512	1.784	2.083
1960	0.369	0.503	0.746	0.987	1.230	1.482	1.748	2.038
1961	0.376	0.482	0.716	0.950	1.187	1.432	1.691	1.974
1962	0.365	0.509	0.757	1.005	1.258	1.520	1.799	2.107
1963	0.360	0.511	0.760	1.008	1.260	1.523	1.802	2.110
1964	0.352	0.515	0.766	1.017	1.274	1.542	1.828	2.145
1965	0.357	0.528	0.785	1.043	1.306	1.581	1.875	2.201
1966	0.348	0.560	0.836	1.113	1.400	1.701	2.029	2.397
1967	0.399	0.556	0.828	1.102	1.383	1.677	1.996	2.353
1968	0.388	0.557	0.831	1.109	1.395	1.697	2.024	2.394
1969	0.391	0.557	0.831	1.109	1.395	1.697	2.024	2.394
1970	0.394	0.536	0.800	1.066	1.339	1.626	1.937	2.284
1971	0.396	0.536	0.802	1.070	1.347	1.640	1.958	2.316
1972	0.401	0.526	0.786	1.049	1.320	1.605	1.915	2.262
1973	0.397	0.534	0.797	1.065	1.341	1.633	1.951	2.308
1974	0.395	0.537	0.802	1.070	1.347	1.640	1.958	2.316
1975	0.397	0.527	0.787	1.049	1.320	1.604	1.913	2.259
1976	0.398	0.527	0.787	1.049	1.320	1.604	1.913	2.259
1977	0.402	0.508	0.757	1.009	1.268	1.539	1.831	2.157
1978	0.402	0.506	0.756	1.008	1.266	1.538	1.830	2.156
1979	0.404	0.506	0.756	1.008	1.266	1.538	1.830	2.156
1980	0.403	0.502	0.749	0.997	1.250	1.516	1.801	2.117
1981	0.406	0.487	0.726	0.967	1.214	1.472	1.749	2.055
1982	0.412	0.460	0.686	0.913	1.145	1.387	1.644	1.925
1983	0.414	0.459	0.685	0.911	1.143	1.384	1.640	1.922
1984	0.415	0.456	0.680	0.906	1.136	1.376	1.633	1.914
1985	0.419	0.459	0.685	0.914	1.148	1.394	1.656	1.946
1986	0.425	0.449	0.671	0.895	1.124	1.364	1.620	1.901
1987	0.426	0.437	0.653	0.871	1.094	1.328	1.577	1.850
1988	0.427	0.435	0.651	0.868	1.092	1.325	1.574	1.848
1989	0.431	0.427	0.640	0.855	1.077	1.310	1.559	1.832
1990	0.428	0.434	0.650	0.868	1.092	1.325	1.575	1.849
1991	0.428	0.430	0.642	0.856	1.075	1.304	1.547	1.813
1992	0.434	0.413	0.617	0.823	1.033	1.251	1.482	1.733
1993	0.454	0.375	0.563	0.753	0.950	1.154	1.372	1.609
1994	0.456	0.381	0.572	0.766	0.967	1.176	1.400	1.644
1995	0.450	0.392	0.589	0.790	0.998	1.217	1.452	1.710
1996	0.455	0.381	0.572	0.766	0.967	1.176	1.400	1.644
1997	0.459	0.376	0.566	0.759	0.958	1.167	1.390	1.634
1998	0.456	0.376	0.566	0.759	0.958	1.167	1.390	1.634

18 Internal migration, household size and income inequality in Turkey

Süleyman Özmucur and Jacques Silber

18.1 Introduction

Since the beginning of the Republic in 1923, Turkey has experienced significant changes in its demographic structure. The population, which was 13.6 million in 1927 (the first population census), reached 67.8 million in 2000 (the last census). This indicates an average annual growth rate of 2.22 percent. During this period, the urban population grew at an annual rate of 3.61 percent. Thus, while in 1927 the urban population represented only 24.2 percent of the total population, this share was equal to 64.9 percent in the year 2000.

Internal migration and urbanization became in fact important phenomena in the 1950s (Shorter 1985). Note that in addition to natural increase and internal migration, the enormous increase in the urban population was also affected by the reclassification of municipalities since by Turkish law a municipality becomes a city once its population reaches ten thousand inhabitants. Some studies have estimated that this reclassification accounts for approximately 25 percent of the rural to urban migration flows. Population movements were not only from rural to urban areas but also within areas.

There were several reasons for this internal migration, though the relative significance of these factors was not stable throughout the entire period. During the 1950s, 1960s and 1970s, state-supported rapid industrialization was probably the most important but not the sole determinant of urbanization. Social services such as education and health developed faster in urban areas. Rising education and employment opportunities led to the perception of a better life in urban than rural areas, hence the increased demand for moving to urban areas. Developments in transportation and communications and the presence of former migrants in urban areas made these movements less costly. The limited supply of rural resources was also an important determinant of rapid urbanization (SIS 1995).

After the liberalization of 1980 there were additional reasons for such an internal migration. This liberalization allowed an environment where interest rates and exchange rates were determined by market forces. The differential interest rate system that had been in favor of the farmers had now been abolished. The agricultural support pricing system was also gradually abolished, and international prices were offered that were much lower than support prices for major crops. Subsidized prices for the major agricultural inputs such as fertilizers or tractors were abolished and credits by the agricultural bank were reduced because of financial problems. These factors evidently precipitated the exodus from regions with a large agricultural base (East, Southeast and Black Sea). In fact the share of agricultural income in national income declined significantly at that time.

The purpose of this chapter is, however, not to determine the macro-economic factors that precipitated the migration from rural to urban areas. It is rather to take a look at the impact that such an internal migration had on income inequality in Turkey. Several studies (see, for example, SIS 1997) have actually attempted to analyze the changes in the distribution of income in Turkey that took place in recent years. An interesting survey of individual income distribution in Turkey is presented in Gürsel *et al.* (2000). Their study determines the exact impact of various income sources on the overall income inequality, examines the impact of various household characteristics on poverty levels and finally compares the results with those available for other EU countries. Selim and McKay (2000) propose a more detailed analysis of the relationship between characteristics of households' heads and poverty levels but their study is mainly descriptive. This is also generally the case of Özmucur and Silber's (2000) study of inequality in Turkey in 1994. None of these studies, however, took a detailed look at the link between internal migration and changes in the distribution of incomes.

Our hypothesis is that a move from a rural to an urban area has at least two important effects on a household. First, it will increase its income. Second, for various reasons that will not be examined here, it will ultimately decrease its fertility. These two effects will evidently lead to changes in the income distribution in Turkey and hence to variations in income inequality. The present study will attempt to determine the specific impacts on income inequality of differences between rural and urban areas or between regions in the sizes of the households.

This chapter is organized as follows. The following section explains the methodology that will be used. It emphasizes in particular the role played by the way the welfare of household members is measured as well as the importance of the definition of the unit whose welfare distribution is analyzed (individuals or households). Then, in another section, an empirical illustration based on the Income Survey that was conducted in Turkey in 1994, confirms the relevance of this emphasis on the concepts of welfare measurement and observation units and the usefulness of the proposed methodology. Concluding comments are given in the final section. Throughout the chapter the income inequality index that is used is the Gini index.

18.2 Analyzing the impact of internal migration on income inequality: the methodology

18.2.1 A simple formulation for the decomposition of income inequality by population subgroups.

Let G_{TOT}, G_{BET}, G_{WITH} and G_{OVERL} refer respectively to the overall value of the Gini index of income inequality in a given country, to the between-areas inequality in this country, to the within-areas income inequality and finally to the residual term of the decomposition of overall inequality. Note that this residual measures in fact the degree of overlap between the income distributions in the various areas (see Silber 1989). We may then write (see Silber 1989, and Deustch and Silber 1999) that:

$$G_{TOT} = G_{BET} + G_{WITH} + G_{OVERL} \qquad (18.1)$$

The within-areas inequality G_{WITH} may be expressed (see Silber 1989 for more details) as:

$$G_{WITH} = \Sigma_{r=1\,\text{to}\,R}\, p_r\, s_r\, G_r \qquad (18.2)$$

where p_r refers to the population share of area r, s_r to the share of area r in the total income of the country, G_r to the Gini index of income inequality within area r while R represents the total number of areas in the country. Let us call respectively y_m and y_{mr} the average incomes in the whole country and in area r.

Since s_r may be also expressed as:

$$s_r = p_r\, (y_{mr}/y_m) \qquad (18.3)$$

we may also write (18.2) as:

$$G_{WITH} = \Sigma_{r=1\,\text{to}\,R}\, (p_r)^2\, (y_{mr}/y_m)\, G_r \qquad (18.4)$$

The within-areas inequality index G_{WITH} is therefore expressed as a function of only three sets of variables: the shares of the various areas in the total population of the country, the ratios of the average incomes in the various areas over the average income in the whole country and the within-areas Gini indices.

We will now show that is possible to express the between-areas inequality index G_{BET} as a function of only two sets of variables: the shares of the various areas in the total population and the ratios of the average incomes in the various areas over the average income in the whole country.

It may in fact be shown (see Silber 1989) that if $[p_r]'$ represents the row vector of the population shares of the various areas while $[s_r]$ refers to the column vector of the shares of the various areas in the total income of the country, the areas in both vectors being ranked by decreasing values of the average incomes of the areas, the between-areas Gini inequality index G_{BET} may be expressed as:

$$G_{\text{BET}} = [p_r]' \, G \, [s_r] \qquad (18.5)$$

where G, called the G-matrix, (see, Silber 1989) is a n by n matrix whose typical element g_{hk} is equal to 0 if $h = k$, to -1 if $k > h$ and to $+1$ if $h > k$.

Combining then (18.3) and (18.5) one derives that:

$$G_{\text{BET}} = [p_r]' \, G \, [p_r(y_r/y_m)] \qquad (18.6)$$

where as before the elements of the row vector $[p_r]'$ and of the column vector $[p_r(y_r/y_m)]$ are ranked by decreasing values of the regional incomes y_r.

18.2.2 Measuring the respective impacts of income and size of the household on inequality differences

In the previous section no attention was given to two important questions:

- on which measure of the welfare of the household members should the inequality analysis or comparison be based?
- which are the units (households, individuals) whose distribution of welfare we want to analyze?

These issues have been analyzed in Danziger and Taussig (1979) and we summarize here their main ideas.

(a) Measuring the welfare of household members

The question here is in fact to determine which part of the goods and services consumed by the household should be considered as purely private goods (whose consumption cannot be shared, e.g. food) and which part as public goods (e.g. a kitchen). Buhman *et al.* (1988) proposed a nice formulation to tackle this problem by expressing the welfare x_i of household members as:

$$x_i = y_i/(n_i)^a \qquad (18.7)$$

where y_i is the total income of the household, n_i is the size of the household and a is a parameter included in the interval [0,1]. It may be observed that if a = 0, the welfare of the household members is equal to the total household income, so that it is then assumed that all goods and services are considered as public goods. On the contrary, when a = 1, the welfare indicator is equal to the per capita income, in which case one supposes that all goods and services are private. A more general case occurs when $0 < a < 1$ which implies that part of the goods and services consumed are public, part private.

It is also possible to make a difference between adults and children and write (cf. Coulter *et al.* 1992) that:

$$n_i = a_i + \lambda\, c_i \tag{18.8}$$

where a_i is the number of adults in the household and c_i *is the number of children, while λ is* a parameter indicating how the consumption of a child should be converted into an adult's consumption.

(b) The selection of the unit whose welfare distribution is analyzed

This question is different from the previous one. Whatever measure of welfare is analyzed, we may ask whether we want to look at the inequality between households or between individuals. Given that we have four measures of welfare and two units of observation (individuals or households), we will have eight different ways of measuring inequality.

To measure inequality we use the algorithm based on the G-matrix as in expression (18.5) and express the Gini index of inequality G_r within a given area r as:

$$G_r = [e']\, G\, [s] \tag{18.9}$$

where e' is a row vector of the shares in the total population of the different subgroups distinguished (these subgroups may for example be the deciles of the total population in area r), G the G-matrix defined earlier and s a column vector of the shares of the different subgroups in total income, the elements of e' and s being ranked by decreasing values of the average income of each subgroup.

Calling respectively h_i and n_i the number of households and individuals in subgroup i and y_i the average household income in this subgroup, we summarize in Table 18.1 the way expression (18.9) will be expressed in the eight cases distinguished.

(c) Analyzing the respective impacts of household income and size on inequality comparisons

Let us for example compare the value of the between households Gini index of income per equivalent adult in two areas. Table 18.1 indicates that for area r this index may be expressed as:

$$G_r = [h_i/\Sigma_i h_i]'\, G\, [(y_i/(n_i)^{0.5})h_i/\Sigma_i[(y_i/(n_i)^{0.5})h_i] \tag{18.10}$$

Assuming that the data are given by decile so that $(h_i/\Sigma_i h_i) = 0.1$ for every i, we

Table 18.1 Various ways of expressing the Gini index

Welfare Indicator	Inequality between households	Inequality between individuals
Total household income	$[h_i/\Sigma_i\,h_i]'\ G\,[y_i/\Sigma_i\,y_i]$	$[n_i/\Sigma_i\,n_i]'\ G\,[y_i/\Sigma_i\,y_i]$
Per capita income	$[h_i/\Sigma_i\,h_i]'\ G\,[(y_i/n_i)h_i/\Sigma_i\,(y_i/n_i)h_i]$	$[n_i/\Sigma_i\,n_i]'\ G\,[(y_i/n_i)n_i/\Sigma_i\,(y_i/n_i)n_i]$
Income per equivalent adult	$[h_i/\Sigma_ih_i]'\ G[(y_i/(n_i)^{0.5})h_i/\Sigma_i[(y_i/(n_i)^{0.5})h_i]$	$[n_i/\Sigma_in_i]'\ G[(y_i/(n_i)^{0.5})n_i/\Sigma_i[(y_i/(n_i)^{0.5})n_i]$
Alternative formulation of the income per equivalent adult	$[h_i/\Sigma_ih_i]'G[(y_i/(a_i+0.5c_i)^{0.5})h_i/\Sigma_i[(y_i/(a_i+0.5c_i)^{0.5})h_i]$	$[n_i/\Sigma_in_i]'\ G[(y_i/(a_i+0.5c_i)^{0.5})n_i/\Sigma_i[(y_i/(a_i+0.5c_i)^{0.5})n_i]$

may write G_r as a function $f\,(y_{ir},n_{ir})$ where the subscript r indicates to which area the function r refers. The difference ΔG between the values of the Gini index in two areas r and s may therefore be expressed as:

$$\Delta G = f\,(y_{ir},n_{ir}) - f\,(y_{is},n_{is}) = 0.5(C_1 + C_2) + 0.5(C_3 + C_4) \qquad (18.11)$$

where:

$$C_1 = f\,(y_{ir},n_{ir}) - f\,(y_{ir},n_{is}) \qquad (18.12)$$

$$C_2 = f\,(y_{is},n_{ir}) - f\,(y_{is},n_{is}) \qquad (18.13)$$

$$C_3 = f\,(y_{ir},n_{ir}) - f\,(y_{is},n_{ir}) \qquad (18.14)$$

$$C_4 = f\,(y_{ir},n_{is}) - f\,(y_{is},n_{is}) \qquad (18.15)$$

It is easy to show that the expressions $0.5(C_1 + C_2)$ and $0.5(C_3 + C_4)$ measure respectively the impact of differences between areas r and s in the sizes of the households and in total household income. A similar decomposition may be obtained when the alternative definition of income per equivalent adult is used.

In the case where one measures inequality between individuals, expression (18.9) will be expressed as:

$$G_r = [n_i/\Sigma_in_i]'\ G\,[(Y_i/(n_i)^{0.5})n_i/\Sigma_i[(Y_i/(n_i)^{0.5})n_i\,] \qquad (18.16)$$

where Y_i is the total income of all households belonging to subgroup i (e.g. deciles of households).

The ratio $(Y_i/(n_i)^{0.5})$ may be also expressed as:

$$(Y_i/(n_i)^{0.5}) = (Y_i/h_i)/((n_i)^{0.5}/h_i) = (z_i/e_i) \qquad (18.17)$$

where z_i and e_i measure respectively the per household income and the number of equivalent adults per household.

The difference ΔG between the values of the Gini index in two areas r and s may therefore be expressed in this case as:

$$\Delta G = f(z_{ir}, e_{ir}, n_{ir}) - f(z_{is}, e_{is}, n_{is}) \tag{18.18}$$

Using decomposition techniques quite similar to those given in expressions (18.12) to (18.15) but applied to the case where we have three explanatory variables (z_i, e_i, and n_i), it is possible to measure the respective impacts on this gap ΔG of differences between the subgroups (e.g. household deciles) in the total number of individuals (role of differences in n_i), in the total household incomes (role of z_i) and in the number of equivalent adults per household (differences in e_i).

18.3 An empirical illustration: spatial inequality in Turkey in 1994

18.3.1 Differences between urban and rural areas

The results of this analysis are reported in Tables 18.2 to 18.5. Table 18.2 indicates that the average income, whether of households or of individuals, in urban areas is about 25 percent higher than in Turkey as a whole while in rural areas it is about 70 percent lower. Table 18.3 then indicates that, whatever concept of inequality one uses, inequality is much higher in urban than in rural areas. If one decomposes the overall inequality in Turkey into between areas (urban and rural), within areas and an overlapping component, Table 18.4 shows that close to 50 percent of the overall inequality is attributed to within-areas inequality, the between-areas inequality accounting for 34 to 37 percent and the overlapping component for 16 to 18 percent of the overall inequality.

Note also (see Table 18.3) that the difference between the two areas in within-areas inequality is highest when per capita income is the measure of welfare chosen and lowest when total household income is used, this being true for both inequality between households and between individuals.

In Table 18.5 we have decomposed the difference between the inequality of per capita or per equivalent adult income in urban and rural areas into two components measuring respectively differences between the two areas in total household income and in the average size of the households. It appears that the latter component (role of the household size) explains approximately 40 percent of the difference while the former component (role of total household income) accounts for the remaining 60 percent.

The important role played by differences in the size of the household appears clearly in Table 18.2 which shows that not only the average size of the household is smaller in urban areas but also its standard deviation and the

Table 18.2 Summary data for the urban and rural areas

Region	Share in total number of households	Share in total number of individuals	Share in total income	Average size of household	Standard deviation of size of household	Coefficient of variation of size of household	Relative income of household	Relative income of individuals
Urban areas	0.562	0.536	0.689	4.24	0.22	0.052	1.23	1.29
Rural areas	0.438	0.464	0.311	4.71	0.68	0.144	0.71	0.67

Table 18.3 Summary data on within-areas inequality

Region	Between households–per household income	Between households–per capita income	Between households–per equivalent adult income	Between households–alternative per equivalent income	Between individuals–per household income	Between individuals–per capita income	Between individuals–per equivalent adult income	Between individuals–alternative per equivalent income
Urban areas	0.458	0.443	0.451	0.447	0.452	0.439	0.446	0.442
Rural areas	0.384	0.321	0.353	0.351	0.370	0.313	0.342	0.341
Turkey as a whole	0.442	0.414	0.428	0.425	0.434	0.408	0.421	0.418

Table 18.4 Summary table of decomposition of inequality for urban and rural areas

Concept of inequality and measure of welfare of household	Total (whole country) inequality	Between-areas inequality	Within-areas inequality	Overlap	Share of between-areas inequality in total inequality	Share of within-areas inequality in total inequality	Share of overlap in total inequality
Inequality between households							
Inequality of household income	0.479	0.178	0.229	0.072	0.37	0.48	0.15
Inequality of per capita income	0.443	0.149	0.216	0.078	0.34	0.49	0.18
Inequality of per equivalent adult income	0.462	0.164	0.223	0.075	0.35	0.48	0.16
Inequality of alternative measure of per equivalent adult income	0.458	0.163	0.221	0.074	0.36	0.48	0.16
Inequality between individuals							
Inequality of household income	0.467	0.183	0.220	0.064	0.39	0.47	0.14
Inequality of per capita income	0.433	0.153	0.207	0.073	0.35	0.48	0.17
Inequality of per equivalent adult income	0.450	0.168	0.214	0.068	0.37	0.48	0.15
Inequality of alternative measure of per equivalent adult income	0.446	0.167	0.212	0.067	0.37	0.48	0.15

Table 18.5 Decomposition of the difference* in inequality between urban and rural areas

Areas	Inequality between households			Inequality between individuals			
	Total difference between urban and rural areas	Gap due to difference in household incomes	Gap due to differences in size of households	Total difference between urban and rural areas	Gap due to difference in population shares	Gap due to difference in household incomes	Gap due to differences in size of households
Comparison of urban and rural areas	+0.122 (0.097)	+0.076 (+0.075)	+0.046 (+0.022)	+0.126 (+0.104)	+0.004 (+0.006)	+0.078 (+0.077)	+0.044 (+0.021)

* The number not in parenthesis refers to the case where the welfare of the household (individual) is measured by the per capita income while that in parenthesis corresponds to the case where this welfare is assumed to be equal to the per equivalent adult income. The component 'population shares' which appears in the case where one measures inequality between individuals is due to the fact that the data were given for deciles of the household population, not of the population of individuals.

coefficient of variation of the size of the households. Moreover, a look at more detailed data indicated that the average size of the household, in both urban and rural areas, increases with the average income, whether of households or of individuals.

Remembering that our analysis is based on data collected for quintiles, we have computed also the ratio of the average size of the households in the richest over that in the poorest quintile. This ratio turns out to be equal to 1.12 in urban areas and to 1.56 in rural areas. We have similarly computed the ratio of the average total household income in the richest over that in the poorest quintile and found that this ratio was equal to 11.8 in urban and 8.6 in rural areas. Combining these two types of results one derives that the ratio of the per capita income in the richest over that in the poorest quintile is equal to 10.3 in urban and 5.5 in rural areas.

These data imply that migration from rural to urban areas induces an increase in the inequality of per capita income (inequality between households or individuals). The first reason is that the inequality of total household incomes is higher in urban areas. The second factor refers to the fact that so is also the inequality of household size.

18.3.2 *Regional differences*

The results of this analysis are presented in Tables 18.6 to 18.9. Table 18.6 indicates that, whether for household or per capita income, the average income is highest in Marmara and the region of the Aegean Sea and lowest in Eastern and Southern Anatolia (see the data in Table 18.6 on the relative income of the various regions, the comparison being made with Turkey as a whole). Table 18.7 then shows that the within-region inequality is highest for total household income and lowest for per capita income, this being true whether one looks at the between-households or the between-individuals inequality. The data of Table 18.7 indicate also clearly that, whatever concepts of inequality are used, the within-region inequality is highest in the three richest regions (Marmara, Aegean Sea and the Mediterranean region) and lowest in the two poorest regions (Eastern and Southern Anatolia). Note also that the greatest difference between the regions is observed when per capita income is the measure of welfare used and the smallest one when total household income is used, this result being similar to that observed when comparing urban and rural areas.

A look at Table 18.8 shows that when regions are compared, the between-regions inequality is much higher than the within-regions inequality, whatever measure of welfare is used and whether one looks at inequality between households or individuals. In fact 40 to 60 percent of the overall inequality is explained by between-regions and only 15 to 18 percent by within-regions differences.

In Table 18.9, we have decomposed the difference between inequality within a given region and that in Turkey as a whole into three components

Table 18.6 Summary data for the regions in 1994

Region	Share in total number of households	Share in total number of individuals	Share in total income	Average size of household	Standard deviation of size of household	Coefficient of variation of size of household	Relative income of household	Relative income of individuals
Marmara	.266	.247	.386	4.12	0.36	0.088	1.45	1.56
Aegean	.157	.136	.139	3.85	0.52	0.136	0.89	1.02
Mediterranean	.125	.127	.111	4.54	0.31	0.068	0.88	0.87
Central Anatolia	.179	.172	.154	4.27	0.44	0.102	0.86	0.90
Black Sea	.128	.135	.109	4.68	0.43	0.093	0.85	0.81
Eastern Anatolia	.071	.088	.057	5.51	0.75	0.136	0.80	0.65
Southern Anatolia	.074	.096	.045	5.72	0.56	0.098	0.61	0.47

Table 18.7 Summary data on within-regions inequality in 1994

Region	Between households—per household income	Between households—per capita income	Between households—per equivalent adult income	Between households—alternative per equivalent income	Between individuals—per household income	Between individuals—per capita income	Between individuals—per equivalent adult income	Between individuals—alternative per equivalent income
Marmara	0.490	0.460	0.475	0.472	0.482	0.454	0.468	0.466
Aegean	0.401	0.347	0.375	0.373	0.388	0.340	0.365	0.363
Mediterranean	0.423	0.399	0.411	0.407	0.417	0.395	0.406	0.402
Central Anatolia	0.412	0.380	0.397	0.394	0.400	0.372	0.386	0.384
Black Sea	0.414	0.376	0.395	0.394	0.405	0.370	0.388	0.387
Eastern Anatolia	0.342	0.279	0.311	0.309	0.329	0.271	0.301	0.299
Southern Anatolia	0.351	0.306	0.329	0.325	0.345	0.304	0.325	0.321
Turkey as a whole	0.442	0.414	0.428	0.425	0.434	0.408	0.421	0.418

Table 18.8 Summary table of decomposition of inequality

Concept of inequality and measure of welfare of household	Total (whole country) inequality	Between regions inequality	Within-regions inequality	Overlap	Share of between-regions inequality in total inequality	Share of within-regions inequality in total inequality	Share of overlap in total inequality
Inequality between households							
Inequality of household income	0.549	0.339	0.085	0.125	0.62	0.15	0.23
Inequality of per capita income	0.442	0.182	0.0078	0.182	0.41	0.18	0.41
Inequality of per equivalent adult income	0.494	0.261	0.081	0.152	0.53	0.16	0.31
Inequality of alternative measure of per equivalent adult income	0.490	0.259	0.081	0.150	0.53	0.17	0.31
Inequality between individuals							
Inequality of household income	0.548	0.352	0.079	0.117	0.64	0.14	0.21
Inequality of per capita income	0.439	0.191	0.073	0.175	0.44	0.17	0.40
Inequality of per equivalent adult income	0.493	0.273	0.076	0.144	0.55	0.15	0.29
Inequality of alternative measure of per equivalent adult income	0.488	0.269	0.076	0.143	0.55	0.16	0.29

Table 18.9 Decomposition of the difference* in inequality between Turkey as a whole and the various regions

Region	Inequality between households			Inequality between individuals			
	Total difference between Turkey and the region	Gap due to difference in household incomes	Gap due to differences in size of households	Total difference between Turkey and the region	Gap due to difference in population shares	Gap due to difference in household incomes	Gap due to differences in size of households
Marmara	−0.046 (0.047)	−0.050 (−0.049)	+0.004 (+0.002)	−0.046 (−0.048)	0 (0)	−0.051 (−0.050)	+0.004 (+0.002)
Aegean	+0.067 (+0.053)	+0.042 (+0.041)	+0.024 (+0.011)	+0.068 (+0.057)	+0.003 (+0.004)	+0.043 (+0.042)	+0.022 (+0.011)
Mediterranean	+0.015 (+0.017)	+0.019 (+.019)	−0.004 (−0.002)	+0.013 (+0.015)	−0.001 (−0.002)	+0.019 (+0.018)	−0.004 (−0.002)
Central Anatolia	+0.034 (+0.031)	+0.030 (+0.030)	+0.004 (+0.002)	+0.037 (+0.035)	+0.002 (+0.002)	+.0032 (+0.031)	+0.003 (+0.001)
Black Sea	+0.033 (+0.033)	+0.029 (+0.029)	+0.005 (+0.004)	+0.038 (+0.033)	0 (0)	+0.029 (+0.029)	+0.009 (+0.004)
Eastern Anatolia	+0.135 (+0.117)	+0.104 (+0.l02)	+0.031 (+0.015)	+0.137 (+0.120)	+0.002 (+0.003)	+0.105 (+0.103)	+0.030 (+0.014)
Southern Anatolia	+0.108 (+0.099)	+0.097 (+0.094)	+0.010 (+0.005)	+0.104 (+0.096)	0 (0)	+0.094 (+0.091)	+0.010 (+0.005)

* The number not in parenthesis refers to the case where the welfare of the household (individual) is measured by the per capita income while that in parenthesis corresponds to the case where this welfare is assumed to be equal to the per equivalent adult income. The component 'population shares' which appears in the case where one measures inequality between individuals is due to the fact that the data were given for deciles of the household population, not of the population of individuals.

(see the methodology previously described). The first component is due to differences between the quintiles in population shares (this is a consequence of the fact that, whereas the share of the households in each quintile is by definition equal to 20 percent, that of individuals is not necessarily equal to 20 percent). The second component reflects differences between the quintiles in total household income while the third element is a consequence of differences in the size of the households. It appears that in the poor regions (Eastern and Southern Anatolia) the component reflecting differences in total household income accounts for 80 to 90 percent of the total gap while that due to differences in household size explains 10 to 20 percent. In rich areas (Marmara and Aegean Sea) the results are not clear, total household income contributing to even more than 100 percent of the overall difference in Marmara but to only 60 percent in the Aegean Sea area.

As far as the size of the households is concerned it appears (see Table 18.6) that first this average size is much higher in poor regions (the average there being equal to 5.5 to 5.7 individuals) than in rich regions (average varying from 3.85 to 4.12). Similarly the standard deviation of household size is lower in rich than in poor regions but the results for the coefficient of variation of household size are not clear.

When comparing household size with relative (to Turkey as a whole) total household income or per capita income in the various regions we find a negative correlation between average household size and total household income (correlation: −0.61) or per capita income (correlation: −0.77). A similar analysis shows a negative correlation between the standard deviation of household size and relative total household income (correlation: −0.48) or per capita income (correlation: −0.55).

The results of this regional analysis are thus quite similar to those derived in the urban versus rural areas comparison, though sometimes less clear-cut conclusions may be derived because some of the regions are not specifically urban or rural areas. But as a whole they seem to confirm the important role played by internal migration which affects inequality both through its impact on the inequality of total household incomes and on the size of the households.

18.4 Concluding comments

This chapter has attempted to analyze the impact of internal migration on spatial inequality in Turkey, whether it be inequality between urban and rural areas or regional inequality. It appears that there are two reasons why internal migration from rural to urban areas and between regions induces an increase in the inequality of per capita income, whether one looks at inequality between households or individuals. First, the inequality of total household income is higher in urban areas; second, that of the size of households is higher in rural areas.

References

Buhmann, B., Rainwater, L., Schmaus, G. and Smeeding, T. (1988). 'Equivalence Scales, Well-Being, Inequality and Poverty: Sensitive Estimates Across Ten Countries Using the Luxembourg Income Study (LIS) Database', *The Review of Income and Wealth*, 34: 115–142.

Coulter, F. A. E., Cowell, F. A. and Jenkins, S. P. (1992). 'Equivalence Scale Relativities and the Extent of Inequality and Poverty', *Economic Journal*, 102: 1067–1082.

Danziger, S. and Taussig, M. K. (1979). 'The Income Unit and the Anatomy of Income Distribution', *Review of Income and Wealth*, 25: 365–375.

Deutsch, J. and Silber, J. (1999). 'The Decomposition of Inequality by Population Subgroups and the Analysis of Interdistributional Inequality', in J. Silber (ed.), *Handbook on Income Inequality Measurement*, Dordrecht and New York: Kluwer Academic Publishers, 363–403.

Gürsel, S., Levent, H., Selim, R. and Sarica, O. (2000). *Individual Income Distribution in Turkey. A Comparison with the European Union*, Istanbul: TUSIAD Publication.

Özmucur, S. and Silber, J. (2000). 'Decomposition of Income Inequality: Evidence from Turkey', *Topics in Middle Eastern and North African Economies, Electronic Journal*, Vol. 2, Middle East Economic Association and Loyola University Chicago, http://www.luc.edu/orgs/meea/volume2/ozmucur2.pdf (accessed 12 January 2007).

Selim, R. and McKay, A. (2001). *The Changes in Income Poverty in Turkey over a Period of Economic Liberalization*, Paper presented at the Workshop on Poverty and Governance in the Middle East and North African Region, 2–3 August, Yemen.

Shorter, F. C. (1985). 'The Population of Turkey After the War of Independence', *International Journal of Middle East Studies*, 17: 417–441.

Silber, J. (1989). 'Factor Components, Population Subgroups and the Computation of the Gini Index of Inequality', *Review of Economics and Statistics*, 71: 107–115.

State Institute of Statistics (1995). *The Population of Turkey, 1923–1994, Demographic Structure and Development with Projections to the Mid-21st Century*, Ankara: State Institute of Statistics Publications.

State Institute of Statistics (1997). *Income Distribution Survey Results, 1994*, Ankara: State Institute of Statistics Publications.

Index

Please note that references to Notes will have the letter 'n' following the note. Page references to non-textual information such as Figures or Tables will be in italic print.